Ovid's Homer

Ovid's Homer

Authority, Repetition,
and Reception

———◦◉◦———

BARBARA WEIDEN BOYD

OXFORD
UNIVERSITY PRESS

OXFORD
UNIVERSITY PRESS

Oxford University Press is a department of the University of Oxford. It furthers
the University's objective of excellence in research, scholarship, and education
by publishing worldwide. Oxford is a registered trade mark of Oxford University
Press in the UK and certain other countries.

Published in the United States of America by Oxford University Press
198 Madison Avenue, New York, NY 10016, United States of America.

© Oxford University Press 2017

CIP data is on file at the Library of Congress
ISBN 978–0–19–068004–6

1 3 5 7 9 8 6 4 2

Printed by Sheridan Books, Inc., United States of America

For my parents, Peter and Elizabeth Weiden, in loving memory

sit uobis terra leuis

Igitur, ut Aratus ab Ioue incipiendum putat, ita nos
rite coepturi ab Homero uidemur. Hic enim, quem
ad modum ex Oceano dicit ipse amnium fontiumque
cursus initium capere, omnibus eloquentiae partibus
exemplum et ortum dedit.

QUINTILIAN, Inst. 10.1.46

Nunc me Pierios cupiam per pectora fontes
Irriguas torquere vias, totumque per ora
Volvere laxatum gemino de vertice rivum;
Ut tenues oblita sonos audacibus alis
Surgat in officium venerandi Musa parentis.

JOHN MILTON, Ad Patrem 1–5

Contents

Preface

FEW ANCIENT POETS, if any, have received more critical attention and acclaim than Homer, whose *Iliad* and *Odyssey* are as fundamental to virtually every aspect of modern classical studies as they were to the lives and imaginations of their first audiences, and to very many generations of readers since. Homeric studies nourish the investigations of contemporary historians of the ancient Mediterranean much as they did the first ancient writers of history; Homeric studies fueled the explorers of the eighteenth and nineteenth centuries, whose work, for better or worse, nurtured the development of the discipline of archaeology—among the contemporary practitioners of which are many for whom the search for Homer's Troy remains an abiding concern. Last but not least, the literary scholars who today continue to debate the precise nature of Homeric composition and textual transmission and of the world depicted by Homer look back for inspiration not only to those nineteenth-century scholars who first attempted to use the modern scientific art (or artistic science) of philology but also to their predecessors in Hellenistic Alexandria, for whom the poems of Homer were nothing less than the preeminent cultural patrimony of all Greek-speaking people—and, eventually, of the Romans as well.

Indeed, it might be said with at least some accuracy that all classicists are engaged in Homeric studies, at least to the extent that the *Iliad* and *Odyssey*, and the humane comprehension that informs both of them, are at the core of the rationale for our discipline's centrality to the study of the human condition, even in times, places, and circumstances far removed from those in which we find ourselves today. The professional specializations that distinguish us from each other, and that at times even divide us, all nonetheless yield to Homer, as they should: the image evoked by Quintilian, of Homer as the Ocean from which all streams of knowledge flow, takes as its source the image of the Ocean that flows around the circumference of Achilles's shield in *Iliad* Book 18, embracing as it does so all human experience within its vastness.

Thus, as I began this book, the work that awaited me appeared daunting at best: simply to control the most important scholarly literature not only on Ovid but also on Homer that has been published during the last fifty years or so is a prospect that can inspire only fear in most of us. It was clear that any concerted effort to do at least a fraction of this work would require time without interruption or distraction, the two most prominent features of a teaching career. I am therefore deeply indebted to the two entities that recognized some merit in my proposal and provided the funds necessary to permit me to take a full year of sabbatical leave, the National Endowment for the Humanities, which provided a fellowship for research, and the National Humanities Center, which supplemented the NEH funds with its own Rockefeller Fellowship and provided besides a remarkable haven of quiet and concentration that allowed me to work intensively on this project for nine months. Third but no less important is my own institution, Bowdoin College, which allowed me to supplement a year of external funding with an additional semester of leave. Among the many supportive staff members at Bowdoin I want to single out for thanks Cara Martin-Tetrault, who helped me every step of the way with the process of applying for funding. Of course, with my salutatory words I do not mean to imply that the task I began is fully done; rather, I invoke these benefactors as incomparable helpers in a never-ending process of discovery. I hope this book will be seen as a beginning, rather than an end.

Financial support and time are among the basic *sine quibus non* of scholarly work; the other crucial factor is access to excellent library resources. I want therefore to single out the libraries and librarians who made my work so enjoyable and productive: all the librarians at Bowdoin, especially Guy Saldanha and Jaime Jones, who swiftly found and provided materials not in our collection; the truly remarkable library staff at the National Humanities Center, Brooke Andrade, Sarah Harris, and Jason King, for their ability to make books appear out of thin air overnight; and Sebastian Hierl and the staff of the library at the American Academy in Rome, where I spent the last two months of my leave and where I finished the first draft of the book.

Equally important are several people who graciously offered to read the manuscript for me: in every case, I benefited from their ideas and suggestions, and with their help removed inconcinnities and inconsistencies in language, style, and content. Christopher Brunelle and Louise Pratt read the entire manuscript and offered invaluable assistance; among those who read drafts of individual chapters, or of more than one chapter, I single out Sergio Casali, Jennifer Clarke Kosak, Sharon James, and Birgit Tautz for their encouragement. Several sections of this book originated as talks—in some cases, as talks I conceived of long before this book came into being; I thank audiences at Duke University, the University of North Carolina at Greensboro, the University of Kansas, and Università degli Studi di Roma Due (Tor Vergata), as well as colleagues in attendance at the meetings of the Classical Association (UK) in Exeter and Edinburgh; of the Classical Association of Canada in Québec; and of the Fédération Internationale des Études Classiques in Bordeaux. And then, there are the steadfast colleagues who supported this project from its inception, Peter Knox and Richard Thomas: I am fortunate indeed to be able to call them my friends. I also thank my fellow travelers at the National Humanities Center, with whom I shared fellowship, cookies, and poetry; I am particularly grateful to the director of the Fellowship Program, Cassie Mansfield, for the confidence she placed in me, and to my fellow Fellow Gordon Teskey, who led our discussions of some modern poets and who introduced me to Milton's Latin verse.

I offer special gratitude to the anonymous readers for Oxford University Press, both of whom provided invaluable guidance on matters great and small. And it has been a pleasure to work with my editor, Stefan Vranka, who welcomed the idea for the book and ushered it through to publication almost painlessly. His assistant, John Veranes, cheerfully, swiftly, and astutely answered my many emails and supported the process of putting all the pieces together. My copy editor, Susan Ecklund, has brought consistency and clarity to every page; and as production editor Sivaranjani of Newgen has promptly and efficiently handled questions great and small. Finally, I thank my student Andrew Raisner, who read much of the manuscript aloud to me in the search for repetitious wording and other potential flaws of style.

Sections of several chapters of this book appear (in unrevised form) in edited collections of papers published previously or in journals. I have cited these earlier publications at the appropriate points in the text of this book; here, I offer my thanks to the volume editors, including Alison Keith and Jonathan Edmondson, and Laurel Fulkerson and Tim Stover, and their publishers, the presses of the University of Toronto and the University of Wisconsin, respectively. I also thank the editors of *Materiali e discussioni* and *Paideia*, Rolando Ferri and Giuseppe Gilberto Biondi, respectively, for allowing me to republish material they first read and published. Finally, I am grateful to the University of Michigan Press, which allowed me to reprise the discussion of one of Ovid's *Amores* that appears in my first book, and to its Classics editor, Ellen Bauerle, who has taught me a lot over the years about the art of editing.

Sic paruis componere magna solebam: for those of us whose primary or sole professional responsibility is to teach undergraduates, Homer's poems are both a godsend and a constant challenge. Even students with no knowledge of Greek or Latin are drawn to these poems and to the great stories they tell, to the heroes whose names are synonymous with an uncommon greatness and to the gods whose existence is too vivid to be entirely fictional; and so Homer continues to serve as the great teacher, just as he did in the ancient world, introducing youth and indeed all readers to the concepts of human potential, fate, inventiveness, love, grief, and so much else besides. And Homer is held out as the ultimate prize for those students who can persevere through the rigors of seemingly countless verb forms and rules for accents in order to learn enough Greek to experience the poems without the obscuring filter of a translation. Thus, even a Latinist like me will jump at the chance to teach an undergraduate Homer course—and not simply because the poet does all the important teaching; even a Latinist like me will welcome the combination of awe and immediacy that comes with every reading of the *Iliad* or *Odyssey*. I am therefore also greatly indebted to my students at Bowdoin, especially those with whom I've had the pleasure over the years of reading and thinking about Homer; and those with whom I've shared my love for Ovid, a love that has only grown as I have taught his poems in a variety of contexts and guises. In fact, this book is at least in part a result of the serendipity that results from teaching broadly as well as deeply: I was teaching a course in translation on intertextuality in ancient epic (a challenge to discuss without Latin or Greek, but well worth it) when I first began to think about Homeric resonances in Ovid.

Last but not least, I thank my family, Michael and Rachel Boyd. My husband Michael has read every word of this book—in some cases, several times—and has commented astutely on everything from my style to the strength of my argument. And our daughter Rachel, a brilliant scholar in her own right, has taught me the importance of fundamental questions about influence, repetition, and creativity, all with her inimitable charm, sense of humor, and enthusiasm for life. They are really the ones who make it all worthwhile.

Acknowledgments

EARLIER VERSIONS OF several sections of this book have been published previously elsewhere and are indicated as such in the text. I am grateful to the following editors and publishers for allowing me to reprint parts of those earlier publications here:

"Repeat after Me: The Loves of Venus and Mars in *Ars amatoria* 2 and *Metamorphoses* 4," in *Repeat Performances: Ovidian Repetition and the Metamorphoses*, edited by Laurel Fulkerson and Tim Stover (Madison: University of Wisconsin Press, 2016), 47–68. ©2016 by the Board of Regents of the University of Wisconsin System. Reprinted courtesy of The University of Wisconsin Press.

"Ovid's Circe and the Revolutionary Power of *carmina* in the *Remedia amoris*," in *Roman Literary Cultures: Domestic Politics, Revolutionary Poetics, Civic Spectacle*, edited by Alison Keith and Jonathan Edmondson (Toronto: University of Toronto Press, 2016), 111–23. ©2016 by the University of Toronto Press.

"Ovidian Encounters with the Embassy to Achilles: Homeric Reception in *Metamorphoses* 8 and *Heroides* 3," *Paideia: Rivista di filologia, ermeneutica e critica letteraria* 70 (2015): 27–41. ©2015 by Editrice Stilgraf.

"On Starting an Epic (Journey): Telemachus, Phaethon, and the Beginning of Ovid's *Metamorphoses*," *Materiali e discussioni per l'analisi dei testi classici* 69 (2012): 101–18. ©2012 by Fabrizio Serra Editore.

Finally, sections of the discussion of *Amores* 1.7 that appears on pages 52–64 of this book are revised from a briefer discussion in *Ovid's Literary Loves: Influence and Innovation in the Amores* (Ann Arbor: University of Michigan Press, 1997), 123–29. ©1997 by the University of Michigan.

Texts and Abbreviations

THE FOLLOWING EDITIONS of Greek and Latin texts are those most frequently quoted in this book:

For Homer:

> Allen, T. W., ed. 1917. *Homeri Opera: Odyssea.* 2 vols. Oxford: Oxford University Press.
>
> Monro, D. B., and T. W. Allen, eds. 1920. *Homeri Opera: Ilias.* 2 vols. 3rd ed. Oxford: Oxford University Press.

For Ovid:

> Alton, E. H., D. E. W. Wormell, and E. Courtney, eds. 1985. *Ovidius: Fasti.* Leipzig: Teubner.
>
> Dörrie, H., ed. 1971. *P. Ovidii Nasonis Epistulae Heroidum.* Berlin: De Gruyter.
>
> Kenney, E. J., ed. 1995. *P. Ovidi Nasonis Amores, Medicamina Faciei Femineae, Ars Amatoria, Remedia amoris.* 2nd, corrected edition. Oxford: Oxford University Press.
>
> Owen, S. G., ed. 1915. *P. Ovidi Nasonis Tristium Libri Quinque, ex Ponto Libri Quattuor, Halieutica, Fragmenta.* Oxford: Oxford University Press.
>
> Tarrant, R. J., ed. 2004. *P. Ovidi Nasonis Metamorphoses.* Oxford: Oxford University Press.

For other ancient authors, I use the Oxford Classical Text or Teubner edition wherever possible and as seems appropriate; very occasional divergences are discussed in the relevant footnotes. All references to the Homeric scholia are based on the edition of H. Erbse (1969–88. *Scholia Graeca in Homeri Iliadem.* 7 vols. Berlin: De Gruyter). All references to Ennius's *Annales* are based on the edition of O. Skutsch (1985. *The Annals of Q. Ennius.* Oxford: Oxford University Press). All references to Callimachus are based on the edition of the fragments by R. Pfeiffer (1949–53. *Callimachus*. 2 vols. Oxford: Oxford University Press; abbreviated Pf.), but I have noted those places where the fragment number differs in the edition of Massimilla, or of Harder, or of both.

For abbreviated references to ancient authors and works, I generally follow the list found in the *Oxford Classical Dictionary*, supplemented by those in Liddell, Scott, and Jones's *Greek-English Lexicon* and the *Oxford Latin Dictionary*; for journals and other serial publications, I generally follow the list used by *L'Année philologique*. Exceptions and other abbreviations are as follows:

AJP	*American Journal of Philology*
CA	*Classical Antiquity*
CP	*Classical Philology*
D-K	Diels, H., ed. 1912. *Die Fragmente der Vorsokratiker, griechisch und deutsch*. Revised by W. Kranz. 2 vols. in 3. 3rd ed. Berlin: Weidmann.
EGF	Davies, M., ed. 1988. *Epicorum Graecorum Fragmenta*. Göttingen: Vandenhoeck & Ruprecht.
FGrH	Jacoby, F., ed. 1923–69. *Die Fragmente der griechischen Historiker*. Berlin: Weidmann (1923–57); Leiden: Brill (1957–69).
FHG	Müller, K., ed. 1878–85. *Fragmenta Historicorum Graecorum*. 5 vols. Paris: Firmin Didot.
HSCP	*Harvard Studies in Classical Philology*
IE^2	West, M. L., ed. 1989. *Iambi et elegi Graeci ante Alexandrum cantati*. 2 vols. 2nd edition. Oxford: Oxford University Press.
IG	*Inscriptiones Graecae*. Berlin: De Gruyter, 1873–.
LSJ	Liddell, H. G., R. Scott, and H. S. Jones, eds. 1996. *A Greek-English Lexicon*. 9th edition, revised. Oxford: Oxford University Press.
M-W	Merkelbach, R., and M. L. West., eds. 1967. *Fragmenta Hesiodea*. Oxford: Oxford University Press.
Nauck	Nauck, A., ed. 1926. *Tragicorum Graecorum Fragmenta*. Leipzig: Teubner.
OCD	Hornblower, S., A. Spawforth, and E. Eidinow, eds. 2012. *The Oxford Classical Dictionary*. 4th ed. Oxford: Oxford University Press.

OLD	Glare, P. G. W., ed. 1968–82. *Oxford Latin Dictionary*. Oxford: Oxford University Press.
Pf.	Pfeiffer, R., ed. 1949–53. *Callimachus*. 2 vols. Oxford: Oxford University Press.
Powell	Powell, J. U., ed. 1924. *Collectanea Alexandrina: Reliquiae minores poetarum Graecorum aetatis Ptolemaicae, 323–146 A.C.: Epicorum, elegiacorum, lyricorum, ethicorum*. Oxford: Oxford University Press.
TAPA	*Transactions of the American Philological Association*
TrGF	Snell, B., ed. 1986–. *Tragicorum Graecorum Fragmenta*. Göttingen: Vandenhoeck & Ruprecht.

I use consonantal *u* in place of *v* throughout in the quotation of Latin texts; in some titles, however, and in postclassical Latin quotations, I retain *v* as it appears in my source. For the spelling of Greek names, I generally use Latinized forms (e.g., Achilles rather than Akhilleus) except in quotations from the works of other scholars; with Odysseus/Ulysses, I use "Odysseus" when discussing the character as he appears in the Homeric poems and other Greek texts, but "Ulysses" for the character depicted in Latin texts.

Introduction

> He did not want to compose another *Don Quixote*—
> which would be easy—but *the Don Quixote*. It is
> unnecessary to add that his aim was never to produce
> a mechanical transcription of the original; he did not
> propose to copy it. His admirable ambition was to pro-
> duce pages that would coincide—word for word and
> line for line—with those of Miguel de Cervantes.
>
> —JORGE LUIS BORGES, "Pierre Menard, Author of
> Don Quixote"

IN THE HISTORY of modern classical philology, much has been said and written about the relationship of Ovid to his predecessors and models. Because the elegiac couplet appears from the available evidence to have been Ovid's meter of choice, his relationship to the elegists who preceded him—particularly Gallus, Propertius, and Tibullus—has naturally earned interest and attention, and his pursuit of all things Callimachean, or more generally Hellenistic, has been regularly and profitably traced. More recently, scholarly attention has broadened its focus: Philip Hardie and his disciples have reoriented the perspective modern readers take on the Roman poetic landscape to include Lucretius, whose philosophical science regularly informs Ovidian cosmography; Alessandro Barchiesi, Stephen Hinds, and others have drawn lively attention to Ovid's engagement with the *Homeric Hymns*, long considered outsiders in the history of ancient poetry; and a new generation of younger scholars is now bringing to light Ovid's poetic immersion in texts as disparate as Sappho's lyrics, on the one hand, and the Hesiodic *Catalogue of Women*, on the other.[1]

---

1. Lucretius: Hardie 1988, 1995, 2007b; Garani 2013; *Homeric Hymns*: Barchiesi 1999; Hinds 1987a; Sappho: Thorsen 2014; *Catalogue of Women*: Ziogas 2013.

No poet besides Virgil, however, has so strongly influenced our reading and reception of Ovid. Ovid's indebtedness to Virgil—inescapable, inimitable, nonpareil—has been recognized as a rich source of intertextual complexity; it has also at times obscured our view of the remarkable creativity of Ovid on his own terms. Indeed, for scholars and readers of ancient poetry, particularly Latin epic poetry, the *synkrisis* of the two has informed to a great extent the way these two poets are read and interpreted. This has meant that, at least in the modern period, Ovid's poetry has been read as the embodiment of belatedness, with all of its pitfalls. As Joseph Farrell has argued, the second half of the twentieth century was an important time for the recuperation of Ovid, a recuperation that has gained so much in both speed and force that comparisons of Virgil and Ovid are no longer predictable, no longer grounded in the stereotype that, while Virgil is an "important" poet, Ovid is simply rhetorically adept, but so shallow and so handicapped by his own bad habits that there is no real substance in his work.[2] Rather, it has become far clearer, especially since the mid-1980s, that this truism begins with Ovid himself, who sets up the *synkrisis* between himself and Virgil at the beginning of his career (*Arma graui numero uiolentaque bella | parabam, Am.* 1.1.1), and for the next several decades at least challenges his readers not to forget it.[3] It is clear as well that the medieval and early modern traditions surrounding the pairing of Virgil and Ovid have also played an important role in the understanding with which Ovid entered the twentieth century: as Séverine Clément-Tarantino and Florence Klein show, a vivid picture emerges from postclassical writings about the two poets as "frères ennemis," mirror images of each other who are trapped for life, as it were, in their inseparability—an inseparability that is reflected in their identification with the genres of epic and elegy, respectively.

Virgil's supremacy in this matchup has long seemed inevitable; but in this context it is worth observing that in another classic instance of the phenomenon Virgil's place is less stable: I refer to the *synkrisis* of Virgil and Homer. This comparison too has a long and familiar history: from the time of Quintilian, if not earlier, discussions of the complementary characters of Greek and Latin literature (itself a fundamental comparison that

---

2. Farrell 2001, esp. 21–28. On stereotypes about Ovid, see Hinds 1987a; Hardie 2007a develops the Virgil-Ovid *synkrisis* in some detail.

3. On Ovid's creation of the juxtaposition with Virgil, see Farrell 2004; Hardie and Moore 2010:5–6; and Clément-Tarantino and Klein 2015.

shapes our contemporary discipline) have turned to Homer and Virgil as a sort of "matched pair" of epic poets, each one the greatest in his respective tradition (Quint. *Inst.* 10.1.85–86);[4] and the literary analysis of Virgil, of which we find abundant evidence in the remains of Servius's commentary and in Macrobius's *Saturnalia*, is rooted in the idea that Virgil is the Roman Homer. Changes in literary taste along with changing social and political contexts have caused the relative rise or decline of each of the two from one era to the next, but the pairing itself is remarkably stable. Even the discovery of, say, fifteen books of Ennius's *Annales* would do little to alter the status quo, however fervently we would wish it for other reasons,[5] because the Homer-Virgil *synkrisis* has such a long and richly elaborated tradition in the field.[6] The very dominance of Virgil on the Latin side of the equation, meanwhile, has obscured other forms of Homeric reception in Latin poetry, except in those instances in which Virgil has provided the "window," so to speak, through which a later poet looks back at Homer.[7] Such instances are legion, especially in the appearance of tropes closely identifiable across linguistic borders, such as extended similes and repeated epithets, and sometimes it is enough to understand them as saying that a post-Homeric, post-Virgilian poem is competent to "speak" the language of epic it has learned from the masters.[8]

In this book, I propose to add a new *synkrisis* to these two well-established examples by juxtaposing Ovid's work not with that of his Latin predecessor but with Homer. My purpose is not to complete a perfect triangle (although this project does, serendipitously, show how it might be done), but to continue the progress that has been made in the last three

---

4. *Idem nobis per Romanos quoque auctores ordo ducendus est. itaque ut apud illos Homerus, sic apud nos Vergilius auspicatissimum dederit exordium, omnium eius generis poetarum Graecorum nostrorumque haud dubie proximus. utar enim uerbis isdem quae ex Afro Domitio iuuenis excepi, qui mihi interroganti quem Homero crederet maxime accedere "secundus" inquit "est Vergilius, propior tamen primo quam tertio." et hercule ut illi naturae caelesti atque inmortali cesserimus, ita curae et diligentiae uel ideo in hoc plus est, quod ei fuit magis laborandum, et quantum eminentibus uincimur, fortasse aequalitate pensamus. ceteri omnes longe sequentur.*

5. Although the recent work of Elliott 2013 demonstrates how important Ennius's position between Homer and Virgil could well have been: see especially her chapter 2.

6. It would be impossible to catalogue the studies, both monumental and minor, that have had recourse in some way to the comparative approach. I single out here a few rather obvious examples: Heinze 1993 (1928); Knauer 1964; Dekel 2012. For a succinct but informative discussion of the history of the comparison, see Vogt-Spira 2007.

7. Further on "window reference," a term coined by Thomas 1986, see chapter 2, n.74.

8. Exemplified by von Glinski 2012.

decades of dispelling the large Virgilian shadow that for so long shaded our reading of Ovid. This is not to suggest that that shade has been entirely harmful; like Virgil's Tityrus, Ovid has flourished in the recent past, especially as we have come to appreciate the authority with which Ovid asserts his poetic originality, frequently doing so precisely through allusion to Virgil. But the contiguity of Ovid to Homer, on the other hand, is a vast and little-explored territory; it is likely, and entirely understandable, that the structures of learning so long in place have obscured a vital element in the literary history that produces Ovid. As a result, readers of this book may be surprised at the outset to discover that, by and large, I bypass both Virgil and Ovid's reception of him. I do so, however, quite intentionally, since my goal is to decenter the nature of the discussion about Ovidian intertextuality writ large by focusing on one important but obscured area. This does not mean that Virgil is entirely absent from this book: given Ovid's evident immersion in everything Virgil wrote, it would be foolhardy—if not impossible—to attempt to overlook his importance when the occasion demands. But I have intentionally recentered my focus by selecting Ovidian episodes, poems, and characters that do not immediately demand my reader's opening of his or her text of Virgil. I have, I hope, good reason to be confident that my reader will be persuaded to stay the course with me as I sketch a new map through Ovidian territory.

Of course, Ovidian intertextuality with the Homeric poems has not been entirely overlooked: not only in the numerous new commentaries on various books of Ovid's works but in articles focusing on individual poems or episodes, a number of scholars have recently drawn attention to the Homeric presence in Ovid. I single out here as particularly influential for my own thinking the discussions of the Calypso episode in *Ars* Book 2 by Alison Sharrock; of Nestor's narrative of the battle of Lapiths and Centaurs in *Metamorphoses* Book 12 by Margaret Musgrove; of the *Heroides* by Megan Drinkwater and of the double *Heroides* 16 and 17 in particular by Elizabeth Mazurek; and of Ovidian elegy generally by Jean-Christophe Jolivet.[9] Each in its own way takes seriously Ovid's engagement with Homer and his sophisticated reading of the Homeric poems, and each opens up the intertextual and metatextual possibilities of Homeric allusion in Ovid. But a central distinction between these scholars' work and mine is its episodic

---

9. Sharrock 1987; Musgrove 1998; Drinkwater 2007, 2013a; Mazurek 2013; Jolivet 1999, 2004, 2005. The latest addition to this list that I am aware of is Heslin 2016.

character; with few exceptions,[10] a broader approach to Ovid's reception of Homer has yet to be advanced.

It is my purpose, therefore, to sketch at least the outlines of a broader framework for Ovid's reception of the Homeric poems. Readers inspecting the table of contents may notice with some surprise that I have no chapter devoted to Ovid's "little *Iliad*" (or "little *Aeneid*," for that matter), nor do I devote much attention to battle scenes generally; chapter 2, on Diomedes, does engage briefly with the theme of *nostos* inherited from the *Odyssey*, but as I attempt to suggest, shows that Ovid's poetic memory of Homer can sometimes play with the idea of its own evanescence. Nor do I attempt to catalogue the many allusions to Homer that fill Ovid's works: such a catalogue would be a fool's errand, I think, given the ubiquity of such echoes and the inescapability of repetition that is at the heart of poetic language.[11] I should also mention here that I range widely across the corpus of Ovidian poetry, and intentionally so. From the earliest elegies to the exile poetry, and from the Roman calendar to Greek myth (and back again), there is, I suggest, a saturation of Ovidian poetry in and by Homer: the lessons learned in those early years (*pueriles anni*; cf. *Fast.* 6.417) link Ovid not only to Livius and Ennius, whose poems were the substance of his early education, but indeed to Homer himself, whose peerless poems must have been close at hand as Ovid thought and wrote.[12]

I shall return in chapter 1 to the role of Livius and Ennius in the transmission of Homeric poetry and poetics to the Roman audience. First, however, I shall introduce the basic ideas and concepts that inform this book. As its title indicates, a central theme is authority; that is, what strategies does Ovid use to assert his readiness to be matched with Homer, and how archly antagonistic is this assertion? This is a subject that has already been discussed amply and well by other scholars vis-à-vis other poets, Virgil in particular; while the idea is not a new one, it nonetheless takes on a new importance when Homer enters upon the scene. Homer

---

10. The one real standout is Baldo 1986; cf. also Baldo 1995:111–41; but he limits his project to the *Metamorphoses*.

11. Conte 1986:40–41 characterizes poetic discourse as *Wiedergebrauchsrede*, "language that can be reused": "Language that is reused is inevitably *preserved in the poetic memory*" (Conte's italics).

12. See also Quint. *Inst.* 10.46–51, giving Homer pride of place among the authors deemed most suitable for an orator's education.

is, after all, "a father as well as the Ocean," to quote Philip Hardie, refer-ring both to Harold Bloom's Freudian reading of the relationship between poetic fathers and sons and to the ancient imagery representing Homer as the river of Ocean, from which all streams of poetic inspiration flow.[13] In my first chapter, I look in some detail at how the poetic stream of Homeric inspiration from which Ovid drinks is likely to have reached him, and at how bold Ovid's move is in actively pursuing a career-long engagement with Homer in his elegy as well as in the *Metamorphoses*.

Bloom's idea of a writer's inspirational model and source of influence as a father figure is developed by him in fundamentally Freudian terms. While it is not my purpose to obscure this dynamic, my focus is instead on the metatextual dimensions of this relationship—that is, not on an interper-sonal but rather on an intertextual relationship, and on the ways in which Ovid himself draws attention to his status as heir in the context of the ines-capability of Homeric influence. Ovid's ostentatious self-awareness vis-à-vis his predecessors takes on the character of a kind of literary footnoting: that is, he regularly engages his reader in the pursuit of his models, in a process that is part game, part intellectual challenge, and then permits this reader—at least, the cleverly successful reader—to make what she will of the result. I shall generally attempt to avoid, therefore, falling into the trap of trying to determine a "winner" or "loser" as we proceed; the game, it seems to me, is of far greater interest than the concluding score, especially when that score itself seems to shift as we move from one poem, or one episode, or one character to another. This is one of the tendentiously didactic lessons, I believe, that Ovid embeds in the narrative of Arachne's tapestry, when he juxtaposes its never-ending expansiveness to the teleologically complete nar-rative of Pallas Athena's work (*Met.* 6.70–128).[14] Clarity, as exemplified by Athena, results in a single unified vision that is both all-encompassing and limiting; its intentional obfuscation, on the other hand, can lead to a rich

---

13. Hardie 1993:117 in a discussion of Bloom 1973. For Homer as Ocean, see the collection of sources by F. Williams 1978:98–99, as well as his note on Callim. *Hymn* 2.105–13. Quint. *Inst.* 10.1.46 captures the image well: *Igitur, ut Aratus ab Ioue incipiendum putat, ita nos rite coepturi ab Homero uidemur. Hic enim, quem ad modum ex Oceano dicit ipse amnium fon-tiumque cursus initium capere, omnibus eloquentiae partibus exemplum et ortum dedit. hunc nemo in magnis rebus sublimitate, in paruis proprietate superauerit.*

14. The metatextual nature of the scene has been the subject of many scholarly discus-sions, among which I note Leach 1974; Lateiner 1984; Harries 1990; Rosati 1999:248–53; 2002:292–97; Johnson 2008:74–95; and Pavlock 2009:3–6.

and fertile profusion of ideas, as exemplified by Arachne and as we find in Ovid's poetry.

But I anticipate myself; let us return to the image of poetic paternity that Hardie proposes for Homer's relationship with those poets who follow him. In what follows, I suggest that the trope of paternity is a powerful presence in Ovid precisely because, as an astute reader himself of Homer, Ovid recognizes the centrality of paternity both in the plotting of the *Iliad* and *Odyssey* and in his relationship, as reader, to their creator. In other words, paternity is already a central theme and a central legacy of the Homeric poems; Ovid uses both the thematic and the metatextual potential of this trope to define his place in an unbroken tradition of poetic narrative by assuming the role of Homer's son and heir. Ovid's bold claim to this Homeric inheritance serves to bolster rather than to undermine his assertion of poetic authority, as he anticipates the durability of his name and his work. We might pursue the imagery of paternity a bit further with the suggestion that Ovid legitimizes his transformative poetics through his claim to Homeric paternity: the limitless scope of "father" Homer's poetic vision enables Ovid to achieve his own equally ambitious goals.

Of course, this is not to say that the role model provided by the Homeric poems is not regularly interrogated by our poet: indeed, Ovid's assumption of the role of Homer's poetic son allows him on occasion to play fast and loose with the model as he considers the implications of their relationship figured as one between a father and his son. Familial resemblance and ancestral exemplarity are central to the Roman concept of identity—that is, a man's character and actions are inextricably bound up with his ancestral line, and the importance placed upon each succeeding generation to retain the "family resemblance" can not be overstated.[15] Good sons are those who emulate their fathers and forefathers; competition in the achievement of excellence is integral to this emulation, so that sons may demonstrate their ability to "live up" to the family name through their accomplishments. The goal is generally not differentiation, except in the degree of excellence achieved; maintenance of tradition is an elemental obligation that sons owe to their fathers and family. For Ovid and his poetry, however, the replication of tradition is double-edged: he recognizes that, while a poetic father instills into his

---

15. Flower 1996 is crucial to an understanding of the dynamics of *mos maiorum* as the central organizing principle in Roman ideas about familial relationships.

son the desire to keep a tradition alive, he also has the potential to stifle his offspring, to strip his son of individuality and will. Ovid responds to this challenge repeatedly by asserting his independence, at some times changing course entirely, at others, rejecting the limitations of tradition—but with a rejection that is almost always arch and self-aware, a fiction that draws attention to Homer's prominent role in his imagination, and to the course that his poetic ship cannot help but take upon the inescapable ocean of Homer. Poetic authority and the trope of paternity are therefore closely linked in this book; over the course of chapters 2 through 6 in particular, I shall explore how Ovid deploys this trope in surprising but effective ways, often exploiting the Callimachean conceit of "childishness" (cf. *Aet.* fr. 1.5–6 Pf.) to characterize his metatextual relationship with his poetic father.[16]

A second central theme in this book is repetition. "Repetition" and "repetitiousness" are thorny literary concepts: sometimes repetition can be highly effective, as with the figure of *epanelepsis* (the repetition of a word or phrase in two or three contiguous lines of verse), but it has often encouraged even learned readers of Ovid to think of the contemporary connotation of the word: "boring" or "tedious."[17] Fortunately, a more nuanced approach to repetition in general, and to Ovidian repetition in particular, has begun to take shape in recent years. Several of the most influential studies of Ovid from the past few decades approach him as a repetitious poet, even when the poetics of repetition is not their explicit theme; taken together, they also illustrate that repetition itself can take many forms and lend itself to a variety of interpretive models. These books include Stephen Hinds's analysis of Ovid's two versions of the Ceres and Proserpina myth, with particular attention devoted to the differences linked to generic expectations; Alison Sharrock's focus on the psychological and cognitive pleasure aroused in the reader by the combination of didactic repetition with subtle differences of context and perspective; and Jeffrey Wills's brilliant examination of how the echo of phrases, half lines, and other word-patterning

---

16. On the Callimachean poetics of childishness, see Cozzoli 2011; on Ovid's adaptation of the trope, see L. Morgan 2003. I return to this idea in chapter 1.

17. See the prescient caution of Bickel 1950:308–9: "Quodsi hoc urgemus, Ovidium nusquam fere sine variatione flosculos, hemistichia, nedum solidos versus iteravisse, lassitudo et socordia minimum locum retinent inter causas, quibus eius imitatio sui declaretur. sed vide, ne Ovidium, cuius ex ore facundo versus lepidissimi per lustra et decennia innumeri proruebant, delectaverit, artem suam etiam sic ostentare, ut variandae elocutionis potentissimum se praestans, ea quae antea eleganter dixerat, etiam elegantius repeteret."

devices can establish subtle but firm networks of allusion between and among different poems and poets.[18] The recent appearance of a collection of essays devoted precisely to the theme of Ovidian repetition is evidence of the growing maturity of the subject, as the inter-, intra-, and metatextual potential of repetition in Ovid elicits a new appreciation.[19] While the idea of repetition is in some form at least inescapable throughout this book, it becomes the particular focus of chapters 7 through 9, in which I develop the idea that Ovid's repetitions of Homer are both the expression and the fulfillment of Ovid's desire to embody a distinctly Homeric poetics in his work, to make his work a true heir to the legacy left by his poetic father.

This repetitious desire, as I call it, is not a physical form of desire (although the flexible boundaries of Ovid's relentlessly metamorphic poetic corpus sometimes flirt with physicality),[20] but an expression of Ovid's distinctive relationship with the Homeric poems. By looking at how Ovid's emulation of Homer can also be seen as one poet's desire to become the other, we can better appreciate Ovid's decision to continue and to renovate the inherited poetic tradition, especially as expressed in stories and characters that are closely identified with repetitious physical desire.

Repetition is, after all, a central feature of Homeric style, evidence of a long tradition of oral composition and reworking of traditional themes and stories; in other words, it is "formulaic," to use Milman Parry's term. Following in the footsteps of several generations of Homeric scholars, however, I consider formulaic repetition to contribute to the subtle expression of meaning in the poem, and to indicate not meaningless patterns but resonant poetic memories of other speeches, episodes, and poems.[21] For Ovid, Homeric repetition is both a clever technique and a potential model for the assertion of authority: Ovid uses repetition repeatedly not only to evoke something in the Homeric poems but even, on occasion, to

---

18. Hinds 1987b, with its homage to Heinze 1919; Sharrock 1994b; Wills 1996.

19. Fulkerson and Stover 2016b. In their introductory essay to the volume, esp. 3–15, Fulkerson and Stover 2016a provide a superb overview of how our understanding of Ovidian repetition has changed in tandem with our broader understanding of Ovidian poetic practice.

20. Further on poetic embodiment in Ovid, see Farrell 1999.

21. For Parry's original definition of "formula," see Parry 1971: TE 13. I shall not enter into the continuing fray over the significance of formulaic language in Homer, beyond the assertion made here that it makes an important contribution to the poems' meaning: as I suggest in this book, Ovid certainly read it in this way. For a helpful overview of the scholarly study of the Homeric formula, see Clark 2004; and cf. Calhoun 1933 [1944] for an early appreciation of the contribution of repetition to meaning in Homer.

claim Homeric authorship for a disputed episode. In so doing, he projects his own signature, so to speak, onto the Homeric corpus by demonstrating the thoroughness of his Homeric scholarship. Ovid's repetitious desire, then, entails not only an appropriation of language, style, and subject matter but also the suggestion that Ovid is a devoted reader and editor, whose emulation of his model is grounded in an intimate appreciation for and knowledge of the text: in other words, Ovid's Homer.

This brings me at last to the final element in my title, reception. The general concept of reception needs no introduction to my readers, as the field of classical reception writ large has grown over the past decade or so into an area of disciplinary specialization, with scholarly journals, book series, and conferences dedicated to a vast array of reception studies.[22] But the idea of reception as something that can describe not simply the ways in which later ages reread and revised the classics, and not simply as the way in which we read ancient texts today, but as a phenomenon of the reading experience that can aptly describe how Roman literature itself entails, in many instances, a renegotiation of its relationship with the Greek literary past, is an idea that is only now coming fully into its own. In this book, I use the term "reception" to describe the perspective that Ovid brings to his reading of Homer, and the ways in which that perspective contributes to the transformation that the Homeric poems undergo in Ovid's appropriation of themes, episodes, and diction. A focus on reception can help us to grasp not only the inevitability of intertextuality but also its inexhaustible metamorphic power. Ovid's poetry, in other words, is not only a repository of reused language and stories but a matrix for the living classical tradition.

---

22. A good introduction to classical reception is offered by Hardwick 2003; for further development of method and theory, see the essays in Martindale and Thomas 2006.

I

Starting from Homer

"ἕτερος ἐξ ἑτέρου σοφός | τό τε πάλαι τό τε νῦν"
. . . οὐδὲ γὰρ ῥᾷστον "ἀρρήτων ἐπέων πύλας | ἐξευρεῖν"

—BACCHYLIDES, fr. 5[1]

Allusion is itself a way of looking before and after,
a retrospect that opens up a new prospect.

—CHRISTOPHER RICKS, *Allusion and the Poets*, 86

I. Homer in Fragments

Our knowledge of Roman literary culture in the third century BCE is a perfect example of the random and contingent nature of knowledge in general. Scholars and other learned writers of later ages happen to mention, usually in passing, the titles of earlier works or to quote, usually quite briefly, something particularly memorable or exceptional, or both, from a familiar classic. Thus it is that a few more than thirty fragments remain from a Latin version of Homer's *Odyssey* transformed into Saturnian verse by Livius Andronicus; and the same or similar sources also tell us what little we know about the remainder of Livius's career and work: he is said to have been a freedman from Tarentum who taught both Latin and Greek to the children of the general M. Livius Salinator (cos. 207 BCE); to have written tragedies and comedies, including one of each produced at the Ludi Romani of 240 BCE, and at least one hymn for public performance; and to have employed grander diction in his translated epic than in the plays.[2]

---

1. "One becomes a skilled poet from another, now as in the past,". . . for it is not easy "to find the gates of unspoken words" (quoted by Clement of Alexandria, *Strom.* 5.68.5).

2. For the fragments of all of Livius's works with testimonia, see Blänsdorf 1995:17–38 and Livingston 2004; also Warmington 1936. On Livius's life, career, and works generally, see

Similarly scattered and random, though somewhat more abundant, is our knowledge of the life and career of Quintus Ennius, who belongs to the generation following Livius. By tradition born in 239 BCE in southern Italy, in 204 he was brought by M. Porcius Cato to Rome, where he too appears to have been a *grammaticus*. Also like Livius, he wrote plays, primarily tragedies of the Euripidean type but also comedies; and yet again like Livius, he tried his hand at Homeric-style epic—but here, the differences are what matter. Livius's *Odysia* appears to have followed Homer closely, although the precise length of the poem is debated;[3] Ennius's epic, however, seems to have positioned itself not as a "translation" like that of Livius but as a real complement, a poem on the grand scale (initially, fifteen books) employing Homeric hexameter and deploying Greek gods but treating a distinctively Roman theme, the history of Rome's ascent to greatness from its origins at Troy: *Annales*.[4]

Fraenkel 1931 (still a model of the genre) and his successor, Suerbaum 2005; on problems of chronology in what little we know of Livius's career, see Kaster 1995 on Suet. *Gram.* 1.2; on the language and style of the *Odysia*, see also Mariotti 1986 (1952); Broccia 1974; Sheets 1981; Kearns 1990; Possanza 2004:46–56; and McElduff 2013:39–55. Some scholars have seen Livius as an innovator of signal accomplishment, effectively inventing the art of literary translation and deeply influenced by Hellenistic poetics (e.g., Mariotti 1986 [1952]; Ronconi 1962:17–20; Traina 1970:11–28, 55–65; Büchner 1979), while others consider him the modest producer of what was essentially a school text, of little real literary value and of correspondingly little cultural impact (e.g., Goldberg 1995:46–51). My approach, emphasizing the symbolic value of his undertaking as opposed to the product, is intentionally restrained; our very limited access to his work in his own words seems to me good reason to refrain from yet another attempt at defining his strengths and weaknesses as poet and translator. Cf. Fränkel 1932:307–8: "Übersetzung ist an sich ein Akt der Interpretation, und wie jede Übersetzung in vielfacher Hinsicht hinter dem Original zurückbleibt, so wird auch jede in diesem und jenem Zug interpretierend über das Original hinausgehen müssen"; Broccia 1974:116, paraphrasing Arthur Schopenhauer, *Parerga und Paralipomena* 2.25: "Andronico non intendeva dare ai Romani 'caffè di cicoria'"; and most recently Feeney 2016:53–55, 62–64.

3. There is no indication in our testimonia for Livius of book numbers or divisions, as one typically finds with, e.g., the fragments of Ennius; thus, some scholars suggest that Livius's translation was an abridged version, although the abridgment would have had to be quite severe for his *Odysia* to have been contained in a single scroll (e.g., Goldberg 1995:46–47; cf. Feeney 2016:193, suggesting that Livius's poem was an "amazing feat of compression"); others refrain from expressing a view on the poem's length, observing only that his translation predates the Homeric book divisions most likely introduced by Aristarchus early in the second century BCE (e.g., Courtney 1993:46).

4. For the major fragments of all of Ennius's works, see Warmington 1935; for the *Annales*, see Skutsch 1985. Rossi and Breed 2006 offer a good introduction to the status quo in contemporary Ennian studies, although the thoughtful discussion of Elliott 2013 is likely to make even that recent work somewhat dated.

We know of several other writers of Latin verse active in the third century BCE as well, but I focus attention briefly on these two in particular because, in spite of the fragmentary nature of our knowledge about them and their work, one important idea links them: Homer.[5] Homer is of course the traditional name used since antiquity for the composer of the *Iliad* and the *Odyssey* (I intentionally set aside here the abundant variations on my choice of the word "composer," since it is not my purpose here to enter the unending debate over the origins and character of the Homeric text), as well as a metonymy for the poems themselves; but Homer is also, I submit, an idea, a tradition, a poetic system, whose miraculous presence at what are for us the beginnings of the Western literary tradition gives him (I use the pronoun as a convenience) an unparalleled authority over the unbroken and timeless present of creative expression.[6] Thus, Homer allows us to make sense of Livius, about whom we know so little and in whom we can only infer an instinctive desire to become a part of the Homeric tradition by turning Homer's *Odyssey* into Latin, by engaging with a text that embodied both the cultural supremacy of the Greeks and the first threads of a tradition of mythical connections with Italy.[7] Thus, Homer also allows us to make sense of Ennius, who begins his avowedly Latin historical epic with a dream that recalls the poets' dreams of Hesiod and Callimachus but in which the Latin poet is invited to channel Homer himself, and to communicate with Homer not only through the Muses but directly, bridging time, place, and history to transform Homeric epic values into Roman poetry.[8] Finally, Homer allows us to make sense of their shared position as *grammatici* to the Roman elites: culturally mixed themselves, Livius and Ennius can be seen as conduits of the Greek past to the Roman future, combining fidelity to Homeric authority with the instinct to innovate, challenging themselves to accomplish nothing less

---

5. Suetonius also links Livius and Ennius in the first paragraph of *Gram.*, describing them as *poetae et semigraeci*, but speaking somewhat disparagingly of their contributions to *ars grammatica* (*initium . . . mediocre extitit*): see Kaster 1995 ad loc.

6. Zeitlin 2001 focuses on the era of the Second Sophistic in her discussion of "the remarkable cultural authority of Homer" (the phrase is from her opening paragraph), but her discussion is in fact broadly relevant.

7. On the Italian connections of Odysseus/Ulysses, the definitive starting place is Malkin 1998:178–209.

8. On Ennius's dream, see Mariotti 1991 (1951):41–62; Skutsch 1985:147–87; Aicher 1989. Elliott 2013 is a thoroughly persuasive discussion of Ennius's Homeric poetics, especially chapter 2. The general survey of Homeric influence in Roman poetry by Tolkhien 1991 (1900), though dated, is still of use as an overview.

than Homer himself as they instruct a new audience in the tradition of epic values.[9]

As this book proceeds, the role of teaching as an essential means of transmitting cultural memory will appear repeatedly, both as serious business and as a literary convention that invites play—and sometimes as both simultaneously. The Homeric poems are fundamental to ancient education, both in the Greek world and in Rome; papyrus fragments from many centuries and places illustrate the centrality of the Homeric poems from the earliest years of schooling,[10] and the complexity of Homeric allusion so central to the fabric of a poem like Virgil's *Aeneid* bears witness to the degree of Homeric competence at a very sophisticated level possible from a Roman education, not only in the learned poet but in the audience for whom he wrote. As we shall see when we turn to Ovid, this competence can also be translated into an intricate play with and among texts, and can not only activate but demand textual engagement of the first order: Ovid relies on his reader's knowledge of Homer in order to play fast and loose with the Homeric poems, challenging Homeric truths and values even as he shows his intimate knowledge of them. I shall suggest that Homer is indeed Ovid's first and greatest teacher; as we shall see, however, Ovid challenges the traditional hierarchy of the teacher-student relationship by inverting, subverting, and making something entirely new out of familiar and traditional material. Indeed, Ovid personalizes the relationship in a way that surpasses even the intimacy of the teacher-student relationship, endowing his teacher Homer with paternal qualities and figuring himself as Homer's son and rightful heir.

---

9. For a sophisticated appreciation of the political moves underpinning and sustaining Livius's and Ennius's epics, see Sciarrino 2006. Perusal of the collection of fragments of Latin verse in Blänsdorf 1995 indicates the enduring appeal of Homeric translation and adaptation in Roman culture: in addition to the anonymous rewriting of Livius's translation in hexameters (for the scant fragments of "Liuius refictus," Courtney 1993:46–47; Blänsdorf 1995 frr. 37–40), see e.g. the fragments of Cn. Mattius's *Ilias*, Laevius's *Sirenocirca*, and both *Iliad* and *Odyssey* translations by Cicero.

10. Note Pl. *Rep.* 606e, ['Όμηρος] τὴν Ἑλλάδα πεπαίδευκεν. Virtually every modern study of ancient education starts from the premise of the status of the Homeric poems as fundamental, in all senses: see, e.g., Marrou 1956:3–13 *et passim*; Robb 1994:159–82; and Cribiore 1994. Some particularly useful discussions for the Roman context are Hamdi-Ibrahim 1976–77; Bonner 1977:214–49; and T. Morgan 1998:69–73, 97–100, 105–15.

II. Homer Everywhere

Even the casual reader of Ovid—or of most Latin poetry, for that matter—
will be aware of the Homeric poems as a sort of poetic lingua franca.
Traditional tales become traditional through repetition;[11] and the narratives
of the *Iliad* and the *Odyssey*, with their rich store of characters both male
and female, both human and divine, of interrelationships and intrigues
that shape so much of social interaction, and of events that occur at every
point on the emotional spectrum, from horror and sorrow, through doubt
and distrust, to pleasure and joy, constitute an almost limitless supply
of material to be handed on and down from one generation to the next
and in every artistic form imaginable. The subject matter of the Homeric
poems becomes almost synonymous in the process with the concept of
epic: thus, when Catullus echoes the opening lines of the *Odyssey* in the
first verse of his own poem on the death of his brother, *Multas per gentes
et multa per aequora uectus* ("Having traveled through many peoples and
across many seas," 101.1), he "make[s] Odysseus's mythical journey well
up through his words," as Gian Biagio Conte observes;[12] but he also—
and here I diverge from Conte—not only endows his brother's death with
heroic significance but also puts both his brother's death and his own
journey to Troy in mourning into an epic frame, a frame that would be
adequate for the profound emotion stirred by the death and that would
also represent this emotion adequately to his readers.[13] The tension thus
established between elegy, as the traditional form of epitaph, and epic, the
genre of transformative events of world-changing scale, is an expression

---

11. As I noted in the introduction, repetition as a feature of Homeric style will be a recurring
theme throughout this book, as it is a building block of so much of contemporary Homeric
scholarship. For a moving defense of repetition as a feature of Homer's poetic style, see
also Calhoun 1933 [1944]; though inevitably dated by subsequent research, this essay, writ-
ten shortly after Parry's earliest publications on Homeric composition, shows a passionate
appreciation for the essence of poetry generally and for the accomplishment of Homer in
particular.

12. Conte 1986:36.

13. Conte's discussion of the Homeric echo occurs in the context of a discussion of how
Virgil's reuse of Catullus's line in the *Aeneid* entails a recognition of Catullus's allusion to
Homer (1986:32–37); the Catullan line itself is thus of less importance to Conte than is
Virgil's reading of it. Conte does acknowledge (36 n.8), however, that Catullus's language
may endow his brother with heroic features.

of the tension between private emotion and the public display of grief that Catullus enacts.[14]

A similar tension emerges from the Homeric context of the elegy in which Tibullus describes his own illness far from home and imagines his own death (1.3). The poet sets the tone by identifying the place of his convalescence as Phaeacia (*me tenet ignotis aegrum Phaeacia terris*, "Phaeacia keeps me, sick as I am, in unknown regions," 1.3.3)—the exceptional place name, a mythical alternative for the more mundane Corcyra, identifies the setting immediately with the location of Odysseus's near-death in shipwreck and subsequent salvation by Nausicaa and her parents (*Odyssey* Books 5–7).[15] Then, however, the Tibullan lover veers away from the Homeric narrative, at least from its narrative sequence: whereas the Homeric Odysseus arrives in Phaeacia only after the journey to the under-world during which he receives guidance for the future, and only after the storm at sea that kills all his companions, the Tibullan lover envisions a world at endless war, in which stormy seas are inevitable (49–50), and the only escape from which is possible in a lovers' Elysium (57–66). Thus, the poet evokes a momentary reminiscence of the Homeric hero only to undercut it—but also to underscore the potential Delia's love has to be his saving grace, and to celebrate the idea of a love that will outlast them both. This poet is a soldier with no desire to fight; yet the epic paradigm will not be ignored, and the lovers' Elysium thus takes on the character of a death wish, dispelled only at the end of the elegy when a faithful Delia is to be reunited with her lover, Penelope-like (89–94).

It is striking that both the Catullan and Tibullan echoes of Homer cluster around the theme of death, in the first instance commemorative, and in the second, apotropaic. Yet if we recall how well well-educated Roman boys are likely to have known the Homeric poems—especially, perhaps, the *Odyssey*, thanks to Livius—both can be seen as part of a coherent tradition, in which elegy appropriates and transforms the values and assumptions of

---

14. Ready 2004:154–56 comments on Catullus's use of Homeric figures in the similes of poem 61; although Ready's discussion is concerned primarily with the character of Catullan similes, it is worth noting as well that here, too, in the context of an epithalamium, the Homeric imagery is used to suggest a tension between public and private, now not in the context of mourning but as a marker of the significance of marriage ritual in Roman culture.

15. On the Homeric analogy, cf. also Eisenberger 1960; Wimmel 1968:179–80, 218 n.83; Bright 1971; Mills 1974; and Maltby 2002 ad loc. Murgatroyd 1980:100 is less impressed by the Homeric resonance of the elegy; and cf. Lee-Stecum 1998:103–4 for a more open-ended reading of the Homeric allusion.

epic. The conceit of heroicization of the deceased converges with the overpowering emotion that the prospect of death arouses to suggest a point on the spectrum where the two genres meet: thus, epic and elegy face off constantly, as do the hexameter and pentameter verses of which each couplet is composed.[16]

Propertius continues this tradition of generic confrontation—and, perhaps not surprisingly, he too interests himself in imagining death in terms that draw on a Homeric model. In a discussion of Propertius 4.7, in which the shade of the dead Cynthia reproaches her lover-poet for his neglect, Margaret Hubbard has keenly observed the effect of the elegist's appropriation of the scene in *Iliad* Book 23.62–108 in which the shade of Patroclus reproaches Achilles:

> This is Homer not merely recollected but transposed and modernized, to a world where characters of equal authenticity, however remote from the values, the strengths, the limitations of the heroic world, speak in the accents of their great predecessors. It is an acknowledgement that the imagination has power to reach over centuries, that the picture it presents remains valid for persons and in societies utterly different from those the original poet could envisage; far more than any blunt statement we have in other books and other poets, it displays the power of poetry to confer immortality, and not by shunning detail and the contingent. The society Cynthia inhabits is more complex, and her words more full of particularity than those of Patroclus; but Patroclus remains an exemplar for her.[17]

Interestingly, although Hubbard does not use the rhetoric of intertextuality, she has fastened on a Homeric passage—and its simulacrum in Propertius—in which several intertextual signposts can be noted. First of all, both scenes emphasize similarity—the similarity between the appearance of the living character and his or her now dead shade;[18]

---

16. L. Morgan 2010:345–59 offers a highly relevant discussion of Ovid's deployment of the elegiac couplet.

17. Hubbard 1974:150; cf. also Muecke 1974 with the limitations imposed by Yardley 1977. Some scholars have suggested that Propertius 4.8, too, is to be read through a Homeric lens—in this case, as a comic revision of the scene of the suitors' death and destruction in *Odyssey* Book 22: see, e.g., S. Evans 1971 and H. M. Currie 1973.

18. Cf. Hutchinson 2006 on 4.7.7–12.

and in both scenes, the speaking ghost accuses the living sleeper of forgetfulness (Hom. *Il.* 23.65–70, 105–7; Prop. 4.7.7–10, 15–16, 21–22):[19]

ἦλθε δ' ἐπὶ ψυχὴ Πατροκλῆος δειλοῖο,
πάντ' αὐτῷ μέγεθός τε καὶ ὄμματα κάλ' ἔϊκυῖα,
καὶ φωνήν, καὶ τοῖα περὶ χροῒ εἵματα ἕστο.
στῆ δ' ἄρ' ὑπὲρ κεφαλῆς καί μιν πρὸς μῦθον ἔειπεν.
"εὕδεις, αὐτὰρ ἐμεῖο λελασμένος ἔπλευ, Ἀχιλλεῦ.
οὐ μέν μευ ζώοντος ἀκήδεις, ἀλλὰ θανόντος. . . ."

"παννυχίη γάρ μοι Πατροκλῆος δειλοῖο
ψυχὴ ἐφεστήκει γοόωσά τε μυρομένη τε,
καί μοι ἕκαστ' ἐπέτελλεν, ἔϊκτο δὲ θέσκελον αὐτῷ."

The soul of wretched Patroclus came to [Achilles], so like the living man in every way—stature, fair eyes, and voice, and he wore on his body such garments [i.e., as he had worn in life]; and he stood above his head and addressed a speech to him: "You sleep, and you have forgotten me, Achilles; for you are careless of me now that I am dead, though this was not so while I lived . . . ."

"All night long the soul of wretched Patroclus stood above me, weeping and wailing, and bade me each thing; and seemed marvelously like himself."

eosdem habuit secum quibus est elata capillis,
   eosdem oculos: lateri uestis adusta fuit,
et solitum digito beryllon adederat ignis,
   summaque Lethaeus triuerat ora liquor, . . .

   "iamne tibi exciderant uigilacis furta Suburae
      et mea nocturnis trita fenestra dolis? . . .
   foederis heu taciti,[20] cuius fallacia uerba
      non audituri diripuere Noti!"

---

19. Richardson 1993 on *Il.* 23.69–92 notes that the rebuke for forgetfulness by a dream figure is typical in Homer, and gives other examples; but the combination of rebuke with emphasis on similarity makes this the closest model for Propertius.

20. Camps 1965 prints *foederis heu taciti* here, following several of the earliest and most authoritative manuscripts; Heyworth 2007b, however, following Palmer's 1880 emendation, prints *foederis heu pacti*; see also Heyworth 2007a:466. The rarity of the construction—a so-called genitive of exclamation, otherwise found only in comedy—adds to the uncertainty, but the precise reading has no bearing on my discussion. See also Hutchinson 2006 ad loc.

Her hair was the same as it had been when she was carried out, her eyes the same; the garment on her flank was burned, and the fire had eaten away at the beryl ring she always wore on her finger, and the water of Lethe had worn away the edge of her lip, . . .

"Have the stolen pleasures of the wakeful Subura now escaped you, and my window worn by nocturnal deceptions? . . . Alas for the secret pact, whose false words the south winds, never intending to listen, have torn and scattered!"

In both cases, the emphasis on similarity between the living person and the dead draws attention to the continuity that helps humans make sense of lived experience; on a metatextual level, it also suggests the immortality that only poetry can bring, sustaining as it does the reputation of men—that is, the κλέα ἀνδρῶν—more important than life itself; but the promise of poetic immortality can of course only be guaranteed through the active presence and participation of memory, the poetic memory that echoes past texts as it creates space for a new poetic vision. These two interrelated ideas are certainly implied in the Catullan and Tibullan poems I introduced earlier; but Propertius appears to bring this fusion of texts and ideas to a new level of sophistication with a bold inversion of relationships that also suggests—but barely—a sexualized reception of its Homeric model.[21]

More explicit examples of the same approach to Homeric models appear in several other Propertian elegies and constitute what D. T. Benediktson calls an "elegiacization" of Homer.[22] Indeed, with Propertius's treatment of Homer we see what may well be thought of as Ovid's most direct precursor, although my goal is to demonstrate that the generic reversal that has an episodic significance in Propertius becomes a form of full engagement with the Homeric poems only in Ovid. There is no overarching preoccupation or systematic theme determining

---

21. I refrain from entering the debate over the nature of the relationship between Achilles and Patroclus; for strong arguments on both sides, see, e.g., W. M. Clarke 1978 and Halperin 1990:75–87. The issue here is rather the reception of the Homeric characters in later writers, and there the conviction that the relationship is sexual (as well as affective in other ways) appears to be virtually universal: Pl. *Sympos.* 179e–180b is a succinct example of the trend. W. M. Clarke 1978 offers a valuable collection of post-Homeric discussions, including the influential views of Aristarchus and other early editors.

22. Benediktson 1985.

Propertius's Homeric allusions, aside from a logical interest in the epi-
sodes and characters that have the greatest potential for erotic develop-
ment. Thus, in 1.15, lamenting Cynthia's fickleness, Propertius introduces
Calypso as a paradigm of the elegiac beloved, lamenting the departure of
Ulysses (9–16):[23]

> at non sic Ithaci digressu mota Calypso
>   desertis olim fleuerat aequoribus:
> multos illa dies incomptis maesta capillis
>   sederat, iniusto multa locuta salo,
> et quamuis numquam post haec uisura dolebat
>   illa tamen longae conscia laetitiae.

Not thus had Calypso, moved by the Ithacan's departure, once wept
to the deserted seas; she sat there in sorrow for many days, her hair
unkempt, addressing many words to the unjust sea, and although she
would never see him again afterward, she grieved, thinking of their
long happiness together.

The scene is actually quite curious, since Calypso does not in fact lament
the loss of Odysseus in *Odyssey* Book 5, try though she might to convince
him not to go. In fact, the first couplet of this excerpt transfers to Calypso
Homer's description of Odysseus weeping on the beach (*Od.* 5.82–83),[24]
and so adapts the emotion to an elegiac poem. Homer's Calypso does com-
plain to Hermes (*Od.* 5.118–44), directing some anger toward the gods, but
eventually decides to become Odysseus's helper, advising him how best
to manage the solo journey on which he is about to embark. Propertius,
however, dwells on the time and events not narrated by Homer, that is,
the period immediately after Odysseus's departure, and offers a cameo
of Calypso that foreshadows Ovid's treatment of abandoned lovers in the
Heroides and elsewhere.[25]

---

23. Cf. also Prop. 2.21.13–14. Boyancé 1953 notes this and other examples of Homeric allusion
in Propertius but frames them in terms of the value of the Homeric poems as a repository of
myths, particularly regarding mythical females. Berthet 1980 offers a more nuanced reading
but remains focused on *loci similes*.

24. Itself an adaptation of Achilles's mournful posture on the beach at *Il.* 1.348–50.

25. Fedeli 1980 on 1.15.9–14 compares the Calypso episode that appears in *Ars amatoria* Book
2; the similarity is even greater, however, to Ovid's Circe in the *Remedia*. See chapter 7 for a
discussion of both scenes.

Again, in elegy 3.12, the erotic motivation both for Ulysses's odyssey homeward—that is, in order to be reunited with Penelope—and for his romantic encounters along the way is used as an analogy in a poem addressed to Propertius's friend Postumus. The poet attempts to assure Postumus of his wife's loyalty, no matter how long he may be gone and through what trials (23–38):

> Postumus alter erit miranda coniuge Vlixes:
>   non illi longae tot nocuere morae,
> castra decem annorum, et Ciconum mors, Ismara capta,[26]   25
>   exustaeque tuae nox, Polypheme, genae,
> et Circae fraudes, lotosque herbaeque tenaces,
>   Scyllaque et alternas scissa Charybdis aquas,[27]
> Lampeties Ithacis ueribus mugisse iuuencos
>   (pauerat hos Phoebo filia Lampetie),   30
> et thalamum Aeaeae flentis fugisse puellae,
>   totque hiemis noctes totque natasse dies,
> nigrantisque domos animarum intrasse silentum,
>   Sirenum surdo remige adisse lacus,
> et ueteres arcus leto renouasse procorum,   35
>   errorisque sui sic statuisse modum.
> nec frustra, quia casta domi persederat uxor.
>   uincit Penelopes Aelia Galla fidem.

Postumus will be another Ulysses, thanks to his admirable wife. So many long delays did him no harm: the ten years' camps, the death of the Cicones, once Ismara was captured, and the night of your burned eye, Polyphemus; the deceptions of Circe, the lotus and the man-grasping herbs, and Scylla and Charybdis, divided by alternating seas; the bulls of Lampetie, mooing on the Ithacan spit (his daughter Lampetie had pastured these for her father Phoebus

---

26. Of several textual variants in this elegy, the most significant is in this verse. I print verse 25 as it appears in Camps 1966 and Heyworth 2007b; some editors prefer to read the second half of this line as *Ciconum mons Ismara, Calpe*. Calpe is another name for Gibraltar, a place that in post-Homeric tradition is associated with the *nostos* of Odysseus; if its reading is retained here, it also evokes the western Mediterranean associations of Odysseus that become so important for the Romans; see also Fedeli 1985 on 3.12.24–25; Heyworth 2007a:345–46.

27. For another interpretation of this somewhat difficult line, see Heyworth 2007a:346. The issues concerned do not affect my discussion here.

Apollo); fleeing from the bedchamber of the weeping Aeaean girl and swimming through so many days and nights of storm; entering the gloomy dwellings of the soundless shades, and approaching the pools of the Sirens with deafened oarsmen; refreshing the old bow with the death of the suitors, and thus setting a limit to his wandering: and none of this was in vain, since his wife had remained chaste at home. Aelia Gallia surpasses the trustworthiness of Penelope.

Here Propertius offers a sustained comparison of a contemporary couple with a mythological one; and the reader of the *Odyssey* (or, presumably, the reader who had been schooled on Livius's Latin version) would recognize almost all of the specifics as derived from Homer: ten years, the Ciconian cannibals, Polyphemus, Circe, the Lotus Eaters, Scylla and Charybdis, the cattle of the Sun, Calypso, the underworld, the Sirens, the suitors and the contest of the bow—and, last but not least, Penelope.[28] Yet the description of Calypso is in fact rather odd—she is called "the Aeaean girl," but in the *Odyssey* it is Circe, and not Calypso, who lives on Aeaea (*Od.* 10.135–36).[29] This "confusion" between the two is perhaps better considered an instance of conflation, most likely intentional at that; the two paramours are assimilated to each other with some regularity in post-Homeric tradition,[30] and as we shall see, Ovid exploits the possibilities of this assimilation in his own treatment of Circe.

Propertius thus demonstrates not only familiarity with the Homeric poems but a real mastery of them, and an attraction to what Alexander Dalzell calls "a romanticized Homer," by which he means episodes and characters in the Homeric poems in which passion and drama come to the fore.[31] We may want to counter Dalzell's view with the observation that passion and drama are vague, even generic terms, and as such can describe almost everything that happens in Homer; but it is clear that, whatever terms we use, Propertius experiments at least to a limited

---

28. Fedeli 1985 on 3.13.24–37 argues convincingly that the apparent disorder of the list (i.e., not in accordance with the Homeric sequence) is of no real significance. Cf. also the somewhat abbreviated summary of the *Iliad* that appears at Prop. 3.1.25–32.

29. Calypso's island is generally identified as Ogygia, although there is some uncertainty surrounding the name: see Hainsworth in Heubeck, West, and Hainsworth 1988 on *Od.* 6.172.

30. See Fedeli 1985 on 3.12.31–32; Kaiser 1964: 197–99, 210–13.

31. Dalzell 1980:31.

degree with the possibility of using Homer programmatically to assert the claims of elegy, and that he focuses in particular on scenes and characters that present the greatest potential for emotional development. Thus, situations and relationships involving sexual desire have an obvious appeal, and so we find Ulysses, Penelope, Calypso, and Circe as obvious points of focus; likewise, the relationship between Achilles and Patroclus, whatever its true nature ("truth" being a challenge to define in this context), lends itself to an erotic interpretation, and so it too shares at least potential common ground with the erotic terrain of elegy. But Propertius does not go further; he never uses his verse to construct a strong affiliation between himself and Homer, and never suggests that he is Homer's heir. For Propertius, Homer is a poet of great accomplishment, but Virgil is set to outdo even Homer (*nescio quid maius nascitur Iliade*, "something greater than the *Iliad* is born," 3.34.66); and though there may be moments in Homer that suggest the emotional texture of elegy, Homer is no elegist (*plus in amore ualet Mimnermi uersus Homero*, "the poetry of Mimnermus is worth more in love than is Homer," 2.9.11). I suggest, therefore, that we see Propertius's Homeric moments as simply moments, as fundamentally conventional markers of the boundary between genres. For a poet like Ovid, for whom boundaries present themselves as something demanding to be transgressed, Propertius may well be thought to provide some incipient inspiration; but only in the poetry of Virgil and, I propose, of Ovid can we see the real fruits of a Homeric education in the sophisticated and subtle transformation of Homeric ideas into Latin poetry. I turn now to its mature manifestation in Ovid.

III. Homer Meets Ovid

Propertius, as I have suggested, experiments with the possibility of reading Homer through an elegiac lens, but we must wait for Ovid to extend this idea and frame it as a personal challenge. I turn now to three brief passages in Ovid's elegiac verse that can serve, by way of introduction, to illustrate the shift, as subtle as it is profound: in the later chapters of the book, I will focus instead on more detailed instances of Homeric appropriation and transformation in Ovid. But these three passages serve an important purpose, demonstrating as they do the career-long preoccupation of Ovid with the first and greatest poet of them all. They also suggest *in paruo* the distinct tone of challenge combined with affection that Ovid reserves for his poetic ancestor.

I begin with a small example (chosen from among an almost innumerable supply) in which it is no great leap to see the subversive playfulness of a reading by Ovid that refashions Homer as an elegist *avant la lettre*. Simultaneously, we can also trace here the beginnings of a poetic challenge to Homer, involving the subtle alteration of details or even wholesale revision in erotic terms (*Am.* 1.9.33–40):

> ardet in abducta Briseide magnus Achilles—
>   dum licet, Argeas frangite, Troes, opes!
> Hector ab Andromaches complexibus ibat ad arma,
>   et, galeam capiti quae daret, uxor erat.
> summa ducum, Atrides, uisa Priameide fertur
>   Maenadis effusis obstipuisse comis.
> Mars quoque deprensus fabrilia uincula sensit;
>   notior in caelo fabula nulla fuit.

Great Achilles is afire over stolen Briseis—while you can, Trojans, break the Argive resources! Hector was departing from the embraces of Andromache to take up arms, and it was his wife who would give him the helmet for his head. The son of Atreus, chief among the leaders, is said to have been struck dumb when he saw the daughter of Priam, with her hair flowing like a maenad's; and Mars too, once captured, felt the artificer's bonds; no tale was more famous in heaven.

In four swift couplets, Ovid miniaturizes the entire Trojan War—not to mention its divine observers—as a series of erotic episodes: from the wrath of Achilles over the loss of Briseis that initiates the *Iliad*; through an allusion to the marriage of Hector and Andromache; through the love of the Greek general Agamemnon for his Trojan captive Cassandra; to the divine comedy of Venus, Mars, and Vulcan that Demodocus sings in *Odyssey* Book 8, the central events and characters of Homeric epic are refocused through an erotic lens. In fact, careful readers may well notice that some details in these couplets skew Homeric details so as to give them a new centrality, or even allude to events that are not precisely Homeric: in *Iliad* Book 9, while Achilles articulates his feelings for Briseis in sentimental terms (*Il.* 9.337–43; cf. 9.131–34), his sentiment easily yields to the much stronger emotion provoked by Agamemnon's arrogance; after all, she is a "prize" (γέρας) first and foremost, and what matters most to him is the insult and even humiliation of Agamemnon's assertion of superiority.[32] Ovid focuses instead on Achilles's remarkable, if short-lived, affection for Briseis, reframing it as the erotic raison d'être for the *Iliad*. Again, in *Iliad* Book 6, Hector removes his helmet in order to dispel the martial fearsomeness of his appearance in the eyes of little Astyanax, when he meets wife and son back in Troy (*Il.* 6.466–73); the suggestion here that Andromache eventually hands the helmet back to Hector as she bids her husband to return to the battlefield is a detail not found in Homer, however (rather, Hector picks it up himself, *Il.* 6.494–95), but it invites a tendentious reading on Ovid's part of the tension between gender roles in the Homeric scene.[33] Similarly, the allusion to Agamemnon's infatuation with Cassandra is not in fact a Homeric detail: in *Iliad* Book 1, it is rather Chryseis to whom he is attached, and whom he wishes to bring back home with him (*Il.* 1.111–15); Cassandra is linked to him only in *Odyssey* Book 11 and only posthumously, when the ghost of Agamemnon tells Odysseus about his death, alluding to the murder of Cassandra as well (*Od.* 11.421–23). In fact, Aeschylus provides the first surviving hint—and it is only that[34]—of an erotic attachment between Agamemnon and the captive princess, when Agamemnon introduces her to Clytemnestra by describing her as "a chosen flower of many treasures, the army's gift to me" ("αὕτη δὲ πολλῶν χρημάτων ἐξαίρετον | ἄνθος, στρατοῦ δώρημα," *Ag.* 954–55); but it is only in Euripides's *Trojan Women* that the relationship is described in explicitly erotic terms, with Agamemnon now the victim of love's arrow (ἔρως ἐτόξευσ' αὐτὸν ἐνθέου κόρης, "desire for the inspired girl has pierced him [i.e., like an arrow]," *Tro.* 255).[35] Rather, Ovid effectively offers a revised version of the Homeric poems, in which "love at

---

32. Cf. Hainsworth 1993 on *Il.* 9.336: "[W]hat Akhilleus had loved he spurns when it has been soiled." Ovid's eroticization of the relationship probably draws on post-Homeric versions of the story: see McKeown 1989 ad loc.

33. Ovid may wish in particular to recall the boundary-testing exchange between the two characters that occurs as Hector prepares to return to battle: Andromache begins to offer him advice about where to take a stand and how best to resist the Greek onslaught, thus stepping momentarily out of her wifely role and presuming to offer strategic advice (*Il.* 6.433–40); Hector responds by reminding her that war is his concern, not hers ("ἦ καὶ ἐμοὶ τάδε πάντα μέλει, γύναι," *Il.* 6.441; cf. also 490–93). Cf. McKeown 1989 ad loc., who notices the difference in the treatment of the helmet.

34. Cf. Fraenkel 1950 on *Ag.* 954f., advising readers not to read later versions of the relationship into Aeschylus's play.

35. Cassandra's death, along with Agamemnon's, may have been narrated in the epic cycle (see Procl. *Nost.* arg. 5 in West 2003), but the moment of infatuation is not mentioned in any early

first sight," an erotic convention more frequently associated with women than with men—and certainly not commonly with a general introduced as *summa ducum*—characterizes Agamemnon,[36] while the Homeric comparison to a maenad, used in the *Iliad* only of Andromache (*Il.* 22.460; cf. 6.389–90), is now transferred to Cassandra. Ovid is also at pains to advertise his learning, applying the hyper-Greek patronymic Priameis (first here in Latin) to her,[37] while simultaneously trivializing the entire allusion with the suggestion that what really has an effect on Agamemnon is not her prophetic skill—no hint of that here aside from the (somewhat misleading) mention of a maenad—but the beautiful disarray of her hair.[38] The series of Homeric (or pseudo-Homeric) references comes to a close with a knowing summary of the loves of Venus and Mars—few details need to be given, avers the poet, since the story is so well known from the *Odyssey*; what really matters is that even the god of war himself cannot resist love.[39] Thus, the poem's opening gambit—"every lover is a soldier," *militat omnis amans*—can also be inverted, suggesting that "every soldier is a lover."

The example of Homeric referentiality I have just considered comes from one of Ovid's earliest works, the *Amores*; the tone is appropriately playful, and the tongue-in-cheek didacticism of the poem is only underscored by the poet's use of mythological allusions familiar to every

---

source; nor is it entirely clear whether the allusions to her in the *Iliad* show Homer's knowledge of the tradition giving her the power of prophecy: see *Il.* 13.366 with Janko 1994 ad loc. and 24.699 with Richardson 1993 ad loc. See also Gantz 1993:92–93. Clearly, the Euripidean version had its appeal: cf. Hor. *Carm.* 2.4.7–8, *arsit Atrides medio in triumpho* | *uirgine rapta* (with Nisbet and Hubbard 1978 ad loc.) with *Am.* 2.8.11–12, *Thessalus ancillae facie Briseidos arsit;* | *serua Mycenaeo Phoebas amata duci.*

36. For "love at first sight," see, e.g., Ariadne (Catull. 64.86–93) and Tarpeia (Prop. 4.4.19–22); McKeown 1989 on *Am.* 1.8.24 collects several other examples. Ovid may well wish to acknowledge, however, that the first literary instance of the trope describes a male's view of a female: Zeus as Hera presents herself to him at *Il.* 14.293–94 (cf. Janko 1994 on *Il.* 14.294).

37. This patronymic is not in fact found in Greek but is likely to be modeled on other Homeric patronymics, e.g., Chryseis and Briseis; Ovid uses it again of Cassandra at *Ars am.* 2.405; cf. Janka 1997 ad loc. with Kenney 2002:68. Homer uses the masculine patronymic Priamides frequently, often in a formulaic phrase with the name of Hector.

38. A favorite trivializing detail in Ovid: see, e.g., *Met.* 1.527–30 (Apollo's pursuit of Daphne).

39. Cf. Pl. *Sympos.* 196c8–d4: καὶ μὴν εἴς γε ἀνδρείαν Ἔρωτι "οὐδ' Ἄρης ἀνθίσταται." οὐ γὰρ ἔχει Ἔρωτα Ἄρης, ἀλλ' Ἔρως Ἄρη—Ἀφροδίτης, ὡς λόγος—κρείττων δὲ ὁ ἔχων τοῦ ἐχομένου· τοῦ δ' ἀνδρειοτάτου τῶν ἄλλων κρατῶν πάντων ἂν ἀνδρειότατος εἴη (Agathon is speaking, and the phrase in quotation marks is an allusion to fr. 256 *TrGF* [= fr. 235 Nauck], attributed to the *Thyestes*). For a detailed discussion of the Homeric story, see below, chapter 8; and cf. chapter 9, where I consider yet another episode in which Mars's lust is stronger than his martial instincts.

Roman schoolboy. The poet acknowledges as much later in his career, when he gives his own brief summary of the events leading up to the Trojan War at *Fasti* 6.417–36, while introducing a discussion of how the Palladium arrived in Rome and is now protected by Vesta.[40] Troy's walls were new, says the poet, when Minerva sent her image to the city, and the oracle of Apollo told the Trojans that their city would endure as long as the goddess's image was there. And there she stayed, until during the reign of Priam she was stolen—by whom, it is not clear—and brought to Rome. Ovid's version of events elides the *Iliad*, but that he knows it well is clear from one precise detail, the use of the epithet Smintheus (425) for Apollo: this unusual epithet appears prominently at the beginning of the *Iliad* (and only here in Homer), when Chryses prays to the god to avenge the theft of his daughter by the Greeks (*Il.* 1.39), but otherwise is found almost exclusively in writers of prose texts, primarily of a technical nature.[41] Having thus gestured to the *Iliad*'s opening, Ovid knowingly gestures to the end of the war as well, with his lapidary allusion to the loss of the Palladium: *sub Priamo seruata parum* ("protected too little under Priam," 431). The entire summary, meanwhile, is introduced by a telling couplet that indicates how familiar the myths of Troy and the poems of Homer are to him (417–18):

> Cetera iam pridem didici puerilibus annis,
>> non tamen idcirco praetereunda mihi.

> The rest I learned some time ago, in my boyhood; but this is no reason for me to pass it by.

---

40. Littlewood 2006 ad loc. provides general commentary but does not dwell on the matters that are my focus here.

41. These include geographical and grammatical texts, as well as the collections of lexicographers; cf. also Ael. *NA* 12.5.24 and, in verse, *Orph.* 34.4. Ovid uses it on one other occasion, in an allusion to the tenth year of the Trojan War (*Met.* 12.585). His two uses of the epithet thus allude in two different ways to his Homeric model: the *Metamorphoses* instance, introducing the death of Achilles, alludes generally to the narrative time of *Iliad* Book 1 (near the end of the war) without repeating it, while the *Fasti* instance alludes to the Homeric narrator's sequencing (near the beginning of the poem), again without repeating it. Interestingly, in his *Lexicon Homericum* (an abridged form survives: Bekker 1833), Apollonius Sophistes (late first century CE) reported that Aristarchus considered the use of this epithet by Homer to be ἀπρεπές (quoted by Erbse 1969, apparatus on *Il.* 1.39). If Apollonius is correct about Aristarchus, therefore, Ovid's decision to use the epithet may well be an instance of his rejection of Aristarchus's Homeric criticism. See below, chapter 8, n.29, for the scholiasts' reliance on "appropriateness" as a criterion for Homeric authenticity.

This opening appears to have a touch of nostalgia to it;[42] but as the reminiscence closes, the poet reminds us that Troy is not just the subject matter of bedtime stories, but is a, if not the, scholarly subject par excellence (433–35):

> seu gener Adrasti, seu furtis aptus Vlixes,
>   seu fuit Aeneas, eripuisse ferunt;
> auctor in incerto, res est Romana; . . .

> They say that someone stole it—whether it was the son-in-law of
> Adrastus, or Ulysses ready for theft, or Aeneas; the doer of the deed
> is not certain, but the object is Roman.

Different versions of the story are available, acknowledges Ovid; and though he offers us none of the three options he has listed, it is clear that, should he want to, he could.[43]

As Ovid approaches the end of his career, Homer still looms large as a poetic influence—but now, the arch conceit of *militat omnis amans* and the continuities between Greek myth and Roman culture that constituted the basis of his elementary education give way to the serious business of poetry's politics. Indeed, the political becomes personal now, as Ovid articulates not only a scholarly knowledge of the Homeric poems but a deep affinity for the greatest of all poets. Thus, in *Tristia* Book 2, his "autobiographical" elegy, Ovid offers a defense of his work as a poet, particularly as a poet of erotic elegy, by composing a revisionist literary history in which all of Greco-Roman literary tradition is framed in erotic terms.[44] Of particular note here is his elegiac rendering of the Homeric poems (*Tr.* 2.371–80):

---

42. A less nostalgic view of schooldays is given by Horace, who ruefully recalls the tedium of studying Livius Andronicus under the guidance (and threats) of his schoolmaster Orbilius: *non equidem insector delendaque carmina Liui | esse reor, memini quae plagosum mihi paruo | Orbilium dictare, Epist.* 2.1.69–71, with Rudd 1989 on 71.

43. Barchiesi 1997b:209 takes Ovid at his word: "Ovid himself admits that he does not know who brought the sacred pledge away from Troy." My reading is based instead on the idea that Ovid does in fact know that there are three versions of the theft of the Palladium; he makes a point of advertising the very plurality of options, and so revealing his own deep learning in scholarly exegesis (and its limits). Although Loehr 1996 does not include this example in her analysis, *Fast.* 6.433–35 could easily be included in several of the groups of *Mehrfacherklärungen* she describes (see esp. 360–65).

44. Ingleheart 2010:21–24 offers a brief but useful discussion.

Ilias ipsa quid est, nisi turpis adultera de qua
    inter amatorem pugna uirumque fuit?
Quid prius est illic flamma Briseidos utque
    fecerit iratos rapta puella duces?
Aut quid Odyssea est nisi femina propter amorem,   375
    dum uir abest, multis una petita procis?
Quis nisi Maeonides Venerem Martemque ligatos
    narrat, in obsceno corpora prensa toro?
unde nisi indicio magni sciremus Homeri
    hospitis igne duas incaluisse deas?   380

What is the *Iliad* itself, other than a shameless adulteress over whom there was a fight between lover and husband? What in it comes before a burning passion for Briseis, and how a stolen girl made leaders angry? Or what is the *Odyssey* other than one woman pursued by many suitors on account of love while her husband is away? Who other than the son of Maeon tells of Venus and Mars bound up, their bodies held down in the shameful bed? Whence other than from the evidence of great Homer would we know that two goddesses were on fire with desire for their guest?

Several features of this excerpt quickly announce a reminiscence of the passage in *Amores* 1.9 considered earlier: Briseis is here again (373), representing the *Iliad*, and the loves of Venus and Mars again evoke the *Odyssey* (377–78). But other details add something new and introduce themes to which I shall return in greater detail in later chapters: first of all, the *Iliad* and *Odyssey* themselves are personified, as females—and not just any females but the two with whose behavior each poem is respectively concerned: "Ilias" is the adulteress who caused both the war and the poem about the war, just like Helen, and "Odyssea" is a faithful wife but beset by suitors, just like the poem's main female character, Penelope. The personification and gendering of the two epics introduce a theme about which I will have more to say in chapters 6 and 7; the central idea I wish to underscore at this point is the degree to which Ovid reshapes the Homeric poems in elegiac terms, endowing them with the same emotional life as is to be found in Propertius's Cynthia, Tibullus's Delia and Nemesis, and of course, his own Corinna. In the process, Homer himself is figured as poet and lover simultaneously—as if, in fact, the two identities are inseparable.

Other features of this excerpt make it quite unlike the Homeric paradigms of *Amores* 1.9, however. In the first place, Homer himself is identified explicitly, by name or patronymic, not once but twice, in two successive couplets. The explicit naming of poets whose work should not be taken as indicative of their character is a recurring motif throughout Ovid's *apologia* (353–496) as he moves from Accius and Terence to his contemporaries. The implicit logic of this catalogue leads unerringly to Ovid himself, after all, who notes ruefully at the conclusion that, of all the poets who have transgressed social mores in some way or other in their poetry about love, only he has been punished for it (*nempe—nec inuideo—tot de scribentibus unus | quem sua perdiderit Musa repertus ego!*, "as everyone knows—nor do I deny it—out of so many writers, I alone have been discovered to be the one whose Muse destroyed him," 495–96); he is thus both the last in a long parade of poetic heroes, and the first and only member of an exclusive club indeed.

The twofold naming of Homer also invites us to consider the duality of Homer's poetic corpus: both *Iliad* and *Odyssey*—or "Ilias" and "Odyssea"—bear his name. It also casts into relief the allusiveness of the rest of the passage: with the exception of Briseis, Venus, and Mars, we are invited to provide the other names for ourselves. Thus, the *turpis adultera* of 371 is of course Helen, while the two men mentioned in 372 (*inter amatorem . . . uirumque*) can only be Paris and Menelaus (although the jingle created by the two nouns also plays with another Homeric echo, the phrase *arma uirumque* with which, as he opens the *Aeneid*, Virgil gestures to *Iliad* and *Odyssey*, respectively).[45] In the next couplet, the periphrasis *flamma Briseidos* takes the place of Achilles's name, and the phrase *iratos duces* unites Agamemnon and Achilles around the poem's central theme, *ira*. In the next couplet, Penelope is the focus—but she is identified in the hexameter only as *femina*, and only a series of modifying phrases in the pentameter (*dum uir abest, multis una petita procis*) give her a more precise identification.[46] Finally, the mention of two goddesses and a guest (*hospitis . . . duas . . . deas*, 380) looks to other erotic episodes in the *Odyssey*, namely, the one year spent with Circe and the seven with Calypso; but the phrasing is generic enough to leave room for at least momentary

---

45. Cf. Conte 1986:82–87 on the generic significance of the *incipit*; cf. also Ingleheart 2010 on *Tr.* 2.372, following B. Gibson 1999:29.

46. B. Gibson 1999:29 makes the nice observation that with the generic *femina*, Ovid responds to the first word of the *Odyssey*, Ἄνδρα.

speculation about the identity of the characters to whom Ovid alludes. The noun *hospes*, after all, is used prominently by Virgil to describe Aeneas;[47] and encounters with goddesses are frequent enough in ancient literature to require some precision when they are mentioned. But in fact precision is already available to readers who know the earlier works of Ovid: at *Ars am.* 2.124, just before the Calypso episode that will receive my attention in chapter 7, Ovid himself has already mentioned the "sea goddesses" enamored of Ulysses (*aequoreas torsit amore deas*), with a use of the plural that is somewhat puzzling there but that here can be construed straightforwardly.[48]

Perhaps the most clever aspect of this passage, however, is the one that is hiding in plain sight: I refer to my earlier notice of the explicit naming of Homer, and in particular to the claim that it was Homer himself who narrated the loves of Venus and Mars, complete with scandalous details: *quis nisi Maeonides Venerem Martemque ligatos | narrat . . . ?* (377–78). As Bruce Gibson has observed, "There is an immediate rejoinder to Ovid's question . . . . The answer is that it is not Homer but Demodocus . . . who gives the story, which is merely reported by Homer."[49] Of course, Ovid is correct insofar as Homer *is* the external narrator—and, meanwhile, there is a striking lack of direct quotation from Demodocus in this part of *Odyssey* Book 8—but with *quis nisi Maeonides* Ovid does precisely what he accuses his readers of doing when they mistake him for his work, and vice versa, namely, he confuses narrator and narrative, internal narrator and external narrator.

Another aspect of the poet's responsibility for his subject matter can be read in the next couplet, when Ovid claims that readers' knowledge of Ulysses's two divine paramours is a result of Homer's evidence (*indicio magni . . . Homeri*, 379). Bruce Gibson points to the allusion in this line to Ovid's self-defense some twenty lines earlier, *nec liber indicium est animi* ("nor is the book evidence of my disposition," *Tr.* 2.357);[50] but there is also

---

47. R. K. Gibson 1999 begins his discussion of Aeneas as *hospes* in Virgil with an allusion to *Ars am.* 3.39–40, observing Ovid's pointed use of the Virgilian term.

48. See below, chapter 7, for a discussion of *aequoreas . . . deas* and for the phrase's function in linking the otherwise separate episodes of Calypso in *Ars amatoria* Book 2 and Circe in the *Remedia*.

49. B. Gibson 1999:30.

50. B. Gibson 1999:30.

an irony in the suggestion that Homer is an "informant" on matters of morality especially in the context of the Augustan marriage legislation, under the terms of which transgressive behavior such as adultery, formerly a matter for private adjudication, if any, was criminalized, and those who knew of it would themselves be brought up for action unless they lodged a formal public complaint.[51] Homer, Ovid suggests, is a prototype for the Roman *delator*; but as we shall see in chapter 8, Ovid also suggests that being an informant is not at all a desirable role and can in fact lead to real trouble for the informant himself.[52] The poet's role as tale teller thus takes on the potential to be a dangerous—and virtually unavoidable—predicament indeed; but as Ovid at least implies, it is a necessary risk for a poet, one he has inherited from the first and greatest informer on the gods, Homer.

I introduce these three instances of Homeric exempla because they suggest a pattern of thematic coherence and continuing engagement over the course of Ovid's career, while at the same time illustrating the versatility and flexibility not only of the stories themselves but also of Ovid's awareness of their potential. As an indication of what might be seen as the three stages in Ovid's career, they also suggest an increasing identification with Homer not simply as artistic and technical master—though he is always that—but also as a second self, a poet who, just like Ovid, took risks in his devotion to his calling. In an earlier era of critical study and analysis, such exempla would most likely have been seen as perfect illustrations of Ovid's glib and overly casual attitude toward even the serious business of great poetry; and his allusions to Homer might well have been framed as parody or burlesque, sure signs of the irreverence that would prevent Ovid from being taken seriously.[53] I do not mean to suggest that such responses are entirely misguided: I have already invoked the idea of playfulness in describing Ovidian verse, and the concept will appear again

---

51. On the Augustan marriage legislation, see, e.g., McGinn 1998:140–47 and Severy 2003:54–55; cf. also Holzberg 1990 and Sharrock 1994a on the politics of informing in the depiction of the loves of Venus and Mars in *Ars amatoria* Book 2, along with the discussion below in chapter 8.

52. Cf. Keith 1992:95–115 on the rewards and punishments for tale-telling in *Metamorphoses* Book 2. On the terms *index* and *indicium* in Ovid, see McKeown 1998 on *Am.* 2.1.9 and 2.2.53, respectively; on the verb *indicare*, see Barchiesi and Rosati 2007 on *Met.* 4.236–37; and cf. the discussion in chapter 6 of *Tr.* 3.7.71–72.

53. Hinds 1987b provides an appealing introduction to these and other critical stereotypes; see also Boyd 1997:1–18.

repeatedly in the following pages; but as Llewellyn Morgan has suggested in a wide-ranging discussion of Ovid's "childish" poetics,[54] playfulness is itself a strategy for positioning himself vis-à-vis his first great model and teacher. I shall argue that through his career-long engagement with the Homeric poems Ovid positions himself as Homer's heir and successor, and that this positioning can be seen to express itself as both the logical result of an inevitable intertextuality and the carefully crafted product of a highly self-aware metatextuality. Over time, it also becomes a self-fulfilling prophecy, as Ovid's Homer combines fiction and history to effect a seamless bond between the two poets.

IV. Homer in the Details

It is easy enough to imagine Ovid sitting at his desk, Homer's two poems resting in their containers and always close at hand. But what precisely would these books have looked like, and how would the texts have been presented? Our knowledge of such matters is woefully scant; though it is possible to sketch a general picture of the availability of books in Rome from a wide variety of ancient sources, from archaeological evidence to casual references to books by their readers, the nature of the books used by Rome's most learned readers is not easy to visualize.[55] A second, only slightly less opaque issue is the selection process that took place in the centuries preceding Ovid, which established the *Iliad* and the *Odyssey* alone (i.e., as distinct from the rest of the epic cycle) as the work of Homer: although Herodotus is the first extant source to refer to the poems by the names *Iliad* and *Odyssey* (2.116–17), it is only with the edition (however loosely defined) of Antimachus of Colophon (active c. 400 BCE) that we can be sure that these two poems alone were treated as truly Homeric.[56] We know of Antimachus's work, however, only from the subsequent Homeric scholia, the monumental paratexts that accumulated around the poems in the library at Alexandria and elsewhere. The Hellenistic librarian-scholars,

---

54. L. Morgan 2003.

55. Generally on Roman books and libraries, see Houston 2014, who provides an illustration of what one of these book boxes might look like on 182. Nelis 2010 on Virgil's library is nicely suggestive as well.

56. On the nature of Antimachus's edition, see Pfeiffer 1968:94–95; cf. also 69–73 on Aristotle's subsequent Homeric studies, again distinguishing the *Iliad* and the *Odyssey* from the other works. West 2001:63–67 establishes the status quo since Pfeiffer.

acutely self-conscious about the cultural centrality of the poems and appar-
ently determined to fix it firmly in place, strove to elucidate points of detail
in Homer's language and references to archaic cultural, religious, and
social phenomena; and in the effort to insulate the perceived perfection of
the Homeric poems from any taint or contamination by inferior succes-
sors, they challenged words, lines, episodes, and even entire books on the
basis of perceived inconcinnities with Homeric decorum or characteriza-
tion, or inconsistencies with the general plot, or both.[57]

These paratexts and their authors, chief among whom is Aristarchus,
were clearly known and consulted by the Roman poets as they studied
Homer, although the exact form that these materials took is not self-
evident. Several scholars have suggested that even Livius had access to
Hellenistic commentary of some sort, although his translation of the
Odyssey clearly predates some of the important paratexts.[58] By the first cen-
tury BCE, therefore, the cultural environment in which Roman poets were
working appears to have been fully equipped with materials: not just the
Homeric poems themselves (in what had already become a standardized
form of twenty-four books each) but scholia, commentaries, and other
parerga that we might think of collectively as the first stage of Homeric
reception.

Indeed, by the first century BCE the interest in all things Homeric, at
least among learned men, teachers, and librarians, seems to have intensi-
fied, if that is possible: Alexandrian scholars like Aristonicus and, even
more so, Didymus produced mountains of Homeric commentary and
exegesis, combining their own organization and analysis with extensive
excerpts from their Hellenistic predecessors—excerpts that would in turn
be excerpted by the compilers whose work is present in the Homer manu-
scripts now extant.[59] Meanwhile, it is clear also that the Alexandrian taste
and temperament of the poets writing in Rome around the same time that
Aristonicus and Didymus busied themselves with Homer, that is, at the
very end of the Republic and during the principate of Augustus, meant

---

57. Dickey 2007:18–26 gives a valuable summary of the early scholarship on Homer; cf. also
Kirk 1985;38–43.

58. On Livius's knowledge of Homeric commentaries, see Fränkel 1932:306–8; Mariotti
1986:22 follows Fränkel. Livius may well have had access to the work of Zenodotus and
Aristophanes, but Aristarchus's Homeric criticism is likely contemporaneous with or post-
dates Livius's poem.

59. I refer here to the "four-man commentary," to which Aristonicus and Didymus are the
earliest contributors: see West 2001:46–85 for details and context.

that they read the Homeric poems not only actively but critically and seized every opportunity to become a part of the next wave of Homeric reception. These were the poems, after all, to which they had first been introduced as schoolchildren, and which were thus a part of the cultural fabric in which they were enmeshed. The clearest and most fully studied example of this reception is provided by Virgil, whose *Aeneid* in particular shows evidence everywhere of the poet's Homeric learning. Central themes, narrative techniques, tropes, and images all advertise their Homeric affiliations, beginning with the very first words of the poem, *arma uirumque cano*;[60] but an even richer vein of interpretive possibilities can be mined by readers aware of the critical history of the Homeric epics, Virgil's careful reading of which reveals itself both in fine details and in larger structures of ethical and political complexity.[61]

This is the tradition to which Ovid is heir. From the Republican productions of Livius and Ennius down to the literary scene of his own lifetime— during which, as he notes, he just managed to see Virgil (*Tr.* 4.10.51)—the Homeric poems are a constant presence. And something more: as Virgil's engagement with Homer amply demonstrates, the *Iliad* and the *Odyssey* taken together are *provocateurs* of poetic excellence: they provoke their own reception, I suggest, by inviting poet-successors to compete with and, if possible, to surpass them by retelling, renewing, and reinventing their own incomparable store of narratives, characters, and emotions, and to do so not only in broad strokes but also with often playful attention to details.

With this idea in mind, I turn back once more to the image of Ovid with his texts. Again, the precise nature of these texts is tantalizingly out of our reach; but the cumulative result of individual readings offered in this book suggests that the scholarly apparatus introduced by the librarians at Alexandria and others, then further promulgated by Didymus and his fellow compilers, was as well known to Ovid as were the poems

---

60. See above, n.45, for one of several instances of Ovid's treatment of this phrase; cf. also *Tr.* 2.534 with Ingleheart 2010 ad loc., noting Ovid's transformation of the phrase into an obscene innuendo; Ingleheart also lists other instances of Ovidian play with the phrase; and cf. McKeown 1989 on *Am.* 1.1.1–2. On parallels between the epics of Homer and Virgil, see the introduction, n.6; see also Barchiesi 1984 (2015) and, for a brief but enlightening overview, Hexter 2010.

61. First steps toward uncovering Virgil's use of Homeric criticism are those taken by Schlunk 1974, following Heinze 1993 (1928; see especially the index s.v. scholia on Homer). In the last two decades, exploratory projects inspired by Schlunk have begun to multiply but are often limited to individual episodes or books; the premier exception is Schmit-Neuerburg 1999. Cf. also Horsfall 1991:41–42; Hexter 2010.

themselves. I have not constructed this discussion around Ovid's reading
of scholia and commentaries; indeed, when I began this project, I was not
myself aware of the evidence I would find to suggest such a reading. It
nonetheless emerges from my study that Ovid's project entails reception
of Homeric scholarship along with the Homeric poems themselves.[62] Of
course, Ovid never comes out and says explicitly that his treatment of a
particular episode or character is based on a comment by a scholiast; a
statement of that sort would diminish the fun, suggests Ovid, the sheer
intellectual excitement of becoming part of a tradition in the making—and
for his readers, the moment of realization as this tradition asserts itself.
On a variety of occasions throughout this book, therefore, I note the way
in which Ovid appears to be drawing attention to his familiarity with the
scholia—and in particular, I suggest, with scholia that express criticism of
or concern for something in the Homeric text. Ovid is not explicit about
his goals—but the "suspicious reader," as Matthew Robinson terms the
sort of reader who actively seeks in the text for interpretive openings,[63]
will discern, if attentive, a certain curious pattern in the features of the
Homeric poems and the predilections of their first critics that seem par-
ticularly attractive to Ovid.

A prominent characteristic of Ovid's reading and reinterpretation of his
models generally speaking is a distinctly contrarian perspective: truisms
and common knowledge are particular bugbears for the poet-as-critic. One
very obvious example will serve to illustrate this: Ovid's frequent allusions
to the *pietas* of Aeneas (sometimes in the form of a Homeric-style epithet,
i.e., *pius Aeneas*). *Pietas* can be seen as not only a virtually canonical attri-
bute of the protagonist of Virgil's monumental poem but, through a sort of
logical (if unconscious) progression, a metonym in subsequent tradition
for the entire Virgilian project: the reverence with which the poet Virgil
and his poems are venerated by succeeding generations finds its essential
core in his central character and his defining characteristic.[64] Yet when

---

62. I am not the first to observe this: cf., e.g., von Albrecht 1980:44 (in a discussion of
Heroides 3): "Homerrezeption durch eine kommentierte Ausgabe überrascht bei Ovid so
wenig wie bei Ennius oder Vergil." Jolivet 1999 is particularly effective in demonstrating the
possibilities.

63. Robinson 2011:9–11.

64. Ovid's many allusions to the *pietas* of Aeneas include (at least) *Am.* 2.18.31; *Fast.* 1.527,
2.543, 3.601, 4.37, 4.274, 4.799; *Met.* 13.640, 14.109 and 443; cf. also, e.g., *Met.* 13.640 and
15.681; *Tr.* 1.3.86; *Pont.* 2.2.21. (In several other instances, Ovid uses the idea of *pietas* in
connection with a character other than Aeneas—Romulus, for example—but in a way that

Ovid employs the conventional imagery, even using twice the phrase *pietas spectata per ignes* (*Fast.* 4.37 = *Met.* 14.109) and so giving it the complexion of a Homeric formula, he invites us to take a new and more critical look at the character and his actions; the undercurrent of—what is it? irony? sarcasm? doubt?—that pervades Ovid's references to *pius Aeneas* is subtle but constant. On a grand scale, we might even argue that the cumulative effect of such allusions threatens to undermine the entire Augustan project—if even the great ancestor of Rome presents us with an appearance of *pietas* that is never clearly grounded in the "facts," then what are we to make of the great men who claim descent from him and who promote their own right to supreme authority in similar terms?

When we turn back to Ovid's Homeric intertextuality, the terms of comparison are somewhat different, but analogous; here too we see Ovid as contrarian not only in his treatment of individual characters—my discussions of Briseis and Achilles in chapter 3 and of Penelope and Circe in chapter 7 are illustrative—and of the very balancing act that distinguishes epic from elegy but in his response to the critics and editors of Homer. This book is not primarily about Ovid as a reader of Homeric scholia, but I do attempt to indicate regularly throughout my discussion, both in the body of the text and in the notes, points at which it is possible to see in Ovid's treatment of a particular character, event, or other detail a reaction to something he has read in the scholia. In particular, I suggest that Ovid has taken note of a number of challenges to authenticity in various Homeric episodes and uses his own poetic authority to "reinscribe" previously challenged episodes and scenes into the Homeric corpus. Thus, I shall argue in chapter 3 that Ovid's approach to the Embassy to Achilles, a substantial and crucial episode in *Iliad* Book 9, stems at least in part from his interest in reasserting the authenticity of the episode in general and of the character of Phoenix in particular. Ovid's reading of *Iliad* Book 10, the *Doloneia*, asserts itself somewhat differently, but again I would suggest that his interest in the episode is related at least in part to its exceptional

---

invites his reader to associate the two.) On the canonical status of Aeneas's *pietas* after Virgil, see Bömer vol. 6, 1982 on *Met.* 13.623–14.608; Weinstock 1971:253–56; Galinsky 1969:53–61; and cf. Knox 1986:69–70.

It is tempting to suggest that the attribution to Virgil of the epithet Parthenias, appearing for the first time in Aelius Donatus (*Vita* 11), springs from a similar impulse to see Virgil's character in his verse, and vice versa: *cetera sane uita et ore et animo tam probum constat, ut Neapoli Parthenias uulgo appellatus sit, ac si quando Romae, quo rarissime commeabat, uiseretur in publico, sectantis demonstrantisque se subterfugeret in proximum tectum.*

status in the poem. The Byzantine scholar Eustathius, apparently alluding to the Alexandrian editors as his source, reports that the *Doloneia* was not part of the "original" *Iliad* but was a separate Homeric composition, and that it was only during the reign of the tyrant Pisistratus in Athens (i.e., mid-sixth century BCE) that the anomalous book was introduced into the *Iliad*: Φασὶ δὲ οἱ παλαιοὶ τὴν ῥαψῳδίαν ταύτην ὑφ' Ὁμήρου ἰδίᾳ τετάχθαι καὶ μὴ ἐγκαταλεγῆναι τοῖς μέρεσι τῆς Ἰλιάδος, ὑπὸ δὲ Πεισιστράτου τετάχθαι εἰς τὴν ποίησιν ("The ancients say that this song was arranged separately by Homer and was not included among the parts of the *Iliad*, but was integrated into the poem by Pisistratus").[65] This claim, presumably made hundreds of years before Ovid read the works of Homer, continues to be the dominant view in the world of Homeric scholarship: Martin West articulates the status quo in definitive terms:

> It is a lively, exciting episode, certainly composed to stand where it does now in the poem, but structural and stylistic considerations combine to show that it was no part of the original poet's design, nor from his workshop. . . . Nothing in what has gone before points forward to the episode, and nothing that comes later harks back to it. It is particularly noteworthy that the chariot race at the Games for Patroclus, which involves all the other important horses of the *Iliad*, has no place for the marvellous snow-white steeds of Rhesus that Odysseus and Diomedes capture in the Doloneia. All this might be conceivable if the Doloneia were the *Iliad* poet's final afterthought, inserted after the rest was complete. But it is also marked by peculiarities of linguistic usage and by its own unique tone. So it has to be attributed to a different poet.[66]

Of course, this is not—cannot be—the final word, and other scholars continue to attempt to make the case for the book's "Homericity" in the context of oral transmission.[67] While I shall refrain from declaring my own loyalties in this competition, it is important to note that the events narrated in the *Doloneia* constitute one of the most frequently evoked Homeric allusions in the Ovidian corpus: Ovid makes reference to it in

---

65. See also the T scholia on the opening of *Iliad* Book 10.

66. West 2001:10.

67. See especially Dué and Ebbott 2010, following the many studies of Gregory Nagy; for a recent example, see Nagy 2004.

five different works,[68] often treating the episode as a sort of shorthand for the entire Homeric corpus in the process. These allusions occur at *Am.* 1.9.17–28; *Her.* 1.39-46;[69] *Ars am.* 2.129–40; *Met.* 13.98 and 242–54;[70] and *Ibis* 625–28.[71] I have already looked briefly at another selection from *Amores* 1.9, where Ovid summarizes the erotic plots of both the *Iliad* and the *Odyssey* in four elegiac couplets; in the lines preceding them (21–28), Ovid develops the trope of the lover as a spy in the night, ready to pounce on his prey (as well as on any would-be competitors), and the *Doloneia* provides the perfect epic model for this thoroughly elegiac undertaking. In *Heroides* 1, Penelope includes the *Doloneia* in the list of dangerous activities that Ulysses has engaged in at Troy, and about which she has heard from the various visitors who stop in Ithaca—though her version conveniently omits the participation of Diomedes; and in *Ars amatoria* Book 2, Ulysses is depicted as a brilliant storyteller, who enthralls both Calypso and, apparently, himself with repetitions of (an again highly tendentious version of) the *Doloneia*.[72] In *Metamorphoses* Book 13, in his version of the *iudicium armorum*, the Ovidian narrator locates allusions to the *Doloneia* in the speeches of both Ajax and Ulysses (although tellingly, while Ajax's mention is contained in a single verse, Ulysses's description is developed over thirteen); and in the *Ibis*, the narrator wishes upon his victim as bad a night's sleep as that experienced by Rhesus and his comrades. In short, Ovid uses the *Doloneia* as a sort of metonym for Ulysses as warrior, and indeed for the Homeric poems in general; while this curious focus on an episode whose authenticity was impugned by the Alexandrian critics may have any number of explanations, I venture to suggest that Ovid is

---

68. A sixth allusion to the episode may be thought to exist at *Rem. am.* 282, where the Etoniensis (eleventh century) reads *resus*, but that this is a scribal error for *rursus* is now generally agreed; see the apparatus of Kenney 1995, along with Kenney 1958:172 and Kenney 1959:258.

69. Barchiesi 1992 and Knox 1995 on *Her.* 1.39–46 both note specific verbal and other allusions to *Iliad* Book 10.

70. Cf. Hopkinson 2000 on *Met.* 13.98 and 238–54.

71. Jolivet 2004 surveys these allusions in the context of a discussion of the reception by both Virgil and Ovid of the *Doloneia* and its status in the scholia, concluding that while Virgil's response (i.e., in the episode of Nisus and Euryalus in *Aeneid* Book 9) is more "complex" (53) than Ovid's, Ovid's version focuses more directly on the character of Odysseus and its treatment in the scholia. For a full and useful discussion of Virgil's response to Homer and the scholia in *Aeneid* Book 9, see Schmit-Neuerburg 1999:19–65; Cf. also Hardie 1994:29–30 along with his notes on *Aen.* 9.176–449.

72. See the discussion of both the *Heroides* and *Ars amatoria* episodes in chapter 7.

attracted to it precisely *because* it is controversial. In the process of allud-
ing to the episode not once but repeatedly, moreover, Ovid also, I suggest,
works to "reauthorize" the episode, to assert its Homericity, and indeed to
feature it as in some sense the most "Ulyssean" of all the events surround-
ing the Homeric figure.

Ovid's Homer reflects the influence of tradition—stories transmitted
across and through generations, preserving an essential core of meaning
as they adapt and are adapted—and of an intimate and original percep-
tiveness. Ovid follows in a long line of models who read Homer actively
and insightfully, but he also stakes out for himself a distinctive, and char-
acteristically Ovidian, approach, reading against the grain—not so much
against the grain of Homer but of all those who have read Homer since
the *Iliad* and *Odyssey* took textual form. In the following chapters, I shall
explore some of the ways in which Ovid establishes a dialogue across
space and time with Homer, interrogating and responding to Homeric
narrative on every level. Ovid's reception of Homer is an active process
that he engages in at every stage of his career, from the first elegies he
writes (*Amores* 1.1 and *Heroides* 1) until he composes his last verses in exile.
This Homeric saturation can be insouciant or moralizing, complimentary
or competitive, or all of these things at once: such is the brilliance of Ovid,
a brilliance he nurtures in a lifetime of Homeric moments.

2

Seeing Double: Ovid's Diomedes

"καί ποτέ τις εἴποι πατρός γ' ὅδε πολλὸν ἀμείνων
ἐκ πολέμου ἀνιόντα"

—HOMER, *Iliad* 6.479–80[1]

I. Ovid Reads (and Re-reads) Homer

While Odysseus, as we shall see, provides a number of entry points into Ovid's collected oeuvre, Homer's Diomedes also appears prominently, if less frequently, in several episodes; and it should not be entirely surprising to the metapoetically oriented reader to find that the hero who is deemed second only to Achilles by Homer would attract the interest of a poet who positions himself as a belated but worthy second to Virgil.[2] As we have seen, brief allusions to the most notable Homeric episodes involving Diomedes, his wounding of Aphrodite in *Iliad* Book 5 and his collaboration with Odysseus in the night raid (*Doloneia*) of Book 10, are exploited by Ovid throughout his career, from *Am.* 1.9.21–26, where the *Doloneia* is invoked as a parallel for lovers hoping to catch their prey off guard—in

1. "And some day, may someone say, 'This man is far better than his father,' as he comes home from war" (Hector's words to Andromache about their son Astyanax).

2. On Ovid's emulation of the Virgilian career model, see Farrell 2004. One topic not discussed elsewhere in this chapter but worth keeping in mind is the tantalizing reference in the Horatian scholiast Pseudo-Acron to an epic *Diomedea* by Iullus Antonius, the son of Marc Antony and Fulvia, born, like Ovid, in 43 BCE: see Thomas 2011 on Hor. *Carm.* 4.2.2, along with the discussion by S. J. Harrison 1995:115–22. On the little we know about this writer and his work, see Coppola 1990, who speculates that the story of Diomedes offered the potential for a distinctively anti-Augustan treatment; though we have virtually no hard evidence to go on, it is tempting to consider that this characterization could well have added to the appeal of Diomedes to a poet like Ovid.

fact, asleep—to *Pont.* 2.2.13–14, where Ovid contrasts his own respect for
the gods and their offspring (by implication, Augustus) with the assault
that made Diomedes notorious. Ovid, like Virgil, also makes reference to
the post-Homeric tradition surrounding Diomedes, most notably the theft
of the Palladium from Troy. This last episode is a predictable component
of the Vesta narrative of *Fasti* Book 6, where Ovid makes reference to the
various "thieves" associated with the image's translation to Rome (*Fast.*
6.433–34).[3]

The most frequent basis for allusion to Diomedes, however, is his
exceptional encounter with Aphrodite, an encounter that offers Ovid a
metapoetic model for his identity as a poet of love, an encounter that might
be read, I propose, as Ovid read it, as both intimate and aggressive, as both
playful and threatening, as at once an assault on authority and an assertion
of defiance in the face of divine wrath. The suggestion that he is both like
and not like Diomedes comes to the fore, as we shall see, in *Amores* 1.7, but
it is active as well in other poems, especially the *Remedia amoris*, in which
the erotic metaphors involving wounds, medicine, and healing that per-
meate so much of Latin poetry, especially elegy, are literalized, as "Doctor
Ovid" proposes to cure his pupils of the disease of love (the very same
disease he was instrumental in helping them contract).[4] There, Diomedes
is figured prominently as an anti-Ovid in the opening lines: the Ovidian
praeceptor responds to Cupid's imagined outrage at the offensive title of
the new poem ("*bella mihi, uideo, bella parantur*" ait, " 'Wars, I see, wars
are being prepared for me,' he said," *Rem. am.* 2) with the assurance that
this poet is no Diomedes (*non ego Tydides, a quo tua saucia mater* | *in liqui-
dum rediit aethera Martis equis*, "I am no son of Tydeus, from whom your
mother, wounded, returned to the clear sky with the horses of Mars," *Rem.
am.* 3–4), that is, that he plans no assault on the god of love. Ovid's fasci-
nation with the potential presented by Diomedes for engagement with the
Homeric poems is a constant in our poet's varied career; in this chapter,
I will focus on the two most extensive appearances of Diomedes in the
Ovidian corpus, but it is worth remembering that this hero reappears fre-
quently, if briefly, elsewhere in Ovid's poetry.

---

3. Littlewood 2006 on *Fast.* 6.417–36 offers details of the tradition; see also Börner 1958 on
Fast. 6.417, commenting that this is one of the first indications of the prominent place of
Homerica (probably via Livius Andronicus) in Roman education; see chapter 1, above.

4. The term "Doctor Love" is used by Sharrock 1994b:50 *et passim.* On the probable origins of
the metaphor of *medicina amoris* in the elegies of Gallus, see Ross 1975:66–68; O'Hara 1993.

II. Homer's Diomedes and Family Honor

An extended episode in *Iliad* Book 4, known to ancient critics as the *Epipolesis*, or Tour of Inspection, focuses on Agamemnon's efforts to rally the Achaean leaders in the face of the Trojan assault (4.223–421).[5] Agamemnon circulates through the camp, stopping to speak with various groups of warriors and their individual leaders. The vividness of Homeric narrative combined with the focus on leaders in this episode helps to individuate several of Agamemnon's interlocutors and may well provide a rationale for the episode's length: like the *Teichoscopia* in *Iliad* Book 3, the descriptive direct speech of this episode allows Homer's audience to deepen its familiarity with several characters who will play important roles later in the poem.[6]

Agamemnon's energetic cheerleading is a model for the rallying speech before battle: he begins with a combination of encouragement and praise for those eager to fight and reproach for those who hesitate (4.223–49), in both cases invoking Zeus as the ultimate assessor of the men's relative merits. He then proceeds to focus his attention on a number of individuals, beginning with Idomeneus, leader of the Cretan contingent (4.250–71); after receiving confirmation of Idomeneus's unfailing commitment, he moves on to the two Aiantes, who receive brief but strong words of praise for their battle readiness (4.272–91). Next is Nestor, whose own instruction of the Pylians is already in full swing; indeed, Nestor provides a mirror image of Agamemnon himself—and vice versa—so underscoring the authority of both men and, through a shared reflection on the relative merits of age and youth, hinting at the unbroken tradition that links them (4.292–325). After this triad of increasingly positive encounters, Agamemnon moves on to another twosome, Mnestheus and Odysseus;[7] but this time, he opens with reproach, for, though battle ready, neither man has begun to lead his troops into battle. Mnestheus makes no reply; not surprisingly, Odysseus pre-empts him and speaks for them

---

5. See Kirk 1985 ad loc. for the episode's usefulness in creating a delay before the resumption of hostilities and so adding to the narrative tension.

6. Kirk 1985 ad loc. makes the analogy to the *Teichoscopia*.

7. An odd pairing, as Kirk 1985 on *Il.* 4.338–40 notes; but the fact of pairing itself, seen already with the two Aiantes, may well be more important for the poet than the particular makeup of the pair. In this case, indeed, Mnestheus's relative unimportance is useful, allowing Odysseus to take center stage as he does.

both in rejecting Agamemnon's harsh words and asserting their readiness, already proven many times over, to fight (4.326–63).

Homeric mastery of narrative theme and variation[8] is well demonstrated by this sequence: Agamemnon tailors his address to fit the character of each of his interlocutors, and they in turn constitute a chorus of voices in harmony with their leader. The exchange with Odysseus is particularly telling, suggesting as it does a certain strategic shrewdness: Odysseus's well-known preference for words over deeds is momentarily used against him, before being used by Odysseus himself to invalidate Agamemnon's rebuke.

Thus far, the expectations of Homer's audience have been satisfied: Agamemnon's eloquent leadership is on full display, and its culmination in a matching of wits with Odysseus is highly satisfying. What happens next, however, while a natural extension of Homeric theme and variation, is nonetheless surprising: Agamemnon next turns to Sthenelus and Diomedes, another pair of warriors who, like their predecessors, have not yet joined in battle (4.364–418).[9] With the preceding pair, Agamemnon had at least nominally addressed both men; now, however, he singles out Diomedes for extended rebuke, delivering by far the longest single speech in the episode. Aside from a brief mention in the Catalogue of Ships (2.559–64), this is Diomedes's first appearance in the poem;[10] that his introduction takes the form of a rebuke adds to the unexpectedness of this turn of events. The content of Agamemnon's speech is also exceptional, offering not a promise of the rewards of victory but rather an extended comparison between Diomedes and his famous father, Tydeus. Indeed, Agamemnon delivers a miniature *Thebais*, in which the most important figure by far is Tydeus; the focus is on Tydeus's efforts to assemble an army and to negotiate with Eteocles, and his successful—and bloody—thwarting of an ambush.[11] In fact, this portrait of Tydeus, eliding as it does the infamous and ignominious final

---

8. van Otterlo 1944 uses the term *Ritornellkomposition* to identify the pattern of linear variation seen here; see also Gaisser 1969.

9. Andersen 1978:33–46 offers a good discussion of the contrast between Odysseus and Diomedes in the *Epipolesis*.

10. Noted also by Pratt 2009:147; Slatkin 2011:104.

11. For details, see Gantz 1993:502–3 (on the *Thebais*), 510–13 (on the Homeric story). Torres-Guerra 1995 makes a case for the priority of the *Thebais* to the Homeric poems; Ebbott 2010 considers Homer's *Thebais* allusions as indicative of the "hypertextual" relationship of the Homeric poems to other, now lost and/or fragmentary, poems.

episode in the tale,[12] depicts Tydeus as behaving in the past much as Agamemnon himself is behaving now, taking the initiative, rallying the troops, preparing for battle; the contrast Agamemnon makes between father and son is further underscored by the fact that Diomedes, feeling respect for (αἰδεσθείς, 4.402) this address, says nothing in reply, even though Agamemnon has just concluded his speech with the assertion that Tydeus's son, while excelling less in battle, is greater in the assembly, "i.e. at speaking" (Kirk 1985 ad loc.).[13]

The participle used by Homer to register Diomedes's response to Agamemnon, αἰδεσθείς, is worth lingering on for a moment. Recent commentators on this passage are generally at pains to argue for a sense of respect rather than shame in its use here: Kirk (1985 on 4.401–2), remarking on the unusual features of this scene, notes: "That so great a warrior should accept [Agamemnon's rebuke] in silence is unexpected; even more so that he 'respected', αἰδεσθείς, the royal reproach, especially because at 9.34–6 he will remind the king of his insult." Kirk continues by commenting on "the difficulty of αἰδεσθείς," claiming that it "shows that Diomedes respects the king's office, merely, and understands the kind of behavior it tends to elicit." Willcock (1978 ad loc.) sees the contrast between Odysseus and Diomedes as most important and continues: "Diomedes has the qualities of the ideal junior commander—he is respectful to authority, clear-headed, immensely capable and controlled. All the same, he does not forget this insult . . . . "[14]

Diomedes's surprising silence is set in even higher relief by what happens next: though Agamemnon has not acknowledged his presence, Sthenelus replies, using the eventual failure of the expedition of the Seven to assert the superiority of his own and Diomedes's accomplishments: he argues that while Diomedes's father, Tydeus, and his own father, Capaneus, were among the warriors who perished at Thebes because of their own blindness, he and the other Epigoni had the gods on their side and so were victorious (4.401–10).[15]

---

12. On Diomedes's limited use of his genealogy in the *Iliad*, especially regarding his father, see Christensen and Barker 2011:32–35. While much of that discussion is peripheral to the current study, I want to acknowledge the implicit parallels between my reading and theirs, as evidenced in the discussion that follows.

13. On Diomedes's development as a speaker in the *Iliad*, see Christensen 2009.

14. See also, e.g., Sheppard 1940:52; Christensen and Barker 2011:30; Cairns 1993:95–97.

15. Christensen and Barker 2011:12–23 offer a valuable discussion of this story's resonance with the *Odyssey*.

Sthenelus's bold assertion of superiority is intended to refute Agamemnon; indeed, Sthenelus responds much as had Odysseus in the previous encounter. But while Odysseus's fighting words made Agamemnon back down, the king has no opportunity—or need—to do so now, for Diomedes breaks his silence at last and, rather than replying directly to Agamemnon in his own defense, directs his own rebuke at Sthenelus for speaking against Agamemnon.[16] The episode concludes with Diomedes using action rather than words to indicate his willingness to join the battle, leaping from his chariot with an awe-inspiring clang of weapons (*Il.* 4.419–21):

Ἦ ῥα, καὶ ἐξ ὀχέων σὺν τεύχεσιν ἆλτο χαμᾶζε·
δεινὸν δ᾽ ἔβραχε χαλκὸς ἐπὶ στήθεσσιν ἄνακτος
ὀρνυμένου· ὑπό κεν ταλασίφρονά περ δέος εἷλεν.

He spoke, and from the chariot he leapt with his armor to the ground. The bronze resounded terribly on the breast of the lord as he was moved to action; fear would have seized even a stout-hearted man.

The battle is ready to begin—and it does, with a simile of crashing waves that follows Diomedes's aggressive leap from his chariot (4.422–26).

III. Diomedes Shamed

I open with detailed analysis of this episode because it introduces several themes important for the following discussion. Diomedes is of course one of the most prominent figures in the *Iliad*, identified in Book 5 as a warrior second only to Achilles (5.103 and 414);[17] with the latter's withdrawal from the field, Diomedes is featured prominently in the *aristeia* of *Iliad* Books 5–6 and again in the *Doloneia* of Book 10, among numerous other scenes, especially battle scenes.[18] Several features of the *aristeia* in particular will concern us in what follows, but the call to arms just described, although

---

16. Cf. Higbie 1995:97: "The greatest surprise of this small scene now occurs: Diomedes speaks belatedly, but only to rebuke his friend and to recognize the justness of Agamemnon's criticism (412–18)."

17. Cf. also *Il.* 6.96–101; and Nagy 1979:30–31. On the character of Diomedes in contrast to that of Achilles, Whitman 1958:165–69. Pratt 2009:154–61 summarizes the key themes of the comparison.

18. Higbie 1995:92–93.

generally of less apparent interest to Homeric scholars than the other epi-
sodes, provides a particularly useful basis for considering Ovid's reception
of the Homeric hero.

The first prominent aspect of Agamemnon's interchange with
Diomedes is, for our purposes, the emphasis on talk as opposed to action.
Agamemnon first uses this opposition as a rhetorical strategy in his rebuke
of Odysseus; Odysseus reacts the way the Homeric audience expects him
to, pushing back against the leader's words and asserting his readiness.
In fact, his response is pointedly insulting, using a striking metaphor
to suggest that Agamemnon's words are vapid: "σὺ δὲ ταῦτ' ἀνεμώλια
βάζεις" ("'you speak words of wind,'" 355). Diomedes, on the other hand,
apparently acknowledges through his silence that there is some truth to
Agamemnon's words; and even though Sthenelus's defense is factually
correct—the Epigoni were indeed successful where their fathers had not
been—Diomedes is concerned to win Agamemnon's good will by accept-
ing his challenge. Diomedes's restraint before Agamemnon and his silent
acknowledgment of the appropriateness of the latter's rebuke constitute
a remarkable example of how respect and relative status are negotiated
in the *Iliad*, where the performance of masculinity is generally so depen-
dent on verbal competition.[19] Furthermore, although commentators are at
pains to explain the sense of αἰδεσθείς as containing no shading of shame,
but only of the respect expressed by Diomedes toward Agamemnon, it
is impossible entirely to exclude the idea of a sense of shame, however
transitory, from the appearance of the word here; and it is certainly pos-
sible for a reader to "misread" the term αἰδεσθείς, whether he does so ten-
dentiously or ingenuously.[20] Kevin Crotty perhaps comes closest to this
treatment of the participle in a brief reference to this scene: "Agamemnon
uses the exploits of Tydeus . . . to shame the son into action (see 4.370–
400). Sthenelus seems to rebuff Agamemnon's invitation to feel shame
by insisting that he and Diomedes are better warriors than their fathers
were . . . . Diomedes, on the other hand, feels shame (*aidestheis*, 402), and
bids Sthenelus be silent. Sthenelus' response suggests that shame may

19. On the subtle negotiations of status and privilege in Homer, see van Wees 1992, esp. 109–
25; with an emphasis on the interactive dynamics of respect and honor in Homer, Scodel
2008 refines some of van Wees's ideas.

20. A good example of the tendentious reading can be found at Hardie 1993:89, in a context
influential for my discussion generally. For a balanced discussion of the nuance of *aidôs*
and its cognates in Homer, see Cairns 1993:48–106, and cf. G. Zanker 1994:25–27; Scodel
2008:19–20.

not be as strong an incentive when the son has followed and surpassed his father, but Diomedes' reaction indicates that, even so, the appeal to shame is appropriate and effective."[21] "Diomedes Shamed," the tendentious/ingenuous reader might call this episode; and though the spell is broken swiftly enough by the onrush of narrative, it marks this hero as exceptional.

A second and perhaps even more interesting thematic component of this episode is the attention it draws to fathers and sons, and in particular to the problem of intergenerational (dis)similarity—that is, to what extent are sons like or unlike their fathers?[22] The question is a particularly fraught one when the father in question was, or is, a great hero—can the son surpass his father, or at least equal him? Or, rather, is he destined never to live up to his father's standard? Sthenelus's assertion of the superiority of the Epigoni to the Seven is an obvious attempt to offer a definitive answer—but in fact the entire episode leading up to this offers an extended exploration of the topic. Agamemnon's sympathetic conversation with Nestor is premised on intergenerational continuities—Agamemnon addresses Nestor with respect as an adult son might address his father, acknowledging the physical deprivations of time and feeling nostalgia for Nestor's past; Nestor, on the other hand, is a realist and knows that the past cannot return; he also knows that old age brings with it some privileges ("γέρας . . . γερόντων," 4.323), and is satisfied as he must be with his authority.[23] When Agamemnon moves on to Odysseus, on the other hand, there is no generational dimension to his reproach; Odysseus, however, does make a point of including it, defining himself as the father of Telemachus (4.354). "The feeling of pride," as Kirk (1985 ad loc.) calls it, that is expressed here

---

21. Crotty 1994:32–33 n.16; see also his more general remarks on the motif: "The values upheld by the warrior society are exacting standards; feelings of shame act partly as an enforcement device, making the warrior unwilling to act in other than prestige-seeking ways, for fear of others' blame and of losing face . . . . This aspect of shame, that it constrains the warrior to meet the exacting standards of the warrior code, seems also to owe something to the relationship between father and son . . . the youths become warriors in order to live up to the demanding standard of preeminence and superiority imposed on them by their fathers. The father thus ensures that shame will be felt as external pressure enforcing the warrior code on the son from without" (32–33).

22. Schouler 1980 uses this episode as the starting point for a survey of the continuity of the ethos of Homeric *eugeneia* in ancient Greek culture. Crotty 1994:24–41 offers a finely nuanced appreciation for the theme in Homer. See also Christensen and Barker 2011:23–31 on intergenerational politics in the *Iliad*.

23. For further consideration of Nestor as father and teacher, see below, chapter 3.

is clearly important, and there is no need for Odysseus (or Agamemnon, for that matter) to spell it out: Odysseus knows that he sets an example and that even if Telemachus never meets his own father but is destined only to hear about him from the war's survivors, what the son hears will set a high standard indeed.

When we turn to Agamemnon's reproach of Diomedes and the pre-emptive response of Sthenelus, therefore, the comparison of fathers and sons has already served to provide thematic continuity to the episode—in generally sympathetic and nonconfrontational terms. But Agamemnon's rebuke of Diomedes is aggressively direct: Diomedes is nothing like his father, claims the king. The mini-*Thebais* I have already described serves to support Agamemnon's claim with its accumulation of detail: Agamemnon does not simply remind us of Diomedes's father by calling the hero " 'son of Tydeus' " ("Τυδέος υἱέ," 4.370), but uses twenty-three hexameters to detail Tydeus's bravery (4.376–98). The rebuke closes with a stingingly direct comparison: the son is worse than his father in battle, though better at speaking ("ἀλλὰ τὸν υἱὸν | γείνατο εἷο χέρεια μάχῃ, ἀγορῇ δέ τ' ἀμείνω," " 'but he produced a son worse than himself in battle, but better in assembly,' " 4.399–400).[24]

In the face of these challenging words, it is worth recalling that Agamemnon is addressing two men, not only one, and that Diomedes's partner Sthenelus offers a hostile rebuttal to Agamemnon even as Diomedes feels *aidôs*. Agamemnon thus receives two responses to his speech: one rejects the assertion of degeneracy and claims superiority to the predecessor generation, while the other, if only implicitly, allows the possibility of degeneracy and inferiority to linger. From a narrative perspective, this dual conclusion to the episode heightens the tension already created by the delay of battle narrative: Will the warriors now on the battlefield live up to the example set by the ancestors, or not? Is there even a possibility of surpassing them? The subsequent *aristeia* of Diomedes is one way of answering this question.

Let us turn now to the *aristeia* itself. With Achilles's self-imposed absence, the Achaeans are in desperate need of a hero to take his place; and as *Iliad* Book 5 opens, Diomedes steps to the fore, aided by Athena. Together with Sthenelus, he ranges widely across the battlefield, compared as he goes to a winter torrent that sweeps away everything in its path,

---

24. Pratt 2009:146–50 compares Diomedes's relationship with Tydeus as depicted in the *Iliad* with other father-son pairs in the poem.

leaving only destruction (5.87–92). This water simile is worth comparing to the one with which the *Epipolesis* concluded in *Iliad* Book 4: there, when Diomedes leapt into action the Danaans massed on the battlefield began to move as a whole, like crashing waves; now, the focus is on the individual, whose preeminence is accentuated by the individuality of the simile comparing him to a torrent. This central role is further enhanced by a series of "close encounters" with some of the most prominent warriors on the battlefield, including in first place Aeneas, accompanied by Pandarus. So daunting is their aspect, in fact, that Sthenelus recommends to Diomedes that they withdraw to another part of the battlefield; predictably, Diomedes rejects the advice and instead hurls his spear at Aeneas. The Trojan is gravely wounded and close to death; but Aphrodite intervenes to save her son, throwing a protective cloud around him as she takes him from the battlefield. Her actions result in Diomedes's second close encounter, now with the goddess herself. Wounded, she flees, leaving her son in Apollo's protection (5.330–51). Quickly healed by the god of medicine, Aeneas soon returns to the battlefield; before long, the focus shifts to Hector, who is accompanied by Ares as he rushes at the Achaeans. The narrative once more characterizes Diomedes with a water simile—as he sees the Trojan hero with the god, he draws back like a man whose path is interrupted by a flooding river (5.597–600).[25]

Diomedes's step backward is a cue for the development of the narrative more broadly—the focus shifts again, and the gods consider a variety of interventions to bring the fighting to a climax as the mortal warriors they champion show signs of flagging. This frustrating state of indecision is broken only when Athena spurs Diomedes to action once more, challenging him much as had Agamemnon in *Iliad* Book 4. Diomedes is tending to a recent wound; but Athena provokes a response by suggesting that he is hardly like his father, who though small in stature was always battle ready (5.800–813). As commentators generally note, her challenge recalls the generational comparison made in *Iliad* Book 4 by Agamemnon; but as Kirk (1990 on 5.800–834) observes, "The two rebukes . . . might seem repetitious if Athene's tone were not so different from Agamemnon's, half-humorous rather than pompous." And in fact the change of tone suggested by Kirk is implicit in Diomedes's response—for he does respond this time and does so "calmly and skilfully" (Kirk 1990 on 5.815–24). The

---

25. Cf. Kirk 1990 ad loc.

book concludes with the resumption of Diomedes's *aristeia* and reassertion of his control of the battlefield, demonstrated by nothing less impressive than the wounding of a second god, Ares himself. His *aristeia* continues into *Iliad* Book 6, where his encounter with Glaucus dominates the first half of the book; of primary interest for our purposes is not the exchange of armor so frequently discussed but the fact that Diomedes observes in passing that, while he knows about his grandfather Oeneus's relationship with Glaucus's ancestor Bellerophon, he does not remember his own father, Tydeus ("Τυδέα δ' οὐ μέμνημαι," 6.222). Given the reminders of Tydeus's heroism mentioned by Agamemnon and then Athena, it is at the very least ironic that Diomedes now addresses the relationship, only to minimize its psychological force. Even as he acknowledges the strength of guest-friendship over the generations, he suggests the contingent nature of memory; the very idea that a son whose father was absent for an extended period might well "not remember" that father echoes the fragile character of traditional memory depicted by Glaucus when he compares the generations of men to leaves (6.145–49).[26] On this note, the *aristeia* of Diomedes concludes, as we are invited once again to consider the substance and meaning of a son's relationship with his father, and vice versa.[27]

---

26. Cf. Kirk 1990 on *Il.* 6.144–51: "The likening of human generations to the fall of leaves in autumn and their growing again in spring carries no suggestion of rebirth, but means that life is transient and one generation succeeds another." On Diomedes's lack of paternal memory, see also Pratt 2009:157–59. This example should be seen in contrast with the paternal memory of Telemachus, who desires urgently to know his father and so to reconstitute the tradition; see below, chapter 4.

27. Observant readers of Homer will have noticed that I omit here discussion of another exchange between Agamemnon and Diomedes in *Iliad* Book 14: there, in another council of leaders (1–134), Agamemnon floats the idea of abandoning Troy. The rationale for excluding it from my discussion is simple: the Ovidian reception of Homer seems not to have looked to this scene in particular. Insofar as it develops the idea of Diomedes's resilience, however, I include a brief summary: Nestor and Odysseus are present along with Agamemnon and Diomedes, with Nestor urging further discussion and Odysseus quickly rebuking Agamemnon for setting a bad example of leadership. Finally, Diomedes responds to Nestor's request for good advice, urging a speedy return to battle. He prefaces his suggestion with an extensive genealogical excursus, focusing on his father, Tydeus; and while he never actually indicates that he knew Tydeus in person, he shows an intimate familiarity with his father's exploits (eliding again the most notorious deeds). We may see in Diomedes's speech, I believe, a well-thought-out response to the rebuke he received in the *Epipolesis*: by focusing on heredity, he asserts a claim to the bravery and nobility of his father, and does so in a shrewdly calibrated speech, thus implying that he rejects the assertion of degeneracy made by Agamemnon in the earlier scene. There, Agamemnon had claimed that Tydeus was the better warrior, though Diomedes was better in council (*Il.* 4.399–400), but now Diomedes suggests that this constitutes a false dichotomy. See also Janko 1994 on *Il.* 14.1–134, esp. his discussion of Diomedes's speech on 14.110–32.

IV. Alter ego *Diomedes*

It is time now to locate Ovid in this discussion. The two themes I have identified here as central to the development of Diomedes's character in the *Epipolesis* and his subsequent *aristeia*, namely, his susceptibility to awe—even shame—and the equivocation between intergenerational tension and harmony, will prove to be determinative of Ovid's incorporation of the character of Diomedes in his poetry; indeed, the combination of the two as linked in the *Iliad* may well have drawn Ovid to Diomedes in the first place. Diomedes's exceptional status as the one hero who succeeds in wounding a god—and in fact does so with not one but two gods—makes the episode of his *aristeia* particularly appealing as a script for Ovid's elegiac narrator; the reprise of Agamemnon's rebuke in Athena's, furthermore, serves to link the *aristeia* with the *Epipolesis* and to draw added attention to the theme of resemblance and difference between different generations of the same line. A third dimension of Diomedes's epic character—his mythical status as a Trojan War survivor who, like Aeneas, eventually settles in Italy—will be our focus later in this chapter; but because the epilogue to his career moves his story outside the narrative boundaries of the *Iliad*, it will be useful to focus clearly on the Iliadic Diomedes first. I will begin the following discussion, therefore, by considering Diomedes's starring role in the *Amores*; the post-Homeric Diomedes of the *Metamorphoses* will provide us with a fitting conclusion.

Let us return to the participle αἰδεσθείς describing Diomedes's initial response to Agamemnon's rebuke in *Iliad* Book 4. I suggested earlier that it would be at least momentarily possible to (mis)read this participle as meaning "shamed," whether we understand this (mis)reading as ingenuous or tendentious. Ovid, I suggest, revisits the Homeric participle and exploits its ambiguity to sustain a comparison between his elegiac narrator in the *Amores* and the Homeric Diomedes. Other heroic figures—Ajax, for example—are equally susceptible to shame; but Diomedes's shaming—at least as read by the Ovidian narrator—is transitory and is counterbalanced by a resilience that allows him to re-enter the fray after a rebuke. In other words, he is much like the Ovidian narrator himself.

This combination of susceptibility to shame and resilience makes Diomedes the perfect Ovidian foil in *Amores* 1.7. The Ovidian narrator sets the stage at the opening of the poem with two couplets that confess to a violent outbreak of *furor* against his *puella* (*Am.* 1.7.1–4):

Adde manus in uincla meas (meruere catenas),
   dum furor omnis abit, siquis amicus ades.
nam furor in dominam temeraria bracchia mouit;
   flet mea uesana laesa puella manu.

Put my hands into bonds (they have earned chains), friend—if any-
one present is a friend—until all madness is gone. For it is madness
that moved reckless arms against my mistress; now, wounded by a
crazed hand, the girl weeps.

The emphasis on madness here and throughout the poem is hyperbolic—
and the hyperbole is further marked by the fact that, while Ovid soon
acknowledges having thrown the *puella*'s hair into disarray (11–12), the
enormity of the crime is only fully broached at 49–50:

at nunc sustinui raptis a fronte capillis
   ferreus ingenuas ungue notare genas.

But now I, with a heart of iron, have managed to tear the hair from
her brow and to mark her delicate cheeks with my nails.

The physical violence at the heart of this poem is thus trivialized, as Ovid's
own sense of remorse displaces any emotion felt by the *puella*.

But trivialization is only one part of Ovid's strategy; there is also some-
thing grandiose to his self-portrait. After presenting himself as a victim
of post-traumatic stress disorder *avant la lettre*, he moves quickly to intro-
duce a series of exempla that establish a place for him in lofty company;
acknowledging that his physical force could have made him attack his
own parents or mount an assault on the gods (5–6), he draws a paral-
lel between his own *furor* and that of Ajax and Orestes (7–10). His *puella*
then is given her own series of ennobling exempla, all depicting women
abused, emotionally or physically, by their lovers (or would-be lovers, in
the final case): Atalanta, Ariadne, and Cassandra (11–18). Thus, both the
Ovidian narrator and his lover step into heroic tradition, where their emo-
tions are figured not as lived experience but as literary tropes.[28]

---

28. I here revisit my earlier discussion of Ovid's exempla, Boyd 1997:123–24, 157. Missing
from that analysis, however, is recognition of the particular importance of Diomedes here—
an importance that, as this chapter strives to demonstrate, is paramount. J. V. Morrison 1992
offers a discussion of literary predecessors for the exempla in this poem.

Ovid's *exempla* rush forth in a flood of words; his *puella,* on the
other hand, is silent from fear. In the face of her silence, he continues
to express remorse, even wishing to lose his arms (23–28), presumably
so that his hands could bear the brunt of the blame rather than his bear-
ing it himself—a grotesquely humorous desire for detachment from his
crime.[29] For a brief moment, Ovid re-enters a Roman frame of reference,
noting the irony in the fact that assault on a Roman citizen would be an
actionable offense (29–30);[30] but then he shifts back again into the heroic
frame and identifies himself with Diomedes, who like Ovid himself struck
a goddess—this analogy immediately undercut by more hyperbole, as
Ovid claims his own crime to be worse than Diomedes's (31–34):

> pessima Tydides scelerum monimenta reliquit:
>   ille deam prius perculit; alter ego.
> et minus ille nocens: mihi quam profitebar amare
>   laesa est; Tydides saeuus in hoste fuit.

The son of Tydeus left terrible reminders of his crimes; he was the
first to strike a goddess; I am the second. In fact, he did less dam-
age: in my case, the girl whom I professed to love has been hurt,
while the son of Tydeus was violent in the case of an enemy.

Ovid's use of the phrase *scelerum monimenta* to describe the wound-
ing of Aphrodite by Diomedes likewise highlights and problematizes
the analogy: the etymological association of *monimentum* with words
involving memory as well as with warning[31] gives this phrase the flavor
of an Alexandrian footnote,[32] even as it undoes its own ponderousness.

---

29. Cf. McKeown 1989 commenting on *Am.* 1.7.3–4: "the phrasing contributes ingeniously to
Ovid's attempt to dissociate himself from his hands' heinous deeds"; Gössl 1981 also empha-
sizes this detail.

30. I omit from this discussion an analysis of *Am.* 1.7.35–40, lines imagining a Roman trium-
phal procession in which the *puella* is paraded as a defeated enemy, because they are not inte-
gral to the Ovidian narrator's identification with Diomedes; but see P. A. Miller 2010:166–69
for the contribution these lines make to the depiction of violence in the poem.

31. Varro, *Ling.* 6.49: *meminisse a memoria . . . ab eodem monere*; cf. Maltby 1991 s.v.; O'Hara
1996:174; McKeown 1989 on *Am.* 1.7.31–32.

32. Ross 1975:77–78 for the term; J. F. Miller 1993 discusses Ovid's frequent play with *memini*
and its cognates to allude to an earlier version of a story. Although he does not note the
instance discussed here, at 163 he briefly mentions a cross-reference to *Am.* 1.7 at *Ars am.*
2.169—i.e., one poetic "memory" evoking an earlier "memory," that in turn evokes an earlier
"memory."

If a *monimentum* is something that endures, it is hardly appropriate to describe the grazing of Aphrodite's wrist (*Il.* 5.334–40), gone and all but forgotten in fewer than one hundred Homeric hexameters (5.416–17); only Aphrodite herself keeps the memory alive because of its insult to her divinity. For the Roman readers of Homer, however, among whom we may well count the Ovidian narrator of *Amores* 1.7, the episode is in fact memorable, not least because Aphrodite is wounded while saving Rome's national hero, Aeneas, from Diomedes. The use of the phrase here thus invites Ovid's audience to notice, and to appreciate, the difference.

It is also worth pausing here to note that Ovid designates himself the *alter ego* (32) of Diomedes; none of the other comparisons, explicit or implied, is quite so close. The immediate rationale for the comparison is of course the physical violence just noted—he is guilty not simply of a violent act but of one directed against a female; and whereas Venus is a goddess, and so subject only to an ephemeral wound, Ovid's *puella* is truly harmed.[33] Indeed, the Ovidian narrator himself draws out this point, noting that while Diomedes's violence was at least directed at an enemy, his own was directed at the one he claimed to love (33–34). In other words, he has outdone Diomedes at behaving like Diomedes.

Ovid also draws attention here to the fact that madness is a distinguishing feature of Diomedes's depiction in Homer; in this as in other qualities, he is second only to Achilles. Homer's Trojan characters are struck by Diomedes's exceptional madness on the battlefield, and they come close to comparing him to Achilles: at *Il.* 5.185–86, Pandarus describes Diomedes as raging in a manner only made possible by a god ("οὐχ ὅ γ' ἄνευθε θεοῦ τάδε μαίνεται, ἀλλά τις ἄγχι | ἕστηκ' ἀθανάτων νεφέλῃ εἰλυμένος ὤμους," "'nor does he rage thus without a god, but some one of the immortals, shoulders wrapped in cloud, stands near to him'"), and at 6.100–101, Helenus suggests that, in his rage, Diomedes surpasses all others ("ἀλλ' ὅδε λίην | μαίνεται, οὐδέ τίς οἱ δύναται μένος ἰσοφαρίζειν," "'but he rages excessively, nor can anyone vie with him in force'"). The specifically Homeric nature of Diomedes's *furor* is indicated by the Ovidian narrator's use of a simile to describe his assault (43–48):

> denique si tumidi ritu torrentis agebar
> caecaque me praedam fecerat ira suam,

---

33. Cf. Hinds 1987a:9 on Corinna's markedly nondivine epiphany in *Am.* 1.5: "Like her prototype Lesbia, Corinna first appears as, but cannot sustain an appearance as, her elegiac poet's *candida diua*."

nonne satis fuerat timidae inclamasse puellae
    nec nimium rigidas intonuisse minas
aut tunicam a summa diducere turpiter ora
    ad mediam (mediae zona tulisset opem)?

In short, if I was being driven in the manner of a swollen torrent
and blind fury had made me its prey, would it not have been enough
to shout at the timid girl and to thunder less-than-severe threats, or
to sunder her tunic shamelessly from its top edge to her waist (her
girdle would have protected her there)?

This simile is both traditional in Homeric terms and unusual stylis-
tically. The comparison with a raging river looks back at the series of
water similes that cluster around Diomedes in the *Iliad*.[34] The mad-
ness of Diomedes in this poem is thus a continuation of his Homeric
madness—unless, of course, our recollection of the simile extends far
enough to remind us that in *Iliad* Book 5, the raging river is used to
characterize both Diomedes as he roams the battlefield (5.87–92) and
Diomedes's response to Hector (5.597–600); in the latter instance, the
tables are turned, and now it is Diomedes himself who is daunted by a
seeming force of nature.

The structure and diction of the simile are noteworthy as well. The sim-
ile proper fills less than a single hexameter (*tumidi ritu torrentis agebar*);
syntactically, it constitutes half of the protasis in a mixed condition, a con-
dition that is drawn out over the three couplets of a quasi-enjambed rhe-
torical question. This unusually long unit of meaning[35] packs a rapid-fire
series of actions—or imagined actions—into a run-on sentence, in which
the two halves of the protasis are followed by an apodosis that begins with
nonne satis fuerat and that is completed by not one but three infinitives
(*inclamasse, intonuisse, diducere*), the last of which is further qualified by a
parenthetical observation (*mediae zona tulisset opem*). The high-epic tone
of the ensemble is marked at the outset by the archaic use of the ablative

---

34. A comparable simile appears at *Il.* 11.492–97 in a description of Ajax's battle rage. Ajax
has already appeared in this poem as a potential comparandus (line 7, discussed above), but
now Diomedes holds our attention. Cf. also Fenno 2005:489–90 on the unusual character
of Diomedes's association with bodies of water in Homer.

35. Platnauer 1951:27 gives 5 percent as the frequency of elegiac couplets ending with a
comma or no punctuation in Ovid, and the Ovidian examples he does cite (primarily with
vocatives) are not analogous; cf. Kenney 2002:48–53. Christopher Brunelle has pointed out
to me an even longer sentence at *Pont.* 4.10.47–58: six couplets, also about *flumina*.

ritu to mean "in the manner of";[36] and the characterization of the tor-
rent to which he compares himself as *tumidus* recalls the "swollen river"
imagery that Callimachus so famously employs of the poetry he rejects at
Hymn to Apollo 105–13.[37] After the first couplet of the simile, however, the
tone and register gradually change, as the Ovidian narrator first identi-
fies his target not as an armed enemy but as a scared and defenseless
girl (*timidae puellae*), then qualifies his own desire to have "thundered"
at her (*intonuisse*: again, a Callimachean metaphor for epic)[38] by adding
"not too much" (*nec nimium*), and finally wishes he had simply torn her
clothes—even the last of these wishes qualified immediately by the par-
enthetical assertion that, had he done so, her belt would have limited the
damage.[39] In other words, by the conclusion of the sixth verse, the narrator
has damped down his own *furor*, although in the first couplet that force
seemed to be in control of the narrator, rather than the narrator himself
controlling it (*caecaque me praedam fecerat ira suam*).[40]

Ovid thus portrays his narrator as an epic hero trapped in an elegiac
world—knowing he should conform to elegiac stereotypes, and more or
less willing to do so, but not fully in control; it is almost as if the Ovidian
narrator is caught in a generic identity crisis, and so tries to shoehorn his
own epic pretensions into the neatly measured boundaries of the elegiac
couplet; but his efforts to do so are sporadic and his success markedly
limited.

As the Ovidian narrator proceeds to describe the *puella*'s reaction to
his violent blow, it appears that she too is not without extrageneric quali-
ties: though an elegiac *puella*, she manifests an epic response, at least as
constructed by the narrator as he observes her (51–58):

---

36. Cf. Horsfall 2003 on *Aen.* 11.611: "perhaps an Ennianism (or at least an archaism)."

37. See Wimmel 1960:59–70, 222–33; F. Williams 1978 ad loc. assembles much valuable
background on the Callimachean passage. Ovid is fond of the play with genre invited by a
river in flood: see also the description of Achelous as *imbre tumens* at *Met.* 8.550 with Hollis
1970 on 8.549ff. ("[Achelous's] pomposity . . . is shown by the frequent Ennian ring of his
language"); and *Am.* 3.6, in which the Ovidian narrator is prevented from getting back to
his *puella* by a river in flood: cf. Boyd 1997:212–13 with bibliography; Barchiesi 1989:57–60;
Rosati 2002:288.

38. See the words of the Callimachean narrator at *Aet.* fr. 1.20 Pf., βροντᾶν οὐκ ἐμόν.

39. In the introduction to his commentary on *Amores* 1.7, McKeown 1989 describes this as
an "incongruously detached and pedantic parenthesis"; *per litteras* Christopher Brunelle has
observed that parenthesis with polyptoton/repetition is "super-Ovidian," as at *Ars am.* 2.131,
135, 573, and 3.53.

40. Cf. McKeown 1989 on 1.7.43–44 (*agebar*).

> astitit illa amens albo et sine sanguine uultu,
>   caeduntur Pariis qualia saxa iugis;
> exanimes artus et membra trementia uidi,
>   ut cum populeas uentilat aura comas,
> ut leni Zephyro gracilis uibratur harundo
>   summaue cum tepido stringitur unda Noto;
> suspensaeque diu lacrimae fluxere per ora,
>   qualiter abiecta[41] de niue manat aqua.

She stood there in turmoil, her face pale and bloodless, like stone that is cut on the ridges of Paros; I saw her lifeless limbs tremble, as when a breeze fans the poplar's tresses, as when a slender reed is shaken by the gentle west wind or the very top of the wave is grazed by a mild south wind. Tears, suspended in her eyes for a long time, then flowed down her face, as when water flows from piled snow.

Her reaction to her lover's violence is framed entirely in terms of analogies: a dense sequence of similes illustrating almost complete silence and stillness, broken only by trembling and tears. The narrator employs no fewer than five similes in what I am tempted to describe as an overly rich visualization of the *puella*; as I noted in an earlier discussion of this passage, this sequence taken as a whole, with its recollection of Homeric and Hellenistic models, is an intellectualizing device used by the narrator to detach himself from lived experience and to capture the literary nature of his beloved.[42] But there is more to be said, particularly in light of the Homeric analogy that is so strongly developed to characterize the narrator himself. My earlier discussion concerned itself with elegiac decorum and with the interpretation of "Homeric" similes in Ovidian elegy; but now, I would like to press the Homeric resonance of this scene a bit further. Only one of the five terms of comparison in this simile cluster has a clear Homeric model, at least as noted by commentators (see below); but a closer examination of discrete elements in the cluster suggests a sort of Homeric pastiche, at the conclusion of which the one recognizably Homeric simile serves as a signature. In identifying Diomedes as his *alter*

---

41. The reading *abiecta* of the majority of primary manuscripts is problematic, and no fully satisfactory emendation has been proposed. See McKeown 1989 ad loc. for a full but noncommittal description of the problems involved.

42. Boyd 1997:124–30. Cf. also the opening of Propertius 1.3, in which the sleeping Cynthia is compared to the sleeping beauties of myth (1–8).

ego, the Ovidian narrator assumes an epic identity; now, he bestows a similar status on his *puella*, whether she wants it or not.

Let us consider the details of these similes. In the first couplet, the Ovidian narrator focuses on the paleness of his *puella*'s complexion: her pallor is thematized in both the hexameter (*albo et sine sanguine uultu*) and the pentameter, where the marble-like cast of her complexion is jarringly compared to Parian marble—a hard material indeed to characterize the recently bruised *puella*. Yet the comparison to marble, disconcerting though it is, is not without precedent: Callimachus (*Hymn to Apollo* 24) describes the mourning Niobe as "sorrowful marble in place of a gaping woman" (μάρμαρον ἀντὶ γυναικὸς ὀϊζυρόν τι χανούσης);[43] Horace uses Parian marble as a comparandum for Glycera's beauty (*urit me Glycerae nitor | splendentis Pario marmore purius*, "the brilliance of Glycera, gleaming with greater purity than Parian marble, sets me on fire," *Carm.* 1.19.5–6);[44] and Virgil compares the unresponsiveness of Dido in the underworld to the immovability of Marpessan stone—that is, marble, from one of the mountains on Paros (*nec magis incepto uultum sermone mouetur | quam si dura silex aut stet Marpesia cautes*, "nor, when [Aeneas] begins to talk, does she show emotion on her face more than if hard flint or a Marpessan crag were standing there," *Aen.* 6.470–71).[45] Another field of analogy derives from a Homeric simile comparing the white skin of Penelope to fresh-cut ivory; her beauty is enhanced by Athena as she sleeps (λευκοτέρην δ' ἄρα μιν θῆκε πριστοῦ ἐλέφαντος, "[Athena] made her whiter than freshly cut ivory," *Od.* 18.196). As commentators note, Homer is attentive to the freshness of ivory's cutting because the material changes color with time,

---

43. Ovid's allusion to the Callimachean description of Niobe, itself a "reauthorization" of Homeric lines athetized by Hellenistic editors (*Il.* 24.602–20), may be seen as a way of standing with Callimachus vs. Aristophanes of Byzantium et al. Ovid treats the story of Niobe fully in *Met.* 6.146–312—far more fully, indeed, than it is narrated in the *Iliad*—perhaps from the same contrarian response to the scholiasts that seems to motivate several of his other Homeric episodes: cf. the discussion above, chapter 1. Heyworth 1994:52–54, in a study of Prop. 3.10.5–10, draws attention to the silence of Callimachus's Niobe, likewise appropriate in a comparison to Ovid's silent *puella*: on Niobe's silence, see also Cic. *Tusc.* 3.63, and cf. Hollis 1997. Finally, it is also worth noting that the Homeric lines suggest that the rock that was once Niobe now sheds tears—an idea that, as this simile sequence develops, will become relevant to the Ovidian *puella*.

44. See Nisbet and Hubbard 1970 ad loc. for additional comparanda.

45. Boyd 1997:126–27 offers fuller discussion and bibliography. Note also *Met.* 3.418–19, where Narcissus stunned by his own beauty is compared to a statue of Parian marble, with Hardie 2002:146–47; and cf. von Glinski 2012:124 n.27, noting the similarity to Ovid's description of Narcissus at *Met.* 3.480–85.

growing yellow with age; freshly cut, it is at its whitest.[46] The cutting of ivory and marble that is the initial step in transforming the two materials into artworks is also incorporated into the Ovidian narrator's frame of reference—the verb *caeduntur* triggers a momentary suggestion that the narrator is a sort of Pygmalion, whose creation is the beautiful, lifeless form he describes—she is now more like a statue in progress than a living girl.[47] As McKeown notes (1989 ad loc.), "*caedere* is the regular term for quarrying"; but as he also observes, "The general sense 'strike' . . . comes readily to mind and makes the simile more apposite."[48] This observation is worth pursuing to its logical conclusion: the Ovidian narrator suggests that it is his own act of violence that transforms the *puella* into a work of art.

The next three comparisons extend over two couplets, all with the same point of comparison: the Ovidian narrator offers three different analogies for the *puella*'s trembling (*exanimes artus et membra trementia*, 53). In three verses, the narrator describes the effects of a breeze on three different natural phenomena: the leaves of trees, reeds, and the surface of a body of water.[49] The breeze too is identified in three ways: first, as generic *aura*, and then by two names of different winds, Zephyrus and Notus. The narrator thus says the same thing three times, offering again an overly rich array of visual choices; she is like leaves, or reeds, or water, all delicate and

---

46. Boyd 1997:115 with n.56, in a discussion of Ovid's more precise recall of another Homeric simile involving freshly cut ivory: at *Am.* 2.5.39–40, Ovid describes his *puella*'s blush in terms that recall the blush of Lavinia at *Aen.* 12.67–68, itself modeled on Homer's description of Menelaus's pale flesh stained by the blood of a wound at *Il.* 4.141–42. In that Ovidian simile, the Homeric model is guaranteed by Ovid's translation of the Homeric γυνή . . . Μηονίς as *Maeonis femina*, one element of the Homeric comparison omitted by Virgil but that alludes to the supposed genealogy of Homer: Hellanicus (*FGrH* 4 F5) identifies Homer as the son of Maeon, and adjectives derived from his name (also traditionally associated with Lydia, one of the supposed birthplaces of Homer) become commonplace in Latin poetry as epithets for Homer, e.g., Hor. *Carm.* 1.6.2 and 4.9.5–6; Ov. *Am.* 1.15.9 and 3.9.25, *Ars am.* 2.4, *Rem. am.* 373; etc.

47. The comparison of a beautiful *puella* to a statue is frequent in highly stylized poetry: particularly apposite here are Catull. 64.62 (Ariadne) and Ov. *Met.* 4.673–75 (Andromeda); cf. also Narcissus, above n.45.

48. In fact, Ovid uses *caedere* in *Amores* 1.9 (*Militat omnis amans*) in an allusion to the *Doloneia*, where he advances the conceit that lovers, like soldiers, can use the sleep of their enemy to advantage: *saepe soporatos inuadere profuit hostes | caedere et armata uulgus inerme manu*, 1.9.21–22. His mention there of the unarmed condition of the victims (*uulgus inerme*) may well be read as an ironic reminder of the assault described two elegies previously.

49. On the three comparanda in this simile vis-à-vis *Her.* 14.39–41, a double simile describing the effect of a breeze on ears of grain or leaves, see Frings 2005:54.

insubstantial; but of equal note is the implication—and it is just that—that the ruffling force of the breeze, itself insubstantial, is meant to counteract the severity of the blow that has just been characterized by the verb *caeduntur.*

These comparisons are of course Homeric, at least in a generalized way; Ovid does not here direct his reader to a specific instance of the analogy but has created a general aura of Homeric provenance.[50] At *Il.* 2.144–50, for example, Homer uses a double simile comparing the movement of the Achaeans in assembly to waves raised by Eurus and Notus, and to grain stirred by Zephyrus; at *Il.* 7.63–65, he compares the pregnant stillness of the Achaean and Trojan troops to a rippling of the sea by Zephyrus; and at *Il.* 16.765–71, he uses the conflict of Notus and Eurus as they shake the leaves of trees to describe the din of battle.[51] The Homeric similes generally crystallize in a single image the shared movements of masses of men; in Ovid, on the other hand, a multiplicity of images is used to characterize the shuddering of a single person, his *puella.*

The final comparison in this sequence fills the last couplet with a slow and detailed description of tears, long held back, that flow down the *puella*'s cheeks at last like water dripping from melting snow. This simile is typically identified as the one in this sequence of five with a clear Homeric model: at *Od.* 19.204–8, Penelope's tears—and indeed her flesh—are compared to melting snow:

τῆς δ' ἄρ' ἀκουούσης ῥέε δάκρυα, τήκετο δὲ χρώς.
ὡς δὲ χιὼν κατατήκετ' ἐν ἀκροπόλοισιν ὄρεσσιν,
ἥν τ' Εὗρος κατέτηξεν, ἐπὴν Ζέφυρος καταχεύῃ·
τηκομένης δ' ἄρα τῆς ποταμοὶ πλήθουσι ῥέοντες·
ὡς τῆς τήκετο καλὰ παρήϊα δάκρυ χεούσης . . .

As she listened, her tears flowed, and her flesh melted. As when snow melts in the high mountains, snow which the east wind has softened, when the west wind pours down, and the rivers as they flow are filled with it as the snow melts; thus her lovely cheeks melted as she shed tears . . .

---

50. An interesting instance of what Thomas 1986:190–93 calls "apparent reference"; coincidentally, his discussion of this phenomenon in Virgil centers on a passage that is ostensibly Homeric.

51. See Janko 1994 ad loc. for the formulaic features of the comparison and comparanda.

The Homeric comparison is indeed much fuller than Ovid's, sketching as it does an entire landscape and the seasons it experiences: the snow in the mountains, brought by Zephyrus and warmed by Eurus, melts, and as it does so, the rivers are filled with the liquid. In place of lofty mountains and seasonal change, the Ovidian simile compresses both downward motion and the passage of time into the two words *suspensae . . . diu*; there are no longer any mountains, although in the phrase *fluxere per ora*, the final word suggests a pun on Homer's ἐν ἀκροπόλοισιν ὄρεσσιν; and there is no mention of rivers or breezes, perhaps because both flowing water and the movement of air have already figured in the preceding two couplets. We may well wonder whether the Ovidian narrator expects his reader to know the Homeric simile so well that he can supply what is missing, or—even better—appreciate how its individual components have been distributed over the entire sequence of similes.

Of course, the reader who recognizes the Homeric provenance of the simile will also remember that, in the *Odyssey*, it occurs during Penelope's initial interview with Odysseus. He is still in disguise and has just finished an elaborate fiction about having met her husband when he stopped at Crete on his way to Troy (*Od.* 19.171–202). As she listens, she begins to weep; the moving effectiveness of the simile is well captured by Joseph Russo, who comments (Russo, Fernández-Galiano, and Heubeck 1992 on *Od.* 19.204–8):

> A form of τήκω is used in each of these five successive verses, an unparalleled verbal concentration that creates an overwhelming image of melting and overflowing. The verb includes both meanings, which our translation cannot imitate: overflowing is the surface phenomenon; melting is what happens internally. τήκετο δὲ χρώς means her skin ran with liquid from her tears, not that it "melted." What does melt is Penelope's long-standing resistance to yielding herself to the belief that Odysseus is alive and will return . . . ; and as melting snow produces a liquid overflow, so the dissolving of her energies spent in repression of emotion produces an overflow of feeling whose concrete manifestation is tears . . . . Hence the perfect aptness of this simile representing the release of Penelope's strong innermost feelings through the image of snow dissolving under a warm wind.

Russo's nuanced interpretation of the simile brings out its relevance in its context: Penelope's tears are caused not by any physical phenomenon but by the combination of memory and emotion that the disguised Odysseus arouses. The Ovidian narrator thus invites us to think of his *puella* as a modern Penelope—a comparison already hinted at glancingly with the opening comparison of the *puella*'s pale complexion to freshly cut marble. Yet the sustained tension of the compound simile can only heighten the reader's awareness that the situation is anything but Homeric: this *puella* is a victim of abuse, and her tearful trembling is the result not of nostalgia or longing but of a physical blow. The simile sequence thus underscores the faulty reasoning—or sheer perversity—of the Ovidian narrator; he is no Diomedes, and not only is she no Aphrodite, but she is not even like the mortal Penelope.

The Ovidian narrator seems to recognize the outrageousness of his own hyperbole: no sooner do the similes end than he revises the last of them, taking the reader far indeed from the Homeric frame of reference even as, like Sophocles's Ajax or Euripides's Hercules, he recognizes after the fact what he has done. In the next couplet, he redefines the *puella*'s tears (59–60):

tunc ego me primum coepi sentire nocentem;
  sanguis erat lacrimae, quas dabat illa, meus.

Then I first began to perceive myself as doing harm; the tears which she shed were my blood.

The sense of the pentameter is striking, and strikingly ironic: the narrator suggests that the *puella*'s tears are his blood, that is, that her weeping draws the very lifeblood from him.[52] The idea that he is the one losing blood, when she is the one who has suffered blows and whose response renders her complexion, as we saw earlier, *sine sanguine* (51), is an audacious sort of παρὰ προσδοκίαν—surely he cannot mean what he says, can he? But in fact this inversion of roles continues through the remainder of the elegy, as the narrator urges his *puella* to retaliate by turning on him to tear at his face, eyes, and hair (64–65); all she needs are hands, and anger to strengthen them (*quamlibet infirmas adiuuat ira manus*, 66). In other words, the very weapons from which he earlier tried to distance himself and the very wrath that drove him to commit an outrage are now recommended, so that the *puella*—now clearly no Penelope—can reciprocate.

---

52. See McKeown 1989 ad loc.

The request of the final couplet that she rearrange her hair so as to eliminate any evidence of his assault—and, presumably, so that they can resume their affair—is a final rejection of the Homeric persona assumed earlier: as the Ovidian narrator redefines the assault as a lovers' quarrel and no more, both his violence and the epic imagery that sustains it evaporate, leaving only a subtle hint that this episode could well be repeated in the course of their affair.[53] From "Diomedes Shamed" we have arrived at an oxymoron, shameless Diomedes.

V. Diomedes at the Vanishing Point

When we turn to the *Metamorphoses*, Diomedes no longer plays a starring role; in his brief appearance, he functions primarily as the narrator of a metamorphosis not his own, and allusions to him by other narrators offer an ambivalent verdict at best on his heroic status. Not surprisingly, mention of Diomedes occurs first in the so-called little *Iliad* of the *Metamorphoses*, that is, in Book 13: both Ajax and Ulysses use his performance in the Trojan War as evidence supporting their appeals to be awarded the armor of Achilles. Ulysses's famous success in that competition raises an implicit but nagging question about Diomedes's importance, both in the conduct of the war and in the *Iliad*; and the final encounter with Diomedes himself in the "little *Aeneid*" of Book 14 underscores the victory of Ulysses, as Diomedes withdraws from a new opportunity to fight with the Trojans.

The episode known as the Judgment of Arms is not narrated in the *Iliad*; evidence from the fragments of the cyclic epics indicates that this story was featured in the *Aethiopis* and the *Ilias Parva*.[54] We are thus moving away, both temporally and in narrative terms, from the representation of Diomedes in the *Iliad*; yet the Homeric tradition casts its long shadow over this episode as well, at least in Ovid's version of it.[55] As Nancy Zumwalt has suggested,[56] the ecphrastic description of Fama with which Ovid opens his "little *Iliad*" (*Met.* 12.39–63) serves

---

53. On gendered violence as a recurring motif in the *Amores*, see P. A. Miller 2010.

54. See Davies 1989:48–49 (*Cypria*) and 63–68 (*Ilias Parva*) for details; West 2003:65–107 (*Cypria*) and 118–43 (*Ilias Parva*) for texts and translation.

55. I am indebted throughout this discussion to the fine commentary on *Metamorphoses* Book 13 in Hopkinson 2000. That volume should be consulted for many detailed observations concerning Ovid's adaptations of Homeric language and scenes.

56. Zumwalt 1977.

both to acknowledge the territory of epic tradition into which Ovid is now directing his narrative and to remind us of its inherent fragility and mutability: falsehood and truth exist side by side in a vast story world that is constantly shifting, growing and adapting to the desires of its audience (53–58):

atria turba tenet: ueniunt, leue uulgus, euntque
mixtaque cum ueris passim commenta uagantur
milia rumorum confusaque uerba uolutant.
e quibus hi uacuas implent sermonibus aures,
hi narrata ferunt alio, mensuraque ficti
crescit, et auditis aliquid nouus adicit auctor.

Confusion fills the halls: a fickle populace, they come and go, and thousands of rumor-filled remarks mixed with truth wander here and there, and confused words fly about; of these, some fill empty ears with gossip, others take what they have been told to another place, and the measure of fiction grows, as each new author adds something to what he has heard.

Nouus auctor:[57] thus Ovid makes himself a part of the story and incorporates himself into the transmission of epic tradition, simultaneously inviting his reader to question the authority with which he does so.[58] And it is against this background that the comments of Ajax and Ulysses concerning Diomedes are cast into relief: the former, whom we might think of as a unitarian (or, in more recent parlance, multiform)[59] Homerist, sees the actions of Diomedes during the war—in particular the episode generally known as the *Doloneia, Iliad* Book 10, in which Odysseus and Diomedes together ambush the Trojan spy Dolon and invade the camp of Troy's

---

57. Barchiesi 2002:196 notes Ovid's play on the derivation of *auctor* from the verb *augeo*, "augment," and then adds: ". . . for Ovid it is thought-provoking that the word can describe the producer of a text, the guarantor of a [sic] pre-existing information, or the latecomer who brings a little something new to add to the series of fictions." The playful potency of the noun will be exploited repeatedly in a number of the episodes discussed in this book, as Ovid presents himself as a sort of meta-Homer.

58. Hardie 2012:150–68 offers a rich discussion of Ovid's Fama.

59. The term, first expounded by Lord 1960, has been promoted by Gregory Nagy and his students to describe Homeric poetry as constituted not of separable components but of all its parts, including variant versions (although the term "variant" is itself problematic to proponents of the multiformity of Homer): Nagy 2001 presents the basic idea.

Thracian ally Rhesus—as crucial to Ulysses's success (*Met.* 13.98–106, in particular 13.100, *"nihil est Diomede remoto,"* as Ajax puts it succinctly); the latter, on the other hand, is an Ovidian neo-analyst, asserting that Diomedes's choice of him as companion for episodes like the *Doloneia* is itself evidence of Ulysses's preeminence (*Met.* 13.238–54).[60] As Ulysses takes credit for the defeat of both Dolon and Rhesus, his audience may well be inclined to revise their view of the Homeric *aristeia* of Diomedes, hearing it described now as just a small component in a much greater (though not narrated as such by Homer) *aristeia* of Odysseus. Ovid thus invites his reader to question Homer's authority as narrator of the truth, and, with Ulysses's triumphant winning of the weapons of Achilles, offers a sophistic commentary on the power of rhetoric to shape, and reshape, a tradition.[61]

Diomedes himself, it should also be remembered, is an exemplar of rhetorical excellence in the *Iliad*—at least this is the implication of the final words of Agamemnon's rebuke in the *Epipolesis*: at *Il.* 4.399–400, Agamemnon offers what he clearly thinks is a stinging comparison of father and son, saying that Diomedes is worse than his father in battle, though superior to his elder in the assembly (quoted above). As we have already seen, this comparison of father and son is premised on the idea of degeneracy, and Diomedes's respectful (or shamed) response both acknowledges this idea and implies a determination to prove Agamemnon wrong. When Ovid's Ulysses elides the *aristeia* of Diomedes and appropriates to himself all the glory for their shared accomplishments, he replays and revises the terms of the comparison in Agamemnon's criticism and in Diomedes's response: now, it is Ulysses himself who is best in assembly, but also—so he claims—best in confrontations with the enemy; and the version of Diomedes depicted by Ovid's Ulysses effectively reverts to the awe-filled (or shamed) Diomedes of the *Epipolesis*. This Diomedes, claims Ulysses, would never try to compete for the arms of Achilles because he knows that a man who fights is inferior to one who thinks (*Met.* 13.354–56):

---

60. May Ovid simultaneously be inviting his reader to consider the arguments for and against the authenticity of the *Doloneia*, as challenged by Aristarchus? See chapter 1.

61. Hopkinson 2000:16–18 provides a brief but pointed discussion of the triumph of eloquence in this episode and suggests that in this competition Ulysses offers a model for, or reflection of, the sophisticated rhetoric of Ovid himself. It is tempting to extend Hopkinson's train of thought and to suggest that Ovid thus implies a challenge to Homer himself: see the remainder of this discussion.

"qui nisi pugnacem sciret sapiente minorem
esse nec indomitae deberi praemia dextrae,
ipse quoque haec peteret; . . ."

"If [Diomedes] did not know that a fighter is inferior to a wise man
and that rewards are not owed to an uncontrolled right hand, he too
would seek these things . . . . "

Ulysses thus represents Diomedes as a man influenced by respect for
what others would think—in other words, an Ovidian version of Diomedes
αἰδεσθείς. He does so, furthermore, in terms of comparison reminiscent—
but also subversive—of those used by Agamemnon: *pugnacem . . . sapiente
minorem esse* inverts the Homeric assessment of the relative merits of phys-
ical and mental excellence, χέρεια μάχη, ἀγορῇ δέ τ' ἀμείνω (*Il.* 4.400). The
sophistry of Ulysses has revised the Homeric value system anachronisti-
cally, making him sound more like a contemporary Roman noble than a
Homeric warrior; indeed, his implicit self-identification as *sapiens* aligns
him with Stoic philosophical tradition, in which Ulysses is identified as
a model of the *uir sapiens*.[62] In Ulysses's victory over Ajax, then, there is
embedded another victory—of words, if not of deeds—over Diomedes as
well; Homer's hero second only to Achilles is now replaced by a new, up-
to-date hero, the versatile Ulysses.[63]

The eclipsing of Diomedes by Ulysses along with his implicit reluc-
tance to compete anew paves the way for a final episode[64] involving
his doings in the *Metamorphoses*, in the "little *Aeneid*."[65] A lengthy epi-
sode recounting the stories told by two former companions of Ulysses,

---

62. See Bömer vol. 6, 1982 ad loc., and cf. Hor. *Epist.* 1.2.18–19, *rursus quid uirtus et quid
sapientia possit* | *utile proposuit nobis exemplar Vlixem* [sc. *Homerus*] with Mayer 1994 ad loc.;
R. B. Rutherford 1986 is an excellent treatment of moralizing/philosophical readings of the
Odyssey.

63. See chapter 7 for a fuller discussion of Ovid's treatment of Ulysses.

64. Though not the final brief allusion to him: when Venus is anticipating with dread
the assassination of her descendant Julius Caesar (*Met.* 15.761–806), her expression of
dismay is framed in terms of the insult already done to her by Diomedes, as is her intent
to intervene (esp. 15.768–70, 806). It is evident from this echo that, by the end of the
Metamorphoses, the memory of Diomedes has begun to merge with poetic memory: see
the discussion below.

65. For general discussions of many aspects of the "Little *Aeneid*" not touched upon here,
see, e.g., Tissol 1997:177–91; Myers 1994:98–113; and Papaioannou 2005, esp. 143–56. The
commentary of Myers 2009 is an especially helpful introduction to the approach I take here.

Macareus and Achaemenides, who join the Trojans working their way
up the western coast of Italy, fills much of the first half of *Metamorphoses*
Book 14 (158–440); they have met at Caieta, a site just north of the bay of
Naples where Virgil had located the death of Aeneas's Trojan nurse of the
same name (*Aen.* 7.1–4). In a narrative sequence dense with allusions to
and reworkings of details in the *Aeneid*,[66] Ovid reorients his reader to an
epic universe already reoriented by Virgil: the two Greek refugees, now
effectively, if benevolently, held captive by the Trojans, embody the illusion
of "Homericity" that still clings to their stories, an illusion belied by the
obvious fact that they are not actually Homeric characters at all: they thus
suggest simultaneously the continuity of epic tradition and its rupture.

After the long pause at Caieta that enables Macareus and Achaemenides
to trade stories, Ovid "fast-forwards" his narrative: after using the allu-
sion to Aeneas's nurse to gesture to the opening of the second half of the
Aeneid, Ovid summarizes more than four Virgilian books in about seventy
hexameters (14.445–513); and of these seventy verses, most (457–511: fifty-
five verses) are devoted to Diomedes's refusal to get involved in a new cam-
paign against the Trojans. This episode had already been featured in the
Aeneid, of course, but there the scale of the episode in relationship to its
surroundings is well proportioned: *Aen.* 8.9–17 offers a brief description of
the embassy to Diomedes led by Venulus, and at *Aen.* 11.225–95, Venulus
and his companions return, bearing the news of Diomedes's refusal.
Venulus reports what purport to be the words of Diomedes himself (11.252–
93), in seven hexameters of which he alludes to the metamorphosis of
Diomedes's men and attributes it to his assault on Venus (11.271–77). Virgil
marks the significance of the episode—both its inclusion and the rejec-
tion embedded within it—with a simile describing the fearful reaction of
the Italians to this news: their rumbling resembles the crashing of waves
of water on stones and the rippling aftermath (11.296–99). As Nicholas
Horsfall notes (2003 ad loc.), there is no clear Homeric (or Apollonian)
model for this simile; we may wonder whether Virgil thus nods to the fact
that this episode in Diomedes's career is itself not Homeric—or whether
he might intend to evoke the various water similes that Homer uses to
characterize Diomedes, while not actually selecting any single example as
a model.[67] Virgil's inclusion of Diomedes in the post-Homeric world of the

---

66. See Myers 2009 ad loc. for details, following Hinds 1998:107–22; and see Baldo
1995:120–41 for details of the Homeric-Virgilian interplay in Ovid's version.

67. See above, n.50, for the concept of "apparent reference" described by Thomas 1986.

Aeneid brings out the difference between the world of Homeric epic and his own.[68]

But let us turn our attention back to the fact that this episode is not Homeric, nor is there any indication that it appeared in the cyclic epics. Rather, the first detailed extant attestation for the Diomedes-in-Italy tradition is in Lycophron, who in the *Alexandra* gives a riddling but informative description of the location of Diomedes's settlement and the transformation of his companions into birds (*Alex.* 592–632). The story is likely to have much earlier roots: a scholion on Lycophron *Alex.* 610 reports that the archaic poet Mimnermus told of how Diomedes, arriving home in Argos after the Trojan War only to find that his wife, at the instigation of a vengeful Aphrodite, had been unfaithful, fled from his home to the protection of King Daunus in Italy; in the scholiast's report, Daunus treacherously killed Diomedes (fr. 22 *IE²*).[69] There is also ample if fragmentary evidence to suggest that the metamorphosis of Diomedes's men featured in a number of paradoxographies and other Hellenistic compendia of metamorphoses.[70] In Lycophron's treatment, Cassandra's "future reflexive"[71] prophecy locates Diomedes's homeward journey in the future: because of Aphrodite, his wife will be unfaithful, and he will be compelled to wander until settling on the east coast of Italy, where he will found Argyripa and give his name to the Diomedean Islands; he will see the transformation of his men into birds and will curse the land; and after

---

68. The relationship of Homeric and Virgilian Diomedes has been the subject of several recent studies: see Papaioannou 2000; Barbara 2006; Fletcher 2006.

69. Compare the scholiast on Pind. *Nem.* 10.12, reporting Diomedes's subsequent divinization and worship; cf. also Serv. on *Aen.* 8.9. Some scholars (e.g., West in *IE²*) question the attribution of the Mimnermus fragment: see now, however, Grethlein 2007, who makes the ingenious suggestion that Mimn. fr. 14 *IE²* should be contextualized as part of a Diomedes narrative in which the intergenerational comparison of the *Epipolesis* is recalled and inverted, offering a metatextual commentary on the "young" elegy of Mimnermus vis-à-vis the "old" epic of Homer.

For comprehensive overviews of traditions concerning Diomedes in Italy, see Bérard 1957:368–76 and Malkin 1998:234–57. Klein 2009 is a rewarding discussion of Lycophron's presence in Augustan poetry (572–83 on Diomedes in Virgil and Ovid); McNelis and Sens 2016:160–70 look at how Lycophron's depiction of Diomedes reflects larger themes in his poem.

70. Ant. Lib. 37, presumably following Nicander's *Heteroeoumena* (Myers 1994:102 n.35); Antig. Car. 172; [Arist.] *Mir. ausc.* 79; and cf. Plin. *HN* 10.126–27, citing Iuba of Mauretania, author of works on natural history (= *FGrH* 275 F60).

71. The term is from Barchiesi 2001b (1993), who uses it to describe the reorientation of a traditional narrative to a new temporal perspective; his focus is on the *Heroides*.

slaying the dragon that once protected the golden fleece, he will die and be worshipped as a god. Adapting this for his own purposes, Virgil omits the details about the unfaithful wife,[72] as well as about Diomedes's eventual immortality; the focus of this episode is on the harsh experiences Diomedes has had since leaving Troy, among which is the transformation of his men. Ovid likewise focuses on these details—of course, the transformation of Diomedes's companions is the ostensible reason for the inclusion of this episode in the *Metamorphoses* in the first place; we may well suspect, in fact, that Ovid adapts one of the few metamorphoses found in the *Aeneid*[73] precisely in order to assert his "priority" in the tradition of metamorphic epic.

Meanwhile, in incorporating this tale into his *Metamorphoses*, Ovid takes the story of Diomedes even further, both temporally and geographically, away from its Homeric sources than he had done when putting allusions to him into the mouths of the central figures in the Judgment of Arms of Book 13. With the latest episode, we might well describe Ovid's allusivity with a term popularized by Richard Thomas: "window reference," that is, a complex form of allusivity whereby Poet Z (here, Ovid) uses a precise allusion to Poet Y (here, Virgil) but incorporates into that allusion something that recognizes a third poet, Poet X (here, Lycophron), as Poet Y's model, while highlighting differences. In this example, we might further thicken the density of references by locating a Poet H—Homer, of course—at the very beginning of this chain of connections, since it is with Homer in the first place that the story of Diomedes originates, the story that Lycophron engages and then transmits in turn to Virgil and Ovid.[74] A particular novelty attaching itself to this example, however, centers on its inherent mutability: that is, the version of things first reported by Lycophron includes precisely that part of the story that is non-Homeric, and in the further extensions of the tradition in Virgil and Ovid, the presence of Diomedes is defined precisely in terms of absence—that it, he participates in the narrative only

---

72. See Horsfall 2003 on *Aen*. 11.270.

73. Hinds 1998:104–7.

74. For the term "window reference," see Thomas 1986:188–89. In his original articulation of the concept, Thomas sees window reference as a particularly pointed form of "correction," or *oppositio in imitando*; my use of the term here is somewhat loose, therefore, since the corrective character of the allusion is not, I think, the most noteworthy thing about it.

long enough to express the explicit desire *not* to participate in it (and in Virgil's case, he does not even speak directly but is only reported to do so, at a safe distance, by Venulus). In this case, in other words, the referential window opens onto nothing, creating the illusion of a palimpsestic repetition of tradition while underscoring the distance that both Diomedes and his audience have traversed since he was first singled out in the Catalogue of Ships in *Iliad* Book 2.

VI. *The Memory of Diomedes*

The distinctiveness of Diomedes's heroism is a defining characteristic; from his Homeric origins to his self-erasure in Virgil and Ovid, Diomedes is solitary. I do not mean by this that he has no companions—at his first appearance in the Catalogue of Ships (*Il.* 2.559–64), he is paired with Sthenelus, and Sthenelus again accompanies him in the *Epipolesis* of *Iliad* Book 4, where, as we have seen, this ally asserts the superiority of the younger generation to their fathers. In *Iliad* Book 10, Diomedes chooses Odysseus to accompany him on his night raid; and the post-Homeric Diomedes who, in Virgil and Ovid, has settled in ancient Apulia, arrives there leading a troop of companions. Yet in crucial ways Diomedes sets himself apart, or is set apart by the events that happen around him: we have already considered the way in which, surprisingly, he sides with Agamemnon against Sthenelus in the scene in which Agamemnon rebukes him; and his wounding of Aphrodite (as well as of Ares) in *Iliad* Book 5 is a feat of daring—or foolhardiness—which no other Homeric hero even attempts to approximate. The exceptionalism of this act then becomes, willy-nilly, his destiny: when we encounter him (or hear the report of Venulus's encounter with him) in southern Italy, he is isolated again, since the companions who traveled with him have been transformed into birds. His solitary state reverberates in his choice to stand apart, and not to join the Latins in their war with the Trojans; his withdrawal from the narrative thus signifies a withdrawal from history and into myth, where he and his story change no more.

Memory and its opposite are important components in Diomedes's narrative fate. Earlier in this chapter I drew attention to the Homeric Diomedes's striking assertion that he does not remember his father (*Il.* 6.222), a claim that underscores the fragility of poetic memory. Virgil relocates that forgetfulness, transferring it from Diomedes's forgetfulness of

his father to forgetfulness—at least wishful[75]— of the Trojan War itself and
a desire to consign the past to oblivion (*Aen.* 11.279–80):

> "nec mihi cum Teucris ullum post eruta bellum
> Pergama nec ueterum memini laetorue malorum . . . . "

> "Neither do I have any war with the Trojans since their city fell, nor
> do I take pleasure remembering the old troubles . . . . "

Forgetting the past is nonetheless hard to do; when we meet Diomedes
in *Metamorphoses* Book 14, he still has not forgotten, in spite of himself,
and so forces himself to revisit the past a final time in order to convince
Venulus that his reasons for not wanting to join the fight are sound (*Met.*
14.464–66):

> "neue haec commenta putetis,
> admonitu quamquam luctus renouentur amaro,
> perpetiar memorare tamen . . . . "

> "And lest you consider these things to be fabrications, I shall endure
> to recall them, although grief is renewed by the bitter memory . . ."

As Diomedes proceeds, however, it becomes clear that, while he may be
glad to forget his past, another entity more powerful than he will not—
namely, Venus, who pushes him along his course out of vindictive mem-
ory, unwilling to allow the episode of her wounding to be forgotten: *"et
antiquo memores de uulnere poenas | exigit alma Venus"* ("'and maternal
Venus exacted a penalty mindful of her ancient wound,'" *Met.* 14.477–
78).[76] Metamorphosis nonetheless trumps even Venus: for while her
memory of the old insult (*ueterem . . . iram,* 14.495) reacts vengefully to
the disdain shown to her by one of Diomedes's companions, Acmon, and
leads her to punish him and the other companions with transformation,
it also ensures that no human other than Diomedes himself will be able
to bear witness to the old wound. With the gradual but inexorable loss of

---

75. Cf. Horsfall 2003 ad loc. on the hendiadys *memini laetorue.*

76. On the prominence and power of Venus in Augustan poetry, see also Johnson 1996 and
Barchiesi 1999, as well as the discussion below, chapter 9.

that memory, the identity of Diomedes himself begins to crumble, and no mortal offspring stand by to keep his memory alive. The Diomedes of *Metamorphoses* Book 14 thus brings us back to a revised version of the point where we began: in place of a son with no memory of his father, Ovid leaves us with a hero defined not by his paternity but by his self-effacing desire to have no future.

3

Fathers and Sons, Part One: A Success(ion) Story

Ni la gloire ancestrale, ni la valeur paternelle ne fond-
ent un privilège, mais elles engendrent un devoir, elles
mettent devant les yeux du fils de famille un double
projet: faire aussi bien que ses ancêtres est la moindre
de ses obligations; faire mieux que son père, au mérite
de ne point déroger, ajoutera la gloire qui légitime réel-
lement son rang.

—BERNARD SCHOULER, "Dépasser le Père"

I. The Poetics of Paternity

In my discussion of Ovid's deployment of the Homeric Diomedes, the
threat of degeneracy was ever-present: in his own desire to present him-
self as second only to Homer, Ovid develops a character who is second
only to Achilles, but the Homeric character himself embodies textual
anxiety about measuring up to one's predecessor. In the conceit of
"Diomedes shamed," we saw the vulnerability to which the Homeric fig-
ure is at least sporadically subject: the alleged superiority of his father,
Tydeus, on the battlefield is a constant reminder, or threat, of the poten-
tial for decline.

The relationship between fathers and sons is fertile ground for meta-
poiesis: the constant tension between similarity and dissimilarity, between
sameness and otherness, between repetition and loss—as well as between
repetition and innovation—characterizes the interactions between self-
consciously competitive characters, whether they are characters of the
imagination or the fashioners of imaginative narrative themselves. In the
following chapters, I shall develop the idea that Ovid explores alternatively

the role of father or of son in his poetic relationship with Homer: the father who creates, instructs, and controls and has at least the ability if not the desire to limit freedom of choice, and the son who models himself on his father—or who experiments with cutting himself loose, going out on his own, and, at least potentially, making a distinctive new path for himself, but risking his very selfhood if he fails.

The relationship between fathers and sons has a powerful Homeric resonance: from the very first line of the poem we are invited to consider the central character in terms of his relationship with his father (μῆνιν ἄειδε, θεά, Πηληϊάδεω Ἀχιλῆος, "Sing, goddess, the wrath of Achilles, son of Peleus"), and this relationship is also central to the resolution of both Achilles's wrath and the poem: Priam's nighttime visit to Achilles's camp to retrieve the body of Hector is premised on the potential for commonality arising from the shared love of fathers for their sons and from sons' recognition of the duties owed to fathers.[1] Of course, in the study of classical cultures, generational themes, with both positive and negative associations, are ubiquitous; in the next chapter we will consider an instance of this pattern with striking implications for Augustan mythopoiesis itself. And, while tradition passed from father to son may be seen as a defining preoccupation of epic, it is hardly absent from other literary forms: indeed, one may think in particular here of tragedy, where Sophocles's *Oedipus Tyrannus* is just the most obvious example of a pattern of repetition that only becomes more toxic as its imperatives, figured by fate, invite resistance. In the following analysis, therefore, I emphasize that my reading of the episodes and characters considered here, while privileging the Homeric intertext, is not intended to obscure or occlude other frames of reference; rather, as we shall see, the Homeric intertext frequently sharpens our comprehension of Ovid's all-embracing poetics as it constructs a rich genealogy for ancient narrative.

II. *The Power of Paternal Guidance*

When the funeral games for Patroclus described in *Iliad* Book 23 are about to begin, Nestor offers his son Antilochus advice on how to excel in the chariot race (23.306–48). As Richardson notes in his commentary on the

---

1. For a classic statement of the theme, see Whitman 1958:218–19; and cf. Greene 1963:47–48. See also Finlay 1980; Lynn-George 1988:241–50; Edwards 1991:10; Redfield 1994 (1975):110–13. Crotty 1994:24–41 offers a valuable complement to my discussion.

speech, "Nestor himself is ἱππότα by tradition . . . , and he is descended from Poseidon, god of horses"; Richardson then lists the several other episodes in the poem in which Nestor presents himself as an authority on chariot racing.[2] It has been observed since antiquity that Nestor's speech here is among the most straightforward examples of didactic rhetoric in Homer; indeed, some have seen this speech as evidence that Homer rather than Hesiod is the father of didactic poetry.[3]

The suggestion that Homer is the father of didactic poetry (whether true or not is not at issue here) is mirrored in the character of Nestor, who in this scene is cast as both father and teacher. Nestor's instruction is long and detailed, as are so many of his speeches; but the specifically didactic nature of his theme is brought out near the opening, when Nestor uses two forms of the verb διδάσκειν to introduce his discourse ("Ἀντίλοχ', ἤτοι μέν σε νέον περ ἐόντα φίλησαν | Ζεύς τε Ποσειδάων τε, καὶ ἱπποσύνας ἐδίδαξαν | παντοίας· τῶ καί σε διδασκέμεν οὔ τι μάλα χρεώ," "'Antilochus, though you are young, both Zeus and Poseidon have loved you and have taught you horsemanship of all sorts; there is really no need for me to teach you this,'" 306–8). These lines are intended to compliment Antilochus at the same time as anticipating the theme of his comments, for, Nestor proceeds, although Antilochus may need no advice about horsemanship per se, his horses are slowest at racing (309–10). Success, therefore, according to Nestor, lies not in swiftness but in cleverness, μῆτις; and he underscores the point by using the noun μῆτις and its associated verb five times in eight verses (311–18):

---

2. Richardson 1993 on *Il.* 23.301–50 (he refers here to the epithet ἱππότα, which is applied to Nestor first at *Il.* 2.336; see Kirk 1985 ad loc.). For a comprehensive study of the character of Nestor, see Frame 2009, who focuses attention on the irony inherent in Nestor's speech; after all, later during the games (23.638–42) he mentions that, when as a younger man he participated in the funeral games for the Epeian king Amarynceus, he was successful in all the competitions except one: the chariot race. Frame uses this information as part of the case he builds to argue that Antilochus's behavior in Book 23 entails a sort of displacement of Nestor's earlier failure, inverting the roles of deceiver and deceived so that Nestor's son can succeed where his father did not (2009:131–72). While most of Frame's interests lie outside the scope of this discussion, his insight about patterns of repetition (and of its avoidance) along generational lines complements my analysis. On the potential for irony in Nestor's epithet ἱππότα, cf. Stanley 1993:106, 276–77.

3. I am indebted throughout the following discussion of Nestor's speech and the opening of *Ars amatoria* Book 1 to Citroni 1984 (specific details in the following notes). On the debate regarding the priority of Homer vis-à-vis Hesiod, or vice versa, cf. West 1978:27 n.2, rejecting the "ingrained belief that epic comes before everything else." On the didactic character of much Homeric narrative, particularly *exempla*, see Howie 1995.

"τῶν δ᾽ ἵπποι μὲν ἔασιν ἀφάρτεροι, οὐδὲ μὲν αὐτοὶ
πλείονα ἴσασιν σέθεν αὐτοῦ <u>μητίσασθαι</u>.
ἀλλ᾽ ἄγε δὴ σύ, φίλος, <u>μῆτιν</u> ἐμβάλλεο θυμῷ
παντοίην, ἵνα μή σε παρεκπροφύγῃσιν ἄεθλα.
<u>μῆτι</u> τοι δρυτόμος μέγ᾽ ἀμείνων ἠὲ βίηφι·
<u>μῆτι</u> δ᾽ αὖτε κυβερνήτης ἐνὶ οἴνοπι πόντῳ
νῆα θοὴν ἰθύνει ἐρεχθομένην ἀνέμοισι·
<u>μῆτι</u> δ᾽ ἡνίοχος περιγίγνεται ἡνιόχοιο."

"Their horses are swifter, but they themselves do not know more
than you do about how to contrive with cleverness. But come, dear
one, put all sorts of cleverness in your heart, so that the prizes do
not elude you. By cleverness, to be sure, is the woodcutter far bet-
ter than by force; by cleverness in turn does the helmsman on the
wine-dark sea keep his ship on a straight course when it is buffeted
by winds; by cleverness does one charioteer prevail over another."

The fivefold repetition of words derived from μῆτις, itself striking, is
amplified in force by the threefold anaphora of the dative μῆτι at the begin-
ning of three of the last four verses of this excerpt. Ancient commentators
call this an example of ἐπαγωγή, a word frequently used by Aristotle to
describe inductive reasoning;[4] in fact, Aristotle seems to be recalling this
very passage of Nestor's speech when, in describing ἐπαγωγή as a type of
argument that progresses from particulars to universals, he gives as an
example the idea that, if the skilled ship's pilot is the best ship's pilot and
if the skilled charioteer is the best charioteer, then generally speaking the
skilled person is the best at any given thing (*Top.* 1.12):

ἐπαγωγὴ . . . ἡ ἀπὸ τῶν καθ᾽ ἕκαστον ἐπὶ τὰ καθόλου ἔφοδος, οἷον
εἰ ἔστι κυβερνήτης ὁ ἐπιστάμενος κράτιστος καὶ ἡνίοχος, καὶ ὅλως
ἐστὶν ὁ ἐπιστάμενος περὶ ἕκαστον ἄριστος.

Inductive reasoning . . . is a means of progressing from individual
items taken separately to universals; e.g., if the best helmsman is
the knowledgeable/skilled one and the best charioteer is the knowl-
edgeable/skilled one, then as a rule the one who is knowledgeable/
skilled is best.

---

4. *LSJ* s.v. 5b; see, e.g., schol. bT 23 on *Il.* 23.315–18, commenting that Homer is the first to
employ ἐπαγωγή, with the discussion below; also Eust. *Il.* 1302.49; Citroni 1984:164.

Aristotle's two particulars, the κυβερνήτης and the ἡνίοχος, are identical with two of the three particular examples in Nestor's speech.[5]

The identification of this part of Nestor's speech as an instance of ἐπαγωγή is valuable for two reasons: first of all, because this form of reasoning is fundamental to the didactic process: teachers use specific exempla, or *paradeigmata*, to argue for universal truths;[6] and second, because the didactic function of these exempla can be shown to have a direct link with Ovidian didacticism. Let us look at the opening lines of *Ars amatoria* Book 1 (1–8):

> Si quis in hoc *artem* populo non nouit amandi,
>   hoc legat et lecto carmine doctus amet.
> *arte* citae ueloque rates remoque mouentur,
>   *arte* leves currus: *arte* regendus Amor.
> curribus Automedon lentisque erat aptus habenis,
>   Tiphys in Haemonia puppe magister erat:
> me Venus *artificem* tenero praefecit Amori;
>   Tiphys et Automedon dicar Amoris ego.

If anyone in this people does not know the craft of loving, he should read this; once the poem has been read, let him love learnedly. By craft swift ships are moved with sail and oar, by craft is moved the light chariot; by craft should Love be controlled. Automedon was clever with chariot and slowing reins, Tiphys was master on the Haemonian ship: in my case, Venus made me the artificer in charge of tender Love; I shall be called the Tiphys and Automedon of Love.

In a discussion of the second couplet, Mario Citroni has identified a direct allusion by Ovid to Nestor's speech, suggesting that Ovid must have had access as well to ancient Homeric exegesis.[7] His discussion, starting from a passing observation by William Race about Ovid's "nice parody" of the

---

5. Technical details mentioned later in Nestor's speech are quoted by Pl. *Ion* 537a–b and Xen. *Sympos.* 4.6, suggesting the episode's special notoriety: see Citroni 1984:160–61.

6. Cf. Arist. *Rhet.* 2.20.1393a 26ff., equating *paradeigma* with ἐπαγωγή (noted by Citroni 1984:163 n.15). Nünlist 2009:261–64 comments on instances in which the Homeric scholiasts mention the didactic function of *paradeigmata*, especially when voiced by old men like Nestor.

7. Citroni 1984:165 and n.19.

Homeric lines,[8] focuses on the striking anaphora of μῆτι in Homer, replicated by Ovid with the threefold anaphora of *arte* in *Ars am.* 1.3–4. As West notes in his commentary on Hesiod's *Works and Days*, "formal devices such as anaphora" tend to characterize ancient poetry in which "someone endeavour[s] to persuade another."[9] It is also worth observing that, as in Homer, the threefold anaphora is complemented by another two instances of the same or related words in the same passage: in Homer, μητίσασθαι and μῆτιν, and in Ovid, *artem* (1) and *artificem* (7). In each excerpt of eight verses, then, the key word—"craft," "cleverness," or "skill"—is sounded five times. The Ovidian version, furthermore, pays homage to the Homeric model while personalizing it. After all, in *Ars amatoria* Book 1, the last of these repetitions, *artificem*, is the Ovidian *praeceptor*'s designation of himself: he thus not only appropriates but effectively embodies the didactic principle first enunciated by Nestor.[10]

Another crucial dimension of Nestor's speech—a simple point, but of central importance here—is its addressee, all but ignored up to this point in my discussion: Antilochus, Nestor's son. In fact, the episode that begins with Nestor's speech is the most prominent scene involving Antilochus at any point in the Homeric poems—generally, his presence on the battlefield is in a supporting role, and when he delivers the news of Patroclus's death to Achilles, his sorrow, though observed by the poet, disappears from sight as the narrative focuses in on the grief of Achilles.[11] The character sketch of

---

8. Race 1982:146; cf. also 39 n.16.

9. West 1978:27 and n.4; on *Erga* 5ff., West collects the few examples of threefold (+) anaphora in Homer and Hesiod.

10. The inclusion of himself as *artifex Amori* (and *amoris*) in third place on the *praeceptor*'s list of individuals with special expertise also nods to the fact that Nestor's original set of exempla consisted of three; the *praeceptor* has replaced the Homeric woodcutter with the love-teacher, rearranging the sequence so that now the most important of the three, the love-teacher, comes last—just as in Nestor's speech to Antilochus the charioteer is mentioned last.

11. Willcock 1983:479–80 lists and briefly describes all the *Iliad* scenes featuring Antilochus, before using the youth as an example of the Homeric art of characterization. Antilochus's appearances at *Il.* 5.561–89, 15.568–91, and 17.651–701 are all in connection with Menelaus, a fact that may help to explain the latter's eventual willingness to compromise (see the discussion below); cf. also 17.377–80. In *Il.* 17.651–701, Menelaus bids Antilochus bring the news of Patroclus's death to Achilles; the youth does so in *Il.* 18.1–34. Briefer references to his death at the hands of Memnon occur in the *Odyssey: Od.* 3.108–12 (Antilochus's death recalled by his father) and 4.186–88 (Antilochus's death recalled by his brother); he appears in the underworld in *Od.* 11.467–70 and 24.15–19; and he is catalogued among the sons of Nestor at Hes. fr. 35.10 M-W. According to Proclus, his death at the hands of Memnon was described in the *Aethiopis* (*Aeth.* arg. 2 and 4 in West 2003), while at Pind. *Pyth.* 6.28–42 Antilochus dies

Antilochus that we receive in Book 23 is therefore worth our attention, as he moves from supporting to central character;[12] and the sketch that emerges is a curious one indeed. The character of Antilochus is developed in the first place by his behavior rather than his words; Homer reports no reply to Nestor's speech but moves instead to a description of the allotting of places in the lineup of chariot racers—Antilochus is allotted the first place in the lineup (352–54)—and then to the race itself, reported in very general terms until the horses have reached the final stretch of the course (373–75). Antilochus finally comes into individual focus at *Il.* 23.402, after an extended description of Diomedes's performance in the race that culminates in the intervention of Athena. At this, Antilochus finally speaks, addressing his horses to urge them on—not to win first place, which is now guaranteed to Diomedes, but to take second place, ahead of Menelaus (403–16).

Antilochus's next action is definitive: at a point where the track narrows, he turns his horses aside from the straight course and pursues Menelaus, who, fearing a collision, pulls back (417–37).[13] Angrily, Menelaus shouts after Antilochus, reproaching him for his bad behavior (439–41); the Homeric narrator then leaves his external audience in suspense about the outcome in order to describe the suspense of the internal audience, the Argives watching the chariot race. Their debate as they attempt to determine, through a cloud of dust, who is in the lead continues for more than fifty verses, at the conclusion of which Diomedes arrives at the finish line and is awarded first prize (448–513).

Antilochus indeed arrives second at the finish line—but the Homeric narrator is quick to observe that his accomplishment in surpassing Menelaus is the result not of swiftness but of cunning (κέρδεσιν, οὔ τι τάχει γε, "by cunning, and not by speed," 515). Thus, Antilochus's performance in the funeral games is marked by something close to deceit: he has indeed taken his father's advice about μῆτις to heart, in the process behaving in an objectionably shrewd manner.[14] The ambiguity depicted throughout this episode is remarkable, marking it as one of the most exciting episodes

---

while protecting his father; cf. also Xen. *Cyn.* 1.14 (with Delebecque 1970:39–46, arguing for the authenticity of the opening chapter).

12. Willcock 1983:481–84 emphasizes the Homeric poet's subtle development of the character of Antilochus in connection with Achilles and Patroclus.

13. Roisman 1988 offers a convenient discussion of differing scholarly reconstructions of Antilochus's stratagem to pass Menelaus.

14. Nestor uses the word κέρδεα to describe the shrewdness required to go safely around the turning post at *Il.* 23.322–25. For the closeness in meaning of the two words, note also

among so many in the *Iliad*—the narrator seems to be prolonging the suspense as his audience is forced to wonder whether Antilochus will in fact be awarded the second prize or will be rebuked, perhaps even penalized, for his underhanded sportsmanship.

The narrator's clever invitation to his audience to feel ambivalence about Antilochus can be seen to replicate on a small scale the narrative thrust of the poem as a whole.[15] The arousing of Achilles's wrath by Agamemnon in Book 1 invites the audience to participate in a sustained debate about the merits of both sides of the argument, a debate that is simultaneously played out within the poem by the human actors in the war and by the gods on Olympus and that will only be resolved at the poem's close. Achilles, who as convener of the games in *Iliad* Book 23 is the one to award prizes, can be seen to try to avoid deciding how to address the circumstances of Antilochus's second-place showing by announcing that he will give the second prize neither to Antilochus nor to Menelaus but to another charioteer, Eumelus, who crashed and actually came in last; the Homeric narrator has Achilles explain this surprising choice with the comment that, though last in the race, Eumelus is the best man of all ("λοῖσθος ἀνὴρ ὥριστος ἐλαύνει μώνυχας ἵππους," "'the man who is the best drives his single-hoofed horses in last place,'" 536). Achilles's sympathy for Eumelus may well be a result of his heightened awareness of the injustice he feels he himself has suffered; this sense of injustice is then replicated again in the reaction of Antilochus, who wants the prize he believes he has earned and suggests that Achilles give Eumelus something else from the vast stores of booty he has amassed (543–54). As he does so, Antilochus speaks in a manner highly reminiscent of the arguments Agamemnon had used in Book 1 in refusing to give up Chryseis, and Achilles himself had used in the same book in hopes of avoiding the

---

Od. 13.299, μήτι τε . . . καὶ κέρδεσιν; and cf. Roisman 1990:23–26 for a discussion of κερδ-words in Homer (at 25 she comments, "Explicit mental faculties are the most common companions of the base κερδ- in its noun and adjectival usages"). On μῆτις, see Detienne and Vernant 1974:17–31, who use the episode from *Iliad* Book 23 to launch their study of the centrality of μῆτις in Greek thought.

15. Cf. Richardson 1993 on *Il.* 23.499–652: "The quarrel over the second prize also develops in a way which echoes the main theme of the poem: like both Agamemnon and Akhilleus in Book 1, Antilokhos feels that he is being unjustly deprived of his due and refuses to accept this. Akhilleus' resolution of this issue sparks off the following protest of Menelaos: once again injured honour is at stake and he demands justice. But this quarrel takes a very different course from the quarrel of Akhilleus and Agamemnon, for first Antilokhos yields to the older man, and then Menelaos gives way to him in turn . . ."

loss of Briseis to Agamemnon.[16] At this point, however, the similarity with Book 1 ceases: Achilles now smiles ("for the first and only time in the whole poem," observes Richardson 1993 ad loc.) at Antilochus and acknowledges the youth's claim, thus ending Antilochus's wrath before it can begin (555–65). The spell is broken and, as is only appropriate with funeral games, the threat of disharmony evaporates.

Or rather, it almost evaporates—for Menelaus remains to be appeased. Still angry, he rises to address Antilochus before the assembled Argives, reproaching him for his behavior in the race and appealing to the Argives for adjudication. Menelaus puts Antilochus on the spot, inviting him to affirm with an oath that he did not obstruct Menelaus's chariot through deceit (δόλῳ, 585). Of course, Antilochus cannot in all honesty take such an oath; instead, therefore, he replies with a speech that again confirms that he has learned well his father's lesson about μῆτις.[17] Antilochus does not address the race directly but reminds Menelaus that he is young, while Menelaus is both older and better ("πολλὸν γὰρ ἔγωγε νεώτερός εἰμι | . . . σὺ δὲ πρότερος καὶ ἀρείων," "'For I am much younger . . . you, on the other hand, are older and better,'" 587–88). Then, rather than speaking about himself in particular, he uses a generalization about the transgressive behavior typical of youth (589–90):

"οἶσθ' οἷαι νέου ἀνδρὸς ὑπερβασίαι τελέθουσι·
κραιπνότερος μὲν γάρ τε νόος, λεπτὴ δέ τε μῆτις."

"You know the nature of the aggressiveness that arises in a young man: for his mind is more impetuous, but his skill is slight."

Finally, Antilochus announces that he will after all hand over his prize to Menelaus and furthermore will give Menelaus whatever he may want in the future, if only he may thereby avoid the older man's fault-finding (591–95).

---

16. Note especially *Il.* 23.553, "τὴν δ' ἐγὼ οὐ δώσω," with Richardson 1993 on 23.543–54, summarizing Eust. *Il.* 1315.29ff.: "Akhilleus knows by experience what it means to be robbed of one's prize." The article τὴν here, functioning as a demonstrative, refers to the mare that has been awarded as second prize—but the ellipsis of the noun (i.e., τὴν ἵππον) causes Antilochus's declaration to have the potential to refer to a female of his own species as well.

17. Antilochus even uses the word μῆτις in this speech, ironically claiming to defuse the skill whose achievement had been of such paramount importance in his father's advice. Cf. also Richardson 1993 on *Il.* 23.589–90.

Antilochus's rhetorical dexterity here is brilliant: as Richardson (1993 on *Il.* 23.587–95) comments on the speech, "Antilokhos' reply is a masterpiece of honourable conciliation, putting all the emphasis on the rashness of youth, paying respect to Menelaos' age, reminding him of their past friendship . . . , and of his own accord offering extra recompense. He cleverly avoids having to take the oath, but at the same time does not actually admit that he cheated!" As if to underscore Antilochus's shrewdness, the Homeric narrator concludes this episode—The Wrath That Might Have Been—by allowing Menelaus to have the last word. Apparently charmed by the youth's acknowledgment of Menelaus's superiority—for so Menelaus seems to interpret Antilochus's subtle speech—he abandons his claim to the prize after all and restores it to Antilochus (596–611).[18] Antilochus is, finally, no Achilles, and so the narrator can soon shift his, and our, focus away from this scene.

I have devoted prolonged attention to this scene not simply because of Ovid's redeployment of Nestor's words in the opening of *Ars amatoria* Book 1—although that in itself is a telling indication of Homeric resonance in Ovid—but also because of a broader pattern of interconnected motifs that it introduces: the relationship between fathers and sons that so often, and naturally, has a didactic dimension; the use of *paradeigmata* for instruction in classical narrative; and the constant interplay between similarity and difference that makes the father-son relationship a central concern in ancient culture generally and in the literature of heroic identity in particular. The ambivalence about Antilochus's behavior in the chariot race that I have described above adds, as we have seen, to the tension and excitement, and even to the delightfulness, of the scene; the Homeric poet cleverly keeps his audience guessing about the eventual outcome of the scene right up until its conclusion, when both the older Menelaus and his younger counterpart indicate a willingness to compromise. But another dimension of the episode is equally worthy of consideration: given the influential role of Nestor as a teacher figure in this scene, does Antilochus's behavior in the race constitute a cleverly obedient reliance on the very μῆτις counseled by his father, or is it rather a subversion of his father's advice—is he, in other words, to

---

18. The narrator signals the resolution of the conflict with a simile that compares the warming of Menelaus's heart at the youth's words to dew on a crop of ripening grain (*Il.* 23.597–600), in keeping with a tendency to use similes as closural devices. On the controversy surrounding the precise meaning of this simile, as well as its reception, see Richardson 1993 ad loc.

be seen as at least temporarily disobedient? Menelaus, we recall, labels Antilochus's actions with the word δόλος rather than μῆτις; if there is any justice to his choice of words—and certainly the poet allows his audience to entertain the possibility—then Antilochus has undermined the code of conduct established by Nestor rather than affirming it.

I press this point because it opens up a range of possibilities and in so doing introduces a theme of rich potential both in the Homeric poems and in Ovid's reception of them. Should sons follow in their fathers' footsteps, or not? Should sons obey their fathers, or not? What happens to disobedient sons—and not only to them but also to their fathers? And what of the sons who effectively displace their fathers? Indeed, the genealogical imperative of ancient narrative is so crucial to its logic that one might argue that every (male) character in ancient myth is another character's son, and another character's father, ad infinitum; and, aside from a few notably childless characters, this claim is in fact quite true. But its ubiquity does not make it less central to ancient thought; rather, one might even assert—or at least argue—that it is a structural principle of ancient narrative and as such both demands and repays attention.

These questions are also of relevance to the relationship between Homer and Ovid as poets. To what extent, if any, is Ovid an Antilochus figure, taking his poet-father's advice about μῆτις (and *ars*) even as he innovates in ways not foreseen by Homer? Is Ovid in fact to be seen as disobedient or wayward, or is his behavior exactly what the counsel to use μῆτις prescribes? The paradigm we turn to here is a central theme of Ovidian poetry and poetics and as such provides a window onto Ovid's Homeric intertextuality writ large.

To organize this discussion somewhat, I have divided it into three chapters. In this chapter, I shall turn to another Homeric variation on the paradigm of father as teacher and consider the role of Phoenix in the Embassy to Achilles; this discussion will lead us in turn to a discussion of the Meleager paradigm embedded within it, and to Ovid's reinterpretation of the paradigm in episodes involving Meleager, or the embassy, or both. In a second chapter, I shall introduce a number of non-Homeric episodes in Ovid's poetry—or perhaps it would be better to call them episodes without a precise Homeric intertext—to consider how the Homeric paradigm and its variations are used repeatedly, metapoetically, and politically by Ovid. Finally, I turn to the language of paternity and the implications of obedience and waywardness in Ovid's poems from exile.

III. Phoenix and the Embassy to Achilles

In *Iliad* Book 9, Nestor finally persuades Agamemnon to reconsider his rash alienation of Achilles. After an elaborate face-saving exchange of speeches, Agamemnon declares his willingness to shower Achilles with gifts as an indication of honor and in compensation for the threat of force in asserting his claim to Briseis. The delivery of this message is entrusted to an embassy consisting of Odysseus, Ajax, and Phoenix; while the first two of these emissaries are both by now familiar presences in the poem, and can therefore be expected to command as much authority with Homer's audience as, it is expected, they will exert with Achilles himself, Phoenix is a new and surprising addition to the cast of characters: he appears first here (and elsewhere in the poem only at *Il.* 16.196, 19.311, and 23.360; cf. also 17.555), and does not elsewhere play an important role.[19] Indeed, his presence here has been used to support a traditional analytical argument that sees the poem as an accretion of individual stories sometimes roughly stitched together rather than as a coherent whole shaped by one master poet (or even several); even scholars inclined to argue for the integration and coherence of the episode are therefore at pains to explain Phoenix's inclusion in this pivotal scene.[20] The difficulties here are exacerbated by the notorious presence of dual verb forms in the passage—Aristarchus himself proposed a solution with the suggestion that the duals are used of Odysseus and Ajax, since Phoenix was sent on ahead of them; and more recent attempts to explain the oddities here, while equally ingenious, continue to provoke doubt or, at the very least, speculation.[21]

---

19. He is mentioned in a fragment of the *Cypria* (fr. 16 *EGF*) as having given Achilles's son the name Neoptolemus; see also Hainsworth 1993 on *Il.* 9.168–69 for references in the scholia.

20. Hainsworth 1993 on *Il.* 9.168–69 summarizes the problem: "The poet does not explain why he chose Phoinix, Odysseus, and Aias as the Achaeans' emissaries, but it is not difficult to guess why the last two are designated . . . . Odysseus . . . is professionally well-qualified . . . . Odysseus is a φίλος ἀνήρ (197) to Akhilleus at this point . . . . Aias was not only ἄριστος . . . after Akhilleus himself . . . , but also excelled in ἰδρείη (7.198) in his own estimation. Agamemnon thought him a possible alternative to Odysseus at 1.145 . . . . On the other hand Phoinix is an unknown quantity . . . . His introduction here as if he were as well-known a figure as Hektor . . . , and a natural choice, is awkward . . . ."

21. Hainsworth 1993 on *Il.* 9.182 provides a useful survey of the different explanations that have been put forward and offers a suggestive rationale for the integral presence of Phoenix here: ". . . It may be that there is an insight at this point into the mind of Homer at work, as he improves an embassy of two heralds (Agamemnon's first idea, it appears), to one with two major heroes besides, to one also including Phoinix—whose contribution alone advances the plot of the *Iliad*." See also the summary of Griffin 1995:51–53, with

I shall return shortly to Phoenix's contribution to this scene; first, however, it will be useful to review the substance of the embassy. Upon arrival at Achilles's tent, Odysseus begins, presenting the elaborate list of gifts Agamemnon has offered in recompense: his speech is a notable example of extended formulaic repetition in Homer, replicating almost verbatim Agamemnon's original pronouncement (aside from the shift from first to third person, 122–57 = 264–99).[22] The rich and abundant list of gifts culminates with the offer of marriage to one of Agamemnon's daughters, and Agamemnon's emissaries seem to be as convinced as he himself is that Achilles will be unable to resist the general's almost boundless generosity, index as it is of his own remorse and of the honor in which he holds Achilles. Achilles's refusal comes as a surprising, even illogical, response—but the brooding anger it reflects is clearly articulated in Achilles's own rehearsal of the list of proffered gifts, now not echoed verbatim but with selective emphasis, and underscored by sarcasm (see especially 393–400, the rejection of the marriage offer).[23]

Achilles's highly charged outburst is in turn complemented by the speech of Phoenix, who now steps forward to present himself as a mentor able to command Achilles's respect. Phoenix's long speech is fundamentally didactic: he offers three different arguments meant to persuade Achilles that even a warrior with a justifiable grudge, like Achilles himself, can and should come to the aid of his comrades in need.[24] The first is autobiographical: Phoenix tells how he was compelled by strife with his father, Amyntor, to leave home, was taken in by Peleus, and served as a surrogate parent for the infant Achilles (444–95). I shall return later to several features of this reminiscence; for now, it is worth noting the significance given by Phoenix to the father-son relationship even when it is not strictly biological: he both notes Peleus's role as his own surrogate father (481–82) and addresses Achilles as his child (φίλον τέκος) twice (437 and

Mackie 1997. For the classic exposition of the analytic alternative, see Page 1959:297–315; and for a novel and sensitive interpretation of the inconsistency, see Nagler 1990:225–31; other challenging approaches are offered by Louden 2006:122–34 and B. Currie 2006:42–43.

22. Hainsworth 1993 on *Il.* 9.264–99.

23. Hainsworth 1993 on *Il.* 9.307–429 provides instructive background on Homeric eloquence generally and on the contribution of this speech to the characterization of Achilles.

24. For the didactic value of Phoenix's speech, see Mackie 1997:4–5 on Phoenix as teacher of "community" skills.

444).[25] The implied importance of conformity embedded in the tale is thus framed in terms that encourage the cultivation of resemblance and obedience to authority. He then moves on to a personification of prayers, Litae (Λιταί), to suggest that even the gods can be assuaged by prayer (499–523); the Litae are a powerful presence in an episode so generally filled with forms of λίσσομαι and related words (501, 511, 520, 574, 581, 585, and 591).[26]

Finally, Phoenix presents a *paradeigma* drawn from the world of epic song beyond the events surrounding Troy: this *paradeigma*, a story within a story, substitutes one set of characters and events for another, with the internal narrative reflecting in concentrated form the central themes of its outer frame (524–99).[27] This *paradeigma* is about another hero, Meleager, who suffers (what he considers) an undeserved insult; the cropped allusiveness of Phoenix's version strongly suggests that a fuller version— presumably a no longer extant epic *Meleagris*—preceded the narrative time of the *Iliad* and was known to the *Iliad*'s original external audience; certainly Phoenix's audience within Book 9 is assumed to know it already.[28] In Phoenix's narrative, the Aetolians and Curetes, previously allied, were now at war, in the aftermath of a boar hunt in which one of the Curetes, Meleager's uncle, was killed. The boar hunt was provoked in the first place by the wrath of Artemis, who had been omitted from the divine recipients of a sacrifice by king Oeneus and therefore sent a wild boar to lay waste the Aetolian people and countryside. With the help of comrades, Meleager successfully defeated the Calydonian boar; but the Aetolians and Curetes then fought over control of the booty, and Meleager's uncle was killed in the conflict; Meleager's mother then called down a curse on him because of her brother's death. Meleager therefore withdrew, although the Curetes's threat continued. His retreat to his bedchamber concluded

---

25. On Phoenix as a surrogate father figure, cf. Finlay 1980; Lynn-George 1988:131–40; Pratt 2007:34–35.

26. See Hainsworth 1993 on *Il.* 9.501. The thematics of λίσσομαι and related terms are central to the extensive discussion of the episode by Alden 2000:179–290; see also Rosner 1976:316, 321.

27. Willcock 1964 is the place to begin for a thorough discussion of the form and function of *paradeigmata* in Homer (discussion of the Meleager story at 147–54). Similar readings are offered by March 1987:27–46 and Edmunds 1997:425–32. For a useful approach to the dynamics of Homeric *paradeigmata* generally, see Lang 1983. Grossardt 2001 offers a comprehensive analysis of the development of the Meleager story, including its prominence as *paradeigma*. See also the connection between ἐπαγωγή and *paradeigma* discussed above.

28. On the *Meleagris* and pre-Homeric epic, see Bremmer 1988; for a summary of views of the pre-Homeric tradition, see Grossardt 2001:3–6.

only when Meleager's wife was finally able to convince him that he should return to the defense of his people.

I have already noted the appeal of Phoenix to the analytically minded critics of Homer: the content of his speech only adds to this appeal, since some internal inconsistencies as well as the exceptionality of each of the three sections of his speech can be (and have been) used to argue that the very character of Phoenix is simply not "originally" Homeric.[29] A greater sympathy has emerged, however, over the last several decades, as scholars have directed greater attention to the subtle concinnities of this character and his speech with the larger narrative frame: in particular, Phoenix's anticipation of the poem's concluding encounter of Achilles with Priam can be seen as a foreshadowing of the resolution of Achilles's wrath and of the narrative as a whole.[30] From an Ovidian perspective, in turn, I suggest, the episode is attractive not only because it provides a model for the story-within-a-story form, but also because it combines examples of intensive and extended repetition on the one hand (Agamemnon's initial speech ≈ Odysseus's delivery of the offer) with several features that make its authenticity suspect; as with the *Doloneia*, so here Ovid appears to have been drawn to a particular Homeric scene at least in part because of its controversial status.

Most important for Ovid, however, I suggest, is the emphasis placed on fathers and sons throughout the passage—in particular, on the highly fraught dynamic of competition and strife that this relationship can provoke; and it is this emphasis, furthermore, that makes the specifically Homeric dimension of Ovid's version of the Meleager story worth our attention. Lest I be thought to want thereby to minimize the importance of several other intertexts for Ovid's Meleager, I propose that the following discussion be seen as fundamentally supplemental, not substitutive; the observations made here only add to an already rich vein of texts— many no longer extant, but clearly known to Ovid—shaping what Ovid has done. I single out here the commentary of Franz Bömer on the episode of the Calydonian boar hunt in *Metamorphoses* Book 8 as an essential starting point for scholars interested in those other influences;[31] in fact, since

29. In addition to the references cited in n.21, above, see Fowler 2004:227–29.

30. Among many recent discussions I note also Braswell 1971:22–23; Rosner 1976; Scodel 1982; Held 1987; Swain 1988; and Yamagata 1991.

31. Bömer vol. 4, 1977 on *Met.* 8.273–546; see also Hollis 1970 on *Met.* 8.260–546; Grossardt 2001:149–55. Renaud 1993 offers a synthesis of the myth in support of its Homeric integrity.

Ovid's narrative of the Calydonian boar hunt is the fullest extant version
to survive from antiquity, Bömer's survey of the evidence and analysis are
essential for anyone examining the traditions concerning Meleager, even
for Homerists.[32] There are nonetheless some features of Ovid's version
of the story that have gone without notice but that lend themselves to a
Homeric perspective; in the following discussion, therefore, I limit myself
to those features of Ovid's narrative—both in *Metamorphoses* Book 8 and
in *Heroides* 3, Briseis's letter to Achilles—that can help us to see Ovid's
interest in the Homeric version.

IV. Ovid's Meleager: Genres at the Crossroads

The narrative of the Calydonian boar hunt that appears in *Metamorphoses*
Book 8 is a showpiece of Ovid's virtuoso ability to mix genres and styles.[33]
Features of epic, tragedy, comedy, elegy, and epigram all jostle for domi-
nance in the episode, creating a story that is by turns heroic, bathetic, grue-
some, romantic, violent, and humorous; the overall effect is of a narrative
repeatedly undone by its own pretentions, a narrative that instantiates
Ovid's polymorphous poetic style.[34] It is also worth observing here that
its placement at the very center of the central book of the *Metamorphoses*
makes it both a hinge and a point of focus: this aspect of the story will
gain in significance after we consider it in detail.[35] The transition to this
episode is provided by Theseus's defeat of the Minotaur, celebrated at
Athens (in spite of his abandonment of Ariadne and the suicide of his
father, Aegeus);[36] it causes his name to become known elsewhere, even
in Calydon, currently under attack by a dread boar sent by Diana. So, says
Ovid, even though they already had Meleager, the Calydonians begged
for Theseus's assistance, too (*Met.* 8.267–71)—and so Theseus left Attica
behind, as does Ovid's narrative.

---

32. Hainsworth 1993 on 524–605 acknowledges the value of Bömer's collection of evidence
and bibliography.

33. Earlier versions of this and the following section appear in Boyd 2015. I thank the editors
of *Paideia* for allowing me to reuse that material here.

34. For a discussion of the various models informing Ovid's Meleager narrative, see
Segal 1999.

35. Hinds 1985:22–23 emphasizes the centrality of the story as "the middle myth of the very
middle book." See also below, chapter 4, n.73.

36. On Ovid's *Theseid*, see Boyd 2006:190–99.

The narrative that follows thus elides the frame given it by Homer's Phoenix: there is no longer strife between Aetolians and Curetes; instead, the story centers entirely on the boar. In choosing a version of the story that does not entail civil war,[37] Ovid not only offers a fundamentally simplified version of what was in the *Iliad* a compressed and somewhat confusing story but also allows the focus to shift from the epic battlefield to the mock-epic hunt, for a confrontation in which the enemy is neither human nor divine and the reward of victory is not the defeat of a kingdom but the hide of a boar. This shift quickly draws the narrative toward dangerously funny territory—a danger that is in turn quickly embodied in the boar, the description of which anticipates nothing so much as the Japanese horror movies of the 1950s.[38] In classical literature, of course, boar hunts are generally serious business—no humorous response is provoked, for example, by Odysseus's memory of the boar hunt in which he received the scar recognized by Eurycleia (*Od.* 19.428–73), and a boar hunt is the occasion of the death of Croesus's son Atys (Hdt. 1.34–44). But the Calydonian boar that enters Ovid's narrative is an over-the-top creation that instills fear into even the doughtiest of Greek heroes.[39] Nothing could be more different from Phoenix's brief but effective description of the boar, as fierce as it is large but effectively dispatched in five hexameters by Meleager and friends (*Il.* 9.539–43).

What follows in Ovid's version is entirely non-Homeric in substance, though in form and style the prototype is the Catalogue of Ships in *Iliad* Book 2: a catalogue of the many heroes who join Meleager's entourage (8.298–323).[40] The rapid assemblage of names, many ornamented with patronymics or epic-sounding epithets, is star-studded, although unfamiliar figures appear, too: most notable is the last on the list, Atalanta, whose surprising presence—decidedly non-Homeric again—signals the

---

37. Perhaps an innovation by Euripides in his *Meleager*? This shift in emphasis may well have been a byproduct of the playwright's desire to focus on Meleager's love for Atalanta; see the summary of the play's likely contents, with fragments, by Collard and Cropp 2008:613–31.

38. Compare *Met.* 8.281–97 with the original *Godzilla*, or *Gojira* (http://www.imdb.com/title/tt0047034/).

39. Horsfall 1979 provides a valuable introduction to the humor of the episode.

40. Other important intertexts are the catalogues of Apollonius (*Argon.* 1.20–228) and Virgil (*Aen.* 7.641–87): see Kenney 2011 on *Met.* 8.301 for brief comments on catalogues as a subgenre, and cf. the careful analysis of Tsitsiou-Chelidoni 2003:198–217.

erotic coloring of the version to follow.[41] At least some members of this
gathering are known from other models: in addition to the pre-Homeric
Meleagris (about the precise content of which we know very little), Hesiod's
Ehoiai is clearly an important predecessor,[42] as are the numerous Greek
dramas, known to us now only in fragments or from testimonia, with the
Calydonian boar hunt as a central theme.[43]

The catalogue moves so rapidly, offering so little background detail on
the individual heroes as it does so, that it is tempting to see the ensemble as
of little more significance than the catalogue of Actaeon's dogs that appears
in *Metamorphoses* Book 3: there, the names are playful and punning—as
the names of pets often are—and have virtually no connection with other
mythical narratives; rather, they display Ovid's effectiveness at creating a
jarring contrast between the dogs' pet names and the subsequent gruesome
scene in which they dismember their master (*Met.* 3.206–52).[44] The "all-
star" cast of Ovid's Calydonian catalogue likewise invites us not to worry
about the details excessively—the overall effect might be thought to matter
far more than the individual details. Indeed, the welter of heroic names
invites this response, I think—but even as it does so, Ovid teases his read-
ers, reminding them that there is in fact a Homeric resonance here: and
that resonance appears in the person of Phoenix, whose identity as he
joins the entourage is further specified through one important detail, the
name of his father: *cretus Amyntore Phoenix*, 307.[45] Commentators on this

---

41. Mythical celebrities on the list include Castor and Pollux (301–2); Theseus and Pirithous
(303); pre-Iliadic heroes like Telamon, Peleus, and Nestor (309–13); and a crowd of unem-
ployed former Argonauts (302, 304, 306, 311, etc.); most of the others, although less imme-
diately familiar, are attested elsewhere, but note Hyleus (312), of whom we know nothing.
Atalanta's placement at the conclusion clearly recalls the appearance of Camilla at the end of
the catalogue of Italian heroes in *Aeneid* Book 7: see Boyd 1992, and cf. Keith 1999:223–30.

42. Although very little remains of Hesiod's Meleager narrative: see fr. 25 M-W (Meleager is
the son of Ares rather than of Oeneus, and is killed by Apollo), and fr. 280 M-W (Meleager
is son of Oeneus); and cf. Ziogas 2013:133–34.

43. Invaluable assistance with the dizzying variety of names found in one source or another is
the carefully and clearly sorted collection of Bömer vol. 4, 1977 on *Met.* 8.298–328. Cameron
2004:265–66 provides a context for Ovid's list in the ancient mythographers.

44. Barchiesi and Rosati 2007 on *Met.* 3.206–25 provide a detailed survey of the sources and
etymologies for the names of the dogs; they note that Ovid's list of names in the Actaeon
episode may owe something to an earlier narrative of the Calydonian boar hunt, in which the
hunting dogs were named. Cf. also Cameron 2004:266–67.

45. Although Ovid's Roman readers may well have known the story of Phoenix and his father,
Amyntor, from Euripides's and Ennius's plays on the subject (Collard and Cropp 2009:405–13
and Jocelyn 1967:389–94, respectively), the inclusion of Amyntor's name by Ovid may also
be intended to trigger in his readers a memory of the scholarly debates surrounding four

passage generally have little to say about Phoenix's presence on the list, or pass over him entirely in silence;[46] Bömer (1987 ad loc.) indicates that his name does not appear in any of our other sources for lists of Calydonian hunters. Given the fact that Phoenix narrates the Meleager story in *Iliad* Book 9, however, it is worth pressing the significance of his name's inclusion here: Is he, then, of approximately the same age as Meleager, and when he narrates Meleager's story in the *Iliad*, is he calling on his memory of something witnessed years before? Ovid's version suggests as much; in fact, Homer's Phoenix suggests that the Meleager story is a memory he has carried with him for years (*Il.* 9.524–28):

"οὕτω καὶ τῶν πρόσθεν ἐπευθόμεθα κλέα ἀνδρῶν
ἡρώων, ὅτε κέν τιν᾽ ἐπιζάφελος χόλος ἵκοι·
δωρητοί τε πέλοντο παράρρητοί τ᾽ ἐπέεσσι.
μέμνημαι τόδε ἔργον ἐγὼ πάλαι, οὔ τι νέον γε,
ὡς ἦν· ἐν δ᾽ ὑμῖν ἐρέω πάντεσσι φίλοισι."

"And thus have we learned the fame of men who were heroes of old, when violent anger would overtake a man: they were appeased with gifts and moved by words. I personally recall this deed from long ago, nor was it at all recent; and I shall tell it to all of you, who are dear to me."

Thus, although Ovid's version of the Meleager story is much later than Homer's in terms of literary history, he positions his version as preceding

---

hexameters quoted by Plutarch but not appearing in any of the Homeric manuscripts, generally numbered *Il.* 9.458–61 (*Mor.* 26 = *De aud. poet.* 26f): τὸν μὲν ἐγὼ βούλευσα κατακτάμεν ὀξέι χαλκῷ | ἀλλά τις ἀθανάτων παῦσεν χόλον, ὅς ῥ᾽ ἐνὶ θυμῷ | δήμου θῆκε φάτιν καὶ ὀνείδεα πόλλ᾽ ἀνθρώπων, | ὡς μὴ πατροφόνος μετ᾽ Ἀχαιοῖσιν καλεοίμην. Plutarch reports that these verses, in which Phoenix reveals that he considered killing his father, were removed by Aristarchus; see Hunter and Russell 2011 ad loc. Scholars are generally agreed that Plutarch is unreliable here, because there is no evidence elsewhere for removal of lines by Aristarchus; rather, he would have athetized them, but left them as he found them in the parodosis had they been there to begin with. See Hainsworth 1993 ad loc. for further discussion; also Apthorp 1980:91–99; Janko 1994: 27–28; Griffin 1995 ad loc. The mention of Amyntor and Phoenix together by Ovid suggests that he knew of these lines and the controversy surrounding them, and so may offer yet another example of Ovid's contrarian reading.

46. Neither Hollis 1970 nor Kenney 2011 ad loc. has any discussion of Phoenix's presence on the list. Grossardt 2001 relies on the lists of Bömer vol. 4, 1977, and does not discuss Phoenix. Tsitsiou-Chelidoni 2003:201 observes that Phoenix is included in close proximity to the mention of Peleus (*Met.* 8.309) but says nothing about Ovid's mention of Phoenix's father.

Homer's: for Homer's Phoenix, the hunt is a memory, but for Ovid's, it is lived experience.[47]

As Ovid's narrative of the hunt itself ensues, several of the group's members (e.g., Castor and Pollux at 301–2 and again at 372–77; Telamon at 309 and again at 378–79) are singled out a second time—only to have their abject failure described in some detail; in the chaotic bloodbath, a few new names are added to the list of participants (e.g., Hippalmon and Pelagon at 360), contributing thereby to the mock-heroic feel of the entire scene. Phoenix is not among those mentioned again, but neither are several others from the original catalogue; and as the episode moves inexorably toward its conclusion, this one brief reminder of a Homeric provenance is likely to fade from the reader's attention—if it even held that attention briefly to begin with. Instead, Ovid lavishes narrative attention on two aspects of the story that are either entirely non-Homeric or only momentarily alluded to in the Homeric *paradeigma*: Meleager's awarding of the spoils to Atalanta and the consequent hostilities (380–444), and the curse that Meleager's mother, Althea, pronounces on her son, complete with dramatic monologue, and his subsequent death (445–546). The indebtedness of these parts of the story to models beyond Homer is clear, in spite of the loss of so much of ancient literature.[48]

But Ovid does not conclude the Meleager story without a final acknowledgment of Homeric inspiration. The tale's inclusion in the *Metamorphoses* is in the first place premised on its character as a story involving a transformation, but that transformation only comes at the very end, when Meleager's sisters (with the exception of two) are transformed into birds (536–46). We know from the version of this metamorphosis told by Nicander (as transmitted to us by Antoninus Liberalis 2) that these birds are called Meleagrides, and that they lament their brother's death annually. This is arguably the feature of the story that most clearly dissociates it from the world of Homeric poetry—and yet it is at the moment of this transformation that Ovid makes his most explicit allusion to Homer,

---

47. On Ovid's fondness for repositioning his versions of stories vis-à-vis his models', see above, chapter 2, n.71.

48. See Bömer vol. 4, 1977 on *Met.* 8.273–546 for a comprehensive overview of the evidence. It is tempting to speculate that Ovid has signaled the complex intertextuality of this episode through his repeated emphasis on the word *auctor*, appearing at 349, 418, 430, 436, and 449. For his play with *auctor* elsewhere, see chapter 2, n.57; and cf. below, chapter 5, n.8.

introducing the sisters' transformation with an adaptation of the "many mouths" trope (*Met.* 8.533–35):

> non mihi si centum deus ora sonantia linguis
> ingeniumque capax totamque Helicona dedisset,
> tristia persequerer miserarum dicta sororum.

> Not if a god had given me mouths sounding with a hundred tongues and a capacious talent and all of Helicon would I be able to set forth to the end the sad words of his miserable sisters.

This trope first appears in *Iliad* Book 2, where the Homeric poet prefaces his performance of the Catalogue of Ships with a declaration of the sheer impossibility of doing the catalogue justice (*Il.* 2.488–92):

> πληθὺν δ᾽ οὐκ ἂν ἐγὼ μυθήσομαι οὐδ᾽ ὀνομήνω,
> οὐδ᾽ εἴ μοι δέκα μὲν γλῶσσαι, δέκα δὲ στόματ᾽ εἶεν,
> φωνὴ δ᾽ ἄρρηκτος, χάλκεον δέ μοι ἦτορ ἐνείη,
> εἰ μὴ Ὀλυμπιάδες Μοῦσαι, Διὸς αἰγιόχοιο
> θυγατέρες, μνησαίαθ᾽ ὅσοι ὑπὸ Ἴλιον ἦλθον·

> Neither shall I recall nor shall I list the multitude, not if I had ten tongues and ten mouths, and an unbreakable voice, and my heart were bronze, were it not for the Muses dwelling on Olympus, daughters of aegis-bearing Zeus, who recalled all the men, as many as came beneath Troy.

This declaration of poetic incapacity has a long history of echoes: it is brought into Latin by Ennius (*Ann.* 469–70 Sk.) and is subsequently transformed by Ennius's successor Hostius, who raises the number of imagined voices from ten to one hundred.[49] Virgil uses it twice (*Geo.* 2.43–44 and *Aen.* 6.625–27),[50] and Ovid contributes another three variations on the theme (*Ars am.* 1.435–36, *Fast.* 2.119–20, *Trist.* 1.5.53–56),

---

49. Courtney 1993: fr. 3, and p. 52 for a discussion of the likely date and content of Hostius's poetry.

50. Farrell 1991:232–34 describes Virgil's treatment of the trope in *Georgics* Book 2 as "surely . . . one of the most broadly humorous" passages in the poem, because of the incongruous comparison it suggests between the Homeric Catalogue of Ships and Virgil's catalogue of methods of tree cultivation—an incongruity that, I suggest, may well have attracted Ovid's interest. On the *Aeneid* version, see the suggestive discussion of Gowers 2005.

multiplying the number ten times yet again in the second of these.[51] Whenever Ovid uses it, he clearly invites his reader to compare his narrative with Homer's—but in the conclusion of the Meleager story, on what grounds? Is it simply a kind of grotesquerie, as the Ovidian narrative "degenerate[s] into a totally unepic near-necrophilia"?[52] Is it an indication of structural formalism, meant to recall the Homeric-style catalogue with which the episode began? Certainly ring composition is itself a feature of Homeric narrative.[53] This trope might also be seen as a framing device that completes the offer of a *maius opus* made at *Met.* 8.328, where Ovid recalls the words Virgil uses at *Aen.* 7.45 to announce the start of the Iliadic half of the *Aeneid*.[54] I suggest that we consider this explicit evocation of Homer as a mark of Ovid's broad grasp of Homeric epic, as an indication that, even when his poem is least Homeric, the legacy of Homer is inescapable. This literary relationship is enacted in the presence of Phoenix: when the Homeric Phoenix reminds Achilles of the role of surrogate father played by Peleus to him and by himself to Achilles, he also raises, at least implicitly, a reminder of his own wayward escape from his home and his natural father, Amyntor. This pattern of what I would call "the paternal imperative" is inescapable, though elastic and flexible; and Ovid's Meleager narrative exemplifies this paradox, springing from Homeric roots but assuming a distinctive, even "disobedient," identity as it takes shape.

V. Elegiac Eavesdropping: Briseis on the Embassy to Achilles

In *Metamorphoses* Book 8, Ovid uses the tension between epic subject matter and epic style to explore the nature of literary dialogue, suggesting that even at its most non-Homeric his poem is an offspring of Homeric tradition and, by implication, that he is a "wayward son" of Homer: just as Phoenix

---

51. Skutsch 1985 on *Ann.* 469–70 collects these and other examples; cf. also R. G. Austin 1977 on *Aen.* 6.625ff. Hinds 1998:34–47 uses the "many mouths" image to support his discussion of the relationship of topoi to intertextuality.

52. Galinsky 1975:136.

53. For the classic discussion of Homeric ring composition, see Whitman 1958:249–84 (chapter 11); also Notopoulos 1951:97–100 for a clear and valuable overview.

54. Horsfall 2000 on *Aen.* 7.37–45 offers a thorough discussion of literary models in *Aeneid* Book 7.

cannot escape identification with his father even as he slips almost inevitably into a pattern of surrogate paternity with Achilles, so Ovid's Meleager episode betrays its genetic inheritance even in the apparent absence of the Homeric narrative. Conversely, Ovid adheres closely (albeit selectively) to the Homeric episode of the Embassy to Achilles in *Heroides* 3, the letter of Briseis to Achilles—in other words, he is most Homeric in an elegiac poem that presents itself not as a narrative of κλέα ἀνδρῶν (the term used by Phoenix to introduce the Meleager *paradeigma* at *Il.* 9.524) by a traditional male bard for an audience of men but as a private missive for Achilles's eyes only from a woman, indeed, a slave woman, who is all but silent in the *Iliad*.[55] The ironic inversion of epic and elegiac themes from *Metamorphoses* Book 8 to *Heroides* 3 is complemented by Briseis's inversion of the trope of *militia amoris* so familiar in Roman elegy:[56] she has been turned over to Agamemnon (cf. *Il.* 1.345–48) but wants to be restored to Achilles, a prospect possible only if Achilles relents, agrees to return to the battlefield, and resolves the current impasse. In fact, we shall see that a number of specific allusions to episodes in the *Iliad* in her letter allow us to place the letter temporally with some precision: she was apparently out of sight but not out of earshot during the embassy, and actually recapitulates the substance of the embassy in this letter; Patroclus has yet to die, however, and to be mourned by Briseis. We are therefore to imagine Briseis writing shortly after the events of *Iliad* Book 9, and perhaps also after the *Doloneia* of Book 10;[57] her letter is thus most likely to be composed during the long day of fighting that follows, but before Patroclus's entry into battle.[58]

---

55. Briseis speaks in the *Iliad* only to deliver a funeral lament for Patroclus when his body is restored to Achilles (*Il.* 19.282–300). For an analysis of Briseis's lament as an indication of epic compression, see Dué 2002. Verducci 1985:87–120 focuses on Briseis's status (or lack thereof) as a slave. Jolivet 1999 offers a nice complement to my discussion, demonstrating that throughout *Heroides* 3 Ovid reads Alexandrian scholarship alongside the Homeric intertext, and responds in particular to three *quaestiones Homericae*.

56. For an overview of elegiac *militia amoris*, with bibliography, see Drinkwater 2013b; for the complementary trope of *servitium amoris*, literalized here in the person of the slave Briseis, see Fulkerson 2013. Spoth 1992:63–84 traces the combination of both conventions in *Heroides* 3; and cf. Bolton 1997 for further discussion.

57. Barchiesi 1992 on *Her.* 3.27–40 suggests that the fear expressed by Briseis about going out at night (*si progressa forem, caperer ne nocte, timebam*, 19) glances at the night raid in Homer.

58. Barchiesi 1992 on *Her.* 3.27–40 develops the temporal placement of the letter with further details.

Briseis quickly shows herself in full command of her Homeric identity. After opening the letter with a reproachful address to Achilles (*Her.* 3.1–8), she refers to her own first appearance in the *Iliad* (9–10):

> nam simul Eurybates me Talthybiusque uocarunt,
> Eurybati data sum Talthybioque comes.

For as soon as Eurybates and Talthybius summoned me, to Eurybates and Talthybius was I handed over as a companion.

In the *Iliad*, the heralds Talthybius and Eurybates are introduced at 1.320–21, where they are summoned by Agamemnon and commanded to fetch Briseis. Arriving at Achilles's hut, they are greeted by the hero, who then bids Patroclus to bring out Briseis and hand her over to them; Patroclus does so, and she moves off with the heralds (345–48). Ovid's Briseis knows the names of her escorts from Homer; and her repetition of their names in a single couplet compresses the more extended Homeric scene, where the two heralds' movements mark the scene's opening and close (*Il.* 1.327 and 347).[59]

In the Homeric scene, description of Briseis is limited to two words: one is the conventional epithet καλλιπάρῃος ("fair-cheeked," *Il.* 1.323 and 346), used repeatedly of female characters in Homer to describe female beauty from the perspective of an observer or observers. The other, however, marks Briseis as a character with emotions: ἀέκουσα ("unwilling," *Il.* 1.348)—unwilling, that is, to be taken from Achilles and handed over to Agamemnon.[60] Ovid's Briseis develops this emotion, recalling her reluctance to leave and her sorrow that Achilles has not tried to get her back (*Her.* 3.13–16). She then rehearses the reassurances given to her by Patroclus as he delivered her to the heralds (23–24):

---

59. Jacobson 1971:333–35 uses Briseis's knowledge of Eurybates's name, rarely attested outside of Homer, to launch his discussion of Ovid's familiarity with Homer; cf. also Jacobson 1974:15–16. Barchiesi 1992 on *Her.* 3.9 develops the Homeric resonance: "La ripetizione dei nomi degli araldi fra esametro e pentametro sottolinea appunto la pronta e scrupolosa esecuzione de comando, un po' al modo di certe ripetizioni formulari omeriche che descrivono la fedele consegna di un messaggio. La stretta associazione dei due nomi fa pensare agli aulici *duali* del modello . . ." (Barchiesi's italics).

60. Wilkinson 1953:227–30 begins his discussion of this letter with an astute observation regarding the importance of Homer's ἀέκουσα for Ovid; the remainder of his essay, though dated in its approach, is still of interest. See also Nünlist 2009:249, and cf. Verducci 1985:99 on Homer's spare description of Briseis.

Ipse Menoitiades tum, cum tradebar, in aurem
 "Quid fles? hic parum tempore" dixit "eris."

At the time when I was being handed over, the son of Menoitius
himself spoke into my ear: "Why do you weep? You will be back
here in a short time."

This couplet exhibits in concentrated form Ovid's ability to mark even a
supremely non-Homeric moment with a precise allusion to Homer: in the
Iliad, there is no exchange of words between Patroclus and Briseis; but
Ovid explodes the decorum of the Homeric scene by putting on Patroclus's
lips an intimately whispered reassurance, that if examined closely enough
threatens to destabilize entirely our understanding of the wrath of Achilles.
Even as he does so, however, Ovid has Briseis introduce her mention of
Patroclus with his patronymic—not simply as an indication of her epic
competency (though it is that) but also of Ovid's careful reading of *Iliad*
Book 1, where Patroclus's entrance into the poem occurs not under his
proper name but by his patronymic, *Menoitiades* (1.307).[61] The patronymic
also stands out here as a reminder of the father-son axis that reverber-
ates throughout the mirroring stories of Phoenix's and Meleager's rela-
tionships with their fathers, as well as in Phoenix's surrogate paternity of
Achilles: Ovid's Briseis indicates her competency as a reader of Homer
even as she suggests that it can be replaced by the erotic relationship that
characterizes her longing for Achilles, and that distinguishes the priorities
of elegy from those of epic.[62]

Meanwhile, Patroclus's promise has yet to be matched by Achilles's
deeds—in fact, Briseis is convinced that Achilles's continued inaction
shows his lack of care for her. Support for this inference is to be found, she
argues, in his rejection of the embassy and their offer (27–40). She begins
this reminiscence of the embassy in *Iliad* Book 9 with the names of the three
emissaries, *Telamone et Amyntore nati* (27) and *Laerta . . . satus* (29)—or,

---

61. Cf. Kirk 1985 ad loc.: "This is the poem's first mention of Patroklos, as 'son of Menoitios'
simply—an allusive reference which suggests (proves, indeed, unless it be the result of
minor oral insouciance) that the audience was already familiar with him." The same can be
said of Ovid's Briseis.

62. Alison Keith also has pointed out to me that Briseis's quotation of Patroclus's words
incorporates another kind of quotation as well—namely, from Prop. 2.20.1, addressed to his
puella: Quid fles abducta grauius Briseide? quid fles . . . ? Ovid's Briseis thus demonstrates her
competency as a reader of elegy as well as of the *Iliad*, in which Thetis addresses Achilles
with the same words: "τί κλαίεις;" (*Il.* 1.362, noted by Barchiesi 1992 on *Her.* 3.24).

rather, not their names but the names of each of their fathers together with participles designating paternity. The general effect is to signal yet again Briseis's Homeric competence—she not only knows these men but also has learned of their lineage.[63] On the other hand, we may wonder about her choices: while the mention of Telamon allows for a quick and familiar distinction between Telamonian and Oilean Ajax, and the reference to Laertes evokes an important character in the *Odyssey*, the identification of Phoenix as "son of Amyntor" is likely to puzzle at least momentarily even the most learned of Homer-literate readers—as I have already noted, the embassy of *Iliad* Book 9 is the only episode in which Phoenix plays a significant role, and in that scene the reference to Amyntor comes in the context of Phoenix's autobiographical reminiscence about strife, potentially patricidal, between father and son. Briseis has clearly eavesdropped attentively on the embassy; her recollection pointedly focuses our attention on the intergenerational strife that informs it, implying that the relationship she would prefer is free of such ominous undertones.

Briseis then proceeds to summarize the material offer of recompense made by Agamemnon (31–38):

> uiginti fuluos operoso ex aere lebetas
>> et tripodas septem pondere et arte pares.
> addita sunt illis auri bis quinque talenta,
>> bis sex adsueti uincere semper equi,
> quodque superuacuum est, forma praestante puellae
>> Lesbides, euersa corpora capta domo;
> cumque tot his—sed non opus est tibi coniuge—coniunx
>> ex Agamemnoniis una puella tribus.

Twenty tawny cauldrons of finely crafted bronze, and seven tripods of comparable weight and artistry. To these were added twice five talents of gold, twice six horses accustomed to win, and—what is superfluous—Lesbian women of exceptional beauty, chattel captured when their homes were destroyed; and along with all of these, one girl to be your wife—though of a wife you have no need—chosen from the three daughters of Agamemnon.

---

63. Cf. Jacobson 1974:27, interpreting Briseis's use of references to paternity here as an indication of her tendency "to see people in their roles as kin"; I suggest that this is not so much an indication of her psychological vulnerability as it is a reflection of a Homeric pattern of thought.

As Barchiesi notes, "The list of gifts repeats with refined precision that pronounced by Agamemnon at 9.122–57 and faithfully reproduced by Odysseus at 9.264–98."[64] In the two Homeric lists, the sequence is seven unused tripods; ten talents of gold; twenty burnished bowls; twelve prize-winning racehorses; and seven women of surpassing beauty skilled in crafts from Lesbos—in other words, aside from the relocation of the bowls to the start of Briseis's list, all but identical.[65] Barchiesi continues by suggesting that the precision of Briseis's list is meant as a sort of Ovidian homage to Homer's repetitive code, offering as it does a third instance of repetition. Her precision also has the effect of making the next detail in the passage, in which she diverges from Homer, stand out as a marker of the changed perspectives reflected in changes of gender and genre: whereas the Iliadic catalogue of gifts next includes Briseis herself, with in addition the promise of a bride to be chosen from one of Agamemnon's three daughters, Ovid's Briseis omits mention of herself among the chattel, instead complaining that the offer of a wife is superfluous—that is, since Achilles already has her. With the word *coniunx*, Briseis of course plays with the levels of meaning that the word can have, taking advantage of the euphemism to identify herself as the only sexual partner Achilles needs, or should want.[66] She simultaneously "corrects" the speech by Achilles she has overheard, since while the Homeric hero does—strikingly—refer to her once as his ἄλοχος (*Il.* 9.336), he firmly locates his emotional attachment in the past; now that Agamemnon has taken her, he declares, let him keep her (*Il.* 9.342–45). But Ovid's Briseis places the erotic relationship with Achilles firmly in the present and wills it to continue in to the future—she is now and is determined to remain his *coniunx*.[67]

---

64. Barchiesi 1992 on *Her.* 3.31–38: "L'elenco dei doni repete con raffinata precisione quello enunciato da Agamennone in 9, 122–57 e fedelmente ripetuto da Odisseo in 9, 264–98."

65. Barchiesi 1992 on *Her.* 3.36 notes that these lines contain the first instance of the Grecism *Lesbis* in Latin, which thus comes directly from Homer.

66. Presumably Briseis knows the *Aeneid* as well as the Homeric poems and has learned to obfuscate from Dido: *nec iam furtiuum Dido meditatur amorem:* | *coniugium uocat, hoc praetexit nomine culpam, Aen.* 4.172–73 (cf. also Serv. on *Aen.* 4.23); Adams 1982:160.

67. Ovid's/Briseis's use of *coniunx* here may also reflect the poet's familiarity with the Homeric scholia: the bT scholia suggest that Achilles's use of the term ἄλοχον θυμαρέα to describe Briseis is rhetorically strategic, since by enhancing her status he enhances the gravity of Agamemnon's offense: "ηὔξησε τὴν ὕβριν ἄλοχον αὐτὴν εἰπὼν καὶ θυμαρέα." Clearly, Briseis's interpretation of Achilles's language is different from Ovid's. On "correction" as a gesture of intertextuality, see Thomas 1986:185–88.

The remainder of Briseis's letter is equally rich in its Homeric intertextuality: she recalls Achilles's threat to set sail at dawn and return to Phthia (57–58 and 65–67 ≈ *Il.* 9.357–63); she imagines herself enduring the fate that the Homeric Hector had foreseen for Andromache (69–76 ≈ *Il.* 6.456–58); and she dwells on Achilles's *ira*, focalizing it with the identification of herself as its cause—and so identifying it (and, by implication, herself) as the theme of the *Iliad* as a whole (85–90).[68] Nonetheless, allusions to the embassy continue to be a major factor in shaping the poem's logic: immediately after urging Achilles to set aside his *ira*, she recalls the Meleager *paradeigma* that Phoenix had recounted and which she apparently overheard (92–98). As Barchiesi notes, she thereby compresses into seven verses what had been a narrative of seventy lines in Homer;[69] but the Homeric color of the passage remains strong, in the first place because Briseis uses yet another patronymic, *Oenides*, to tell the story, rather than using Meleager's proper name. She also displays her ability to get to the heart of the story's significance: her version contains no mention of the Aetolians and Curetes, no boar hunt, not even Phoenix as its narrator; instead, the words *bellum erat* (95) suffice to set the scene. The emphasis in Briseis's version in fact falls primarily on the wife through whose intercession Meleager is finally convinced to take up arms in defense of his homeland, and with whom Briseis herself clearly identifies: *coniugis* is the first word of her version of the story, and the wife's role is underscored by the repetition of the word near the end of Briseis's version, *sola uirum coniunx flexit* (97).[70] In turn, embedded within this summary focusing on Meleager's wife is a pregnant allusion to the curse of Althea (93–94)—as in Homer, a reference filled with foreboding but never developed.

In the section of the letter that follows, Briseis continues with her version of the embassy and Achilles's reaction to it, evoking the image Homer had offered of Achilles's pastime in retirement. When the Homeric envoys reach Achilles's hut, they find him playing the lyre, entertaining Patroclus with a performance of the κλέα ἀνδρῶν, "the glorious achievements of warriors" (*Il.* 9.185–91):

Μυρμιδόνων δ' ἐπί τε κλισίας καὶ νῆας ἱκέσθην,
τὸν δ' εὗρον φρένα τερπόμενον φόρμιγγι λιγείῃ,

---

68. See Barchiesi 1992:188.

69. Barchiesi 1992 on *Her.* 3.91–98.

70. Jolivet 1999:23–28 suggests that Meleager's wife, Cleopatra, is a role model for Briseis.

καλῇ δαιδαλέῃ, ἐπὶ δ' ἀργύρεον ζυγὸν ἦεν,
τὴν ἄρετ' ἐξ ἐνάρων πόλιν Ἠετίωνος ὀλέσσας·
τῇ ὅ γε θυμὸν ἔτερπεν, ἄειδε δ' ἄρα <u>κλέα</u> <u>ἀνδρῶν</u>.
Πάτροκλος δέ οἱ οἶος ἐναντίος ἧστο σιωπῇ,
δέγμενος Αἰακίδην, ὁπότε λήξειεν ἀείδων . . .

And they came to the huts and ships of the Myrmidons, and found him pleasing his mind with the clear-sounding lyre, lovely, of detailed craftsmanship, and there was a bridge of silver on it; he had chosen it from the spoils after destroying the city of Eëtion; he cheered his heart with this, and he sang the glorious deeds of heroes. Patroclus alone sat opposite him in silence, waiting for whenever the descendant of Aeacus should cease from singing . . .

In this momentary *mise en abyme*, Achilles takes on the role of a Homeric bard, singing verses that have as their theme something resembling the *Iliad*: indeed, he is like Homer himself—or would be, if his audience were large and communal rather than private and solitary.[71] Briseis translates this scene, both literally and figuratively, into elegy: she too describes Achilles as a warrior who prefers song to battle, taking pleasure in the lyre, but now he resembles not Homer so much as an elegiac poet (113–20):

At Danai maerere putant—tibi plectra mouentur,
    te tenet in tepido mollis amica sinu.
et quisquam quaerit, quare pugnare recuses—
    pugna nocet, citharae noxque Venusque iuuant.
tutius est iacuisse toro, tenuisse puellam,
    Threiciam digitis increpuisse lyram,
quam manibus clipeos et acutae cuspidinis hastam
    et galeam pressa sustinuisse coma.

But the Danaans think that you are grieving—in fact, you play the lyre, and a pliant girl holds you in her warm embrace. And whoever asks why you refuse to fight: fighting does harm, while the lyre, and

---

71. Jolivet 1999:17–23 notes that this Homeric scene provokes a flurry of anxious scholiastic reaction, as the ancient critics attempt to distinguish the behavior of Achilles here from that of lyre-playing Paris in *Iliad* Book 3, and suggests that Achilles's *secessus ab armis* is transformed by Briseis into a *recusatio* of epic (cf. *Her.* 3.115, *et quisquam quaerit, quare pugnare* <u>*recuses*</u>).

nighttime, and Venus all create pleasure. It is safer to lie in bed,
to hold your girl, to make the Thracian lyre sing with your fingers,
than to pick up in your hand shields and a spear with sharp point,
and to wear a helmet, hair pressed beneath.

The first couplet of this excerpt exhibits a typically Ovidian play with
genre—the hexameter alludes to Achilles's sorrow and his lyre playing, both
featured in the *Iliad*, but the pentameter "elegiacizes" the entire scene with
a strikingly non-Homeric detail, the girlfriend lying in Achilles's embrace.
This pattern is more or less repeated in the second couplet: again, the hex-
ameter focuses on Achilles's refusal to fight, well known from Homer, but
in the pentameter his leisure time is filled not with songs of κλέα ἀνδρῶν,
as in Homer, but with erotic pleasures. In the third couplet, this picture of
erotic luxuriation is developed in three parallel clauses, juxtaposing bed,
girl, and lyre, while the fourth couplet lists the three military accoutre-
ments that Achilles rejects: shield, spear, and helmet. In short, the life and
values he appears to prefer are those validated by the elegiac lover of the
Amores, who at *Am.* 2.11.31–32 rejects, in terms that parallel *Her.* 3.17–18, a
heroic career in favor of a life filled with love and love poetry:[72]

tutius est fouisse torum, legisse libellos,
    Threiciam digitis increpuisse lyram.

It is safer to keep to the bed, to read books of poetry, and to make the
Thracian lyre sing with your fingers.

In implying this parallel between Achilles's song and that of the Ovidian
lover, then, Briseis revises the generic orthodoxy; and with the intimate
details she offers regarding Achilles's emotional life—details occluded by
Homeric decorum—she suggests that even Homeric epic is subordinate
to elegiac love.[73]

The inversion Briseis proposes culminates with her suggestion that
she should be freed from Agamemnon by the Danaans so that she herself
can go as an envoy to Achilles and plead for his return to battle (127–28):

---

72. See also Barchiesi 1992 on *Her.* 3.113–20, identifying a further important intertext in
Tibullus 1.1.46, *et dominam tenero continuisse sinu.*

73. Fulkerson 2005:96–97 notes the elegiacization of Achilles here but does not develop the
suggestion that he is depicted as an elegiac poet as well; cf. also Spoth 1992:79–80.

Mittite me, Danai! dominum legata rogabo
   multaque mandatis oscula mixta feram.

Send me, Danaans! As an envoy I will ask my master many things,
and will bring him kisses mingled with commands.

In a single couplet Briseis throws all generic order into confusion, suggest-
ing that she, a woman and captive, has the power to accomplish something
that warriors representing the allies of Achilles are unable to achieve.[74]
This confusion is replicated by the way in which she describes how she
will approach Achilles, namely, with a mixture of *mandata* and *oscula*; the
two words, side by side in the pentameter, juxtapose the public setting
for heroic epic with the intimate world of elegy, the exclusively masculine
politics of epic with the sexual juncture that defines elegy. Simultaneously,
she inverts the very nature of the elegiac world, since a successful embassy
by Briseis would, at least hypothetically, put an end to Achilles's elegiac
dalliance and send him back into battle—or would it? The *mandata* she is
likely to bring him, after all, will be erotic, and so will undermine the epic
imperative driving the men around her. The potential for chaos embedded
in her proposal is amplified in the next couplet, when for a final time she
invokes *Iliad* Book 9 as a model (129–30):

plus ego quam Phoenix, plus quam facundus Vlixes,
   plus ego quam Teucri, credite, frater agam.

I shall accomplish more than Phoenix, more than Ulysses, good with
words though he is, and more than the brother of Teucer: believe me.

With this final listing of the Homeric envoys, Briseis reminds us of their
failure and invites us to imagine, however evanescently, a world in which
women can accomplish more than men and elegy can trump epic. As read-
ers of Homer we know—at least we think we know—the sequel; but in the
upheaval proposed by Briseis, Ovid hints at an ever-expanding horizon of
untold stories, whose consequences we can only imagine.[75]

---

74. The observation by Barchiesi 1992 on 127, *legata*, is apropos: "Il femm. di *legatus*
è, come è facile immaginare, del tutto eccezionale, e riceve un supplemento di intensità
dall'accostamento con *dominum*"; and cf. Spoth 1992:80–81.

75. Alison Keith has suggested *per litteras* that Briseis hints at (without articulating) an anti-
epic tradition that rejects the poets of paternity for an elegiac poetics of women, slaves, cap-
tives, foreigners, and mourners.

4

Fathers and Sons,
Part Two: Paternity as Paradigm

τὰ γὰρ τῶν νέων ἤθη πολλὰς μεταβολὰς ἐν τῷ βίῳ
μεταβάλλειν ἑκάστοτε πέφυκεν

—PLATO, *Laws* 929c[1]

I. Theme and Variation: Paradigm Shifts

The Homeric episode of the Embassy to Achilles establishes a model of
pattern replication; that is, within a brief narrative sequence we are pre-
sented with three variations on the same theme, the son who rejects and
may even lash out at his father. Phoenix tells the story of Meleager, whose
anger at his father makes him retire from the defense of their community;
Phoenix himself is a voluntary exile, forced into leaving his home because
of insoluble strife with his father; and Achilles enacts the pattern as the
story unfolds, rejecting the gifts offered to him by Agamemnon—not only
his senior and playing a broadly paternal role but a man who specifically
offers himself as a prospective father-in-law to Achilles. A second theme,
although less precisely developed, centers on the resolution of the first
pattern: conflict ends, and relations between father and son are restored.
Here, the three versions show some variation: in the simplest version,
involving Meleager and his father, Oeneus, Meleager's wife intervenes and
the hero comes to his country's defense; in an alternative development
of the pattern, Phoenix, unable to live in peace with his father, "adopts"
a surrogate father, Peleus, and becomes himself a surrogate father to the
young Achilles; and in the unfolding narrative, Achilles will go on to a

---

1. "For young men's characters are disposed by nature to experience many changes from one
period to the next."

resolution of his conflict with Agamemnon through the intercession of
another father, Priam, who is acting on behalf of his own son.

Difference and similarity: *referre aliter idem*. Each of these versions of the
succession story is refracted through the others, and each is made richer
and more complex by a consideration of the other narrative routes it might
have taken: What if Phoenix had in fact killed his father? What if Meleager
had rejected his wife's counsel and had refused to fight? What if Achilles
had relented and had married a daughter of Agamemnon? The fact that
these things do not happen confirms the strength of the pattern and its inev-
itable progression. It also demonstrates indirectly how the strong thematic
patterning that shapes so much of classical myth can import into one story
the same resonance, mutatis mutandis, found in another. That is why and
how a *paradeigma* like the Meleager narrative functions in the first place: it
contains many of the same elements that are central to the primary narra-
tive of the *Iliad* but reduces them to a comparatively brief tale involving an
entirely different cast of characters and events. While not connected causally
or circumstantially in any way to the primary narrative, the *paradeigma* nec-
essarily distills the key motifs or themes of the primary story into a concen-
trated version; the resulting mirror image is both different from its model
and repetitious of it. Using the character of the *paradeigma* as an analogy,
I shall temporarily move the discussion away from its close focus on the
Homeric intertext to consider how Ovid exploits the succession theme else-
where in his poetry. Readers concerned that this course of action diverges
from the focus of the book can, I hope, take some pleasure in knowing that
what goes around, comes around—the Homeric poems will in fact work
their way back into our discussion as they inevitably must, following the pat-
tern of ring composition that is a basic element of the Homeric *paradeigma*.[2]

In the *Metamorphoses*, several otherwise unconnected stories involve a
repetition of this pattern. In Book 8 itself, the Meleager story is preceded
by another variation, in which even a son who otherwise seems pliable
disobeys his father—in this case only once, the one occasion that proves
to be fatal. I refer to the story of Daedalus and Icarus (*Met.* 8.183–259), told
immediately after the description of the labyrinth, mastered, together with
the Minotaur inhabiting it, by Theseus.[3]

---

2. On the centrality of ring composition to the functioning of *paradeigmata*, see Willcock
1964:147.

3. Boyd 2006:175–84 offers a detailed analysis of Ovid's labyrinth narrative; see also Pavlock
2009:61–66.

The monitory burden of the Daedalus and Icarus story is fully developed by Ovid, working from a far more partial and elusive version of the story that appears at *Aen.* 6.14–33.[4] Virgil's treatment of the episode there strongly suggests that he is responding to a model that would have been known to his readers; unfortunately, that hypothetical model has not survived, although a remarkably unhelpful scholion on *Il.* 2.145 seems to indicate that Daedalus and Icarus figured in Callimachus's *Aetia* as well as in a work by Callimachus's student Philostephanus.[5] Many Greek dramas, both tragic and comic, treated aspects of the Daedalus saga;[6] unfortunately, only fragments survive, and Ovid's treatment is therefore the fullest version we have from antiquity. In fact, two versions of the same story survive in Ovid: the first, in elegiac couplets, appears in Book 2 of the *Ars amatoria*; the second, in hexameters, is the one I shall focus on here, although the two treatments are so close—including the verbatim repetition of some verses, and the close echo of others—that the repetition has yet to be satisfactorily accounted for. Heinze of course focused on the generic differences between the two narratives,[7] while others are more interested in metaphorical interpretations that associate the characters with a display of *hybris*.[8] The framework for each version is important as well: the *Ars* treatment is explicitly didactic, used by the Ovidian *praeceptor* to warn his pupils about the importance of moderation even in love,[9] while that in the *Metamorphoses* serves as a narrative bridge, moving us away from tales centered on Athens, in the process flirting with the introduction of a non-metamorphic story into the poem—a flirtation that concludes when, in the aftermath of Icarus's demise, the narrator describes the transformation

---

4. For bibliography on the Daedalus ecphrasis in Virgil, see Boyd 2006.

5. For an allusion to Icarus in Callimachus, see Harder 2012 on *Aet.* fr. 23.2–3 (also Massimilla 1996 on *Aet.* fr. 25.3); and for Daedalus cf. Harder 2012 on *Aet.* fr. 43.48–49; Massimilla 1996 on *Aet.* fr. 50.48–49. Callimachus's contemporary Philostephanus also told the story of the flight, thereby providing the aetiology for the Icarian sea, but the precise context is unknown (*FHG* fr. 36).

6. See Bömer vol. 4, 1977 on *Met.* 8.183–235 for a collection of tragic titles and bibliography thereon.

7. Heinze 1919:74–76; see also Sharrock 1994b:87–195 for a full treatment of the intertextuality of the two versions.

8. For a summary (not overly sympathetic) of various readings of the episode, see Janka 1997 on *Ars am.* 2.21–98. Wise 1977 is an influential instance of the focus on *hybris*; cf. also Pavlock 2009:66–68.

9. Generally on moderation in the *Ars amatoria*, see Gibson 2007:105–9; and cf. Kenney 1993:462–65.

of Daedalus's nephew Perdix into a pheasant (8.236–59).[10] Repetition is, as we have already seen, a Homeric signature and is exploited by Ovid on numerous occasions to bring out the nuance in even slight details; it can also, as we shall see in a later chapter, allow Ovid to foreground his own close reading of Homeric scholarship. In the context of the Daedalus and Icarus story, however, I want to remain focused on another crucial aspect, its juxtaposition of fatherly advice and filial disregard, ending inevitably in disaster (203–8, 223–25):

> instruit et natum "medio"que "ut limite curras,
> Icare" ait, "moneo, ne, si demissior ibis,
> unda grauet pennas, si celsior, ignis adurat.
> inter utrumque uola, nec te spectare Booten
> aut Helicen iubeo strictumque Orionis ensem;
> *me duce* carpe uiam."

. . .

> cum puer audaci coepit gaudere uolatu
> deseruitque *ducem* caelique cupidine tractus[11]
> altius egit iter . . . .

He instructed his son, and he said, "I advise you, Icarus, make your course in the middle region, so that, if you go somewhat lower, the moisture from the sea not weigh down your wings, and if you go higher, the fire not burn them. Fly between the two; and I bid you not look upon Bootes or Helice, or the drawn sword of Orion: let me lead as you follow the path!"

. . .

when the boy began to take pleasure in his audacious flight and abandoned his guide and, drawn by a desire for heaven, made for a loftier route . . .

---

10. A similar divergence of functions can be seen in Ovid's two repetitions of the tale of the loves of Venus and Mars: see below, chapter 8.

11. The consensus of the earliest manuscripts is *tactus* rather than *tractus*; Tarrant prints *tractus* with the eleventh-century Laurentianus Marcianus (before corrections were made), and Kenney 2011 ad loc. follows suit. Hollis 1970 ad loc., however, makes a good case for *tactus*; the option preferred does not have a bearing on my discussion.

Daedalus's identification of himself as Icarus's *dux*, echoed as the boy decides to disobey, indicates the merging of his roles as father and teacher: fathers, like teachers, are to go first, while sons, like pupils, are to follow.[12] The limits of this paradigm were posited in a variety of ways in Homer's embassy scene, and its basic tensions were seen to be central to the relationship between Nestor and Antilochus; in the *Metamorphoses* version of the Daedalus and Icarus story, Ovid's narrator chooses to follow a version that is both speedy and fatal: disobedience leads to death, a devastating conclusion for both father and son.

The story of Daedalus's flight has long invited symbolic and/or metapoetic readings, in which the clever artist Daedalus serves as a model—and warning—for the Ovidian poet: his desire to master through flight the realm normally reserved for the gods, and to demonstrate thereby his ability to escape the consequences of virtually anything and everything, has been seen as an analogue for the Ovidian poet's aspiration to surpass all who have preceded him and to acquire poetic immortality.[13] The death of his immature son is read as a metaphor for failure and for hopes dashed—he has lost any hope of immortality through the offspring he leaves behind, whether these offspring consist of children or of poems. From another perspective, however, Ovid invites us to identify his poet not only with Daedalus but also with Icarus himself—that is, with the youngster who wishes to branch out on his own and fly higher than his father would dare to go. As a metapoetic analogy, this would suggest that we put Homer in the paternal role, and the Ovidian poet in the role of the son, wanting to obey but also wanting to strike out on his own, torn between the safe authority of tradition on the one hand and the risks of innovation on the other.

The disastrous consequence of Icarus's decision to depart from the course set by his father is equally ironic, at least from a metapoetic point of view: his name lives on as the name of the waters in which he drowns, the Icarian Sea (*oraque caerulea patrium clamantia nomen | excipiuntur aqua, quae nomen traxit ab illo*, "and his mouth, as it shouts

---

12. Cf. the similar sequence in the *Ars amatoria* Book 2 version: Daedalus's directions: *"me pinnis sectare datis; ego praeuius ibo: | sit tua cura sequi, me duce tutus eris,"* 57–58; Icarus's disobedience: *cum puer incautis nimium temerarius annis | altius egit iter deseruitque patrem,* 83–84.

13. Among the many contributions to this discussion, I note Leach 1974; Solodow 1977; and Tissol 1997:97–105, all of whom in turn provide ample supplementary bibliography.

his father's name, is captured by the sky-blue sea, which took its name from him," 8.229–30).[14] This aetiology for the name of a body of water is a typically Hellenistic signature, ironically applied here to a trope that symbolizes impermanence and the erasure of memory: running water.[15] The association of text with water is itself a logical oxymoron: naming ensures permanence, but water never stands still.[16] At the same time, the name of the sea does in fact have poetic resonance: Homer mentions the Icarian Sea at *Il.* 2.145. Yet again, then, Ovid locates his narrative, and his poetic authority, at a point in time preceding the Homeric poems; Ovid implies that the Ovidian story of Icarus's death enables the Homeric poet to imagine a heroic world in which there is a sea known as Icarian. The roles of father and son, teacher and pupil, so carefully delineated in Homeric narrative begin to be confounded as Ovid repositions himself vis-à-vis Homer.

II. The Wayward Son

The complexity that Ovid suggests in this rewriting of a Homeric paradigm is far more fully developed in another father-son narrative in the *Metamorphoses*, the story of Phaethon and his father, the Sun (*Met.* 1.748–2.328).[17] Parallels with the Daedalus and Icarus story are obvious: the father gives his son clear and firm instructions about how to fly, emphasizing the importance of moderation, but the son throws caution to the wind and disobeys, with disastrous results. But there are differences, too: where Icarus is a child, generally malleable and oblivious to the world around him, Phaethon is older—albeit no more mature from an emotional perspective—and all too aware of peer pressures; furthermore, because of his father's absenteeism, he is insecure about his social standing. In a

---

14. Cf. also *Ars am.* 2.96, *aequora nomen habent.*

15. Cf. also Catull. 70; Soph. fr. 811 *TrGF* (= fr. 742 Nauck), ὅρκους ἐγὼ γυναικὸς εἰς ὕδωρ γράφω (the play from which this comes is unknown).

16. May there also be a bit of metatextual play at work here? The sea is itself an epic metaphor for Callimachus (e.g., *Hymn to Apollo* 108–9), who uses it in a negative metaphor for the kind of poetry Apollo disdains; but the Hellenistic association of Homer with water as a source of inspiration is equally available to Ovid, as he indicates at *Am.* 3.9.25–26: *adice Maeoniden, a quo ceu fonte perenni | uatum Pieriis ora rigantur aquis.* Icarus's "drowning" in the "sea of epic" therefore enhances the oxymoron, as he is thus immortalized.

17. Parts of the following discussion of the Phaethon episode are drawn from Boyd 2012; I thank the editors of *MD* for their permission to reuse some of that material here.

previous analysis of this episode, I was concerned with the placement of the Phaethon episode in the *Metamorphoses*, bridging as it does the close of Book 1 and the beginning of Book 2; in that discussion, I pursue a line of argument initiated by Niklas Holzberg's study of book endings in the *Metamorphoses*[18] to suggest that Ovid's Phaethon episode is modeled on Homer's *Telemacheia*, and in particular on the motif of a son's search for a father he has never (at least not consciously) met. It will be worthwhile to revisit some aspects of that analysis in the current discussion, particularly insofar as they help us to appreciate the metapoetics of Ovid's presentation of the relationship between fathers and sons. Simultaneously, this episode can elucidate the delicate balance between Ovid's sense of his own belatedness and his powerful desire to prove himself a son worthy of— perhaps even greater than—his poetic father, Homer. In the process, we will also see that the possibilities inherent in the repetitious nature of the *paradeigma* can be cleverly exploited to complicate an otherwise familiar tale and allow it to turn back upon itself as it hints at not one but multiple Homeric intertexts.

The story of Phaethon with which *Metamorphoses* Book 1 concludes sets up the episode of his disastrous chariot ride by giving a character sketch of the youth and of his motivation for visiting the Sun god. Stung by teasing that suggests he is illegitimate, Phaethon accosts his mother, Clymene, with a request for the truth; she tells him that the Sun god is indeed his true father and suggests that, if he does not believe her, he should visit Sol and find out for himself. The question of lineage in general and of paternity in particular is, as we have seen, a central and recurring theme in ancient myth and features repeatedly in myth's deployment as the language of epic and tragedy;[19] one of its earliest literary explorations is in the *Odyssey*, in which Telemachus, the son of the absent hero, questions his own paternity and embarks on a dangerous journey away from home to discover for himself the truth about Odysseus's fate.[20]

---

18. Holzberg 1998.

19. Cf. Aesch. apud Ath. *Deip.* 8.347e, describing his tragedies as "steaks" (τεμάχη) from the banquet of Homer.

20. Discussion of the placement and function of the *Telemacheia* in the greater *Odyssey* narrative continues unabated, with particular attention devoted in recent decades to the issues of character development and identity formation: see, e.g., H. W. Clarke 1963; G. P. Rose 1967; N. Austin 1969; Belmont 1969; Jones 1988; Patzer 1991; Roisman 1994; Olson 1995: *passim*, esp. 65–90; Felson 1997:68–91; Beck 1999; Wöhrle 1999:117–44; Clark 2001; Heath 2001; Toher 2001; Wöhrle 2009.

Following a pattern set out in the *Odyssey*, Ovid uses the motif of a young man who determines to make a journey in search of his father not only to create narrative tension and complexity but also to acknowledge his own poetic indebtedness to the Homeric model as he embarks on his own first epic journey. The striking lack of closure to *Metamorphoses* Book 1 gestures to the *Odyssey*, where the journey of Telemachus is plotted in Book 1 but does not actually begin until arrangements for the trip are completed in Book 2.

But the similarities do not end here. Let us look more closely at some details of Ovid's Phaethon story; I shall return to Telemachus later. The narrative of Phaethon is introduced through a connection with Io, whose tormented journey to Egypt after her transformation into a cow ends with the restoration of her human form and the birth of her son Epaphus, believed, the narrator tells us, to be the son of Jupiter (*Met.* 1.748–61):

nunc Epaphus magni genitus de semine tandem
creditur esse Iouis perque urbes iuncta parenti
templa tenet. fuit huic animis aequalis et annis   750
Sole satus Phaethon, quem quondam magna loquentem
nec sibi cedentem Phoeboque parente superbum
non tulit Inachides "matri"que ait "omnia demens
credis et es tumidus genitoris imagine falsi."
erubuit Phaethon iramque pudore repressit   755
et tulit ad Clymenen Epaphi conuicia matrem;
"quo"que "magis doleas, genetrix" ait, "ille ego liber,
ille ferox tacui. pudet haec opprobria nobis
et dici potuisse et non potuisse refelli.
at tu, si modo sum caelesti stirpe creatus,   760
ede notam tanti generis meque adsere caelo."

Epaphus is at last believed to have sprung from the seed of great Jupiter, and throughout the cities possesses temples joined to those of his parent. Equal to him in spirits and in years was the Sun's son, Phaethon. One day, when the latter was boasting and obnoxiously asserting his descent from father Phoebus, Inachus's descendant Epaphus couldn't take it, and he said, "you're crazy to believe everything your mother says, and swollen with the fantasy of a false father." Phaethon blushed, and suppressed his anger through shame, and took Epaphus's insults to his mother Clymene; "and even more painful to you, dear mother," he said, "I said nothing, though I am freeborn and spirited. These taunts are an embarrassment—both the fact that they could be said, and the fact that they couldn't be refuted. But, if I really am descended from divine lineage, give me a sign of my great birth, and claim me for heaven."

Epaphus is an age-mate and friend of Phaethon (*animis aequalis et annis*, 750); the similarity between them is reflected in the fact that the description of Epaphus's lineage (*nunc Epaphus magni genitus de semine tandem | creditur esse Iouis*, 748–49) with which Io's story concludes is mirrored in the opening reference to lineage as Phaethon is introduced. The youth's name appears for the first time in the text preceded by that of his father: *Sole satus Phaethon* (751); he is the son of Sol—and thus Ovid's description of him as Epaphus's *aequalis* takes on another meaning. But Phaethon is boastful and even obnoxious about his lineage (*nec sibi cedentem Phoeboque parente superbum*, 752), and Epaphus finally challenges him, suggesting that his pride is ill-founded—he was wrong to believe his mother, and his boast is an empty one (753–54). Embarrassed and ashamed, Phaethon goes to his mother and angrily asks for proof (760–61). In the speech quoted earlier, Clymene swears that Phaethon is indeed the son of Sol and urges him to go to find out for himself.

The details of this sequence of events indicate that Ovid is actively manipulating the tradition surrounding the myth. Unlike the Daedalus and Icarus story, for which no dramatic models have survived, the substantial fragments of Euripides's *Phaethon* provide solid evidence for how Ovid has drawn on both Homeric and dramatic versions of the myth. In his study of both the evidence for the Phaethon story and critical attempts to reconstruct Euripides's play on the subject and its sources, James Diggle has argued that, while the episodes of Phaethon's driving of the Sun's chariot, its disastrous conclusion, and the mourning of his sisters all predate Euripides's tragedy, the play is of central importance for Ovid, even when their narratives diverge.[21] Diggle's discussion, albeit

---

21. Diggle 1970:3–32 (on sources for the myth) and 180–200 (on the vexed question of the relationship, if any, between Ovid's version of the Phaethon story and that found in Nonnus's *Dionysiaca*). Few pre-Euripidean references to the myth of Phaethon survive, and all that do are fragmentary: see Gantz 1993:31–34.

slightly compromised by concern for what he considers inconsistencies in Ovid's version, has encouraged scholars to abandon the phantom of a lost Alexandrian poem on the topic and to look more closely at the tragic character of Ovid's Phaethon narrative; a number of productive readings of Euripides as intertext for Ovid have resulted.[22] I follow Diggle's lead in positing an important role for Euripides's play in the Ovidian narrative; but it will become clear as well that the *Odyssey* too is a central model text for Ovid's Phaethon.

At least as far as the play can be reconstructed, plot and motivation run roughly as follows.[23] Phaethon's desire to drive the Sun's chariot in the first place is the result of the revelation by his mother, Clymene, that he is the son not of Merops, as he had believed, but of Helios; she reveals this information in the context of Phaethon's impending marriage to a divine princess. Clymene tells Phaethon to seek confirmation of his true paternity from Helios, who will fulfill a single request he desires. The fragmentary state of the text provides few details about the nature of his interaction with Helios once they meet, but the outcome is clear: as reported by a messenger, Phaethon's request to drive the chariot of Helios is successful, and he dies as a result of his inexperience and audacity. His mother, wracked with grief, tries to hide the corpse of her dead son, but Merops eventually learns that Phaethon is dead.

A significant difference between Euripides's and Ovid's versions of the story emerges from this plot summary: Phaethon has not been challenged about bastardy in Euripides, and so he does not come to his mother angrily seeking reassurance; rather, he is apparently concerned about his social standing vis-à-vis his new bride, and Clymene for her part appears to be concerned to conceal from Merops the visit to Helios. In Ovid, on the other hand, the charge of bastardy by Epaphus is what provokes Phaethon's challenge to his mother, and insecurity is a driving force in the narrative both in his encounter with her and in his conversation with Sol. The provocation of Phaethon's insecurity opens up a psychological dimension in

---

22. Following Diggle's discussion of the hypothetical relationship between Ovid and Nonnus, Knox 1988a offers a thorough review of the evidence and concludes that Nonnus was not dependent upon Ovid but that both show familiarity with earlier sources, including but not limited to Euripides. Ciappi 2000 offers an exhaustive and highly successful attempt to show the importance of Euripides for Ovid; see also Seng 2007.

23. In addition to the reconstruction and commentary of Diggle 1970, see the helpful text and notes of Collard in Collard, Cropp, and Lee 1995. I follow the numbering of verses as they appear in both of these editions. Collard's reconstruction of the play is at 196–97.

Ovid's narrative that is not evident in the fragments of Euripides's play but that closely resembles what we see in Homer's Telemachus.[24]

One other feature of Euripides's play that is recoverable at least in part offers further evidence of an important difference between Euripides's and Ovid's versions of the story, a difference that once again by contrast highlights the similarity between the journeys of Homer's Telemachus and Ovid's Phaethon. It is not at all clear from the fragments of the play how Phaethon convinced his father to let him drive the chariot; but the messenger's speech describing the disaster alludes to the presence of Helios on the flight, sitting on his horse and directing his son. Thus, at least at the outset Helios accompanies the boy (175–77):

πατὴρ δ' ὄπισθε νῶτα Σειρίου βεβὼς
ἵππευε παῖδα νουθετῶν· "Εκεῖσ' ἔλα,
τῆιδε στρέφ' ἄρμα, τῆιδε."

Having mounted onto the back of Seirios, the father rode behind, guiding his son: "Drive there, now turn the chariot in this direction, now that . . ."

Helios's paternal guidance of Phaethon here is clearly didactic and may well have informed the lengthy set of instructions Ovid's Sol gives to his son (*Met.* 2.126–49); but Sol delivers his speech on terra firma, and for all intents and purposes Phaethon ignores it. A much closer resemblance to the Euripidean scene can be found in Ovid's story of Daedalus and Icarus, in which, as we have seen, father Daedalus gives his son precise instructions on where and how to fly and offers himself as a guide.[25] Euripides's Helios shows concern for his son and desires to offer guidance, as does Daedalus with Icarus; in fact, the two fathers share a common predecessor in the Homeric figure with whom I initiated this discussion of the succession paradigm, Nestor, who as we saw earlier offers Antilochus extensive advice about controlling the chariot before

---

24. Ciappi 2000:127–28 and n.59 recognizes the psychological motivation in Ovid that appears not to have been a major concern in Euripides. On the paternity of Merops in Ovid, see Kruschwitz 2005.

25. On thematic connections between the Ovidian narratives of Phaethon and Daedalus, see Wise 1977; and cf. L. Morgan 2003:75–82, to whose discussion I shall return below. Although the evidence permits nothing more than speculation, it is quite plausible to imagine that Ovid drew on Euripides's play for many details of the father-son relationship in his versions of the Daedalus and Icarus myth; cf. Ciappi 2000:141 n.109.

the race that is part of the funeral games for Patroclus (*Il.* 23.301–50).[26] Both Sol's ineffectiveness and Phaethon's lack of trust in Sol, on the other hand, underscore the difference between this father-and-son pair and the others mentioned here, sending us back yet again to Homer's Telemachus for a closer model.

I have already mentioned the psychological insecurity that is central to Ovid's version of the Phaethon story. Comparison with Euripides's play indicates that Ovid's emphasis is new in the tradition of the Phaethon story; but it is not without parallel. Rather, Ovid looks to Homer for this motif, recognizing the insecurity that plagues Telemachus when the *Odyssey* opens as a prototype for the emotions that young men feel when they doubt not only their own ability to live up to their fathers but their paternity itself. We first see Telemachus in the *Odyssey* through Athena's eyes; she has descended from Olympus and has taken on the semblance of a Taphian named Mentes, and as she stands at the door is seen first by Telemachus, who has been sitting among the suitors but is grieving at heart, imagining the reappearance of his father; his father's presence would mean, he thinks, not only the dispersal of the suitors but also the restoration of his father's honor and position (*Od.* 1.113–22):

τὴν δὲ πολὺ πρῶτος ἴδε Τηλέμαχος θεοειδής,
ἧστο γὰρ ἐν μνηστῆρσι φίλον τετιημένος ἦτορ,
ὀσσόμενος πατέρ' ἐσθλὸν ἐνὶ φρεσίν, εἴ ποθεν ἐλθὼν
μνηστήρων τῶν μὲν σκέδασιν κατὰ δώματα θείη,
τιμὴν δ' αὐτὸς ἔχοι καὶ κτήμασιν οἷσιν ἀνάσσοι.
τὰ φρονέων μνηστῆρσι μεθήμενος εἴσιδ' Ἀθήνην,
βῆ δ' ἰθὺς προθύροιο, νεμεσσήθη δ' ἐνὶ θυμῷ   120
ξεῖνον δηθὰ θύρησιν ἐφεστάμεν· ἐγγύθι δὲ στὰς
χεῖρ' ἕλε δεξιτερὴν καὶ ἐδέξατο χάλκεον ἔγχος,
καί μιν φωνήσας ἔπεα πτερόεντα προσηύδα·

Godlike Telemachus was by far the first to see her; for he was sitting among the suitors gnawing at his poor heart seeing in his mind his dear father, if only he would come home and set upon the house a scattering of the suitors, and then he himself might have honor and

---

26. Both Homer's Nestor and Euripides's Helios are depicted as teachers of horsemanship and charioteering: see also the comment by Richardson 1993 on *Il.* 23.301–50, noted above (chapter 3, n.2).

rule over his possessions. Thinking this while sitting among the
suitors, he looked upon Athene, and straightaway he went to the
threshold, angered in his heart that a guest was standing so long at
the door; and standing near, Telemachus took the other's right hand
and received the bronze spear, and addressing her, spoke winged
words . . .

After Mentes explains who he is and provides the information he has, such
as it is, about his last sighting of Odysseus, he asks Telemachus if the latter
is really Odysseus's son, noting the physical resemblance. Telemachus's
response reveals the boy's insecurity (*Od.* 1.206–20):

> "ἀλλ' ἄγε μοι τόδε εἰπὲ καὶ ἀτρεκέως κατάλεξον,
> εἰ δὴ ἐξ αὐτοῖο τόσος πάϊς εἰς Ὀδυσῆος.
> αἰνῶς μὲν κεφαλήν τε καὶ ὄμματα καλὰ ἔοικας
> κείνῳ, ἐπεὶ θαμὰ τοῖον ἐμισγόμεθ' ἀλλήλοισι,
> πρίν γε τὸν ἐς Τροίην ἀναβήμεναι, ἔνθα περ ἄλλοι   210
> Ἀργείων οἱ ἄριστοι ἔβαν κοίλης ἐνὶ νηυσίν·
> ἐκ τοῦ δ' οὔτ' Ὀδυσῆα ἐγὼν ἴδον οὔτ' ἐμὲ κεῖνος."
> τὴν δ' αὖ Τηλέμαχος πεπνυμένος ἀντίον ηὔδα·
> "τοιγὰρ ἐγώ τοι, ξεῖνε, μάλ' ἀτρεκέως ἀγορεύσω.
> μήτηρ μέν τέ μέ φησι τοῦ ἔμμεναι, αὐτὰρ ἐγώ γε   215
> οὐκ οἶδ'· οὐ γάρ πώ τις ἑὸν γόνον αὐτὸς ἀνέγνω.
> ὡς δὴ ἐγώ γ' ὄφελον μάκαρός νύ τευ ἔμμεναι υἱὸς
> ἀνέρος, ὃν κτεάτεσσιν ἑοῖς ἔπι γῆρας ἔτετμε.
> νῦν δ' ὃς ἀποτμότατος γένετο θνητῶν ἀνθρώπων,
> τοῦ μ' ἔκ φασι γενέσθαι, ἐπεὶ σύ με τοῦτ' ἐρεείνεις."   220

"But come, tell me this and speak clearly, if being so big you are the
son of Odysseus himself. For terribly like him you appear, both your
head and your lovely eyes, since back when ever so often we associ-
ated with each other before going to Troy, where the other captains
of the Argives went in the hollow ships. For since then I have not
seen Odysseus, nor he me." Telemachus, taking courage, addressed
her in reply: "Guest, I shall indeed speak clearly to you. My mother,
to be sure, tells me I am his, but I myself don't know; for no one
ever really knows his own father. How I wish I were the son of a for-
tunate man whom old age overtook among his possessions. But as
it is, he who was the most unfortunate of mortal men, they say I am
his son, since you ask me this."

Telemachus emphasizes in his response to Mentes that his knowledge of his paternity is based entirely on hearsay ("μήτηρ μέν τέ μέ φησι τοῦ ἔμμεναι, αὐτὰρ ἐγώ γε | οὐκ οἶδ'," 215–16; "τοῦ μ' ἔκ φασι γενέσθαι," 220); he does not know it for himself, and he doubts his mother's truthfulness. A shrewd psychologist, Mentes seizes the opportunity to become Telemachus's confidant and suggests that the youth make a journey to learn news of his father: the results of this inquiry will help Telemachus, suggests Mentes, to settle his mother's fate and to deal with the suitors (*Od.* 1.271–305).[27]

The psychological perspicuity of Homer's portrayal of Telemachus is the prototype for Ovid's Phaethon. The absent father is the direct cause of his son's insecurity and even causes the son to question his paternity; only by displaying the ability to take his father's place can the son truly assimilate himself to his father. And, of course, this is played out all too literally in Ovid's version of the Phaethon story, as the boy tries to do the work of his father. Whereas, as I have noted, Ovid introduces Phaethon in Book 1 as the son of Sol (*Sole satus Phaethon*, 1.751), the boy reappears in Book 2 as *Clymeneia . . . proles* (2.19), and his insecurity and sense of alienation

---

27. The subtlety of interpersonal dynamics in this scene is indicative of Homer's understanding of Telemachus's situation; and while the issue of character development in Homer remains a focus of scholarly debate (see above, n.20), it is clear that many of Homer's ancient readers saw the *Telemacheia* as a whole as a narrative about the maturation of a youth into a man, one who develops successfully by slowly but surely becoming more and more like his father. This reading has long been identified with the late third-century CE scholar Porphyry, whose interpretation of the episode as a model of παίδευσις was a staple support for unitary readings of Homer in earlier scholarly generations; see Wissmann 2009 for a useful discussion. The publication of a fragment from Philodemus's *On the Education of the Good Prince* (*PHerc.* 1507, col. 23) in the 1980s, however, has allowed scholars to assign a date at least three hundred years earlier to this interpretation of the episode. As translated by Fish (1999:71–74, supplementing the text of Dorandi 1982; I omit a few unconnected words at the margins of Fish's translations), this fragment reads in part: ". . . and to be one who has constantly lived among people not living according to his will, since it is necessary for him to be one who has neither seen nor heard of many things and has had no experience of free speech between equals, and in many respects uneducated" (11–19) and "the poet . . . to lead Telemachus to Pylos and Sparta where he was to have dealings with such great people, for he was certainly not going to do any good about his father any longer, since he was already near Ithaca. And making Athena say that it was because of the things which have been said . . ." (24–37). It is clear from the context that Telemachus is the subject of the first excerpt, and that his need for education is a central concern. Fish has suggested (1999:77) that in writing about the education of a future ruler, "Philodemus may have intended the pattern of Telemachus's education to resonate with the manner of education for Roman nobility of the 1st century BC"; among those elites who might have made such a connection, I suggest, was Ovid, whose interest in finding contemporary Roman analogues for hallowed myths is a familiar characteristic of his verse (one need only think of the notorious description of Olympus as *Palatia caeli* at *Met.* 1.176).

from his father manifest themselves physically as he enters Sol's palace (2.19–23):

> Quo simul accliui Clymeneia limite proles
> uenit et intrauit dubitati tecta parentis,
> protinus ad patrios sua fert uestigia uultus
> consistitque procul; neque enim propiora ferebat
> lumina.

> When the offspring of Clymene arrived by a steep route and entered the halls of his doubted parent, straightaway he turned his steps to his father's face, and stopped far off; nor did he bring his eyes any closer.

Phaethon turns in the direction of Sol but then stops; as Ovid puts it, he brings his eyes (*lumina*, 23) no closer, a detail that plays with both the uncomfortable brilliance of Sol and the hesitation of Phaethon, who seems to realize unconsciously that his own "light" cannot compete with Sol's. Sol notices the boy, trembling at the novelty of his surroundings (*rerum nouitate pauentem* | . . . *iuuenem*, 2.31–32), and asks him the reason for his journey; he then quickly identifies the boy as his offspring who must be acknowledged ("*progenies . . . haud infitianda parenti*," 2.34). But even this immediate acknowledgment does not entirely assuage Phaethon's fears: instead, his reply indicates the continuation of his doubt, as he asks Sol for some token that will affirm his paternity: "*pignora da generis per quae tua uera propago* | *credar, et hunc animis errorem detrahe nostris*," 2.38–39).[28]

Ovid's emphasis on the hesitation of Phaethon before Sol underscores the importance of paternity to this version of the story; this hesitation also opens up a certain divergence from the Homeric analogue, since while Telemachus's doubts make him uncertain what course of action to follow vis-à-vis the suitors, he does not hesitate to approach the stranger—whom we know to be Athena disguised as Mentes—when the latter appears on the threshold (*Od.* 1.113–24, quoted earlier). Homer's emphasis on Telemachus's visual perception of the disguised Athena is underscored by

---

28. Ciappi 2000:134 rightly emphasizes Phaethon's doubt and distrust of Sol; cf. also S. Wheeler 2000:66–69 for a discussion of the Phaethon episode as an example of the failure of "intergenerational continuity" as a narrative principle in the *Metamorphoses*.

repetition (τὴν δὲ πολὺ πρῶτος ἴδε Τηλέμαχος θεοειδής, 113; εἴσιδ' Ἀθήνην, 118); it also sets up a contrast with the intervening lines, in which Homer describes how Telemachus fantasizes about his father's return and the vengeance that would ensue: Telemachus sees his father, says Homer, in his heart (ὀσσόμενος πατέρ' ἐσθλὸν ἐνὶ φρεσίν, 115). If we look again at the Ovidian analogue, we can see that Ovid likewise emphasizes the importance of sight;[29] but whereas the sight, even the imagined sight, of his father encourages Telemachus, in Phaethon's case sight is daunting. This is in part, of course, the result of Ovid's play with the appearance of Sol himself—his light is truly overpowering ("*o lux immensi publica mundi*," says Phaethon, 2.35); but Ovid also uses this difference to acknowledge yet another Homeric model and in so doing points his reader to a fundamental departure from the trajectory of the *Telemacheia*. While Phaethon does indeed behave like the son of a Homeric hero, the hero's son in question now is not Telemachus but Astyanax, whose cameo appearance in the *Iliad* is as memorable as it is brief.[30]

In *Iliad* Book 6, during his visit to the city, Hector seeks out Andromache, who has gone out to the Scaean gate with a nurse carrying the infant; after a solemn speech explaining to Andromache the reasons for his determination to return to the battlefield, Hector turns his attention to the child and reaches out for him; but the infant, lying in his nurse's embrace, is struck dumb by the sight of his father, seeing as he does the gleaming bronze helmet with its horsehair plume (*Il.* 6.466–75):

> Ὣς εἰπὼν οὗ παιδὸς ὀρέξατο φαίδιμος Ἕκτωρ·
> ἂψ δ' ὁ πάϊς πρὸς κόλπον ἐϋζώνοιο τιθήνης
> ἐκλίνθη ἰάχων, πατρὸς φίλου ὄψιν ἀτυχθείς,
> ταρβήσας χαλκόν τε ἰδὲ λόφον ἱππιοχαίτην,
> δεινὸν ἀπ' ἀκροτάτης κόρυθος νεύοντα νοήσας.   470
> ἐκ δὲ γέλασσε πατήρ τε φίλος καὶ πότνια μήτηρ·
> αὐτίκ' ἀπὸ κρατὸς κόρυθ' εἵλετο φαίδιμος Ἕκτωρ,
> καὶ τὴν μὲν κατέθηκεν ἐπὶ χθονὶ παμφανόωσαν·
> αὐτὰρ ὅ γ' ὃν φίλον υἱὸν ἐπεὶ κύσε πῆλέ τε χερσίν,
> εἶπε δ' ἐπευξάμενος Διί τ' ἄλλοισίν τε θεοῖσι·

---

29. The visual dimension of the entire scene is established by the opening ecphrasis: see R. Brown 1987.

30. Pratt 2007:26–31 offers a fine discussion of the father-son relationship foregrounded in this scene and its repercussions for the rest of the *Iliad*.

Speaking thus, radiant Hector reached out for his son; but immediately the child lay back on the bosom of his beautifully clad nurse, crying, and bewildered at the sight of his father, frightened at the bronze and the horsehair plume, as he saw it nodding dauntingly on the peak of the helmet. His loving father laughed aloud, and his mistress mother, and straightaway gleaming Hector took the helmet from his head, and he placed it, as it shone brightly, on the ground. Then he kissed his dear child and tossed him in his hands, and praying to Zeus and the other gods he said . . .

Hector and Andromache laugh at the child's reaction, and Hector removes his helmet, placing it on the ground, so that he can play with the child. Ovid cleverly adapts this scene, replacing Hector's helmet with the solar crown of Sol (*Met.* 2.40–43):

dixerat, at genitor circum caput omne micantes
deposuit radios propiusque accedere iussit
amplexuque dato "nec tu meus esse negari
dignus es, et Clymene ueros" ait "edidit ortus."

He finished speaking; but his father set down the rays gleaming all around his head and ordered the boy to approach, and embraced him, and said, "You deserve not to be refused as mine, and Clymene told you of your true origin."

Phaethon does not manifest his fear at the sight of his father as openly as does Astyanax; nonetheless, apparently sensing the fear behind Phaethon's demand for a token of paternity, Sol removes and sets down his crown (*genitor circum caput omne micantes* | *deposuit radios*, 2.40–41).[31] He then orders the boy to come closer, and, embracing him, affirms that Phaethon is indeed his son. In short, Ovid has encouraged his reader to think that Phaethon will embark on an epic journey preparing him for manhood much as does his Homeric model Telemachus; but instead, just before Phaethon demands Sol's chariot, Ovid subverts this parallel, and replaces it with another equally Homeric, but far less promising, episode: doomed father fondles doomed son, a son far from being mature

31. The Homeric model is noted by Bömer vol. 1, 1969 ad loc., citing von Albrecht 1968 (1963): 423.

enough to take his father's place or live up to his father's model. The sig-
nificance of Ovid's poetic sleight of hand here is indicative, I think, of what
we are to expect of the *Metamorphoses* as a whole; indeed, we might say that
Phaethon undergoes a metamorphosis himself as he abandons his earlier
role model Telemachus for a new—and less auspicious—one, Astyanax.
The successful journey that brings Telemachus home, prepared to deal
with the suitors and ready to meet his father, has no Ovidian analogue;
instead, Phaethon enacts the fall from his father's citadel (*Met.* 2.304–13)
that Andromache had foreseen as a possible fate for her son Astyanax (*Il.*
24.732–39).

This intertextual sequence, involving as it does a number of stories
concerning the relationship of fathers and sons, plays repeatedly with
the ideas of similarity and difference that contribute to the discourse of
lineage, in both (mythical) biological and literary senses. A natural resem-
blance (in character as well as in physique) to one's father works against
a son's desire to strike out on his own and to differentiate himself from
others in his line; as I have already suggested, this struggle is played out
repeatedly by Ovid both in the myths he chooses to narrate and in his
articulation of his relationship to Homer. When we read Ovid's narra-
tive describing Phaethon's rejection of his father's prudent advice not to
attempt to drive the chariot of Sol, this paradigm would suggest that we
can also see this on the metapoetic level as Ovid's "rejection" of Homer as
model and guide—a rejection that informs in the first place Ovid's rejec-
tion of a Homeric narrative of successful maturation and intergenera-
tional harmony.[32] Yet Ovid's "rejection" of the Homeric tradition is not so
simple as that; rather, the substitution of Astyanax for Telemachus offers
an alternative to either acceptance or rejection of the model text, play-
fully juxtaposing the two very different fates of two Homeric sons and
so suggesting a relationship between Homer and Ovid that challenges
linear authority. Ovid's use of Homeric models for Phaethon invites us to
reread Homer, using the variation between Telemachus and Astyanax as
a way to open up the Homeric poems to the possibility of interaction and
cross-fertilization.

The circular reading this interaction invites directs us back also to the
opening words of the *Metamorphoses: in noua fert animus.* The phrase *fert*

---

32. See L. Morgan 2003:74: "Childishness . . . was identified from early on as a characteristic
of Ovid's engagement with epic."

animus occurs only once elsewhere in the *Metamorphoses*,[33] near the start of the Phaethon episode, as Phaethon's mother, Clymene, concludes a speech urging her son to visit the Sun god himself to ascertain his parentage (*Met.* 1.768–75):

> "per iubar hoc" inquit "radiis insigne coruscis,
> nate, tibi iuro, quod nos auditque uidetque,
> hoc te, quem spectas, hoc te, qui temperat orbem,
> Sole satum. si ficta loquor, neget ipse uidendum
> se mihi, sitque oculis lux ista nouissima nostris.
> nec longus patrios labor est tibi nosse Penates;
> unde oritur domus est terrae contermina nostrae.
> *si modo fert animus*, gradere et scitabere ab ipso."

> "On this heavenly splendor," she said, "distinguished by shimmering rays, which hears and sees us, son, I swear to you, you are descended from this Sun whom you see, who moderates the globe. If I speak falsehoods, he himself should deny that he is to be looked upon by me, and this light should be the last for my eyes. Nor is it a lengthy task to discover your ancestral Penates: his dwelling is where he rises, and coterminous with our land. *If the spirit moves you*, go and ask him himself."

Thus, the "idea" or "impulse" suggested by the word *animus* is in its first appearance that of the Ovidian narrator and in the second that of Phaethon; the parallel journeys of the two thus frame the book.

Ovid's "rejection" of Homeric epic in fact contains within itself a simultaneous appropriation of the Homeric endorsement of poetic inspiration as articulated by Telemachus in *Odyssey* Book 1. Penelope, upon hearing Phemius's songs of the Trojan War, wants to silence the singer but is prevented from doing so by her son, who says, "Why, mother, do you begrudge our trusted singer the opportunity to delight us however/wherever his mind urges him?" ("μῆτερ ἐμή, τί τ' ἄρα φθονέεις ἐρίηρον ἀοιδὸν | τέρπειν ὅππῃ οἱ νόος ὄρνυται;" *Od.* 1.346–47). The Oxford commentators on this line astutely observe that "Telemachus' reply embodies the earliest literary criticism in Greek literature; he is surely the poet's spokesman in his plea for artistic

---

33. The observation is made by Holzberg 1998:91 and is central to his discussion of the structure of the *Metamorphoses*.

freedom and his emphasis on the importance of novelty."[34] The phrase Ovid's poet uses to launch his epic journey not only acknowledges its Homeric intertext but endorses the earlier poem's declaration of poetic values. *In noua fert animus* ("My mind takes me into new regions") is not simply modeled on Telemachus's phrase νόος ὄρνυται but also responds to Telemachus's expression: Telemachus's ὄππη is completed by Ovid's *in noua*.[35]

Homeric epic is the central (and unavoidable) intertext for the journeys of both Phaethon and Ovid's narrator, and the negotiation of a relationship with their poetic "fathers" poses an initial challenge for both. While traversing uncharted poetic territory both travelers will escape—one more successfully than the other—from the narrative "map" provided by Homer as they venture into the uncharted terrain of the *Metamorphoses*.

III. Fathers in Eclipse

In a discussion of the behavior of the gods in Statius's *Thebaid*, Denis Feeney points to Apollo's disappearance from the narrative after his failure to save his favorite, Amphiaraus (*Th.* 7.771–93); reappearing two books later (9.644–45), the god is still in mourning, and his sorrow is complemented by an appearance that is not at all usual for him (*in nube corusca* | . . . *haud solito uisu*, "in a gleaming cloud . . . with an appearance not at all customary").[36] Feeney suggests that Statius is here creating an analogy between an eclipse of the sun and a metaphorical eclipse of the god's power, and notes that Statius's description of Apollo is reminiscent of Ovid's depiction of Sol after the tragic chariot ride of Phaethon (*Met.* 2.381–85):[37]

> Squalidus interea genitor Phaethontis et expers
> ipse sui decoris, qualis cum deficit orbem
> esse solet, lucemque odit seque ipse diemque
> officiumque negat mundo.

---

34. Heubeck, West, and Hainsworth 1998 ad loc.

35. von Albrecht 1961 notes the similarity between the two phrases but does not develop its significance. The "newness" of Ovid's foray into epic is underscored by the appearance of the word *nouitas* in the description of Phaethon's reaction to his father, *rerum nouitate pauentem* (2.31).

36. Feeney 1991:372–73.

37. Feeney 1991:373 n.192. The lines I print here exclude that traditionally numbered 2.384 but bracketed by Tarrant.

Meanwhile, the father of Phaethon, mournful-looking and lacking his usual splendor, just as he is accustomed to appear when his orb is eclipsed, hates the light, and himself, and the day, and denies his responsibility to the world . . .

In fact, the imagery of eclipse that Ovid employs here completes an eclipse that began some fifty verses earlier, immediately after the nymphs mourning for Phaethon bury him and mark his grave with an epitaph (2.325–28). There, Sol, wracked with grief, covers his head and allows an entire day to pass without sunlight (2.329–32):

Nam pater obductos luctu miserabilis aegro
condiderat uultus et, si modo credimus, unum
isse diem sine sole ferunt; incendia lumen
praebebant aliquisque malo fuit usus in illo.

For the father, wretched with sick grief, covered his face and hid it, and, if only we believe it, they say that one whole day passed without sun; instead, the fires provided light, and there was some utility in that evil thing.

After this passage, narrative time stands more or less still as the Ovidian narrator moves on to describe several metamorphoses that occur in the wake of Phaethon's cataclysmic fall: his sisters, whose unceasing grief gradually gives way to their transformation into poplar trees, the branches of which their mother, Clymene, tears at and causes to bleed; and his cousin Cycnus, whose cries of sorrow give way to the song of the swan into which he is transformed. The two sets of lines describing Sol's eclipse, approximately equal in length, thus bookmark the opening and close of the sunless day. In his commentary on *Met.* 2.329–32, Barchiesi notes that the two passages describing Sol's display of grief through eclipse serve to "stop the world and the narrative of the poem";[38] forward movement resumes only as a result of the intervention of an even greater father figure, Jupiter (*pater omnipotens*, 401), as he sets to work restoring order in the universe.

---

38. Barchiesi 2005 on *Met.* 2.329–32: ". . . questo cordoglio che blocca il mondo e la narrazione del poema."

Until now we have considered a number of characters for whom competition with one's father is a driving force: whether the dominant motive is a possibility of degeneracy, as with Diomedes; an instance of interfamilial strife, as with Phoenix and Meleager; or doubt about paternity, as with Telemachus and Phaethon, in all the examples of the father-son dynamic we have considered so far the father's greater power and/or authority has ultimately been upheld. Even with Icarus, whose immaturity only exacerbates the unequal standing of father and son, the father ultimately, if ironically, prevails; Daedalus's mythical career never reaches a conclusive end, even though he may in fact be the most basic cause of his son's death.

But what happens when a father is eclipsed by his son? As I noted in my opening discussion of Nestor's charioteering advice to Antilochus, there is an implicit irony in the fact that Nestor himself, though ἱππότα, failed at an earlier chariot race;[39] but this irony, while available to Homer's audience, remains always beneath the surface of the narrative. The distinction between the instructions of the Homeric teacher par excellence and his own performance contributes to the characterization of Nestor as one who has learned from experience; Nestor's early failure only adds, so it would seem, to his present authority, so that at least in the world of the *Iliad*, the only eclipse Nestor experiences is the very natural kind resulting from age. When we turn to Ovid, however, the previously implicit prospect of eclipse is activated in a variety of ways. In Sol's case, as we have seen, that eclipse is self-imposed; thanks to Jupiter's intervention, it is temporary; and in any event, the suicidal conflagration of Phaethon means that Sol no longer has a living son who can attempt to surpass him. But the flexible and capacious nature of ancient myth offers a number of opposing examples, of cases in which a son outdoes his father almost naturally, in which the son's superiority is framed as a product of fate itself. Indeed, Homer presages this view of fate, when he allows another father—Hector, whose resonance with Ovid's Sol we have already noted—to pray to Zeus regarding the greatness that awaits Astyanax (*Il.* 6.476–81):[40]

"Ζεῦ ἄλλοι τε θεοί, δότε δὴ καὶ τόνδε γενέσθαι
παῖδ᾽ ἐμὸν, ὡς καὶ ἐγώ περ, ἀριπρεπέα Τρώεσσιν,

---

39. See above, chapter 3, n.2.

40. The quote from Bernard Schouler that serves as an epigraph for chapter 3 concludes his introduction to a discussion of family dynamics that opens with Diomedes and Sthenelus in the *Epipolesis* (see above, chapter 2) and moves to this speech by Hector (Schouler 1980:1–6).

ὧδε βίην τ᾽ ἀγαθόν, καὶ Ἰλίου ἶφι ἀνάσσειν·
καί ποτέ τις εἴποι ‘πατρός γ᾽ ὅδε πολλὸν ἀμείνων’
ἐκ πολέμου ἀνιόντα· φέροι δ᾽ ἔναρα βροτόεντα
κτείνας δήϊον ἄνδρα, χαρείη δὲ φρένα μήτηρ.”

"Zeus and the other gods, grant that this my son be outstanding among the Trojans, just as I am, and excellent in his force, and may he rule Troy with might; and at some point in the future, as he departs from battle, may someone say, 'this man is far better than his father'; and may he carry off the bloody spoils after he has killed a fierce enemy, and may his mother delight in her heart."

Of course, Hector's prayer is not answered, and fate steals his son; he thus becomes an unwitting prototype for Sol in this regard as well, as his own willingness to yield to his son is all for naught.

IV. *The Son Also Rises*

For Ovid, the idea of a son greater than his father has the potential to be not only a literary conceit but a way of making sense of paternity and its discontents in Augustan Rome. Near the close of the *Metamorphoses*, Ovid provides a list of examples of fathers surpassed by their sons, as he explains the logic of Julius Caesar's deification by his son Augustus. In this excerpt from the scene, the Ovidian narrator describes how Venus raises Caesar's *anima* to the heavens (*Met.* 15.848–60):

> luna uolat altius illa
> flammiferumque trahens spatioso limite crinem
> stella micat natique uidens bene facta fatetur   850
> esse suis maiora et uinci gaudet ab illo.
> hic sua praeferri quamquam uetat acta paternis,
> libera fama tamen nullisque obnoxia iussis
> inuitum praefert unaque in parte repugnat.
> sic magnus cedit titulis Agamemnonis Atreus,   855
> Aegea sic Theseus, sic Pelea uicit Achilles;
> denique, ut exemplis ipsos aequantibus utar,
> sic et Saturnus minor est Ioue. Iuppiter arces
> temperat aetherias et mundi regna triformis,
> terra sub Augusto est; pater est et rector uterque.   860

[His soul] flies higher than the moon, and trailing a flame-bear-
ing tail through the wide region it twinkles as a star; and when he
sees the accomplishments of the son, he acknowledges that they
are greater than his own, and delights that he is surpassed by the
younger one. And although the younger man won't allow his deeds
to be considered above those of his father, fame, free of constraints
and bound by no commands, shows him preference, however
unwilling he may be, and so resists in one way. Thus great Atreus
yields to the achievements of Agamemnon; thus Theseus surpasses
Aegeus, and Achilles, Peleus; indeed—if I may employ a compari-
son worthy of these men—thus even Saturn is lesser than Jupiter.
Jupiter regulates the heavenly regions and the kingdoms of the tri-
form realm, while the earth is under the control of Augustus:[41] each
is father and guide.

The accomplishments of Caesar make him worthy of deification; nonethe-
less, the deification is of primary importance because it paves the way for
Augustus himself to be deified—an event which the Ovidian narrator pre-
dicts with confidence even as he prays that it may happen only long into
the future (15.868–70).

The Ovidian narrator's allusions to characters of heroic epic
(Agamemnon, Theseus, Achilles, and their fathers) and Hesiodic cos-
mogony (Jupiter and Saturn) in this passage suggest that the relationship
of Augustus and Julius Caesar be seen in terms of mythic genealogy as
well as in a historical framework. Appearing at the conclusion of Caesar's
apotheosis, they also send Ovid's readers back to the scene that preceded
it, a scene that similarly bridges history and myth: this is the episode
depicting the coming of the god Aesculapius to Rome (*Met.* 15.622–744).
Coming soon after the stunning oration of Pythagoras that dominates
more than half of Book 15, this episode is all but dwarfed by what has
preceded it; and in spite—or perhaps because—of its substantial length,
it seems an odd man out in the poem, where its historical Roman sub-
ject matter comes as a great surprise after more than fourteen books
of divine and heroic myth. The marginalizing effect of the shadow cast

---

41. Of course, the distinction between *augustus* and *Augustus* (*terra sub A/augusto est*) is a
modern concern; for Ovid, there is a playful ambiguity here, as Jupiter has been his most
recent subject, and it is only at the end of this verse—indeed, with the last word—that the
reader can be sure that Jupiter is now paired with his earthbound analogue (*pater est et rector
uterque*).

by Pythagoras is further amplified by two other unusual features of the narrative: the unique appeal to the Muses with which the episode opens (15.622–25) and the subsequent transition from Aesculapius to Julius Caesar, whose apotheosis, also at about 125 lines (15.745–870), all but closes the book and the poem—only the 9-line coda forecasting Ovid's own immortality remains. I shall suggest that, while this marginalization might be seen in somewhat negative terms—as if, in other words, Ovid had simply tacked on an incongruous episode—it in fact serves the aggressively positive purpose of drawing attention to the survival of Homeric poetics in contemporary Rome, most particularly in the work of Ovid himself.

Let us begin with the first of these two distinctive features, the invocation of the Muses. In a study focusing primarily on the ends of *Fasti* Book 6 and *Metamorphoses* Book 15, Alessandro Barchiesi compares Ovid's address to the Muses at the opening of the tale of Aesculapius with Lucretius's only invocation of the Muses, embedded in the last book of his poem (6.92–95).[42] These two invocations are not particularly similar in terms of diction or even specific content; rather, as Barchiesi suggests, it is their status as delayed proems that hints at a relationship, a relationship that is in turn underscored by their complementary contexts:

Pandite nunc, Musae, praesentia numina uatum,
(scitis enim, nec uos fallit spatiosa uetustas)
unde Coroniden circumflua Thybridis alti
insula Romuleae sacris adlegerit[43] urbis. (*Met.* 15.622–25)

Now, Muses, the ever-present powers supportive of bards (for you know, nor does vast antiquity deceive you), reveal whence the island around which the deep Tiber flows selected the son of Coronis, Asclepius, for inclusion in the religious rituals of Romulus's city.

tu mihi supremae praescripta ad candida calcis
currenti spatium praemonstra, callida musa
Calliope, requies hominum diuomque uoluptas,
te duce ut insigni capiam cum laude coronam. (Lucr. 6.92–95)

---

42. Barchiesi 1994:254–56; cf. *idem* 1997a:188–89.

43. I print Tarrant's text; he reads *adlegerit* for *adiecerit* (vel sim.), following a conjecture in Housman 1890; see also Hardie 2015 ad loc.

O skillful muse, as I proceed go before me and show me the finish line
marked out for me with chalk, o goddess Calliope, respite and delight
of men and gods, so that with you as my guide I may seize the crown
with outstanding honor.

These delayed proems both serve to introduce episodes concerning plague;
but while the Lucretian instance introduces a profoundly ominous nar-
rative, the plague at Athens, Ovid tells of how the arrival of Aesculapius,
called *salutifer urbi* (15.744), brings to an end the plague in Rome, an event
traditionally dated to 293 BCE. The characterization of Aesculapius as savior
or healer has tempted scholars to read in the Aesculapius episode an alle-
gory or analogy of some sort for Augustus himself, who, like Aesculapius,
put an end to the city's suffering when he assumed supreme authority in
27 BCE.[44]

The plague of Lucretius Book 6.1090–1286 is of course a retell-
ing of the Athenian plague narrative of Thucydides (Book 2.47–54),[45]
and it in turn clearly played a formative role in Virgil's narrative of
the cattle plague at Noricum in *Geo.* 3.478–566.[46] From the opening
lines of the *Iliad*, plague is a central theme of ancient literary tradi-
tion, and Sophocles's use of the leitmotif as a setting for the tragedy
of Oedipus, played out as it is against the contemporary background
of the Athenian plague, exemplifies the activation of the metaphor of
plague as an index of cultural and social pollution. The broader trope
to which this metaphor contributes, that of the troubled state as a body
weakened by disease, is particularly relevant to a poem that closes in
the historical moment symbolized by Caesar's assassination and deifi-
cation.[47] But before discussing the valence of this episode for a reading
of the *Metamorphoses* as a whole or as some sort of allegorical com-
ment on the new regime, I want to consider the implications of the fact
that Aesculapius is the powerful son of a powerful father, and that the
Delphic oracle that sends the Romans to Epidaurus in the first place
to fetch the young healing god—an oracle that appears to be Ovidian

---

44. See, e.g., S. Wheeler 2000:137–38; Wickkiser 2005; Papaioannou 2006; and cf. Barchiesi
1994:258–65 with *idem* 1997a:191–96.

45. See Gale 1994:112–14, 224–28.

46. As demonstrated by Farrell 1991; see also Papaioannou 2006:139–40.

47. Cf. Papaioannou 2006.

invention[48]—emphasizes the fact that it is not Apollo who will assuage
the plague at Rome, but Apollo's son (*Met.* 15.637–40):

"quod petis hinc propiore loco, Romane, petisses,
et pete nunc propiore loco; nec Apolline vobis,
qui minuat luctus, opus est, sed Apolline nato.
ite bonis auibus prolemque accersite nostram."

"What you seek from here, Roman, you should have sought in a
closer spot; in fact, now seek in a closer spot. You do not require
Apollo to lessen grief, but the son of Apollo. Go with good auspices
and call on my son."

The emphasis in this oracle on Aesculapius's status as son of Apollo is
underscored through repetition—the new god is identified twice as
Apollo's son in the phrases *Apolline nato* and *prolem nostram*; and when the
Ovidian narrator resumes his story after reporting this oracle, he makes
the point a third time with the appellation *iuuenis Phoebeius* (15.642). Not
once but three times, then, Apollo's paternity is asserted, so overshadowing
the description with which Aesculapius is first introduced in Book 15: as
we have already seen (in the address to the Muses, quoted earlier), the god
is first identified as *Coronides* (15.624), in a use of the matronymic that
sends the reader back to the episode of the god's birth that was narrated in
Metamorphoses Book 2.[49] There, the Ovidian narrator introduces Coronis
as beloved by Apollo (2.542–43) but unfaithful to him. When Apollo learns
from an informer of Coronis's unfaithfulness, he swiftly takes up the
bow, his customary weapon, and shoots her (2.598–605). With her dying
breath, Coronis informs Apollo that he has taken the life of not one but

---

48. J. F. Miller 2009:364–65; Stok 1992:136–44; and cf. S. Wheeler 2000:133–34. According
to Livy 10.47, Aesculapius's importation was the result of a consultation of the Sibylline
books; cf. the summoning of Cybele to Rome at a time of crisis (i.e., during the second Punic
War), also as a result of the consultation of the Sibylline books (Livy 29.10). Interestingly,
in his retelling of the later episode (*Fast.* 4.179–348), Ovid appears to be following Livy: see
Stok 1992:141 n.19; Boyd 2003. Gebhard 2001 discusses narrative conventions in stories of
cult transfer.

49. Of course, Ovid's employment of a patronymic (or, as in this case, a matronymic), as
well as of other periphrases for Aesculapius's name, may also be attributed to metrical con-
venience: the proper name simply cannot be used in dactylic verse. I hope nonetheless to
provide an adequate rationale here, as elsewhere in this book, for Ovid's thoughtful choice of
words, and to dispel the idea that convenience is an appropriate explanation for his choices.
Cf. Stok 1992:158–59 n.79; also 170 n.110.

two (2.608–9); he attempts to reverse the effects of his fatal assault, but to
no avail. But at least, thinks Apollo, he can save the child in utero; he seizes
the infant from the flames of Coronis's pyre and entrusts the baby forth-
with to Chiron, centaur and famed tutor of heroes (2.626–30).[50] It is in
Chiron's care that the child's future role as *salutifer orbi* (2.642) is first pre-
dicted; but in the narrative of the *Metamorphoses*, that prediction achieves
its fulfillment only with the plague episode in Book 15, as the now-mature
youth is brought to Rome in his role as *salutifer urbi* (15.744).[51] Meanwhile,
his change in status is paralleled by the shift that occurs as he goes from
being identified as the son of Coronis to his new and more potent associa-
tion with his father, Apollo.

The prominence of Aesculapius as healing god throughout the
ancient Mediterranean world is a phenomenon supported by abundant
historical evidence, especially (but not exclusively) the inscriptions found
at his shrine in Epidaurus;[52] perhaps most significant from a perspec-
tive that seeks to merge literary themes with historical evidence, how-
ever, is the arrival of Aesculapius in Athens in 420 BCE, an event linked
by many historians at least in part to the Athenian plague described by
Thucydides.[53] I shall return shortly to consider the role played both in
the historical record and in Ovid by the god's ability to appear in the
form of a snake; but first, I want to draw attention to the way in which
the advent of Aesculapius in the *Metamorphoses* is paralleled by the
eclipsing of his father Apollo's identity as god of medicine. The transfer
of power from father to son in this relationship has recently been the
focus of discussions by John Miller and Gareth Williams, both of whom
use it as background against which to analyze the presentation of the

---

50. On the relationship of the episode to the larger narrative of *Metamorphoses* Book 2, see
Keith 1992:63–76.

51. The relationship between the Aesculapius episodes in Books 2 and 15 and their intertex-
tuality with the references to Aesculapius that frame the six books of *Fasti* are the subject
of several recent discussions: see especially Barchiesi 1997a:187–96; S. Wheeler 2000: 133;
Papaioannou 2006; J. F. Miller 2009:353–54; G. D. Williams 2010:73–84. On the play
between *salutifer orbi* and *s. urbi* in particular, see the bibliography provided by S. Wheeler
2000:136 n.130.

52. Edelstein and Edelstein 1945 (1998) is a rich souce of evidence for the cult throughout the
ancient world; for representative inscriptions, see test. 423–24, 431–32, and 561–63.

53. See, e.g., Clinton 1994; Gebhard 2001; Mitchell-Boyask 2008:3–5; cf. also Mikalson
1984:223–25 and Wickkiser 2008:63–66, both of whom offer a somewhat more complicated
interpretation of the association between plague at Athens and the cult of Aesculapius.

relationship between Julius Caesar and Augustus in the conclusion of *Metamorphoses* Book 15.[54] Williams discusses at some length the pattern of divine failure developed throughout the *Metamorphoses* in episodes involving Apollo: beginning with the programmatic scene in Book 1 in which Apollo defeats and destroys Python but is unable to deflect the single arrow with which Cupid wounds him (1.438–77), Apollo repeatedly fails, in whole or in part, to achieve success in the very realms of power and influence over which he supposedly presides. In addition to the god's rhetorical failure with Daphne (1.504–24),[55] Williams points to the pattern of medical failure repeatedly experienced by Apollo: unable to find a *medicina* for the wound that made him fall in love with Daphne (1.521–24), he is also unable, as we have seen, to use his healing arts to rescue Coronis (2.617–18), and he fails a third time with the dying Hyacinthus (10.186–89).

Given Apollo's evident weakness, the birth of Aesculapius in Book 2 is fortuitous; the only really surprising thing about his advent in Book 15, implies Ovid, is that it took so long[56]—and indeed, the remarkable delayed proem invoking the Muses that we have already considered underscores the idea, suggesting that, like the poet himself, the suffering city of Rome is now in need of exceptional intercession by the gods. In Ovid's narrative, the new healing god replaces the old one—but he does so not as the result of intergencrational strife but with the full endorsement of his father, as evidenced by the pronouncement of the Delphic oracle. He thus offers us a striking variation on the succession paradigm seen in the other episodes considered here—instead of conflict, the son improves his father's profile, giving new life as well as continuity to old traditions.

This rather upbeat modernization of a difficult paradigm is not without its ironies, however, at least in Ovid's handling. The ostensible rationale for the inclusion of the Aesculapius story in the *Metamorphoses*—aside, that is, from its political message, to which I shall return—is that this is a god who experiences transformation: indeed, the metamorphosis in this

---

54. See J. F. Miller 2009:362–67; G. D. Williams 2010:64–72.

55. G. D. Williams 2010:66–69 suggests that this initial failure is further complicated by the intertextual shadow of his earlier love for Cyrene, hinted at but not fully narrated by Ovid.

56. Cole 2004:412 draws attention to the fact that the reappearance of Aesculapius in Book 15, so long after his birth in Book 2, is an almost unparalleled instance of temporal dislocation in the poem.

episode is not playfully marginal, as it is in so many other episodes,[57] but central both to the narrative and to the shape of the poem as a whole. As Barchiesi has suggested, the very form of the serpent can be seen as a sort of visual pun: a symbol taking the general form of an uppercase *S* was used in ancient book-rolls as a way to mark the end of a text. This closural emblem is given metanarrative life by Ovid, who complements this pun with a description of the creature's curving shape (*deus explicat orbes | perque sinus crebros et magna uolumina labens,* "The god unfolds his coils, gliding through repeated arcs and great folds," 15.720–21), a shape that evokes the book-rolls (*uolumina*) in which a work like the *Metamorphoses* would have been contained. Last but not least, as Barchiesi notes, one name for this serpentine symbol is *coronis*—a perfect symbol, then, for the god who is Coronides, son of Coronis (15.624), and whose story appears near the close of Ovid's monumental work.[58]

Aesculapius's herpetomorphic epiphany is entertaining not simply as a metanarrative pun, however; Ovid provides a uniquely detailed description of the god's metamorphosis into a snake when the god himself appears in a dream and speaks, inviting the Roman who will lead an embassy to Epidaurus[59] to visualize the snake as it is wrapped around the staff on his statue (15.658–62):

> "pone metus: ueniam simulacraque nostra relinquam.
> hunc modo serpentem, baculum qui nexibus ambit,
> perspice et usque nota, uisum ut cognoscere possis.
> uertar in hunc, sed maior ero tantusque uidebor,
> in quantum uerti caelestia corpora debent."

> "Set aside your fear: I shall come, and shall abandon my image.
> Now look at this snake which encircles the staff with its twists, and
> keep taking note of it, so that you can recognize it when you see it.
> I shall change into this, but I will be greater, and will appear as big
> as the heavenly bodies ought as they change."

---

57. See, e.g., the transformation of the Meleagrides which concludes the otherwise metamorphosis-free episode of the Calydonian boar hunt (above, chapter 3).

58. Barchiesi 1994:256–57 (1997a:190–91), developing the discussion of Bing 1988:33–35.

59. Q. Ogulnius, as we know from prose sources: Val. Max. 1.8.2; *De vir. ill.* 22. (No name is given in the brief reference to the event at Liv. *per.* 11.)

The identification of Aesculapius with a snake is nothing new; a number of ancient sources identify the snake either as explicitly an embodiment of the god or, less precisely, as his epiphany.[60] Ovid, however, gives new life to the ancient etymologizing that derived the word snake, δράκων, from the verb for seeing or looking, δέρκομαι,[61] providing an elaborate description in which both the amazing appearance of the serpent-god and its own sharp sight are repeatedly emphasized: at *Met.* 15.674, the newly animate snake causes a supernatural shuddering of his surroundings, raising himself up and moving his flashing eyes about the temple (*oculos circumtulit igne micantes*, "he moved his eyes around as they glittered with fire"); at 685–86, he moves from the temple to the port, gazing back fondly on his former home as he hisses and rolls along (*oraque retro | flectit et antiquas abiturus respicit aras*, "he turns his face to look back, and when about to depart he gazes upon his old altars"); and at 697–99, he mounts the prow to watch the scenery go by (*inpositaque premens puppim ceruice recuruam | caeruleas despectat aquas*, "and weighing down the curved stern, his neck placed upon it, he gazes down at the sky-blue waves"). Finally, after a quick stop at Antium to visit the temple of his father, Apollo (720–27), the *Phoebeius anguis* rises up once more, this time to the top of the mast, to look for Tiber Island (*sedesque sibi circumspicit aptas*, "and he looks around for an appropriate place to settle," 738). Once there, he resumes his usual divine appearance and, in two quick hexameters, saves the Romans from their plague.

The shape-shifting of Aesculapius—is he an anthropomorphic divinity who assumes the form of a snake to instill wonder in the Romans, or simply for convenience while traveling, or is he most at home in serpent form, only assuming human features to appear more approachable?—is itself the cause for further speculation. Several of the other serpents encountered in the *Metamorphoses* (I shall turn shortly to Python's appearance in Book 1; also worth remembering is the snake that Cadmus encounters at

---

60. Paus. 2.10.3 (Sicyon) and 3.23.6–7 (Epidaurus Limera); *IG* 4², 1.22 (Halieis); and perhaps the Telemachus inscription from Athens, detailing Asclepius's installation there (*IG* 2², 4960a = Edelstein and Edelstein 1945 (1998) test. 720). The reading δράκοντα on the Telemachus inscription has been tentatively accepted by most scholars (see, e.g., Beschi 1967–68:412–14; Mikalson 1984; Parker 1996:177–78; Gebhard 2001:468–72), but see now Clinton 1994:21–25 and Wickkiser 2008:67–80.

61. Cf. Macrob. *Sat.* 1.20.3, Paul. Fest. p. 59.9–13. The etymology may well be correct, according to Beekes 2010:1.351 (although Ogden 2013:173–74 with n.157 doubts it).

Thebes, in Book 3) are harmful and potentially destructive.[62] Barchiesi, noting two Virgilian snakes that, like Aesculapius, undergo transformation (the *chersydrus*, the bane of farmers, which grows even more threatening when rejuvenated after sloughing its old skin, *Geo.* 3.437–39; and the rejuvenated snake to which Pyrrhus is compared just before he slaughters Priam, *Aen.* 2.471–75),[63] emphasizes that the sloughing of old skin and subsequent transformation into a new snake are together evocative of apotheosis, and cites Macrobius's interpretation of the shedding of a snake's skin in support of his argument. Let us take a look at this passage, in which Macrobius explains why snakes are commonly depicted on statues and other images of two divinities associated with health and illness, Aesculapius and Salus (*Sat.* 1.20.2):[64]

> ideo ergo simulacris eorum iunguntur figurae draconum, quia praestant ut humana corpora uelut infirmitatis pelle deposita ad pristinum reuirescant uigorem, ut reuirescunt dracones per annos singulos pelle senectutis exuta. propterea et ad ipsum solem species draconis refertur, quia sol semper uelut a quadam imae depressionis senecta in altitudinem suam ut in robur reuertitur iuuentutis.

> And therefore the shapes of snakes are joined to their images [i.e., of Asclepius and Salus], since they provide that human bodies, as if the skin of weakness has been shed, may regain their strength again with the old vigor, just as snakes regain their strength by shedding the skin of old age from one year to the next. And for this reason also the appearance of the snake is associated with the sun itself, since the sun always returns to its height, as if from the old age of its decline it returns to the vitality of youth.

---

62. Papaioannou 2006:126–33 draws a structural and thematic connection between and among these snake episodes in the *Metamorphoses*.

63. On the close relationship of the simile in *Aeneid* Book 2 to the *chersydrus* of *Georgics* Book 3, see Thomas 1988 on *Geo.* 3.437–39. In the context of the current discussion, it is worth noting that Pyrrhus/Neoptolemus, who enters the *Aeneid* compared to a snake, is in many ways the replacement for his father—another potent successor, following a father who was figured primarily as Peleus's son by Homer.

64. For other ancient evidence suggesting a link between the sloughing off of the snake's skin and the physical rejuvenation of Aesculapius's patients, if not their apotheosis, see Edelstein and Edelstein 1945 (1998) test. 701 and 703–5.

The logic of Macrobius's analogy is clear: when humans are restored to good heath by the intervention of a healing god, they flourish with renewed vigor, as if having shed the skin of infirmity; this is just what snakes do when they shed the skin of old age (*pelle senectutis exuta*) each year. Interestingly, Macrobius then goes on to explain in some detail why the appearance (*species*) of the sun and of snakes is similar, and draws an analogy between the decline, or setting, of the sun each evening as if into old age and the reinvigoration, or youthful strength, of the sun as it arises anew each day. The point is well taken if we extend the analogy to the father and son healing gods depicted by Ovid: father Apollo, as I have suggested, is repeatedly seen to be ineffective as a healer as the mythic chronology of the *Metamorphoses* unfolds; meanwhile, his son Aesculapius, *iuuenis Phoebeius*, is in the ascendancy and so can bring a swift cure not simply to single individuals but to the entire Roman people.[65]

Aesculapius is not the only character in this episode whose identity is defined by matro- or patronymic (or both): the Romans who fetch Aesculapius from Epidaurus are twice called *Aeneadae* by Ovid, at *Met.* 15.682 and 695; this patronymic is used only one other time in the poem, to describe Julius Caesar (15.804).[66] At 15.681–82, furthermore, there is a striking juxtaposition of the words *piumque* and *Aeneadae*, at the end of one line and the beginning of the next; in a sort of reverse enjambment, *piumque* belongs syntactically to the line that follows, and the two words together make Aeneas himself a virtual participant in the mission to bring Aesculapius to Rome. The appearance of the patronymic *Aeneadae* here establishes an intertextual relationship between this episode involving Aesculapius's journey westward from Epidaurus to Rome and the comparable journey of Aeneas from Troy to the future site of Rome—an intertextual relationship that is of course grounded in turn in the Homeric *Odyssey*. Fabio Stok has shown with precision how the list of places past

---

65. Macrobius's analogy can also be applied, mutatis mutandis, to Ovid's version of the story of Phaethon and his father, Sol: of course, as we saw earlier, Sol is not permanently eclipsed by his son—but this may well be in part because his eyes are stronger than Phaethon can bear, i.e., like the perspicacious eyes that feature so prominently in ancient descriptions of snakes.

66. Cf. also the two instances of the patronymic in the *Fasti*, at 1.717, in a description of the altar of Augustan peace, and at 4.161, in an invocation to Venus to look fondly on the descendants of Aeneas; and see Bömer 1958 on *Fast.* 1.717.

which Aesculapius sails is modeled on the travels of Aeneas;[67] and Ovid
appears not only to have incorporated the central figure of Virgil's great
poem into this itinerary but to have acknowledged the presence of Virgil
himself in this landscape with his paired allusion to Parthenope (Naples)
and Cumae at *Met.* 15.711–12, *in otia natam | Parthenopen et ab hac Cumaeae
templa Sibyllae* ("Parthenope, born for leisure, and from here, the tem-
ples of the Cumaean Sibyl").[68] The naming of Parthenope, here distin-
guished as a place "born for leisure," is particularly suggestive, recalling
as it does the *sphragis* with which Virgil had closed the *Georgics* (4.563–64,
*Illo Vergilium me tempore dulcis alebat | Parthenope studiis florentem ignobilis
oti,* "At that time, sweet Parthenope nourished me, Virgil, as I took pleas-
ure in the pursuits of lowly leisure").[69] The depiction of Naples as nurse of
leisure-loving Virgil has clearly inspired Ovid to highlight its proximity to
Cumae, and so to link the locations of two influential literary sojourns: that
of Aeneas with the Sibyl, and that of Aeneas's poet Virgil with his seductive
siren Parthenope. But in a narrative gesture that enacts a transformation
of the *Aeneid*, Aesculapius (and Ovid), unlike Aeneas (and Virgil), does
not in fact stop here. Instead, Aesculapius hurries to Antium, where he
lands briefly to visit the temple of Apollo (15.719–22) before coming at last
to the Tiber Island, and Rome.[70] The relationship between Aeneas and
Aesculapius suggested by Ovid is clear: the Trojan hero and the Greek god
have had parallel (but not identical) journeys to the same destination, and
their intertextual identities are overlapped and intertwined by Ovid like
the coils of a great snake. At the same time, Ovid invites us to engage in a
reading that effectively eclipses the *Aeneid*, as *pater* Aeneas is replaced by
the son of Apollo.

With this suggestion I return to our central concern, the succes-
sion theme developed in the narrative of Aesculapius's arrival and

---

67. Stok 1992:144–50, a virtuoso display of the value of a deep familiarity with ancient
topography.

68. Paired only one other time by Ovid, at *Met.* 14.101–4, in Ovid's description of Aeneas's
own journey and his stop at the cave of the Sibyl.

69. The association of Virgil with Naples is also an important detail in the elegiac couplet
alleged by Donatus to have been Virgil's epitaph, where Parthenope is said to be the poet's
final resting-place (*Mantua me genuit, Calabri rapuere, tenet nunc | Parthenope; cecini pascua
rura duces,* Don. *Vita* 36). On the association of Naples with *otium,* see also Hor. *Epod.* 5.43,
otiosa Neapolis.

70. On Ovid's simultaneous avoidance and repetition of the *Aeneid* in the *Metamorphoses,*
see Hinds 1998:99–122.

institutionalization as Rome's new healing god. In particular, I want to look once more at the significance of Aesculapius's epiphany as a snake; already loaded as it is with metatextual meaning, this metamorphosis also reverberates on the narrative level. I begin by directing my reader's attention to another episode that appears much earlier in the *Metamorphoses* and that involves Aesculapius's father, the healing god Apollo. By means of this apparent detour, I propose to arrive at a conclusion that recognizes the father-son relationship of these two gods as an interpretive key, both poetic and political, to the poem's conclusion, offering in the process a new paradigm for genealogical tradition.

In the first myth narrated by Ovid in Book 1 after the receding of Deucalion and Pyrrha's flood, *noua monstra* begin to appear. Chief among them is the snake Python (*Met.* 1.438–51), whose defeat by Apollo is motivated by the threat that Python poses to all the new life on earth and, indeed, to earth herself. Apollo's destruction of the snake is swift, taking all of four verses (1.441–44); Ovid devotes far more time and attention to the narrative of Apollo's pursuit of Daphne. But even in this latter episode Apollo remains the healer: when he at last wins Daphne, fronds and all, after approximately ninety lines of pursuit, Apollo showers her with a proclamation of the rewards that attend his adoption of the laurel as official foliage; and as Ovid brings Apollo's last speech to Daphne to an end, he uses the epithet *Paean,* "healer," for the god (1.566). We might say, then, that Apollo's triumph in Book 1 anticipates the coming of Aesculapius to Rome in Book 15; but the fact that in Book 15 Aesculapius assumes the very serpent shape that Apollo had destroyed in Book 1 is also ominous, reminding us that Aesculapius's arrival in Rome is part of the cyclical repetition of history. The aetiology for the institution of laurel as the crowning material used in the Pythian games is a story that, on one level, marks the end of an era; when Apollo replaces his old oak wreath with the laurel, he moves himself, and Ovid's readers, away from the chaotic disarray following the flood and into a charming world inhabited by nymphs and river gods, almost Arcadian in its simplicity. Yet embedded in the story of Apollo's new crown is a hint that history is not straightforwardly linear, and that the past cannot ever entirely be left behind. Ovid includes an unparalleled detail in his reference to the Pythian victors' crowns, noting that, before laurel was introduced, the wreaths were of oak leaves: *aesculeae . . . frondis honorem* ("the honor of the oak branch," 1.449). This detail, I suggest, merits more attention than most readers have given it.

As Adrian Hollis has demonstrated,[71] Ovid's suggestion that the laurel had not previously existed is not supported by any other source, but the general motif of announcing the introduction of a new ritual feature—in this case, of the reward won in the Pythian games—is found elsewhere in Hellenistic poetry; its appearance here, then, adds to the Augustan panegyric of the scene. Hollis also notes that the specification of the oak (*aesculus*) here as the pre–laurel wreath material at Delphi has no parallel, and suggests that it too contributes to the Augustan flavor of the episode, since the Daphne episode closes with a mention by Apollo of the oak that will stand with the laurel before Augustus's house (*"postibus Augustis eadem fidissima custos | ante fores stabis mediamque tuebere quercum,"* "'Likewise will you stand, a most trusted guard, outside at the doors of Augustus, and protect the oak in your midst,'" 1.561–62).[72] In his commentary, Bömer draws attention to the rare use of the epithet *aesculeus* at 1.449, as opposed to the more common epithets for oak, *querneus* and *iligneus*; as we saw in the passage just cited, *quercus* is the word Apollo will use in his address to Daphne. In fact, the adjective *aesculeus* appears here for the first time in extant Latin literature and demonstrates, as Bömer comments, that "Ovid's mode of expression is as unusual as his point of view."[73] It is also the closest we come to the appearance of *Aescula*pius's name in Ovid's poetry, since, as I have already noted, it is simply not suited to hexameter verse. In *Metamorphoses* Book 1, then, I suggest, Ovid uses this epithet not simply for its novelty but because, through paronomasia suggesting an etymological connection between the oak, *aesculus*, and the god, Aesculapius, it establishes a link between the era of Python and that of Aesculapius. To be sure, the Arcadian world of postcataclysmic Delphi has been left far behind, both temporally and geographically; yet Ovid hints that while the world in which Apollo's son is ascendant is different in regard to specifics, old patterns never die.

---

71. Hollis 1996; cf. also Barchiesi 2005 on *Met.* 1.445–51.

72. Hollis 1996; cf. also Barchiesi 2005 on 1.445–51.

73. Bömer vol. 1, 1969 ad loc.: "Ovids Ausdruck ist ebenso ungewöhnlich wie seine Ansicht." The same adjective also appears (if we accept the reading preferred by Tarrant: see his apparatus) at *Met.* 8.410, in the center of the episode of the Calydonian boar hunt—i.e., at the center of the central book of the poem: perhaps another mark of Ovid's structural sensitivity, and of the cyclical movement of history? On the importance of the poem's center, see also above, chapter 3, n.35. The noun *aesculus* appears once elsewhere in Ovid, in the catalogue of trees in attendance at Orpheus's singing (*Met.* 10.91). For other appearances of *aesculus/ aesculetum* in Augustan literature, cf. Virg. *Geo.* 2.16 and 291; Hor. *Carm.* 1.22.14 and 3.10.17.

That Ovid intends us to link the old serpent and the new through their common connection to Apollo is also, I propose, one of the reasons that he sends the Roman embassy in Book 15 to Delphi—as we have seen, this is a feature of his version that is not found elsewhere, and most of our other sources assimilate the *translatio* of Aesculapius to that of Cybele by having the summoning of both result from a consultation of the Sibylline books.[74] Ovid offers us an explicit reminder of that earlier episode, as well as of the fact that time has indeed been cycled around since then, in his description of Delphi in Book 15: it is home to the laurel of Apollo and his quiver, now standard temple equipment but in Book 1 the embodiment of Apollo's accomplishments and self-definition (*et locus et laurus et quas habet ipse pharetrae*, "the place, and the laurels, and the quiver which he himself carries," 15.634).

The reference to Apollo's Delphic temple here activates another association as well: I refer to a curious anecdote concerning the parentage of Augustus. Augustus's mother, Atia, Suetonius reports, spent the night in a temple of Apollo as part of a ritual for married women. While she was sleeping, a snake crept toward her and departed shortly thereafter; when she awoke and bathed, she discovered an indelible image of a snake on her body, and ten months later she gave birth to Augustus.[75] The child was therefore thought to be the son of Apollo.[76] The political implications of Augustus's association with Apollo are a familiar topic; but we should not inadvertently overlook the fact that the putative epiphany of Apollo as a snake in a dream not only reflects a long tradition of such stories about great men, like Alexander and Scipio Minor, but also is modeled on the very real reports of snake epiphanies involving Aesculapius, such as those

---

74. See also J. F. Miller 2009:364–65.

75. Suet. *Aug.* 94.6: *Atiam, cum ad sollemne Apollinis sacrum media nocte uenisset, posita in templo lectica, dum ceterae matronae dormirent, obdormisse; draconem repente irrepsisse ad eam pauloque post egressum; illam expergefactam quasi a concubitu mariti purificasse se; et statim in corpore eius exstitisse maculam uelut picti draconis nec potuisse umquam exigi, adeo ut mox publicis balineis perpetuo abstinuerit; Augustum natum mense decimo et ob hoc Apollinis filium existimatum.*

Livy 26.19.6–8 reports (and dismisses) a similar story about the birth of Scipio Minor, which incorporates a specific comparison of Scipio with Alexander; Apollo, however, is absent from the description, and there is the clear implication (namely, through a mention of Scipio's habitual visits to the temple of Jupiter on the Capitoline) that the divinity who fathered Scipio (and Alexander) was Jupiter. Cf. also Plut. *Alex.* 2–3.

76. See the discussion by Gurval 1995:100–102, with earlier bibliography; Papaioannou 2006:136–37; J. F. Miller 2009:18–19; and cf. Dio Cass. 45.1.1.

found in the *iamata*, or miracle inscriptions, from Epidaurus.[77] I quote two that are particularly apposite:

B 19
[――]da from Keos. This woman, sleeping here concerning chil-
dren, saw a dream. It seemed to her that in her sleep a snake lay
down upon her stomach. And from this five children were born
to her.

B 22
Nikasiboula of Messene, concerning children. Sleeping here she
saw a dream. It seemed to her the god came bringing a snake creep-
ing beside him and she had sex with it. And from this children were
born to her within a year, twin boys.

These miracle reports not only offer some context for the traditions surround-
ing larger-than-life historical figures like Alexander, Scipio, and Augustus;
they also bear witness to a widespread and enduring belief that Aesculapius
could and did repeatedly take the form of a snake, and that in this form he
assumed the role of a father himself—just like his father, Apollo, in fact,
but better, greater, younger, more powerful. The genealogical paradigm thus
encoded in Ovid's poem gives us a son greater and more potent than his
father—a pattern that reverberates in the parallel of Julius Caesar's pater-
nity of Augustus, and that offers a successful model for succession even as
it leaves some important questions unanswered. Is Aesculapius's journey,
combining as it does a Virgilian model with Ovid's own distinctively humor-
ous description of the snake, indicative of a successful conclusion to both
the poem and a plague-ridden past, or does the form of the snake itself,
with its ambiguous undertones, suggest the circularity of history, and so
signal an inexorable renewal of past troubles, of enduring conflict between
an unresolved past and an overconfident present?[78]

---

77. LiDonnici 1995 provides a full text and discussion; I have adapted her translations (for the
two that appear here, 112–15).

78. A tantalizing but evanescent detail in a major fragment of Hesiod's *Ehoiai* (fr. 204 M-
W = Most 2007: fr. 155) is the location, near the fragment's end, of a sudden transition in the
narrative in which a snake figures prominently. Hesiod has finished cataloguing the suitors
of Helen, her abduction, and the subsequent birth of Hermione; a dramatic description of
seasonal change follows and in turn gives way to an excursus on the life cycle of a snake,
including its reappearance after apparent destruction by Zeus (134–42). West 1985:120 has
suggested the possibility that this remarkable sequence of events is meant as an analogy

V. *A Circular Logic*

Over the course of the past two chapters, we have traversed a wide swath of mythical narratives about genealogical succession. Starting from Homer, we began with a series of stories that have come to shape the relationship of father and son in epic, even as we have traced a long history of dissonance, of sons disobeying their fathers, being unable to measure up, or, in the final instance, eclipsing and so replacing the one who went before. Transpiring as it does in the divine realm, the translation of authority from Apollo to Aesculapius comes without any loss of blood, or of life itself; there is no legacy of intergenerational conflict as besets Phoenix, Meleager, and even Achilles, nor any childish self-destructiveness as with Phaethon and Icarus. But there is just enough ambiguity inherent in the ascendancy of Aesculapius to leave us wondering, I think, about its salutary surface meaning: though Ovid locates the close of his narrative here, he invites us to go back to the beginning, to reactivate our memories of a past that has both literary and historical significance.

The tale of Aesculapius is also ambiguous in metanarrative terms: the implication that Ovid, like Aesculapius, is Apollo's poetic "son" has a nice logic to it, since this would also entail casting Homer in the role of Apollo himself—from the god of poetry to its father is not a difficult stretch.[79] But the suggestion that Ovid replaces Homer as a son replaces his father— new, young, and powerful, rather than old, aged, and weak—is not wholly complimentary and may even be thought (overly) audacious, especially when we also consider the story's political overtones. That is, if Apollo makes way for Aesculapius and Julius Caesar for Augustus, are we to infer that Homer makes way for Ovid, allowing himself to be not only replaced but also displaced, at least within the trajectory of poetic genealogy sketched here? I would suggest that Ovid manages to stay just this side of such invidious comparison at least in part by means of the light, almost humorous touch with which he depicts the snake-god's advent. It

---

of sorts for the passing of one heroic age and the advent of another; J. S. Clay 2005:33–34, following West's suggestion, comments, "[T]he omen of the serpent sloughing off its skin and giving birth can also be understood as an emblem of the cosmic *Zeitwende*, with the end of the old order and the inauguration of something new." It is tempting to imagine the formative influence of this prototype on Ovid's final book, right after the speech of Pythagoras promising the continuity of creation.

79. The association was certainly not far from the mind of Archelaus of Priene as he sculpted the famous relief known by his name: see below, chapter 6.

is also tempting to speculate that the cyclical shape of history adumbrated in the Aesculapius story can be read as a tribute to Homer, whose poetic world opens with the description of a plague (*Il.* 1.2–5), and to the survival and indeed the rebirth of Homeric poetry near the conclusion of the *Metamorphoses*.

5

Paternity Tests

sic iuuenis similisque tibi sit natus, et illum
moribus agnoscat quilibet esse tuum.

—OVID, *Tr.* 4.5.31–32[1]

I. Absent Fatherhood

In the last two chapters, I have surveyed a series of father-son pairs whose relationships are best understood as reflections of an enduring narrative pattern established by Homeric epic. As we have seen, at least on occasion the development of this pattern has played both thematic and metatextual roles: that is, the combination of filial resistance and filial resemblance that pulls at the younger members of each pair can be seen at least at times as a reflection of the relationship Ovid claims for himself with Homer. Phaethon most fully and playfully exemplifies this relationship, in the combination of obstinacy that makes him bound and determined to prove himself worthy of Sol's paternity with the immaturity that dooms him to disastrous failure; but other pairings as well reflect repeatedly, and in nuanced ways, on the relationship. The example set by Nestor and Antilochus suggests that sons can and do learn a great deal from their fathers, and that the mastery of μῆτις/*ars* transmitted from one generation to another may even allow a son to surpass his father, to demonstrate a cleverness not fully envisaged by his father but native nonetheless—and successful. I have also noted in passing the metatextual interpretations to which the story of Daedalus and Icarus have been subject, and have traced the way in which the Aesculapius episode in *Metamorphoses* Book 15 reflects upon its own status as the close of the poem even as it illustrates the circularity of narrative time, with healer-son replacing healer-father as a plague once again threatens historical continuity.

---

1. "So may your son be like you, and may anyone who meets him recognize from his character that he is yours."

I want to close this portion of my discussion with a consideration of the ways in which the metaphor of poetic paternity plays itself out in Ovid's last poems, the elegies from exile. A Homeric or Homeric-Virgilian frame of reference has informed a number of recent studies of the exile poetry, as scholars have explored the ways in which Ovid models his exile on the experiences of several epic characters, among whom Ulysses and Aeneas, along with Jason, are the most prominent.[2] The journey from a beloved home to a place far away, where the hero is separated from all those who know and love him—this scenario describes the exiled Ovid as aptly as it does Ulysses and Aeneas, although each of the two epic heroes moves along a different narrative trajectory: in the case of Ulysses, the destination, Troy, is meant to be a temporary stopping place, and Ithaca stands fixed in the mind and in space as home, the goal to which the hero will return after completing his labors; in Aeneas's case, on the other hand, Troy, that is, home, is effectively lost, and the new destination is permanent, achieved by a definitively one-way trip. For Ovid, both models have the ability to arouse a similar emotional response, as he questions whether his departure from Rome is temporary or permanent, whether Tomis is a stopping place or a new home, and whether his identity as Roman, husband, father, and poet is essential or contingent.

Indeed, the question of identity's ability to persist through radically foreign change of all sorts animates much of Ovid's exile poetry. Strikingly, it expresses itself on several occasions through a familial analogy, as Ovid either personifies his poems, describing them as his sons and reflecting upon their distinctive characters, or discusses his own plight as comparable to that of some of the less fortunate youths who have not followed their fathers' instructions, as we saw earlier. In what follows, therefore, I will be concerned less with Ovid's epic role models per se than with his use of the metaphors of paternity and of wayward youthfulness to talk about his exile poetry and his relationship to it; as we shall see, the Homeric presence continues to exert itself.

II. The Ugly Duckling

I begin with what is perhaps the most physically striking analogy Ovid uses to describe his work: in *Epistulae ex Ponto* 3.9, the poet professes to

---

2. See, e.g., H. Evans 1983:37, 40–41, 48–49 *et passim*; G. D. Williams 1994:30, 66–67, 108–14; Huskey 2002.

feel affection for his poetry in spite of its many defects, just as Agrius, the father of Thersites, is likely to have overlooked his own son's physical flaws.[3] The mention of Thersites is itself definitively evocative of the *Iliad*: shamelessly, he dares to stand up in the assembly of *Iliad* Book 2 to reproach Agamemnon for his weak leadership, in a scene remarked upon since antiquity for its unique portrayal of a character who is most definitely not one of the ἄνδρες ἀγαθοί who otherwise populate the world of Homeric epic.[4] In addition to the scene's exceptional depiction of a "low-class" character, the description of Thersites's physical person is itself remarkable: he is αἴσχιστος, bandy-legged and lame, with hunched shoulders and sporting a stubbly beard on his pointed head (*Il.* 2.216–19).[5] And his speech fits his appearance: he is nasty, crude, and disrespectful, and the Homeric narrator seems to take as much pleasure as do the other Achaeans in the tongue-lashing and physical beating with which Odysseus puts Thersites in his place (*Il.* 2.246–77).[6]

When Ovid mentions Thersites, then, he surely intends this memorable scene to be recalled by his readers, even as he introduces a note of paternal affection into it that is entirely absent in Homer. In this elegy, Ovid is writing to his friend Brutus, who has apparently informed him that someone back in Rome has been critical of the repetitiousness of Ovid's exile poetry; this anonymous critic, says Ovid, accuses him of recycling the same material (*eadem sententia*) repeatedly (3.9.1–4). Ovid first

---

3. Casali 1997:96–102 discusses at length the allusion to Thersites in *Epistulae ex Ponto* 3.9, making the appealing argument that the ugliness of Thersites is a stand-in for the (alleged) ugliness of his exile poetry, but that the real significance of the allusion lies not in Thersites's physical appearance but in the fact that "he also assailed his superiors with abuse" (100). His insolence, suggests Casali, is a key to the irreverence lurking beneath the surface of the exile poems. Casali is not concerned with the imagery of paternity in the poem, however.

4. The T scholiast on *Il.* 2.212 even suggests that this scene shows that Homer himself, rather than Xenophanes, was the first to write satiric lampoons. Kirk 1985 on *Il.* 2.212 notes that, while Thersites is often described as a common soldier or "low" person, the Homeric text does not identify him in these terms; Kirk suggests that he is characterized as "an outrageous person." For other discussions of the episode and the continuing debate over the political and literary ideologies reflected in the character of Thersites, see P. W. Rose 1988; Postlethwaite 1988; Thalmann 1988; Kouklanakis 1999; and Marks 2005.

5. For the details of his physique, described in a number of unusual terms, see Kirk 1985 ad loc. Rosen 2007:67–116 discusses similarities in the physical descriptions of Thersites and Aesop in the context of an analysis of Thersites's relationship to satiric poetic traditions; cf. also Kouklanakis 1999.

6. Note in particular the focalization of the other soldiers: though grieved (ἀχνύμενοί περ) in general terms (perhaps out of a momentary fear that the same thing could happen to them), they take great pleasure in Odysseus's silencing of Thersites (*Il.* 2.270–77).

feigns modesty, claiming that, if this is the only fault to be found, all is well
(5–6);[7] he then proceeds to reveal that he actually knows the weaknesses
of his own poetry better than anyone else, and does not in fact approve of
them, but that, like Thersites's father, he may well be inclined to look past
his child's flaws (7–12):

> ipse ego librorum uideo delicta meorum,
>   cum sua plus iusto carmina quisque probet.
> auctor opus laudat: sic forsitan Agrius olim
>   Thersiten facie dixerit esse bona.
> iudicium tamen hic nostrum non decipit error,
>   nec quicquid genui protinus illud amo.

> I myself see the defects of my books, although everyone approves
> his own poems more than is right. A creator praises his work: so
> perhaps Agrius once said that Thersites was fair of face. This mis-
> take did not deceive our judgment, however, and I do not necessar-
> ily love what I have created.

In the remainder of the elegy, the poet laments his own weakness, observ-
ing that the writing itself still comes easily and is pleasurable; but correct-
ing his own work (*corrigere*, 20, 23) is difficult; so he asks Brutus—and,
by implication, his unnamed critics—for indulgence and understanding.

The mention of Thersites, a character so extremely delineated in the
Iliad as to catch Ovid's reader up short at his mention here, plays with the
idea that a collection of poems has the same qualities as a person's physi-
cal appearance; but the positioning of Thersites here in relationship to
his father, Agrius, simultaneously plays with the idea that a collection of
poems has the qualities of a child and can be thought of as the offspring
of its poet-father. Ovid's use of the two names makes the comparison vivid
and precise; so does the framing language, in which Ovid moves from
describing himself, somewhat ambiguously, as *auctor* (9), to using a verb
that clearly denotes parentage to characterize his relationship with his
work: *genui* (12).[8] He proceeds to observe that loving one's offspring does
not necessarily entail approving of everything about it; his reader is left to

---

7. See also Block 1982 on the importance of reading this poem in light of Ovid's refined tal-
ent for *uariatio*.

8. On Ovid's play with the meaning of *auctor*, see chapter 2, n. 57.

infer that Agrius too knew quite well his son's faults, physical and other-
wise, but chose to overlook them.

The physical comparison of the exile poems to Thersites, then, both
develops the idea of poetic paternity and leaves room for an understand-
ing of the father-son relationship as a complex one, sometimes fraught
with mixed emotions. But Ovid's metatextual engagement with Homer
in *Epistulae ex Ponto* 3.9 does not stop here. First of all, there is the fact
of the naming of Thersites's father: in this most Homeric of allusions,
Ovid includes a genealogical detail *not* found in Homer's poetry itself.
The Homeric Thersites is in fact noteworthy as the only character in the
poem identified neither by patronymic nor by genealogy nor by place of
origin;[9] and while Agrius's name appears in the *Iliad* (14.115, in a speech by
Diomedes detailing his genealogy), he is not connected there in any man-
ner whatsoever with Thersites.[10] Rather, Ovid is likely to have found the
name in the scholia, and its inclusion here is a demonstration, ostensibly
offhand but in fact deeply learned, of his familiarity with Homeric criti-
cism.[11] In fact, shortly after the Thersites exemplum, Ovid uses another
exemplum drawn not from the world of heroic myth but from that of
Homeric criticism to describe the difficulty of improving upon his own
work once written; and while the earlier exemplum is surprising because
of the vivid and unlikely comparison it entails, this exemplum is even
more so—not for its vividness, however, but for the attention it draws to
the work of poetry and to its criticism (3.9.17–26):

> Saepe aliquod uerbum cupiens mutare reliqui,
>   iudicium uires destituuntque meum.
> saepe piget—quid enim dubitem tibi uera fateri?—
>   corrigere et longi ferre laboris onus.

---

9. Kirk 1985 on *Il.* 2.212; and cf. Higbie 1995:11, whose description of Thersites's exceptional
status in the *Iliad* might suit the exiled Ovid equally well, mutatis mutandis: "Without a
patronymic, Thersites appears to be a completely isolated figure, unprotected by family,
friends, or tradition, and easily dismissed or even brutally attacked, no more significant in
the Homeric world than an unnamed servant . . . . "

10. On the Aetolian lineage of both Diomedes and Thersites, see Rankin 1972, who suggests
that "Homer" (Rankin's quotation marks) has intentionally avoided giving Thersites's gene-
alogy so as to suppress any association of Diomedes with a strikingly objectionable character.

11. See the AT scholia on *Il.* 2.212. The mention of Agrius suggests the same sort of fondness
for obscurantist detail seen in the allusions to Phoenix's father, Amyntor, in *Heroides* 3 and
in the episode of the Calydonian boar hunt in *Metamorphoses* Book 8: see above, chapter 3,
and cf. Casali 1997:111–12 n.54.

scribentem iuuat ipse labor minuitque laborem
    cumque suo crescens pectore feruet opus.
corrigere ut res est tanto minus ardua quanto
    magnus Aristarcho maior Homerus erat,
sic animum lento curarum frigore laedit
    et cupidi cursus frena retentat equi.

Often, while wanting to change some word, I have left it, and
strength abandons my judgment. It's often irksome—why, then,
should I hesitate to tell you the truth?—to correct, and to endure
the burden of long labor. The work itself pleases me as I write and
lessens my effort, and as the work grows, it warms with its writer's
emotion; but though correcting is as much less strenuous as great
Homer was much greater than Aristarchus, it bruises the mind
with the sluggish chill of worry and restrains the reins of the horse
eager for a race.

Ovid has been telling Brutus that it is difficult to correct the flaws in his
work even when he sees them—a variation upon the familiar sentiment
"the spirit is willing, but the flesh is weak." Writing itself, he suggests, is a
source of pleasure, since his spirit is lifted by the work; the problem, says
Ovid, is with revision—he simply does not have the heart for it. The verb
Ovid uses to describe the work of revision, *corrigere*, is not seen frequently
in Latin poetry and is likely to be a technical term for textual revision and
editing more generally;[12] the significance of its appearance here is height-
ened by repetition, as the present infinitive appears in the same form
twice, in initial position twice, within an expanse of four verses (and it
will shortly appear yet again, in verse 32, as Ovid tries to capture the harsh
irony of his situation). In confirmation of the verb's technical associations,
Ovid then invokes the relative greatness of the poet Homer and the textual
critic Aristarchus, the great Alexandrian editor of the Homeric poems, to
illustrate how much more difficult it is to achieve what Homer has done
than what Aristarchus has—and so suggests that the "rough drafts" of his
work are like the poetry of Homer in their inspired, albeit imperfect, state.
Ovid thus asserts that his *ingenium*, like Homer's, is still sound—rather,
it is *ars* that is lacking, and its absence is a result of the chilling effect of

---

12. See Hor. *Ars P.* 438, using *corrigere* to describe a critic's instructions to a poet seeking to
improve his work, with Brink 1971 ad loc.

both his physical environment and his emotional isolation.[13] Aristarchus, on the other hand, the archetypal "corrector," is effectively dismissed from Ovid's frame of reference, even as Thersites is treated with unusual, and un-Homeric, kindness.

The logic of this comparison is developed later in the elegy, as Ovid goes on to explain why revision is so difficult for him: the labor entailed provokes emotional strain, as he contemplates with bitterness the context for his writing; the prospect of revising his work with care while surrounded only by wild Getae makes him think he will lose his mind (27–32). This is why, he concludes, his exile poems are so repetitious (*cum totiens eadem dicam*, 39): they simply reflect the repetitiousness of the exile in which he lingers.

The irony of Ovid's situation, then, is mirrored in the poems he writes—and in this poem in particular, in which he both implies a comparison between himself and Homer, and characterizes his paternal feelings for his work in terms that suggest the unloveliest child of all, Thersites—a child so unlovely that Homer avoids mentioning the man's father. Ovid, of course, does not intend to disclaim his poems; his description of their inevitable repetitiousness as a simulacrum of his life in Tomis underscores the symbiotic relationship between him and his work. At the same time, we can detect in this poem, I suggest, an Ovid who is in fact delighted with his own Aristarchean addition to Homer's narrative as he gives Thersites the father who was missing in the *Iliad*. In uniting father and son—even the ugliest of sons—Ovid also writes himself and his poetry into a genealogy that began with Homer, using the trope of repetitiousness to suggest that he faithfully sustains the tradition that links them.

III. The Lost Boys

The preoccupation with family resemblance and paternal affection that provides the basis for Ovid's evocation of Thersites is present in the exile poems from the very start: in the first poem of the first book of *Tristia*, 1.1, Ovid asserts the paternity of his poetry, as he addresses the book of poems that he sends to Rome in his own absence. From the start of the poem, the poet indicates that the appearance of his book is very much a reflection of him: he instructs the *liber* to travel outfitted in the garb of mourning,

---

13. G. D. Williams 1994:86–89 offers a complementary discussion of Ovid's response to Horatian critical theory in *Epistulae ex Ponto* 3.9.

rather than to appear ornamented with the *instrumenta* (9) that usually adorn finely produced books. The edges of the roll are not to be polished, nor are blots to be of any concern; rather, the book should accurately reflect the fate of its author (11–14).[14] The physicality of the book is made prominent by the continuing focus on its appearance; even the book's metrical "feet" are here imagined as physical feet, on which the *liber* makes its journey to Rome (*uade, liber, uerbisque meis loca grata saluta;* | *contingam certe quo licet illa pede*, "Go, book, and greet the pleasant locales with my words; surely with that foot I may touch them," 15–16). The book lives and takes physical shape, in other words, thanks to the attributes Ovid gives it: his poetic *pedes* become the book's physical *pedes*.[15]

The poet's identification with his *liber* is both physical and emotional; and as he imagines the book's Roman adventure, he inverts the original analogy, now not only portraying the book as a projection of himself but wishing that he were his own book: *di facerent, possem nunc meus esse liber* ("I wish the gods would make it so that now I could be my book," 58). That is of course impossible; nonetheless, the *liber* is undertaking a hazardous mission, since it will be virtually impossible for the book to disguise its origins: however much it may try to obscure its appearance, its resemblance to Ovid will be inescapable (59–62). Ovid therefore warns his *liber* that those who recognize the book may try to reject it, and instructs the traveler to point to its *titulus* (i.e., *Tristia*), in order to make clear that it is not the *praeceptor amoris* (65–68).

In my English paraphrase of the poem to this point, I have found it difficult to reflect the intimacy of Ovid's personification of the *liber*: the English pronoun *it* dehumanizes the very humanizing characterization inherent in Ovid's Latin. But Ovid's latest instruction to the *liber*—that it should not identify itself as *praeceptor amoris*—brings out the closeness between the poet and his poems, as between the book and its contents. Ovid's use of the phrase *praeceptor amoris* alerts his reader that he is no longer a poet of love, alluding indirectly to the likely cause of Ovid's exile; it also brings the series of identifications in the poem full circle, linking both poet and book with the book's inspired contents.

---

14. Ovid thus evokes the traditional association of elegy with the poetry of mourning.

15. On Ovid's identification with the *liber* of *Tristia* 1.1, see also Citroni 1986:121–30 and Geyssen 2007; on the *pes* pun, see Hinds 1985:16–17. Casali 1997:111 n.51 points out that Homer's description of Thersites as lame in one foot (*Il.* 2.217) also contributes to Ovid's identification of him with his elegies from exile. Theodorakopoulos 1999 offers a psychoanalytical approach to Ovid's poetic embodiment.

Ovid then develops at some length the difficulty of writing while in exile: the peace and quiet that permit poetry to thrive are out of reach in his current situation (39–44). So difficult are his circumstances, asserts Ovid, that Homer himself would lose his brilliance in such conditions: *da mihi Maioniden et tot circumice*[16] *causas,* | *ingenium tantis excidet omne malis* ("Give me the son of Maeon, and throw so many misfortunes around him: all his inspired talent will fall away at such great evils," 47–48). Ovid thus indirectly implies a parallel between his *ingenium* and Homer's: the downfall of one and the triumph of the other are both the products of chance.

The implied comparison with Homer in turn sets the stage for a series of exempla—none of which are in fact Homeric in provenance, although all reflect, directly or indirectly, on the relationship between a father and his children. The poet imagines the trepidation with which his *liber* might approach the lofty Palatine, since this is the home of the gods (*augusta . . . loca*, 71) and the source of the "thunderbolt" (*fulmen*, 72) that cast him out of Rome and into exile. Ovid again expresses his fear of "Jupiter's weapons" (*Iouis arma*, 81) as he advises the book to seek a humble place to rest rather than any place too lofty (87–88). As Ovid's use of the epithet *augustus* to describe the Palatine makes clear, Jupiter is here a stand-in for the *princeps*, while the heavens over which the thunderbolt-wielding god presides are none other than the imperial residence. To underscore both the loftiness of the imperial heights and their dangerous potential, Ovid frames this analogy with allusions to two mythical characters whose disastrous flights caused their deaths: we have already met these two characters in our discussion of the succession theme in the *Metamorphoses*, in the persons of Phaethon and Icarus.[17]

Phaethon initiates the series: *uitaret caelum Phaethon si uiueret, et quos* | *optaret stulte, tangere nollet equos* ("Phaethon would avoid the heavens if he were living, and would not want to touch the horses which he foolishly desired," 79–80). The contrary-to-fact condition underscores the finality of the story: Ovid addresses his book (and his readers) in terms that presume familiarity with the *Metamorphoses*, and with Phaethon's very definite end. Simultaneously, he suggests that his own plight might well be that of one of his characters—and that he has been as thoroughly destroyed as was

---

16. Owen prints *circumspice; circumice* is Heinsius's emendation.

17. Huskey 2006 discusses these two exempla, along with three others in *Tristia* 1.1, in a study of Ovid's post-exilic rereading of the *Metamorphoses*.

Phaethon. But the conditional form of the analogy also invites his readers to imagine an alternate scenario, in which both Phaethon and he are "once burned, twice shy"—in other words, having learned their lessons, they might in all due modesty continue to live. Ovid proceeds to draw the same analogy in other terms, ranging from the natural world (a lamb once bitten avoiding the wolf) to events following the Trojan War (the Greek sailors avoiding the promontory of Caphereus in the wake of the destruction of the lesser Ajax there by Poseidon in punishment for his disrespect),[18] and concludes with a mention of Icarus—now no longer imagining an alternative reality permitting escape, however, but sealing the list of those who escaped, however barely, with one who had no second chance: *dum petit infirmis nimium sublimia pennis | Icarus, aequoreis nomina fecit aquis* ("While Icarus sought the too-lofty heights on weak wings, he created a name for the watery seas," 89–90). This couplet recalls the definitive end of Icarus's flight in *Metamorphoses* Book 8, complete with its allusion to the etymology of the Icarian Sea (*Met.* 8.230; cf. also *Ars am.* 2.96), concluding as it does so the vain hope of a second chance embedded in the earlier exempla.

Ovid's pairing of Phaethon and Icarus underscores the thematic associations that linked the two in the *Metamorphoses*: both are destroyed by a rash action, and at least in part because of a lack of control. But the analogy can be taken further, particularly if we recall the emphasis placed there on their fathers' losses; Ovid implies that he is the "son" of the *princeps*, whose identity as "father" is here embedded in the comparison to Jupiter.[19] This set of associations allows the poet yet again to begin to hope for a last-minute pardon or reprieve, and he implores the *liber* to represent his interests with all due modesty and prudence (91–104).

As he proceeds with his *liber*'s imaginary homeward journey, however, Ovid also moves from the image of himself as wayward son to that of loving father, whose own children are his books. The poet imagines his earlier books sitting in the bookcase at home, waiting to receive their new brother, and describes their appearance (*Tr.* 1.1.105–22):

---

18. For Homeric reminiscences of the event and its aftermath, see *Od.* 3.151–83 and 276–99, and 4.499–511. Caphereus also figures in post-Homeric traditions surrounding events at the end of the Trojan War: in vengeance for his son's death, Palamedes's father Nauplius is said to have lured the returning Greeks to Caphereus with beacons, so that they would crash and be killed on the rocks. See Gantz 1993:603–8 and 695–97 for a summary of the evidence.

19. Ovid's first readers would also have been familiar with the honorific *pater patriae* bestowed upon Augustus in 2 BCE.

cum tamen in nostrum fueris penetrale receptus,
  contigerisque tuam, scrinia curua, domum,
aspicies illic positos ex ordine *fratres*,
  quos studium cunctos euigilauit idem.
cetera turba palam titulos ostendet apertos,
  et sua detecta nomina fronte geret;
tres procul obscura latitantes parte uidebis:
  sic quoque,[20] quod nemo nescit, amare docent;
hos tu uel fugias, uel, si satis oris habebis,
  Oedipodas facito Telegonosque uoces.
deque tribus, moneo, *si qua est tibi cura parentis*,
  ne quemquam, quamuis ipse docebit, ames.
sunt quoque *mutatae*, ter quinque uolumina, *formae*,
  nuper ab exequiis carmina rapta meis.
his mando dicas, inter *mutata* referri
  fortunae uultum *corpora* posse meae,
namque ea dissimilis subito est effecta priori,
  flendaque nunc, aliquo tempore laeta fuit.

But when you have been welcomed into the innermost part of our house and you have reached your home, the curved book-containers, you will see your brothers placed there in order, for all of whom the same enthusiasm burned the midnight oil. Most members of the crowd will show their titles openly, for all to see, and will bear their names on their uncovered scroll-ends; but you will see three hiding, far off, in a dark spot: and as everyone knows, even so these teach how to love. You should flee from these or, if you have a strong enough voice, you should be sure to call them Oedipuses and Telegonuses. And I advise you, if you care for your father at all, do not love any of the three, though the book itself will instruct you to do so. You will also find there the changed shapes, thrice five books, verses recently snatched from my funeral pyre. I bid you to tell them that the image of my fate can be found among the changed forms, for my fate has suddenly been made different from what it was before, and is lamentable now, though once it was happy.

---

20. *sic quoque* is Bentley's emendation for *hi qui* (or *hi quoque*); cf. Luck 1977 ad loc. Owen prints Vogel's emendation *hi quia*.

Most of them, says the poet, will be recognizable from their prominent *tituli* (109); only three will be hiding themselves, the three who appear to be the cause of their father's demise (presumably an allusion to the three books of the *Ars amatoria*), and they should therefore be carefully avoided. The poet then draws special attention to the fifteen books of the *Metamorphoses* and again writes himself into his poetry, asserting that the dramatic change in his circumstances entitles him to be included among the changed forms of the poem—but the change Ovid describes is emotional rather than physical, since what was once a source of pleasure now causes pain (*flendaque nunc . . . laeta fuit*, 122).

The imagery of family resemblance and of the everyday intimacy of fathers with their children is strong throughout this passage. Stephen Hinds, developing the ideas of Mary Davisson, has drawn particular attention to the function of the mythical analogies here, since the mention of a multiplicity of Oedipuses and Telegonuses immediately—and hyperbolically—calls to mind some of the most feared sons imaginable.[21] Both characters were of course parricides (Oedipus of Laertes, and Telegonus of Ulysses)—in other words, sons who betrayed the most profound of familial ties. Hinds's observation that both Oedipus and Telegonus, while surely parricides, were unwittingly so, is valuable and can be developed a bit further: Ovid's use of these mythical comparisons constitutes not a reproach so much as a recognition that even the three books of *Ars amatoria* are guiltless, and that he will not—cannot—disavow his paternity.

In *Tristia* 1.1, then, Ovid interweaves a number of different themes and analogies that we have already seen elsewhere: direct allusion to Homer as peer is balanced by the indirect suggestion that Ovid is Homer's offspring; and mythical allusions that cast Ovid either in the role of wayward son (Phaethon, Icarus) or in the role of afflicted father (Laertes, Ulysses). These variations are united by an overarching image of the book of poems as a stand-in for the poet himself, as both mirror and receptacle of his most deeply felt love and despair. The sense of intimacy thus created may well be felt to explain how it is that for so long the exile poems have been read as unmediated autobiography; but an analysis of its individual components reveals just how carefully constructed is the identity the poet projects as he writes himself into a literary tradition that begins with Homer.

---

21. Hinds 1985:17–21, following Davisson 1984.

IV. Absent Motherhood

The relationship between Ovid-*pater* and his poetic offspring is highly fraught; as his use of the Oedipus and Telegonus exempla in *Tristia* 1.1 suggests, the poet cannot entirely blame his sons for their treachery—but he can also not entirely forget the consequences, either. The affectionate dimension of this emotional conflict comes out clearly in another elegy, *Tristia* 3.14, at the close of the third book. In this poem Ovid again plays on the physicality of his embodiment in his books, asking an unnamed friend—apparently a supporter of Ovid's work (*uatum studiose nouorum*, "enthusiast of new poets," 7)—to sustain Ovid's "body" in the city (*retine corpus in urbe meum*, "keep my body in the city," 8) even as Ovid himself is absent. The poet argues that his offspring do not deserve to be punished: often an exiled man's children are allowed to stay in Rome (11–12). Ovid then employs a mythical analogy to describe his paternity that is superficially unexceptional, but that has striking implications: he compares his poems to the goddess Minerva, who was born without a mother: *Palladis exemplo de me sine matre creata* | *carmina sunt; stirps haec progeniesque mea est* ("following the example of Pallas, my poems have been created from me, without a mother; this is my lineage, my offspring," 13–14).

Ovid's exemplum draws on a familiar myth, known first from Hesiod: Zeus, having been warned by his Titan parents that the firstborn resulting from his union with Metis would overthrow him, swallows the pregnant Metis instead, thus absorbing the wisdom his mate had possessed; in due time, Athena springs from his head, and so can be thought to be motherless (*Th.* 886–900 and 924–26).[22] Of course, Ovid is on one level asserting his sole responsibility for his poetry—for both its brilliance and its fateful flaws—and simultaneously drawing close the intimate circle that joins him to his work; the absence of a mother figure—again, no Muse is intermediary—also allows Ovid to suggest—just suggest, and no more—that his relationship to his poetry is like that of Zeus to his firstborn daughter, and invites the notice of a bilingual pun on the idea of Metis/μῆτις/*ars*.[23]

---

22. West 1966 on Hes. *Th.* 866–900 provides details of the development of the myth and its various permutations.

23. Cf. Claassen 1990:112–13, who suggests two possible political readings of this exemplum; they have not, however, been taken up in subsequent scholarship on the poem.

The suggestion that Ovid is sole "parent" of his poetry offers a gender-less or disembodied view of Ovid's relationship to his work; but the physical reality of his books is reaffirmed shortly thereafter in the same elegy, as Ovid reflects on the causes of his exile: three of his books (presumably, the three books of *Ars amatoria*) are "infected" or "contaminated" as a result of their contact with him (*tres mihi sunt nati contagia nostra secuti*, "three of my children received my infection," 17).[24] The fifteen books of *Metamorphoses*, meanwhile, are also embodied, but in a different way: Ovid observes that they were "snatched from his funeral" (*carmina de domini funere rapta sui*, 20), and so have not benefited from the revisions he would have made under happier circumstances (*illud opus . . . | nunc incorrectum*, "that work . . . now inedited," 21–23).[25] The mention of a funeral is of course hyperbolic, but it suggests that exile is a sort of living death for the poet; and with the allusion to an object snatched from the funeral, Ovid draws on the imagery of the funeral pyre, so suggesting that these books were nearly burned.

This image is even more fully and physically developed in another exile elegy, *Tristia* 1.7. Here, the poet addresses a friend who possesses a portrait of Ovid; Ovid finds solace in the thought that the presence of his image will ensure that he is remembered even in exile (1–10). But a greater *imago*, claims Ovid, is that presented by his poetry, the *Metamorphoses* in particular (11–14). To illustrate the sense of identification he feels with his work, Ovid then describes how he included his own copies of the fifteen books when he was burning possessions before his forced departure; he now finds solace in the fact that other copies have survived, even though they lack the final revisions he would otherwise have made (*Tr.* 1.7.15–30):

> haec ego discedens, sicut bene multa meorum,
>   ipse mea posui maestus in igne manu.
> utque cremasse suum fertur sub stipite natum
>   *Thestias et melior matre fuisse soror*,
> sic ego non meritos mecum peritura libellos
>   imposui rapidis *uiscera nostra* rogis:
> uel quod eram Musas, ut crimina nostra, perosus,
>   uel quod adhuc crescens et rude carmen erat.

---

24. *OCD* s.v. *contagium* 2a and 2b.

25. Cf. Ovid's expressed dislike for the work of correction and emendation (*corrigere*) in *Epistulae ex Ponto* 3.9, discussed above.

quae quoniam non sunt penitus sublata, sed extant
  (pluribus exemplis scripta fuisse reor),
nunc precor ut uiuant et non ignaua legentem
  otia delectent admoneantque mei.
nec tamen illa legi poterunt patienter ab ullo,
  nesciet his summam siquis abesse manum.
ablatum mediis opus est incudibus illud,
  defuit et scriptis[26] ultima lima meis.

As I departed, with my hand I sorrowfully placed these verses in the fire, along with a good many of my things; and just as the daughter of Thestius is said to have burned her own son in the form of a log, and to have been a better sister than mother, so I placed my most vital parts, my undeserving volumes, on the greedy pyre, destined to die with me—either because I hated the Muses, as if they were reproaching me, or because the poem was still not fully grown, and rough. Since these verses were not completely carried off but survive (I believe they were written up in multiple copies), I pray now that they may live and may delight whoever reads them as products of no worthless leisure, and may remind him of me. They will not be able to be read with tolerance by anyone, however, who does not know that they are lacking my final touch. That work was taken away [from me] in the midst of being hammered into shape, and a final polishing was absent from my writings.

I draw attention first of all to the continuing imagery of embodiment used for poetry here, and in particular to its combination with the trope of filiation: Ovid's poems are his *uiscera* (20), and in destroying them he is like Althea, mother of Meleager, who killed her son by putting into the fire a brand she had been given when he was born, and which was an emblem or body double for the youth.

Several facets of this comparison invite our attention. In the first place, the allusion to Althea's destruction of Meleager sends us back to the aftermath of the Calydonian boar hunt as detailed in *Metamorphoses* Book 8. As we saw in that earlier discussion, in its transformation from the Homeric

---

26. Luck 1967 prints his own emendation *coeptis* for *scriptis*, which appears in several primary manuscripts. Luck's rationale for the change lies in parallels with, e.g., *Met.* 1.2–3 and *Tr.* 2.255–56. Neither reading affects my discussion, although *coeptis* may well be preferable, providing as it does a sharper contrast to *ultima lima*.

version, the story of the hunt, while remaining an inset narrative, has moved from the relatively brief compass of its original mention in *Iliad* Book 9 to take up a substantial and dominant position in Ovid's work, where only the presence of Phoenix son of Amyntor among the hunters and the many-mouths *envoi* tendentiously assert the Homericity of Ovid's narrative. With the sequel focusing on Althea's destruction of Meleager, Ovid diminishes the tale's Homeric character almost to the vanishing point, as he takes a detail that is only briefly alluded to (and inconclusively) in Homer, Althea's unhappiness at the death of her brother(s) (*Il.* 9.565–72), and gives it center stage, substituting a tragic denouement for what had begun as epic-heroic travesty.[27] In fact, the fullest development of Althea's character appears to have been not in narrative epic but on the tragic stage. Fragments of several plays survive that focus on the aftermath of the Calydonian boar hunt, and Ovid's presentation of Althea's soliloquy, at more than thirty hexameters, exhibits many of the features we associate with tragedy.[28]

Of particular interest here, however, is not the content of Althea's internal debate but the interesting shift of setting that the generic transition enables. I refer here to the fact that, while the setting for the hunt is naturally out of doors (cf. *Met.* 8.281, *Olenios . . . per agros*; 329, *silua frequens trabibus*; 340–41, *nemus, et . . . | silua*), Althea's revenge is an interior phenomenon: she is apparently alone within the palace at Calydon when she hears of her brothers' deaths and begins her lament, and the interiority of her curse, delivered as a speech for which she is the only audience, is complemented by a further metaphorical withdrawal from outside to inside: the talismanic log (*stipes, Met.* 8.451) with which she was entrusted at Meleager's birth has been stored away for many years in the innermost regions of the palace (*ille diu fuerat penetralibus abditus imis*, "It had been hidden away for a long time in the innermost chamber," *Met.* 8.458), and she goes now to retrieve it so it may fulfill its fateful purpose.

---

27. Homer mentions a single brother (*Il.* 9.567), but Ovid uses the plural *fratres* (*Met.* 8.446); for the variety, cf. Hainsworth 1993 on *Il.* 9.524–605. See above, chapter 3, for a fuller discussion of this episode.

28. Euripides's *Meleagrus* is likely to have been a, if not the, major influence: see Hollis 1970 on *Met.* 8.445–525 and pp. 67–68, Bömer vol. 4, 1977:97–100, and Kenney 2011 on 8.445–525. For the fragments of Euripides's play with a useful introduction to the reconstruction, see Collard and Cropp 2008:613–31. Generally on tragedy in Ovid, see Curley 2013 (although Althea receives only passing mention).

The pronounced interiority of Ovid's narrative here, reflected in the transition from one model genre to another, and from an exterior landscape against which heroic (or heroic-burlesque) actions take place to an internal one where inner torment is complemented by isolation, is paralleled by the very movements of its sole character, as she withdraws to the hiding place of the *stipes*. Interestingly, in a discussion of the Althea allusion in *Tristia* 1.7 with which I began, Stephen Hinds has made an observation of coincidental relevance about Ovid's use of the word *uiscera* there to describe the *Metamorphoses*, the very poem that at one point he wanted to burn: "Nothing could more clearly emphasise the threat to its [i.e., the *Metamorphoses'*] survival—as recounted, one may add, in the center of this elegy devoted to it" (22). Hinds also notes that, in the midst of his acknowledgment of his work's vulnerability, Ovid alludes to "the middle myth of the very middle book" of the *Metamorphoses*.[29] In other words, if we think of the *Metamorphoses* as organized at least in part around clusters of inset narratives, the Althea episode can be thought of as at its very center, in its *penetralia*; and no Latin word better describes the very center of Ovid's embodied poem, I suggest, than *uiscera*, a term for the innermost and most vital parts of the body.[30] I also think that we may take Hinds's insight a bit further, for the use of *uiscera* in the Althea exemplum of *Tristia* 1.7 is a precise allusion to a moment in the Althea episode in *Metamorphoses* Book 8, when the overwrought mother underscores the intolerable emotional conflict that besets her by using it of the son she now curses: *"rogus iste cremet mea uiscera!" dixit* ("'let this pyre of yours incinerate my vitals!,' she said," *Met.* 8.478).[31]

This brings me to my second point regarding Ovid's use of the Althea exemplum, and of the word *uiscera*, in *Tristia* 1.7 to describe his intimate but highly fraught relationship to his poetry: the emotional conflict he describes is framed in terms suggesting that he experiences his relationship with his work not only as a father would, but in specifically maternal terms as well.[32] The word *uiscera* here is particularly striking: *uiscus* (usually used

---

29. Hinds 1985:21–27, on Ovid's poetic paternity in *Tristia* 1.7; and see also Knox 2016:179–81. The reading of *Tristia* 1.7 I offer here differs significantly from that proposed by Tissol 2005, who reads the elegy as an instance of generic disjunction and comic irony (see especially his comments on the Althea exemplum, 108–9).

30. Of course, as Christopher Brunelle has reminded me, *medulla* has a similar valence: see Rosenmeyer 1999:37–45.

31. For a feminist reading of this imagery that intersects with my discussion, see McCauley 2016:139.

32. For a rich and suggestive discussion of parentage metaphors, especially "poetic maternity," in ancient poetry, see Degl'Innocenti Pierini 2008:15–38. Her discussion, though not

in the plural) can mean "internal organs" in a general sense—as it does, for example, later in the same episode, as Meleager, unaware of his mother's destructive action, feels fire burning within him (*Inscius atque absens flamma Meleagros ab illa | uritur et caecis torrere uiscera sentit | ignibus*, "By that flame is Meleager burned, though absent and unaware, and he feels his vitals afire with unseen flames," *Met.* 8.515–17)—and, by extension, can be used to describe a person's offspring, or "flesh and blood."[33] Ovid often uses it to designate a woman's reproductive organs, her "womb," in particular, applying it in contexts that are both highly charged and strongly gendered.[34] It appears prominently, for example, in *Amores* 2.14, when the Ovidian lover laments Corinna's recent abortion by offering a list of all the great heroes who might never have been born (Achilles, Romulus, Aeneas) had their mothers chosen to abort them: at the close of this list, the lover implores women to explain their otherwise inexplicable actions and uses *uiscera* to describe the fetuses that they have destroyed: *uestra quid effoditis subiectis uiscera telis | et nondum natis dira uenena datis?* ("Why do you gouge out your own innermost organs with weapons applied, and give dread poisons to your unborn children?," 27–28). In the next couplet, the Ovidian lover alludes specifically to the filicides Medea and Procne, so underscoring the association between the destruction of children and maternity—an association perfectly reflected in the vivid violence, both emotional and physical, that the word *uiscera* can suggest. Thus, when in *Tristia* 1.7 Ovid refers to his books of *Metamorphoses* as *mea uiscera*, he not only evokes the painful—indeed, potentially fatal—infliction of violence on oneself and one's children that is most frequently associated in myth with women but also invites his readers to imagine him, if only momentarily, in a stereotypically female role: defenseless, alone, and overpowered by emotion, wishing to inflict harm on those he loves the most because they are his offspring yet whom he hates the most because of the ways in which they have caused, however inadvertently, his suffering.

The comparison of himself to Althea at first seems hardly complimentary: as an infanticide, she, along with characters like Medea and Procne,

---

strongly attentive to the gendered nature of this imagery, has inspired much of what follows in this chapter and the next.

33. The second of these is first seen in Ovid, at *Rem. am.* 59 (of Medea and her children: see *OLD* s.v. 5b), although the word's basic association with internal organs, including the reproductive organs, suggests that the potential extension was always quite clear.

34. For *uiscera* = "womb," Adams 1982:95.

is almost synonymous with (self-)destructive insanity. Here, however, she also serves as a valuable analogy—after all, as he acknowledges in *Tr.* 1.7.21–22, he was driven to destroy his work not only because of its imperfect state but also because he had come to hate the Muses, whom he identifies as *crimina nostra*, that is, his Muse-inspired poetry, and the source of the charges brought against him.

After recalling this earlier emotional conflict, however, Ovid devotes the remainder of the poem not to his destructive desires but to his continuing regret for the less than perfect polish with which he relinquished the *Metamorphoses*. As he moves past the Althea analogy, he also suggests an emotional transformation: from the vantage point of sorrowful exile, he characterizes his relationship to his work no longer as that of a high-strung mother—a mother prey to the extremes of emotion that would allow her to kill a child—but as that of a parent for whom regret is the dominant feeling: in imagining a new preface for the *Metamorphoses*, with parental sympathy he describes the books once again as "deprived of their parent" (*orba parente suo . . . uolumina*, 34).[35] When in *Tristia* 3.14 he compares himself to Jupiter, producing offspring without maternal involvement, therefore, I suspect we are to understand that Ovid is at pains now to present himself as a survivor of exile's trauma, no longer caught up in the throes of grief that accompanied his initial shock—now no longer a dangerous mother, in other words, but a somber father, able to manage, if only barely, in a transformed world not of his own making.

---

35. Claassen 1990:112 notes the emotional shift and suggests that it typifies the pleasure Ovid takes in exploiting the contradictions inherent in such personification. Her dismissal of the phrase *uiscera nostra* as a "casual reference," however, minimizes the intensity of the Althea exemplum.

6

Poetic Daughters

πάντες ἀγαπῶσι μᾶλλον τὰ αὑτῶν ἔργα, ὥσπερ οἱ γονεῖς
καὶ οἱ ποιηταί.

—ARISTOTLE, *Nicomachean Ethics* 1120b.13–14[1]

I. The Poetics of Paternity, Revisited

Ovid's characterization of his poems as his children and as each other's
fratres, and of himself as their parent, animates his relationship to his
work, suggesting that his poems live through him—and he, through
them—in a manner that not only evokes a poetic and metapoetic trope
but constitutes a declaration of the intimacy of the creative experience
and of the vulnerability and risk to which the creative artist exposes him-
self. It will be worthwhile, therefore, to pursue this characterization a
bit further, in the process considering the models for poetic paternity
that existed not only in the Homeric poems themselves but also in the
first centuries of Homeric reception, models with which Ovid was surely
familiar. In chapter 1, I characterized the Homeric scholarship that
emerged in Alexandria during the Hellenistic period as perhaps our full-
est and most explicit source, however fragmented, of this early reception,
and argued for the strong likelihood—indeed, the virtual certainty—of
Ovid's familiarity with this work; as we consider once more the poetic
genealogy of the Ovidian corpus, we turn also to another form that
this reception took, with the personification of the Homeric poems as
"Homer's daughters."

---

1. "All people love best their own creations, as do for example parents and poets."

II. Homer's Daughters

Sometime in the mid-seventeenth century, farmers digging in a field along the Via Appia, close to the area known in antiquity as Bovillae,[2] came upon an unusual object: a marble relief bearing a scene now commonly known as the "apotheosis of Homer,"[3] depicting in fine detail a scene divided into several planes, with the Muses, Homer, Zeus, Apollo, and a retinue of primarily female figures representing various personified poetic values (Arete and Pistis, for example) and the literary genres (e.g., Tragedy), as they prepare to offer a sacrifice (see Plate 1).[4] It is difficult to date the creation of this relief precisely. It is signed by its creator, Archelaus of Priene, but we know virtually nothing else about this artist. Scholars of Greek sculpture are unanimous in describing the work as Hellenistic, but they offer dates of production ranging from the third through the second century BCE.[5] The original function of this sculpture may well have been, as Paul Zanker and others suggest, to serve as a votive offered by a poet victorious in a poetic contest; how, when, and why it traveled to Italy can only be conjectured, although its possession by someone other than its donor in a place other than its intended destination strongly suggests the prestige value it would have held for the Roman who owned it. What matters most

---

2. About ten miles southeast of the center of Rome, on the way to Lago Albano; now a part of the municipality of Marino. See Ashby 1910:282–84 for seventeenth-century discoveries in the area. Sometime not long after the discovery of the relief, the Canon Archangelo de Spagna, hunting in the same area, found another remarkable object that attests to the prominence of Homer and the Homeric poems in the Roman world, and suggests the great social value of the luster reflected by the display of Homeric learning: a marvelously detailed marble sculpture depicting, in exquisite miniature, episodes from the Trojan War, accompanied with inscribed explanatory text; this object, known as the Tabula Iliaca Capitolina, now on view in the Capitoline Museums in Rome (Sala delle Colombe 83), is the most complete fragment among c. 20 such reliefs; of varying subject matter, craftsmanship, and detail, they are collectively known as the Tabulae Iliacae. I do not treat them here because, although they contribute broadly to our understanding of the presence of Homer in the Roman world, too little is known about the contexts in which they were created and used to allow us to draw either inferences from them or analogies to them in support of the current project. The fundamental publication of the reliefs is Sadurska 1964 (for the Tabula Capitolina, see Sadurska 1964:24–37); for recent descriptions and analyses of the many puzzles surrounding these *tabulae* and their interpretation, see the discussions by Squire 2011 and Petrain 2014.

3. The conventional description is not obviously substantiated by the sculpture itself but will be used here for convenience.

4. Now in the British Museum (BM 2191).

5. Pinkwart 1965 is the most complete analysis of the relief's stylistic features. Newby 2007 offers a convenient summary of recent arguments.

PLATE I The Archelaus relief (also known as the Apotheosis of Homer), BM 2191. © The Trustees of the British Museum.

for my discussion, however, is its visual effectiveness, offering, as it does, "a complete vision of Homer as the ancestor of Hellenic culture."[6]

A central part of this "complete vision" consists of the two small female figures who kneel on either side of Homer's chair. One, with a sword, is

---

6. P. Zanker 1995:159. There is a vast bibliography, much of it recent, on the relief; besides Pinkwart 1965, see Brink 1972; Cameron 1995:273–77; Zeitlin 2001:197–203; Newby 2007; cf. also Seaman 2005.

identified as the *Iliad*, the other, holding a ship's prow, as the *Odyssey*.[7] The slight stature of the two figures is noteworthy in a scene with so many other figures, male and female, on more or less the same scale as the figure of Homer. The figures on the same plane as Homer, but facing and approaching him, are preparing to participate in a sacrifice; the sacrificial bull stands behind a small altar, and a youth—presumably a ritual attendant, here identified as Mythos—stands immediately in front of Homer. This attendant is the one other prominently smaller figure on the relief besides the *Iliad* and *Odyssey* personifications;[8] his evident youthfulness in turn leads to the likelihood that the two small females are similarly meant to be understood as children—and not just any children but Homer's two daughters. Indeed, they are the figures to whom he is closest in the scene; the arrangement used by the sculptor suggests a veritable family grouping.[9]

The conceit that Homer's two great epic poems can be imagined as his daughters is not unique to the relief by Archelaus. Two Hellenistic epigrams are motivated by precisely this idea. The first of these, attributed to Antiphilus of Byzantium (first century CE), imagines the two girls as replying to a curious interlocutor (*AP* 9.192):[10]

---

7. Similar accoutrements equip the two female figures flanking Homer on a silver cup from Herculaneum, Museo Archeologico Nazionale di Napoli cat. no. 25301: the female on his right, *Iliad*, wears a helmet and holds a sword, lance, and shield; the female on his left, *Odyssey*, holds a ship's rudder and wears a traveler's hat. See Ruesch 1908:411. P. Zanker 1995:180 thinks the cup is of Augustan date; see also Pannuti 1984, who offers a detailed description of the object, an exhaustive (if aporetic) overview of what is known of its provenance, and and an acknowledgment that, though Alexandrian in technique, it may as easily be a Roman copy as an original, and so cannot be dated other than by the terminus ante quem of 79 CE.

8. I omit from discussion here the small child who appears on the far right of the lowest register but is almost hidden by the robes of the adults who stand with him. He is identified on the relief as (the personification of) Physis.

9. Beaumont has recently argued that the association of stature with age in Greek sculpture, though conventional, can be problematic: height and size "can be 'read' with caution as a clue to the age or life stage of a youthful figure, but should never be used as the sole determining factor" (1995:340 [2012:25]); see also *ead.* 1994, esp. 88–89. She notes that social status as well as the presence of both gods and humans in a given scene can account for the difference, and surveys a variety of types of visual evidence. Her caution is prudent; it is also worth noting, however, that she generally limits her discussion to evidence from Athens in the classical period (cf. also Beaumont 2012), and that there is a discernible change in approach with the growing realism of Hellenistic art: Oakley 2013:167 offers brief but useful comments; and cf. Lawton 2007:43. This is clearly the world of the "apotheosis of Homer" relief, in which the hallmarks of Hellenistic taste are everywhere evident. See further the discussion below.

10. I print the text as it appears at Gow and Page 1968:114, and my translation is a loose adaptation of theirs. In his interpretation of *AP* 9.192, Skiadas 1965:142–46 suggests that the epigram's author, Antiphilus, was actually looking at the Archelaus relief as he composed.

"Αἱ βίβλοι, τίνος ἐστέ; τί κεύθετε;" "Θυγατέρες μὲν
  Μαιονίδου, μύθων δ' ἴστορες Ἰλιακῶν·
ἁ μία μὲν μηνιθμὸν Ἀχιλλέος ἔργα τε χειρὸς
  Ἑκτορέας δεκέτους τ' ἆθλα λέγει πολέμου·
ἁ δ' ἑτέρα μόχθον τὸν Ὀδυσσέος ἀμφί τε λέκτροις
  χηρείοις ἀγαθᾶς δάκρυα Πηνελόπας."
"Ἵλατε σὺν Μούσαισι· μεθ' ὑμετέρας γὰρ ἀοιδὰς
  εἶπεν ἔχειν αἰὼν ἔνδεκα Πιερίδας."

"Books, whose daughters are you? What do you conceal?"
  "We are the daughters of the Maeonian, and learned in Trojan
tales. One of us tells of the wrath of Achilles and the deeds of Hector's
hand, and the trials of the ten-year war; the other narrates the burden
of Odysseus and the tears of noble Penelope over her widowed bed."
  "Together with the Muses, be gracious, for, ever after your
songs, all time has claimed to possess eleven Pierian Muses."

The second epigram is anonymous, and its date is unknown (*AP* 16.292).
In it, the poet addresses Homer; perhaps the epigram was intended to
accompany a portrait bust of the poet:[11]

Υἱὲ Μέλητος Ὅμηρε, σὺ γὰρ κλέος Ἑλλάδι πάσῃ
  καὶ Κολοφῶνι πάτρῃ θῆκας ἐς ἀΐδιον,
καὶ τάσδ' ἀντιθέῳ ψυχῇ γεννήσαο κούρας,
  δισσὰς ἐκ στηθέων γραψάμενος σελίδας·
ὑμνεῖ δ' ἡ μὲν νόστον Ὀδυσσῆος πολύπλαγκτον,
  ἡ δὲ τὸν Ἰλιακὸν Δαρδανιδῶν πόλεμον.

Son of Meles, Homer, you have brought fame for eternity to all of
Greece and to your fatherland Colophon, and you have fathered
these two girls from your godlike soul, writing the twin tablets
from your heart; one sings of the homecoming of much-wandering
Odysseus, and the other, the Trojan war of the sons of Dardanus.

The authors of these two epigrams are, like Archelaus, employing female
personifications to characterize the *Iliad* and *Odyssey*. Although both epi-
grams are brief, and the girls' presence here, as on the Archelaus relief,
does not invite sophisticated character analysis, it is clear that in all three

11. I follow the text that appears in vol. 5 of the Loeb edition of the Greek anthology, edited by
Paton 1916–18, and my translation is loosely based on his.

artifacts the imagery of paternity is meant to suggest a particularly strong tie, not only authorial but also emotional, between Homer and his "poetic offspring." Homer's daughters, I suggest, embody a genealogical loyalty or faithfulness that is beyond question; indeed, they can be imagined to bear a family resemblance to each other, and to their progenitor.[12]

But these depictions, such as they are, invite several tantalizing questions: First, who is the mother of these two daughters? Or are we to imagine a form of asexual reproduction akin to Zeus's fathering of Athena, in which the essential maternal role has been subsumed by an all-powerful father?[13] Perhaps we might imagine, using a certain poetic logic, that the Muses—or, at any rate, one of them—are to be imagined as the maternal progenitor(s);[14] but in the first of these epigrams at least, that possibility seems to be precluded by the suggestion in the last couplet that Homer's two poem-children are to be considered the tenth and eleventh Muses— sisters of the Muses, then, rather than their daughters.[15] The second epigram, too, suggests in its closing address that the Muses are companions of the Iliad and Odyssey, rather than their mothers. More helpful—and suggestive—is a Platonic analogy developed by Diotima in the Symposium. She is elaborating upon an explanation for the rationale behind human desire for the beautiful and uses the language of pregnancy and birth (κύειν, τίκτειν, etc.) to explain its workings. It is human nature, she says,

---

12. A second visual source (with some inscriptional support) for Homer's daughters is a statue group found in the Athenian Agora, dated by scholars to the reign of Hadrian. It appears to have consisted originally of at least three statues, of Homer and the personified Iliad and Odyssey, and has been linked to the discovery of a plinth with an inscription in which the speaker is the Iliad, and identifies herself as the offspring of Homer: see Thompson 1954:62–65; Seaman 2005:177–78. A third example, although unaccompanied by text, is the silver cup from Herculaneum mentioned above, n.7. Homer is at the center, with a female figure on each side. Finally, Homer appears flanked by two female figures, conventionally identified as personifications of the Iliad and Odyssey, on a Sidamara sarcophagus, fragments of which are shared by the Louvre and the Galleria Borghese: the head of the sarcophagus contains the Homer scene, while the two long sides depict the Muses. The Homer scene is in the Louvre; unfortunately, it has been far too damaged by the elements to be able to distinguish which of the two females is which. Shapley 1923 offers a detailed description with plates.

The characterization of poems as a poet's children occurs on a few other occasions: in the Greek Anthology, in AP 7.407.9–10 (Dioscorides), the poet in question is Sappho. Ael. VH 9.15 takes a different point of view, suggesting that Homer's daughter was poor because of her father's poverty.

13. See Hes. Th. 886–900 and 924–26 with West 1966 on Th. 886–900.

14. Cf. Catullus's description of his poetry as dulcis Musarum . . . fetus (65.3).

15. On the Muses as quasi-personifications of creativity, see Murray 2005; cf. also Kaster 1992 on Suet. Gram. 6.2.

to want to beget upon Beauty, not upon Ugliness; Ugliness is discordant with whatever is divine, while Beauty is in harmony with it (*Sympos.* 206c). She proceeds to explain that human nature, though mortal, naturally seeks to be immortal; and the only way it can do this is through generation (γένεσις), since only through generation can one leave something behind (207d). After offering some examples of the risks humans are willing to take to win immortal fame, she moves from the concrete guarantee of fame embodied in human descendants to pregnancy of the soul, a form of pregnancy that is specific to poets and inventors who, by joining with the beautiful, produce immortal virtue (209a):

"οἱ δὲ κατὰ τὴν ψυχήν—εἰσὶ γὰρ οὖν," ἔφη, "οἳ ἐν ταῖς ψυχαῖς κυοῦσιν ἔτι μᾶλλον ἢ ἐν τοῖς σώμασιν, ἃ ψυχῇ προσήκει καὶ κυῆσαι καὶ τεκεῖν. τί οὖν προσήκει; φρόνησίν τε καὶ τὴν ἄλλην ἀρετήν· ὧν δή εἰσι καὶ οἱ ποιηταὶ πάντες γεννήτορες καὶ τῶν δημιουργῶν ὅσοι λέγονται εὑρετικοὶ εἶναι."

"But those who [are pregnant] in the soul—for there are those," she said, "who in their souls rather than in their bodies conceive the things which it is fitting for the soul both to conceive and to bring forth. And what, you may ask, is fitting? Prudent intelligence and virtue generally: and of these things all poets indeed are parents, as are as many of the craftsmen as are said to be inventive."

"Everyone," says Diotima, "would choose to beget such children for himself rather than the mortal kind" ("καὶ πᾶς ἂν δέξαιτο ἑαυτῷ τοιούτους παῖδας μᾶλλον γεγονέναι ἢ τοὺς ἀνθρωπίνους," 209c); just a brief look at Homer, Hesiod, and the other good poets is enough to make one envy them for the offspring they have left behind, offspring that provide these poets with "eternal fame and memory" (ἀθάνατον κλέος καὶ μνήμην, 209d).[16] Diotima clearly implies a correspondence between Homer's poems and children: they constitute the offspring that guarantee Homer's immortal fame.

---

16. Curtius 1953:131–34 offers a brief overview of this and other personal metaphors in Western literature. Seaman 2005:178 notes the importance of Diotima's speech for the personification of the Homeric poems as daughters but does not explore its nuances. Degl'Innocenti Pierini 2008:25–35 offers a sophisticated analysis of Plato's genealogical imagery vis-à-vis poetry, focusing on the dynamics of maternity (as opposed to paternity) rather than the implication of the children's gender.

The intricate details of Diotima's pregnancy metaphor and its philo-
sophical interpretation do not concern us here (though they remain cen-
tral to technical arguments about Platonic metaphor);[17] rather, it is the
existence of the metaphor itself and its circulation outside of philosophi-
cal circles that invite singular attention.[18] It is a short step, after all, from
this genealogical metaphor to the Hellenistic texts and images mentioned
above, in which the metaphorical children *Iliad* and *Odyssey* are themselves
personified—and personified as girls who faithfully bear witness to their
father's inspired creativity (conveniently, both nouns, used as titles at least
since Herodotus's time, are feminine in gender).[19] And this brings me to
a second question: Why identify one's poems as girls rather than as boys?
I hope to have demonstrated in some detail in the preceding chapters how
productive the paternal metaphor can be, but the emphasis throughout
has been on fathers and sons, rather than on fathers and daughters. The
reasons for this are not difficult to guess: long before Freud undertook the
interpretation of gender identification and reinforcement in the human
psyche, the patriarchal character of Western societies, supported by phil-
osophical and protoscientific theorizing, found in sons the perfect mirror
of parental hopes and aspirations; daughters, meanwhile, were seen to
be comparatively weak, physically and emotionally, and their reproductive
function was the one true rationale for their maintenance and inclusion in
societies controlled by men.

But considered from another perspective, the virtues of the daughter
can be seen at least to match if not to outweigh those of the son. The son
can, and indeed must, be competitive, and indeed must strive to outdo
his father; as we have seen, narratives developing the implications of
this paradigm proliferate, from the epic education of Telemachus at one
end of the spectrum to the self-destructiveness of Phaethon at the other,
with multiple variations in between. The daughter, meanwhile, is seen to

---

17. Among many discussions of this metaphor and the role of Diotima generally, I note a
small sample that in turn will lead to a vast bibliography: J. S. Morrison 1964:51–55; Dover
1980 on *Sympos.* 206b1–207a4; Stokes 1986:161–72; Halperin 1990:esp. 137–42; Pender
1992; Sheffield 2001; Hunter 2004:88–92; Imperio 2012:38–41.

18. Although somewhat outside the boundaries of this discussion, it is worth noting that
the metaphor of poetic parenthood appears also in Callimachus, although it is not strongly
developed in the surviving fragments: μηδ' ἀπ' ἐμεῦ διφᾶͺτε μέγα ψοφέουσαν ἀοιδὴν |
τίκτεσθαι "do not expect a loud-thundering song to be born from me," *Aet.* fr. 1.19–20 Pf.
with Massimilla 1996 and Harder 2012 ad loc. (I adopt Harder's translation).

19. See below, chapter 7, on the ancient titulature of poems.

pose no threat, and to sustain the family through loyalty, obedience, and affection; in the best of situations, she internalizes her parents' desires and becomes a faithful reflection of her family's values.[20] The imagery of Homeric paternity as consisting of a father with two daughters thus suggests an early reception of Homer that captures both the fertility of the Homeric imagination, looking always to the maintenance of its future, and the view of Homer's readers who imagined his two "daughters" as the most faithful reflections—without distortion—of Homer himself. As we consider, therefore, Ovid's reception of Homer, together with the deep affection he feels for his own poetic children, I want to turn a final time to the theme of paternity as a source of creative energy—in this case, to an instance of poetic "offspring" that showcases the feminine dimension of Ovid's creativity.

III. A Poetic Daughter

In the discussion so far, paternity has loomed large, particularly in the form of the succession narrative that plays itself out repeatedly in Greek myth and through which Ovid encodes his identification as Homer's "son," worthy heir to the creative aspiration and immortal achievement of his poetic "father." Throughout this exploration of the poetics of paternity, the dominant and wide-ranging father-son narrative has combined a certain tension growing out of the conflicting pressures imposed by tradition and innovation—dangers expressed as waywardness or failure, or conversely as resulting in the father's eclipse by his son. I turn now to another branch of the poetic family and consider what happens when Ovid endows his poetic descendants with feminine features.

Gender has already played a role in Ovid's depiction of his own poetic paternity, although it does so in a severely circumscribed ambit: we have just seen how Ovid takes on both paternal and maternal roles in the exile poetry, using models of mythical parenthood to express alternatively his own destructive impulses toward his poem-children and his intimate embodiment in and through them. In *Tristia* 1.1, the poem-children too were gendered—Ovid tells his traveling *liber* to join his "brothers" (*fratres*, 107) in the bookcase back in Rome. I turn now to one other poetic child, the girl Perilla, to whom *Tristia*

---

20. Of course, tragedy in particular features a number of daughters who deviate wildly from convention and expectation, like Antigone and Electra; but their very exceptionality is central to the dramatic crisis they precipitate.

3.7 is addressed. As we shall see, Perilla is in some ways at least the very image of her father, and unerringly faithful to him—while giving us at least a momentary sense of a new and challenging context for poetic paternity in Augustan Rome.

But who is Perilla? The identity of this mysterious figure has been the grist in many a scholarly mill over the years—Ovid uses a brief simile, *utque pater natae* ("like a father to his daughter," *Tr.* 3.7.18), to describe his tutelage of her and so has led many scholars to conclude that she cannot be his biological daughter.[21] Is she a stepdaughter, perhaps? The question is made all the more difficult by our very limited evidence for Ovid's three marriages; could this be a daughter by his second wife, or is she a child not by him but of his current, third wife (cf. 3.7.3, *dulci cum matre sedentem,* where she is described as currently sitting at home with her mother)? Or could she perhaps be a freedwoman of Ovid's?[22] The difficulties are further complicated by the girl's name: not only is Perilla not a female name known from inscriptions, but it also conjures perplexing associations with two other characters, one apparently historical and one mythical. In describing the use by Latin poets of poetic pseudonyms for their mistresses, Apuleius (*Apol.* 10.4) reports that Ticida used Perilla as a pseudonym for a woman named Metella; this statement has been used in turn to elucidate another Ovidian passage, *Tr.* 2.433–38, in which Ovid mentions Perilla as the apparent pseudonym for Ticida's beloved.[23] The mythical alternative is the character Perillus, who constructed for the tyrant Phalaris the brazen bull in which he roasted his enemies; Perillus was its first victim.[24] While the tale may well be thought to have relevance to Ovid's situation, since he is destroyed by his own creation, it is hard to imagine a logical explanation for Ovid to evoke that myth here, in a poem praising and encouraging his

---

21. Lewis 2012 offers a valuable compendium of virtually all the modern arguments concerning Perilla's relationship to Ovid and proposes as an alternative the theory that Perilla is actually Ovid's third wife. I am indebted throughout this discussion to the first of these components; it will become clear, however, that I disagree with the second.

22. So Courtney 1993:229, suggesting that Latin is not Perilla's native tongue (see *Tr.* 3.7.12).

23. Ingleheart 2010 ad loc. provides a full discussion of textual problems with this passage and consequent challenges to interpretation. See also *ead.* 2012, whose discussion I return to below; and cf. Courtney 1993:228–29 and Hollis 2007:160–62, the latter of whom provides a particularly useful summary of what can be known, and what hypothesized, about Ticida and his work.

24. Pind. *Pyth.* 1.95–98 alludes to the tale, but its details, including the naming of Perillus and his fate, come to Ovid from Callimachus: see Harder 2012 on frr. 44–47, and cf. Hollis 1977 appendix iv.

protégée.[25] We thus have yet another conundrum—is Ovid using Perilla as a pseudonym for someone, and if so, for whom? Or does Ovid intend a strange allusion to Perillus and the Phalaris story? Or does the name imply some combination of both? And whatever conclusion we reach, what special meaning, if any, does the name hold?

In a recent discussion of this poem, Jennifer Ingleheart has suggested a somewhat different approach; my comments here are intended to complement her analysis, while offering a further refinement.[26] At the core of Ingleheart's discussion is the attractive idea, growing out of work on the topic by Maria Wyke, that Ovid's Perilla is actually not a real, historical woman but a poetic construct—a *scripta puella*, to use Wyke's term.[27] Unlike the fictional *puellae* of earlier erotic elegy, however, argues Ingleheart, the *scripta puella* of Ovid's exile poetry "has necessarily undergone a transformation in response to the advertised changes in Ovid's poetic agenda."[28] This transformation does not include a change of subject matter—in other words, Ovid uses this poem not in an attempt to dissuade Perilla from writing love poetry (Ingleheart finds the comparison of Perilla to Sappho [19–20] an important element in understanding this message)[29] but to encourage her to keep writing, in much the same vein as he had before exile, and to assure her that he will not be an informer (*index*) against her (71–72)—indeed, this is why he employs pseudonyms both for her and for other living poets in the exile poetry. And the name he uses, according to Ingleheart, actually entails wordplay: in the first three verses of the poem, "Ovid virtually spells out that the word *Perilla* is formed from a combination of the Latin words *per* and *illa*; . . . Ovid's partial deconstruction of the name makes the point that Perilla is a poetic construct."[30]

Whether or not we accept Ingleheart's etymological speculation here, her reading has many benefits aside from its liberating rejection of the laborious prosopography of Ovid's friends in exile: she invites us to see this poem as programmatic for the exile works, and detects a degree of

---

25. Ovid uses Phalaris as an exemplum of cruelty elsewhere, at *Tr.* 3.11.39–54, *Pont.* 2.9.44, and *Ib.* 437–40; cf. Skinner 1993; G. D. Williams 1994:144–46.

26. Ingleheart 2012.

27. The phrase *scripta puella is* used at Prop. 2.10.8; see Wyke 1987 and 1989 (2006).

28. Ingleheart 2012:228.

29. Ingleheart 2012:235–37.

30. Ingleheart 2012:230.

political defiance in Ovid's stance in the process—this *scripta puella* will carry on Ovid's work, safe thanks to pseudonymity from the censure of the *princeps*. She thus embodies his own determination to persevere even as he writes from the far limits of the empire. Surprisingly, however, Ingleheart does not have much to say about the father-daughter simile (*utque pater natae*, 18) with which I began aside from a brief suggestion, in a footnote, that Ovid is using the image of paternity in a metaphorical sense;[31] yet I think this metaphor has rich potential for interpreting the portrayal of Perilla in light of the poetics of paternity. I turn briefly once more to the exile poetry, therefore, to complete the "family portrait" Ovid creates throughout his works.

I propose that we maintain Ingleheart's suggestion that Perilla is a *scripta puella*—not his beloved, like the Corinna of the *Amores*, but a poetic embodiment for whom he feels paternal affection; indeed, we might well compare her construction to the exile poet's depiction of his wife in *Tristia* 1.6, a poem to which I shall return in the following chapter. Much like the Homeric Nestor with Antilochus, or Phoenix with Achilles, or Daedalus with Icarus, Ovid depicts himself as Perilla's guide and companion (*duxque comesque fui*, "I was both your guide and your companion," 18). He has taught her everything he knows about poetry; now, as she is about to move out from under his wing, he offers her his final words of guidance and encouragement (23–30):

> dum licuit, tua saepe mihi, tibi nostra legebam;
>   saepe tui iudex, saepe magister eram:
> aut ego praebebam factis modo uersibus aures,
>   aut, ubi cessares, causa ruboris eram.
> forsitan exemplo, quo me laesere libelli,
>   tu metuis poenae fata secunda meae.[32]
> pone, Perilla, metum. tantummodo femina nulla
>   neue uir a scriptis discat amare tuis.

While it was possible, I often read your poems to myself, and mine to you; I was often your teacher, often, your critic: either I provided an audience for your recently composed verses, or, when you

---

31. Ingleheart 2012:236 n.47.

32. I print the text of this couplet as it appears in George Goold's revision of the Loeb edition, A. L. Wheeler 1924.

stopped writing, I was the cause of embarrassment. Perhaps from the example by which my books wounded me you fear a fate that will follow in the footsteps of my punishment. Set aside your fear, Perilla: just don't let any woman or man learn to love from your writings.

He does not want her to stop writing out of fear of suffering his fate; rather, he assures her that, though she may not compose exactly as he does (*doctaque non patrio carmina more canis*, "and you sing learned songs that differ from your father's style," 12), her talent (*dotes ingeniumque*, "gifts and inborn ability," 14) is ensured by nature. This appeal to character and talent recalls Phoenix's words to Achilles, reminding the youth of the guidance he received from his tutor; it even more closely recalls Nestor, whose emphasis on μῆτις is central to the advice he gives Antilochus. And as with both those Homeric models, so here Ovid too grants Perilla her independence: as her poetic "father" is eclipsed by forces beyond his control, she is entrusted with the task of keeping the poetic fires burning—while avoiding those other fires that have almost destroyed Ovid: *tu quoque, quam studii maneat felicior usus,* | *effuge uenturos, qua potes, usque rogos* ("and you, for whom I hope that a happier exercise of enthusiasm awaits, flee from the pyres to come in whatever way you may," 53–54).

As we can see, one of Perilla's most distinctive features is fidelity—she can be relied upon to represent the interests of her poetic father faithfully, without striking out on a radically different course or attempting to surpass her father's monumental achievement. Indeed, she embodies that achievement and represents her poetic father's survival into the future. Through her (indeed, we might say *per illam*), the survival of his poetic values is guaranteed. With her creation, then, Ovid enacts a more successful model of poetic paternity than that which led to his exile and so inscribes himself into the poetic genealogy that began with Homer and his "daughters." In spite of the vagaries of circumstance and time that might otherwise isolate him from his own legacy, Ovid asserts a cautious trust in the poetic inspiration he has cultivated in Perilla. She is, of course, no *Iliad* or *Odyssey*; but like them, she supports the survival of this father figure into the poetic future. In fact, her status as his protégée allows Ovid to make a concluding assertion of the certainty of his survival (45–52):

> en ego, cum caream patria uobisque domoque,
>   raptaque sint, adimi quae potuere mihi,

ingenio tamen ipse meo comitorque fruorque:
    Caesar in hoc potuit iuris habere nihil.
quilibet hanc saeuo uitam mihi finiat ense,
    me tamen extincto fama superstes erit,
dumque suis uictrix septem[33] de montibus orbem
    prospiciet domitum Martia Roma, legar.

Consider my case: although I lack homeland, and you, and my
home, and those things which could be taken have indeed been
taken from me, I nonetheless am kept company by and enjoy my
own creative gift: Caesar has had no jurisdiction over this. Though
someone may end my life with a cruel sword, my fame will sur-
vive though I am dead, and as long as Mars's city, Rome, looks vic-
toriously from its seven hills upon the world it has tamed, I shall
be read.

Ovid's bold assertion of the guarantee of poetic immortality, framed as it
is here by words of cautious guidance, is ironically defiant, given his reluc-
tance to let Perilla follow in his footsteps as a composer of love elegy; but
in his defiance, Ovid recalls with the word *superstes*, "survivor," the endur-
ing nature of poetic paternity. This word has a broad range of applications
and does not strongly personify what it describes; Ovid himself had used it
early in his career in predicting the survival of his elegies, in a manner that
animates but does not personify his work as a living thing (*Am.* 3.15.20,
post mea mansurum fata superstes opus, "a work that will endure after my
death").[34] In *Tristia* 3.7, however, the embodied nature of his poetry's sur-
vival is made palpable by the contrast between it and the death by the
sword that Ovid imagines as a possible fate for himself (*saeuo . . . ense*,
49). Ovid's poetic offspring, his poetic "children," constitute his survival.
Perilla, like the exile poetry as a whole, has a small but important role to
play in the staging of this poetic triumph, as she carries the precepts of
Ovid into her own poetic future.

---

33. Owen prints *omnem* rather than *septem*, following several of the primary manuscripts;
septem is found in several of these manuscripts as well and is preferred by Goold in his revi-
sion of A. L. Wheeler 1924.

34. The *Amores* and *Tristia* passages both resemble the *sphragis* of the *Metamorphoses*, but the
imagery of Ovid's poetry as *superstes* appears only in the two elegies. See H. Evans 1983:18–20.

7

Homer in Love

neque tamen te oblitus sum, Laertie noster

—LIVIUS ANDRONICUS, *Odusia* fr. 4 Blänsdorf[1]

I. Repetitious Desires

In this study of Ovid's reception of Homer, I began with a single trope, the intense and complex relationship between a father and his son, and have in the ensuing chapters explored its development throughout the Ovidian corpus. As chapter 6 drew to a conclusion, a novel presence entered on the scene: with Perilla, we focused for the first time on a woman as a figure central to Ovid's poetics. The women who figured earlier in this discussion, notably the unnamed victim of the Ovidian lover's aggression in *Amores* 1.7 (chapter 2) and the poetically sophisticated—and subversive—Briseis of *Heroides* 3 (chapter 3) provided Ovid with different sorts of *tabulae rasae* with whom to explore the elegiac potential of Homer: they are animated in and through Ovid's elegy but otherwise are conveniently lacking in any sort of mythical history or what we might call, mutatis mutandis, an independent existence. Indeed, the same condition defines Perilla in *Tristia* 3.7: the exilic Ovid effectively invents her as he writes to her, using her "safe" poetic talents as a way to talk about his own failure to write safe poetry.

Not all the women who are featured in Ovid's poetry, however, are equally unencumbered by a past; and as Ovid reads and rewrites Homer, he revisits again and again Homer's female characters. Whereas the *puella* of *Amores* 1.7, Briseis of *Heroides* 3, and Perilla of *Tristia* 3.7 all assume literary personalities through Ovid alone, I turn now to a very different cast of characters, to Homeric women and episodes that carry with them what I am tempted to call an excess of "baggage": they do

---

1. "Nor have I forgotten you, our dear son of Laertes."

not appear briefly or namelessly, but display complex emotions and nuanced personalities in central episodes in the Homeric poems.[2] I shall suggest in this chapter that, rather than proving to be an obstacle to his creativity, these characters provoke in Ovid a particularly fertile productivity, one that takes a cue from the repetition that characterizes Homeric narrative.

As we have seen, in an arena of poetic competition that prizes whatever is newest, the attraction of repetition can be dangerous: while inviting comparison, repetition also can be tedious; its inherently double-edged character is nonetheless exactly what I think makes it particularly attractive to Ovid.[3] In the phraseology of Alison Sharrock, poetic repetition is thus "a problematic opportunity":[4] it not only imitates its model but through the very process of repetition comments upon it, allowing even the slightest differences to take on a new importance as it draws attention to its own novelty. Indeed, Ovid's exploitation of poetic repetition does not limit itself to Homeric models: by their very nature mythological narratives invite retellings, with new versions, new emphases, even new characters underscoring the difference. Stephen Hinds's analysis of Ovid's versions of the Medea myth, while not focused on the dynamics of repetition in and of themselves, demonstrates the way in which the very act of repetition can result in something entirely new;[5] while his focus is on Ovid's various treatments of the myth, the same might well be said of Euripides himself, who transformed both the past of Medea and her future with his radical presentation of her story. The remarkable malleability of Greek myth is at least part of what makes the intertextuality of ancient literature particularly intricate and finely wrought; the interaction of this malleability with Ovid's self-consciously "Homeric" repetition is nowhere more evident than in his appropriation of Homer's most prominent female characters. I begin not with Ovid, however, but with the erotic tradition of Homeric reception that Ovid inherited.

---

2. Not to mention in a wide variety of art forms created between the origins of the Homeric poems and Ovid's era, with many of which Ovid is likely to have been familiar. Although my focus here remains Ovid's reading of Homer, the inevitable involvement of other intertexts will make itself apparent.

3. Cf. also chapter 5, above, for the criticism of repetitiousness as a flaw of the exile poetry.

4. Sharrock 1994b:2.

5. Hinds 1993. See also Conte 1986:60–63, developed by Boyd 2010, on Ovid's repeated deployment of the myth of Ariadne. Generally on repetition in Ovid, see the collection of essays in Fulkerson and Stover 2016b.

II. Homer's Women

In the longest extant fragment of his elegiac poem *Leontion*, the Hellenistic poet Hermesianax offers a catalogue of ancient poets and the women they loved. The allusive nature of the catalogue is signaled by the entry for Hesiod,[6] who is said to have been filled with desire for an Ascraean girl, Ehoie: Hermesianax here plays with the famous opening words ἠ' οἵη ("or a woman just as"),[7] that were used by Hesiod in his poem *Catalogue of Women*, or *Ehoiai*, to begin each of the tales of mythical women whose love was the stuff of poetry (Herm. fr. 7.21–26 Powell = fr. 3.21–26 Lightfoot 2009):

> Φημὶ δὲ καὶ Βοιωτὸν ἀποπρολιπόντα μέλαθρον
>   Ἡσίοδον πάσης ἤρανον ἱστορίης
> Ἀσκραίων ἐσικέσθαι ἐρῶνθ' Ἑλικωνίδα κώμην·
>   ἔνθεν ὅ γ' Ἠοίην μνώμενος Ἀσκραϊκὴν
> πόλλ' ἔπαθεν, πάσας δὲ λόγων ἀνεγράψατο βίβλους
>   ὕμνων, ἐκ πρώτης παιδὸς ἀνερχόμενος

I declare that even Boeotian Hesiod, lord of all knowledge, after departing from his home, came in love to the Heliconian town of the Ascraeans; and thence, as a suitor of the Ascraean girl Eoie, he suffered many things, and composed in song entire books of catalogues, starting from the girl first.

Hermesianax imagines that the signature phrase used as a shorthand title for Hesiod's poem is not a practical unit of syntax but, rather, a woman's name; it is tempting to suppose that Hermesianax reached this conclusion (however archly) from the frequency with which the phrase appeared in Hesiod's poem, which is known to have extended to at least five books.[8] Hermesianax's mention of Helicon and Ascra, locales with which Hesiod identifies himself in the *Theogony* and *Works and Days*, allows us to see

---

6. Third in the list, preceded by Orpheus and Musaeus, followed by Homer and Mimnermus, etc., in accordance with a tradition of mythopoetic genealogy.

7. Asquith 2005:280 playfully suggests as a translation "Anne Other."

8. In the extant fragments of the Hesiodic *Catalogue*, however, the ἠ' οἵη-formula appears only nine times: Asquith 2005:272 discusses this surprisingly small number of examples. The likely content of each of the books, as well as the origins of the poem, is conveniently summarized by I. Rutherford 2000:82.

his summary of Hesiod's life and works as a conscious reinterpretation of
Hesiod as love-poet.[9]

Hermesianax's embodiment of Ehoie may seem so extreme as to bor-
der on parody[10]—but, in fact, none of the other examples in his catalogue
invites such a reading; rather, it is clear that he is simply developing a
feature of ancient literature that can be identified with the Homeric tra-
dition itself, namely, naming one's work after its central character.[11] In
a distinctly Hellenistic context, Hermesianax has taken the next logical
step by personifying genres and works as beloved women: we find poetry
books named after the women they memorialize, or thematize, as early
as Mimnermus (his *Nanno* and possibly his *Smyrneis*),[12] and this practice
becomes a standard feature of Hellenistic erotic elegy.[13] By the time we
arrive at the books of Latin elegy composed in the first century BCE, the

---

9. Caspers 2006:22–23 considers the Hesiodic character of Hermesianax's allusions and
discusses the textual difficulties in the passage; see also Hunter 2005:261–63.

10. Bing 1993:627–31 argues that Hermesianax is being ironic and "thereby satirizes and dis-
credits" (631) contemporary conventions of the prose biography. I prefer to see Hermesianax's
intermingling of life and art as less pointed, though not necessarily less playful (perhaps the
characterization of him by Lightfoot 1999:32 as "a prankster" comes closest to the mark); but
without more contextualization my interpretation and Bing's are equally open to debate. For
strong scholarly reactions to Hermesianax, see also n.13, below.

11. Evident beginning with the *Odyssey*; indeed, the bT scholia are at pains to explain why
the *Iliad* bears its name, rather than being called the *Achilleid* (or *Achilleia*): πάλιν ζητεῖται,
διὰ τί Ἀχιλλέως ὡς ἐπὶ τὸ πλεῖστον ἀριστεύοντος οὐκ Ἀχίλλειαν ὡς Ὀδύσσειαν ἐπέγραφε τὸ
σωμάτιον. φαμὲν δ᾽ ὅτι ἐκεῖ μέν, ἄτε μόνως ἐφ᾽ ἑνὸς ἥρωος τοῦ λόγου πλακέντος, καλῶς καὶ
τοὔνομα τέθειται, ἐνταῦθα δέ, εἰ καὶ μᾶλλον τῶν ἄλλων Ἀχιλλεὺς ἠρίστευεν, ἀλλά γε καὶ οἱ
λοιποὶ ἀριστεύοντες φαίνονται· οὐ γὰρ μόνον τοῦτον οἵος ἦν δηλῶσαι βούλεται, ἀλλὰ σχεδὸν
ἅπαντας, ὅπου γε καὶ ἐξισοῖ τινας αὐτῷ. ἐκ τινος οὖν ὀνομάσαι μὴ ἔχων αὐτό, ἀπὸ τῆς πόλεως
ὀνομάζει καὶ τὸ αὐτοῦ καλῶς ὑποφαίνει ὄνομα; and cf. the introduction to *Iliad* Book 10
of Eustathius. West 2001:6–7 suggests that the title *Iliad* indicates that the locality of the
poem's earliest dissemination was the Troad, and that the poem was perceived as coming
from that area; he compares other poems' names such as *Cypria* and *Phocais*, promulgated
in the first place by poets from those regions. See also West 1999:365–66.

12. In the absence of solid evidence some scholars have suggested that Mimnermus's
Smyrneis was named for the city's founder, the Amazon Smyrna: see the convenient sum-
mary in Allen 1993:23–26.

13. Mimnermus's elegiac *Nanno* is generally believed to have been named for a beloved flute-
girl: see Posidipp. *AP* 12.168, with frr. 4, 5, 8, 8, 10, 12, and 24 *IE*², and Allen 1993:20–23.
Hellenistic examples include Antimachus's *Lyde* and Philitas's *Bittis* (but see below, n.21); cf.
also Nicaenetus of Samos's *Catalogue of Women*, Phanocles's Ἔρωτες ἢ καλοί, and Sosicrates's
(or Sostratus's) *Eoioi*. Bing 1993 suggests that this practice reflects the Hellenistic tendency
to look for details of autobiography in an author's works. Sommerstein 2005 surveys numer-
ous examples of such personifications, many in Aristophanes; see also Hall 2000; Imperio
2012. For general discussion of Herm. fr. 7, see also Cameron 1995:318–19 (including his
verdict regarding the poetic qualities of the *Leontion* fragment: "surely the silliest surviving

collapsing of one's love object and the poems written about her (the female gender continues to predominate, for a variety of culturally constructed reasons I shall not explore here)[14] is all but standard practice: from Gallus's collection of *Amores* to Propertius's *Cynthia*,[15] the book as written object and textual idea has become identified with its motive and/or theme. This should not, after all, be surprising: the conceit of the artist in love with his own creation, while perhaps most fully elaborated in Ovid's own Pygmalion narrative,[16] is clearly not new.

The next entry in Hermesianax's catalogue, paired with Hesiod, is Homer; in his case, the beloved is neither an embodied title nor a catch-phrase but Homer's most fully developed female character, Penelope (Herm. fr. 7.27–34 Powell = fr. 3.27–34 Lightfoot 2009):

Αὐτὸς δ' οὗτος ἀοιδός, ὃν ἐκ Διὸς αἶσα φυλάσσει
  ἥδιστον πάντων δαίμονα μουσοπόλων
λεπτὴν ἧς Ἰθάκην ἐνετείνατο θεῖος Ὅμηρος
  ᾠδῇσιν πινυτῆς εἵνεκα Πηνελόπης,
ἣν διὰ πολλὰ παθὼν ὀλίγην ἐσενάσσατο νῆσον,
  πολλὸν ἀπ' εὐρείης λειπόμενος πατρίδος·
ἔκλεε δ' Ἰκαρίου τε γένος καὶ δῆμον Ἀμύκλου
  καὶ Σπάρτην, ἰδίων ἁπτόμενος παθέων.

And this singer himself whom a fate from Zeus protects, the sweetest spirit of all those who serve the Muses, godlike Homer strove to fit to his songs the slender land of Ithaca on account of wise Penelope; and he settled on a small island while suffering many things for her, having left his broad fatherland far behind; and he

---

product of its age" [319]) and Caspers 2006, esp. 22–25 on the pairing of Hesiod and Homer. For a less judgmental approach to Hermesianax and his influence on Latin elegy, see the brief remarks of Farrell 2012:14–17.

14. Interested readers might begin with James 2003 and the bibliography she provides. On the predominance of feminine embodiments of personified abstractions in ancient thought, see generally Stafford 1998. For masculine names as titles of love poems, see the preceding note.

15. On Latin titulature generally, see the cautious discussion of the evidence by Horsfall 1981 (108–9 on the elegists). For Gallus's *Amores*, see Ross 1975:73; for Propertius's *Cynthia*, see Keith 2008:98–99. Wyke 1987 makes the case for Cynthia's objectification by (and subordination to) her poet: the *puella* is "a form of poetic production" (53), identified particularly with elegy.

16. Explored in detail by Sharrock 1991.

sang of the people of Icarius, and the people of Amyclas and Sparta, touching on his personal experiences.

With this conceit, Hermesianax is no longer being overly literal-minded; rather, through a kind of metonymy Penelope is meant to stand for Homer's poems as a whole—and not only the *Odyssey* but, as the references to Amyclas and Sparta (33–34) make clear, to the *Iliad* as well: Sparta is the home of Menelaus, and Amyclas is an ancestor of Helen (though it is worth noting that both of these geographical and/or genealogical references allow Hermesianax to avoid the explicit naming of Helen in the same context as his mention of Penelope).[17]

With these two entries, Hermesianax employs two different but related ways of identifying the relationship between a poet and his work as essentially erotic: in the first example, the beloved embodies Hesiod's genre and style, and in the second, the beloved is a metonymy for Homer's entire narrative, recast now as a narrative driven by the poet's obsession with a central female character. Hermesianax is of course using the elegiac genre to depict these loves; in portraying the first and greatest poets of Greek epic as subject to passion and as infusing their works with their own desire, he implies a subordination of epic to elegy, thereby inverting the standard hierarchy of genres.

III. Penelope

In Hermesianax's eroticized version of the Homeric poems, the poet is in love with Penelope; the poet himself, furthermore, is a replica of Odysseus, traveling far from home across the sea and enduring many things in his desire to reach his beloved (πολλὰ παθὼν . . . | πολλὸν ἀπ᾽ εὐρείης λειπόμενος πατρίδος, 31–32).[18] The love of the poet for his subject is thus metaphorically intensified: he is figured not only as her poet but as her husband. The boundary between biographical fact and narrative fiction is elided, as Hermesianax equates life with art, and vice versa; and while it

---

17. For the extremely murky place of Amyclas in Helen's family tree, see the helpful summary of the evidence by Gantz 1993:216. See Caspers 2006:23–25 on the Homeric allusions in the passage.

18. Caspers 2006:23–24 discusses these and other Homeric allusions. Bing 1993:628–29 wants to identify Homer instead as one of Penelope's suitors, intentionally postponing Odysseus's arrival home; but interpreting the parallels as between Homer-as-lover and Odysseus himself makes better sense of the passage.

may seem perfectly appropriate to reject out of hand Hermesianax's blurring of boundaries as either hopelessly artificial or embarrassingly naive, I remind my readers that there is in fact more than a kernel of truth to this elision in the Homeric *Odyssey* itself, where Odysseus takes on the role of poet and bard in Books 9–12, narrating to his Phaeacian listeners his travels after the war and his costly encounters along the way.[19] The most important internal narrator in Homer is Penelope's husband, Odysseus, who as storyteller mirrors the poem's external narrator, Homer; this suggestive interplay of the singer and his song in turn figures Penelope both as Odysseus's beloved and as Homer's narrative.

Ovid implies not just a similar but the very same blurring of boundaries when he addresses his wife in *Tristia* 1.6, thanking her for the continuing support she provides in his exile. To elevate her faithfulness, he compares her to several literary women—both those who represent the literary work of a famous love-poet and those whose own mythical stories celebrate them as exemplary wives. The opening couplet sets the tone, with its clear allusion to Hermesianax's *Catalogue of Women* (*Tr.* 1.6.1–4):

> Nec tantum Clario Lyde dilecta poetae,
> > nec tantum Coo Bittis amata suo est,
> pectoribus quantum tu nostris, uxor, inhaeres,
> > digna minus misero, non meliore uiro.

Not so dear was Lyde to the Clarian poet, not so much was Bittis loved by her Coan, as much as you, dear wife, cling in my heart, worthy as you are of a less miserable husband, but not a better one.

The opening words, *nec tantum*, neatly invert the Οἵην with which Hermesianax fr. 7 Powell opens[20] and which evokes its Hesiodic ancestor, the *Ehoiai*: Ovid thus swiftly establishes that, while he follows in the catalogue tradition, his intent is to innovate rather than to imitate. Ovid then uses the remainder of the first couplet to identify two such women and the poets who loved them: Antimachus's Lyde and Philitas's

---

19. Plunged into a sea of bibliography on the subject, one would do well to begin with Most 1989; Wyatt 1989; and de Jong 2001 on *Od.* 11.363–69.

20. Of course, we are dealing with a fragment, and what appears now as the "opening" line may originally have followed an introduction or even another catalogue; but within the framework of the poets' catalogue itself, Οἵην does introduce the beloved (and her poet) who must be first in the list, i.e., Eurydice (with Orpheus).

Bittis. Both couples are featured in Hermesianax's catalogue, at 41–46 (Antimachus and Lyde) and 75–78 (Philitas and Bittis), and both of the women named here are said to have given their names to books of poetry:[21] thus, when Ovid compares the wife about whom he is now writing with Lyde and Bittis, he establishes an analogy that is simultaneously erotic and literary.

After these opening comparisons, Ovid continues with a series of analogies intended to illustrate the significance of his wife's interventions on his part: she has been a sturdy beam supporting him in his fall and has kept him afloat after a shipwreck (5–8); she has kept the wolf from seizing him like prey from a sheepfold, and the vulture from pouncing on him (9–12). After several further couplets expressing abject gratitude, Ovid returns to mythological exempla, now drawn from the context of the Trojan War (19–22, 33–34):[22]

> nec probitate tua prior est aut Hectoris uxor,
>   aut comes extincto Laodamia uiro.
> tu si Maeonium uatem sortita fuisses,
>   Penelopes esset fama secunda tuae:
> prima locum sanctas heroidas inter haberes,
>   prima bonis animi conspicerere tui.

Neither does the wife of Hector precede you in upright goodness, nor Laodamia, companion to her husband when he died. If you had been allotted by fate to the Maeonian bard, Penelope's fame would be second to yours: you would have a place first among the sacred heroines, and you would be admired first for the goodness of your character.

---

21. There is, however, a general inclination among contemporary scholars of Hellenistic poetry to doubt that Philitas's *Bittis* was primarily an erotic elegy: see Lightfoot 1999:31–32; and cf. Knox 1993:66, "There is . . . every reason to believe that Philetas wrote a poem named after the woman he loved; the pressing question is whether it influenced Latin love elegy" (Knox concludes that it probably did not). It may be worth noting that Philitas and Antimachus *may* be mentioned together in Callim. *Aet.* fr. 1.9–12 Pf.: on the interpretation of these highly vexed lines, see Massimilla 1996 ad loc. and Harder 2012 ad loc., with their bibliographies.

22. The text as printed here follows the transposition of the poem's final couplet suggested by several textual scholars, following the text as it appears in an early printed edition: for arguments in favor of the transposition, see Luck 1977 ad loc.; see also Kenney 1965:41 and Hinds 1999:126. In any case, the precise placement of this couplet in the elegy is not crucial to my discussion.

Ovid begins with two women who represent symbolically the beginning and the end of the Trojan War: Laodamia, whose husband, Protesilaus, was the first Achaean to leap from the ships onto the Trojan shore and the first to die there;[23] and Andromache, who survives her husband, son, and the city of Troy itself; both are examples of loss and endurance.[24] Both also, it is worth noting, are wives; Ovid has thus moved subtly but importantly from the erotic exempla with which he opened to a set of examples that reflects even more closely than did Lyde and Bittis the nature of his relationship with his wife,[25] especially its underlying permanence.

As with the earlier exempla, Ovid establishes his wife's (and his own) ability to surpass these as well: *nec . . . prior* in verse 19 picks up the competitive note established in the opening line with the words *nec tantum*; "firstness" as the goal of competition is thus enacted on the textual level as well. This metapoetic theme is most fully developed with the next exemplum, however, in which Ovid compares his wife to Penelope: on the narrative level, Ovid thereby positions himself as Ulysses, the absent husband of a faithful wife; but on the metapoetic level, he casts himself as Homer (*Maeonium uatem*)—and following the logic of this conceit, his wife is his greatest literary love. The entire thought is tied together by the emphatic repetition of ordinals underscoring his wife's "primacy" (*secunda . . . prima . . . prima*).

Several scholars have commented on another intertextual dimension of this line, the allusion to Ovid's own *Heroides*: the suggestion in verse 33 (*prima locum sanctas heroidas inter haberes*) that Ovid's wife could be first among heroines had she had Homer to sing her praises is a gesture to the earlier epistolary collection, in which Penelope had indeed come first: the first of the *Heroides* purports to be a letter written by Penelope to her absent husband.[26] As we turn to this poem, I draw attention to its appropriateness as a starting place for at least two reasons: *Heroides* 1 is the earliest text in

---

23. Protesilaus's fate precedes the time portrayed in the *Iliad* and was narrated in the *Cypria* (fr. 18 *EGF* = fr. 22 *IE²*), but a summary of his story, mentioning his (unnamed) wife, appears in the Catalogue of Ships, *Il.* 2.698–702; cf. Gantz 1993:592–93.

24. Cf. Andromache's opening words to Aeneas at *Aen.* 3.315: "*uiuo equidem uitamque extrema per omnia duco.*"

25. Hinds 1999:124 suggests that this elegy is a proem of sorts to a cluster of exile poems that experiment with a new subgenre of spousal love poetry.

26. See Kenney 1965:39–41, developed by Hinds 1985:27–28 and 1999:126–28. Barchiesi 1992:51–55 offers a persuasive rationale for accepting the placement of Penelope's letter as first in the collection.

which Ovid develops a Homeric theme and/or character in real detail; and Ulysses is most noteworthy in this poem for his absence.[27] Penelope uses a form of the verb *abesse* ("be gone," "be absent") five times in this elegy, always in reference to Ulysses: *uirque mihi . . . carendus abest?*, "Must I be deprived of my absent husband?," 50; *uictor abes*, "though victorious, you are absent," 57; *ubi lentus abes?*, "Where, idle one, have you gone?," 66; *neue . . . abesse uelis*, "nor should you want to be absent," 80; and *omnes turpiter absens | . . . alis*, "Do you disgracefully encourage all by your absence?" (*omnes* alludes to the suitors), 93–94.[28] In chapter 1, I noted the prominence of Homeric characters or themes relating to the Trojan War early in Ovid's career, and in chapter 2 we looked at Ovid's impersonation of Diomedes in *Amores* 1.7; but only with the *Heroides*, each of which is voiced by a mythological heroine, do we fully enter the narrative world of Homeric epic. And the unifying premise of each of the *Heroides* is that the woman writing the letter is alone, filled with worry and doubt about her lover's whereabouts; all too often, she has been abandoned, or is in some other way the victim of a deception perpetrated by the man she loves. In *Heroides* 1, the missing lover is of course Ulysses, gone to the Trojan War twenty long years ago; as we shall see, his character thematizes absence and appears repeatedly in Ovid's poetry on the brink of departure, or gone already.

Scholarly studies of *Heroides* 1 have understandably focused attention on Ovid's depiction of Penelope and the closely connected issue of the poem's "Homericity."[29] There is general consensus—in which I participate—that Ovid has "elegiacized" Penelope, that is, has transformed her into an elegiac mistress on the order of Propertius's Cynthia, whose lament in elegy 1.3, provoked by her wayward and drunken lover, itself alludes to her Homeric predecessor.[30] Indeed, every allusion to the Homeric poems is transformed as it is translated into elegy: Troy is an

---

27. See Hardie 2002 for a general introduction to the poetics of absence and presence in Ovid (106–7 on *Heroides* 1).

28. Other language in the poem also adds to the picture, beginning with Penelope's plea in her opening couplet, *ipse ueni* (2), and extending to three adjectives alluding to her sense of abandonment (*deserto . . . lecto*, 7; *relicta*, 8; *uiduas . . . manus*, 10), and to her suggestion that Ulysses's absence is malicious (*in quo lateas . . . orbe*, 58).

29. See, e.g., Jacobson 1974:243–76; Kennedy 1984; Spoth 1992:36–53; Drinkwater 2007:369–75; and the commentaries of Barchiesi 1992 and Knox 1995.

30. Prop. 1.3.39–42, *nam modo purpureo fallebam stamine somnum | rursus et Orpheae carmine, fessa, lyrae; | interdum leuiter mecum deserta querebar | externo longas saepe in amore moras;* compare *Her.* 1.7–10, *non ego deserto iacuissem frigida lecto, | nec quererer tardos ire relicta dies; | nec mihi quaerenti spatiosam fallere noctem | lassaret uiduas pendula tela manus;* and cf. Knox

object of hatred to Greek *puellae* (3), and Penelope's lament is the refrain of abandoned lovers everywhere (*querela*, 70); even the details of matches on the battlefield—derived, presumably, from reports given by earlier visitors to Ithaca—are framed as causes of fear for a timid lover (13–22). What draws our attention now, however, is the way in which Penelope characterizes Ulysses's absence throughout her letter; while she is an elegiac woman now, Ulysses remains outside the poem, tantalizingly close but never quite present in the elegiac world. Of course, Penelope attempts to construct a convincing picture of an elegiac Ulysses, but his continuing absence and the eventual old age to which she imagines herself succumbing (note the final couplet: *certe ego . . . | protinus ut redeas, facta uidebor anus,* "to be sure, as soon as you return, I shall seem to have become an old woman," 115–16) are both indicative of the continuing, and productive, tension between the genres.

The first indication of this tension appears in the first verse, as Penelope gives Ulysses his defining epithet: *lentus.* Given his long absence, Ulysses may indeed be said to be "tarrying" (Knox's translation)—as will become clear later in the poem, the timing of this letter is fine-tuned, coinciding closely with Ulysses's revelation of his presence in the palace;[31] just as at the opening of the *Odyssey,* he has been gone for close to twenty years. In drawing attention to the temporal continuity between this letter and the opening of the *Odyssey,* Ovid also invites us to recall the opening epithet used in that opening by Homer, πολύτροπος; though the sense of the two words is very different, they share a common character trait in the variable meanings each word can have. Homer's readers are led to think from its context at the opening of the poem, in a summary description of his wanderings, that the primary meaning of πολύτροπος has to do with Odysseus's long struggles to get home; but a secondary meaning emerges soon thereafter, as the epithet's active sense, "ingenious" or "versatile," comes to define the hero's character.[32] The effect in Ovid is clearly not identical, but there is an analogous hint that the reader should revise first impressions: though the appearance of *lentus* in the opening hexameter acknowledges the passage of time, the pentameter that follows immediately thereafter makes clear the elegiac

1995 on *Her.* 1.9. See the discussion in chapter 1 of Propertius's modeling of epic elegiacization for Ovid.

31. On the dramatic time of the letter, see Kennedy 1984:417–18; Knox 1995: 87.

32. Cf. Heubeck in Heubeck, West, and Hainsworth 1988 on *Od.* 1.1.

context, and thus, the elegiac connotation of the adjective: Ulysses is characterized by Penelope as a "reluctant" lover, in language familiar from the world of elegy.[33]

In considering the relationship of Ovid's Penelope to Homer's, scholars have agreed that Ovid generally follows the Homeric poems closely; although in virtually each couplet of the poem Penelope uses the elegiac pentameter to redefine the genre of characters and events first identified in the epic hexameter,[34] the sequence of events she follows suggests that Ovid's Homeric frame of reference is all but unmediated by the Homeric cycle or other works treating the same main characters.[35] Nonetheless, several details of her letter stand out as "un-Homeric," that is, inconsistent with details in the *Iliad* and *Odyssey* narratives. The most egregious of these[36] occurs in verses 15–16, when Penelope, referring to a number of Greek warriors whose fates have been reported to her, includes the demise of Antilochus: *siue quis Antilochum narrabat ab Hectore uictum,* | *Antilochus nostri causa timoris erat* ("or if anyone was describing how Antilochus was defeated by Hector, Antilochus became a cause of great fear for me"). This is not consistent with the *Odyssey*, in which Antilochus's death at the hands of Memnon is mentioned (*Od.* 4.184–86); some scholars, therefore, have seen this as unusual evidence of Ovid's forgetfulness of Homeric details. Others postulate the existence of a non-Homeric model now lost, and yet others propose an emendation: in place of *ab Hectore uictum*, they would read *ab hoste reuictum* ("defeated by the

---

33. Barchiesi 1992 ad loc. offers comparanda; see also Knox 1995 ad loc.

34. Cf. Jacobson 1974:252 (describing *Her.* 1.15–22): "Each distich moves from the plains of Troy to the mind of Penelope. Hexameter recounts an event at Troy, pentameter reveals Penelope as its victim."

35. But cf. Porte 1976, with whom Barchiesi 1992 ad loc. expresses some sympathy. The one tantalizing exception here is the presence of Odysseus-in-love stories in Parthenius's *Erotica pathemata*; among the fragments are two such stories, those of Polymela (Parth. 2) and Euippe (Parth. 3); see Lightfoot 1999 ad locc. for details and possible sources. The scantiness of the evidence, however, does not offer an opportunity to draw parallels.

36. Three others are noted by Jacobson 1974:243–44: Ovid's Penelope says that she sent Telemachus to Sparta and Pylos (37–38, 63–65), unlike the Homeric Penelope, who is unaware of her son's plan to travel; Ovid's Penelope identifies Medon among the suitors (91), while in Homer he is a herald; and Ovid's Penelope indicates that the attempted ambush of Telemachus by the suitors took place upon her son's departure (99–100) and is not, as in the *Odyssey*, planned for his return; Barchiesi 1992 and Knox 1995 ad locc. give further details. See, however, the persuasive line of argument pursued by Kennedy 1984:419–22 (". . . deviations from Homer serve to differentiate Ovid's characterization of Penelope," 421). I hope to make clear in the discussion that follows that such apparent discrepancies also serve an important metatextual purpose.

enemy").[37] My own inclination, after weighing the options, is to think it not particularly logical that Ovid would incorporate a single non-Homeric allusion (or even a few) into his portrait of Penelope, especially since it would seem not to have any point; and like other recent readers, I find it equally hard to believe that Ovid was nodding here. Housman's emendation seems to me a satisfactory stopgap, but not the likely permanent solution—its very imprecision makes it stand out.

At the same time, it is perhaps worth noting that elsewhere in this elegy the subject of the mutability of memory (and of forgetfulness) is itself given a thematic place in the poem. Penelope lingers for several couplets on what she has heard about the *Doloneia* (39-44);[38] as befits a good wife, the version she recounts is decidedly partisan, revising as it does the hierarchy of responsibilities that appears in *Iliad* Book 10 so as to give primary credit for the mission to her husband rather than to Diomedes. Even as she does so, however, she uses the episode as an opportunity to reproach her wayward husband, addressing him with the words *o nimium nimiumque oblite tuorum!* ("o you, too forgetful of your family," *Her.* 1.41); three verses later, she comments with acerbity that he is sure to have displayed caution and acted in accordance with her counsel previously (*at bene cautus eras et memor ante mei*, "but previously, you were very cautious and mindful of me," 44). Although neither of the two recent commentaries[39] on this passage draws attention to the emphasis on memory here—in this case, indeed, emphasis on Ulysses's *selective* memory—alert readers will recognize that such imagery is frequently used to signal the presence of an important intertext or to invite the reader to entertain a metatextual reading.[40] If this language is in fact working this way here—and I suspect it is doing so—then what is the point? On one level, Ovid may well here

---

37. Even Barchiesi 1992 ad loc. is bewildered: "È veramente strano cho Ovidio non ricordasse la morte di Antiloco per mano di Memnone, . . . o, quanto meno, la presenza di Antiloco vivo e vegeto negli eventi che seguono la scomparsa di Ettore nell'*Iliade*." Jacobson 1974:243–49 surveys a number of attempts to explain the differences, either forgetfulness on Ovid's part or the use by Ovid of versions other than the Homeric; Jacobson himself thinks that the use of alternate models is likely. The proposed emendation is by Housman 1897:102–3, followed by Knox 1995 ad loc. (who comments that Housman's emendation captures the spirit if not the letter of what Ovid wrote).

38. I include verses 39–40 in the numeration here, although this couplet may well be interpolated: see Barchiesi 1992 on *Her.* 1.37–40 and Knox 1995 on 1.39–40. Its presence (or absence) does not have a bearing on my analysis.

39. Barchiesi 1992; Knox 1995.

40. Conte 1986:57–69; J. F. Miller 1993.

signal his determination to read the *Doloneia* as an integral part of the Homeric *Iliad,* in spite of the critique of the poem's Alexandrian editors;[41] on another, however, Ovid may be inviting his reader to notice that, even as Penelope expertly recounts details from the Homeric narrative, her occasional slips are reminders of the fragility of literary tradition, and of the poet's unique ability to narrate—or to suppress—the truth communicated to him by the Muses.[42]

Commentators regularly observe that Penelope's description of her isolation contains a very precise allusion to the *Aeneid,* and in particular, to Dido; but first, let us consider its broader context. In detailing the ways in which other Greek wives are better off than she, Penelope notes that they have become eager audiences for their husbands' reminiscences about the war (27–36):

> grata ferunt nuptae[43] pro saluis dona maritis;
> > illi uicta suis Troica fata canunt.
> mirantur iustique senes trepidaeque puellae,
> > *narrantis coniunx pendet ab ore uiri.*   30
> iamque aliquis posita monstrat fera proelia mensa,
> > pingit et exiguo Pergama tota mero:
> "hac ibat Simois, haec est Sigeia tellus,
> > hic steterat Priami regia celsa senis.
> illic Aeacides, illic tendebat Vlixes;   35
> > hic lacer admissos terruit Hector equos."

Young wives offer gifts of gratitude on behalf of their saved husbands; the husbands sing of Troy's fates, conquered by their own. Righteous old men and timid girls marvel, and every wife hangs on her husband's words as he tells his story. And now, once the table has been drawn up, one of them illustrates the fierce battles, and draws all of Troy in a bit of spilled wine: "Here flowed the Simois, this is the Sigeian territory, here once stood the lofty palace of old

---

41. See chapter 1.

42. Alison Keith has suggested *per litteras* that the metatextuality of the passage may include a "nod" to Hor. *Ars P.* 358–59, *et idem | indignor quandoque bonus dormitat Homerus.*

43. I follow Knox 1995 in reading *nuptae* for the transmitted *nymphae* here, although neither reading is central to this discussion.

Priam. There Achilles, grandson of Aeacus, had his tent, and there, Ulysses; here, even mutilated, Hector frightened horses into a gallop."

Implicit here is Penelope's envy of the other Greek wives, whose men have returned home and can now treat the Trojan War as a subject of song (*canunt*, 28): each retired soldier is seen as a Homeric bard manqué, narrating to his eager wife and other family members his own version of the events at Troy.[44] Penelope even imagines Homeric settings for these songs and uses the hexameter to depict warriors entertaining their audiences at the banquet table (*posita . . . mensa*, 31); as she moves to the pentameter, however, these Homeric feasts are transformed into the dinner parties of Roman elegy, at which adulterous wives and their lovers communicate by "writing" with wine on the table (*pingit et exiguo . . . mero*, 32). Communicating with wine is a technique of adulterous deception mentioned frequently in Ovidian (and other) erotic elegy;[45] its redeployment here as a means for illustrating epic narrative thus underscores the ironic mixing of genres in this scene.

In this context, Ovid's precise allusion to Dido adds to the generic tensions in *Heroides* 1. Book 4 of the *Aeneid* opens with an extended depiction of Dido's growing and dangerous passion: she has listened to Aeneas's narrative of the end of the Trojan War and his later travels through the preceding two books, two books that are in turn modeled on the four books of the *Odyssey* in which Odysseus narrates to the Phaeacians his post-Troy efforts to return to Ithaca (*Odyssey* Books 9–12). To characterize her now obsessive desire, Virgil describes Dido's wish to renew the banquet and to hear a repetition of Aeneas's story (*Aen.* 4.77–79):

nunc eadem labente die conuiuia quaerit,
Iliacosque iterum demens audire labores
exposcit *pendetque iterum narrantis ab ore.*

---

44. Cf. the stories told by Helen and Menelaus in *Odyssey* Book 4—their intent is to entertain their guests with fond memories (note Helen's τέρπεσθε, 239).

45. Tib. 1.6.19–20, 1.10.32; Ov. *Her.* 17.87–88, *Am.* 1.4.20, 2.5.17–18, *Ars am.* 1.571–72, *Tr.* 2.453–54.

Now as the daylight fades she seeks out the same banquets, and
again, besotted, she demands to hear the Trojan struggles, and
hangs again on his words as he tells his story.

Penelope transposes the imagery of verse 79 to depict not a doomed lover
but a wife pleased at her husband's return; the domestication of the image
of a woman "hanging" on the war stories of the man she loves (*narrantis
pendet . . . ab ore uiri*) is indicated by Penelope's use of the word *coniunx*
to describe the listener.[46] And to confirm the irony, the man imagined as
narrating his war stories is now anyone (*aliquis*, Her. 1.31) *but* Ulysses: the
Apologoi of the *Odyssey* have been depersonalized and stripped of their
deceptive charm to become the benign tales of other wives' husbands.

Penelope's imagined *aliquis* is not, then, Ulysses; then again, might
he not be? The dramatic time of the letter, supposedly composed upon
Telemachus's return, suggests that we are encountering her as she appears
in *Odyssey* Book 17, when mother and son are reunited and Telemachus tells
Penelope what he has learned on his journey (*Od.* 17.85–166). Readers who
know the *Odyssey* well will realize what happens shortly thereafter: Odysseus
arrives disguised as a beggar and enters the palace (17.336–41). Of course,
they will also know that at the moment of her husband's entrance, Penelope
is not in the hall with the suitors but remains above with her attendants
in her private chambers (17.492–506); and it is here that she expresses her
desire to meet the stranger about whom she has just heard (17.508–11). With
an exquisite sense of suspense, Homer then delays their encounter until
Book 19; meanwhile, husband and wife are in separate rooms of the palace.
The narrative embedded in *Heroides* 1 follows, for all intents and purposes,
the sequence of events in Homer; and it is really only later in her letter that
Penelope appears to anticipate this interview (*Her.* 1.59–62):

> quisquis ad haec uertit peregrinam litora puppim,
>   ille mihi de te multa rogatus abit,
> quamque tibi reddat, si te modo uiderit usquam,
>   traditur huic digitis charta notata meis.

---

46. Virgil's use of *pendet* is clearly modeled on Catull. 64.69–70, of Ariadne in love with
Theseus—another instance of the linking of narrative and destructive desire. Ovid's/
Penelope's use of *coniunx* to characterize the fortunate wife whose husband has returned
home may also, in the context of a reminiscence of the *Aeneid*, be intended to remind the
reader of the ambiguity that *coniugium* holds for Aeneas and Dido: see Pease 1935 on *Aen.*
4.172; and see above, chapter 3, on Briseis's use of *coniunx.*

Whoever turns his foreign stern to these shores departs from here after having been asked many questions about you by me; and a letter written with my fingers is entrusted to him so that he may deliver it to you, whenever he may see you anywhere.

Penelope is explaining how it is that she comes to be writing this letter: apparently, she writes it repeatedly, entrusting a copy to each and every traveling stranger (*quisquis*) who happens to stop in Ithaca, in the desperate hope that he will encounter Ulysses later in his travels and deliver the letter as intended. As Duncan Kennedy has observed in his reading of this elegy,[47] Penelope's explanation of her practice takes on particular point if we imagine that the very next recipient of a copy—*this* copy—will be Ulysses himself; thus, she provides a dramatic time for the letter as taking place a little later than the events of *Odyssey* Book 17, and just before the interview of *Odyssey* Book 19.

But I propose that it is worth pursuing the referential possibilities of *aliquis* just a bit further nonetheless, for reasons that will become apparent shortly. First, however, let us return to the content of that imagined disquisition that *aliquis* delivers with the assistance of a little wine spilled on the table to depict Troy (*Her.* 1.33–36; see above for translation):

> "hac ibat Simois, haec est Sigeia tellus,
>   hic steterat Priami regia celsa senis.
> illic Aeacides, illic tendebat Vlixes;
>   hic lacer admissos terruit Hector equos."

As commentators note,[48] these two couplets constitute an elegant variation on Aeneas's description of Troy at *Aen.* 2.29–30: "'hic Dolopum manus, hic saeuus tendebat Achilles; | classibus hic locus, hic acie certare solebant*" ("Here the band of the Dolopes had their tents, and here, cruel Achilles; here was the location of the ships, and here they used to contend in battle'"). Ovid expands upon the four repetitions of *hic* in the Virgilian lines with his own quadruple deployment of the demonstrative (*hac/haec/hic/hic*) and supplements these four uses of one demonstrative with two appearances of

---

47. Kennedy 1984:417–18.

48. Barchiesi 1992 and Knox 1995 ad loc.

another (*illic/illic*). Ovid adopts the Virgilian verb *tendebat* as an acknowl-
edgment of his model, using the same form in the same anachronistic[49]
context at the same point in the hexameter—but simultaneously the model
is trumped, as the verb evokes the presence not only of Achilles (*Aeacides*)
but also of Ulysses himself, the very person whose absence is so central
to this poem, and for whom Penelope longs. The version of events at Troy
that Ovid's *aliquis* presents thus both recapitulates the Virgilian original
and exploits the kind of variation that modern scholarship has come to
identify first and foremost with the poetics of Homeric verse: the use of
topical themes and formulaic expressions in the development of a narra-
tive particularly appropriate to the circumstances of its performance. In
the performance context of *Heroides* 1, Ulysses is the man of the hour, so
to speak; we may therefore infer either that *aliquis* has shrewdly adapted
his version of events to please Penelope in particular, or—just possibly—
that *aliquis* makes a point of mentioning Ulysses together with Achilles
because *aliquis* is talking about himself—in other words, that *aliquis* is
in fact Ulysses, narrating his past just as he does in the *Apologoi* of the
Odyssey.

A central—in some ways defining—feature of Homeric poetry is, as
I have already noted, repetition. In the excerpt under consideration here,
we can see Ovid drawing attention to his repetition, mutatis mutandis,
of a Virgilian moment, as he has Penelope imagine for us a multiplicity
of soldiers back from Troy telling essentially the same story, but each in
his own way, to adoring wives and entire households. Repetition is a fea-
ture of her own letter writing as well—as we have also already noted, she
apparently writes new versions of the same letter repeatedly to entrust to
any travelers who may visit Ithaca, in the hope that one of these itiner-
ants will in turn meet up with Ulysses. Ovid thus suggests an alignment
with Homer himself: that is, his repetition of both Homeric content and
Homeric style replicates Homer's own practice, even as Ovid exploits it to
introduce variations that are distinctively, and pointedly, non-Homeric.
The Penelope of *Heroides* 1 embodies this difference by offering us a ver-
sion of a Homeric character who profoundly challenges the decorum
of Homeric gender and genre expectations, giving voice to an elegiac
response to epic.

---

49. Knox 1995 ad loc.

IV. Calypso

The metatextual aspect of the variation we have just observed is itself redoubled when Ovid playfully recalls Penelope's letter elsewhere, in a context that, if anything, underscores the distance between husband and wife that is thematized in *Heroides* 1. This repetition occurs in Book 2 of the *Ars amatoria*, in the context of advice regarding the cultivation of rhetorical ability: the Ovidian *praeceptor* asserts that, while beauty is only skin deep (*Ars am.* 2.113–20), intellectual ability, rhetorical skill, and linguistic learning (*ingenii dotes*, "the gifts of inborn talent," 112; *nec leuis ingenuas pectus coluisse per artes | cura sit et linguas edidicisse duas*, "nor let it be a trivial concern for you to cultivate your heart through the liberal arts and to learn well two languages," 121–22)[50] have staying power. To prove his point, he introduces an exemplum: Ulysses, whose attractiveness even to goddesses (*aequoreas . . . deas*, "sea goddesses," 122: see below) was a result not of his (modest) physical appeal but of his way with words: *non formosus erat, sed erat facundus Vlixes* ("Ulysses was a good talker, albeit not good-looking," 123).[51] The *praeceptor* then describes how Calypso was hard-pressed to let Ulysses go, and took advantage of his fondness for recalling his exploits at Troy to delay him as long as she could (125–28):

> a quotiens illum doluit properare Calypso
> remigioque aptas esse negauit aquas!
> haec Troiae casus iterumque iterumque rogabat;
> ille referre aliter saepe solebat idem.

Ah, how often did Calypso grieve at his haste, and deny that the waters were right for rowing! She would ask again and again for the fall of Troy: he was wont often to tell different versions of the same story.

This Ulysses is a born storyteller, it appears—and as readers of the *Odyssey* already know well, from the *Apologoi* of *Odyssey* Books 9–12, from the

---

50. For *ingenuae artes* as a periphrasis for rhetorical training, see Janka 1997 ad loc.

51. The contrast between Odysseus's looks and eloquence is set out by Antenor at *Il.* 3.216–24. For the proverbial nature of the character's *facunditas*, see also Quint. *Inst.* 12.10.64: *[Homerus] summam expressurus in Vlixe facundiam et magnitudinem illi uocis et uim orationis niuibus (hibernis) copia [uerborum] atque impetus parem tribuit* (I print the text as it appears in Russell's 2002 Loeb edition).

numerous false autobiographies he gives of himself while in disguise at Ithaca, and from the narrative of his adventures that he delivers to Penelope herself at Book 23.306–43.

In an essay inspired by Kennedy's discussion of the Homeric intertext for *Heroides* 1, Sharrock offers a detailed discussion of this Homeric scene in the *Ars amatoria*.[52] As she observes, verse 128, *ille referre aliter saepe solebat idem*, "expresses the sum of *uariatio*, that great rhetorical and Ovidian technique."[53] In the context of Homeric repetition, we can take Sharrock's observation a bit further and see in the interplay of sameness and difference (*aliter . . . idem*) a concise reflection of Homeric compositional technique as observed by Ovid: like oral poetry itself, Ulysses's stories are always the same *and* always different—and so satisfy another feature of Homeric storytelling (and of Odyssean characterization) noted by Sharrock, namely, that Homer's Odysseus expresses an explicit dislike for telling the same thing twice: "ἐχθρὸν δέ μοί ἐστιν | αὖτις ἀριζήλως εἰρημένα μυθολογεύειν" ("'it is hateful to me to tell again a story told plainly,'" *Od.* 12.452–53). The relevance of this remark to the current discussion is guaranteed, I believe, by the fact that these are the very last words of Book 12—and follow immediately upon a glancing reference to his extended stay with Calypso. In only three and a half hexameters, he elides the longest single stop on his journey home with the suggestion that narrating it would be tediously repetitive, since he has already described it; and, in fact, he has used a precis of this episode to introduce the tale of his troubles when he meets Alcinous and Arete (7.244–66). Commenting on the metanarrative significance of Odysseus's final words in Book 12, de Jong observes: "Arriving at the point in his tale when he lands on Ogygia and stays with Calypso, Odysseus literally begins to repeat himself (447–9 = 7.253–5) and, realizing this, breaks off his story."[54] Ovid's Ulysses, on the other hand, appears to have learned how to vary his narrative just enough so that he (and his listeners) can tolerate some repetition: it is worth noting that, while Calypso's request is always the same

---

52. Sharrock 1987.

53. Sharrock 1987:407 n.4; see also Galinsky 1975:4; Janka 1997 ad loc.

54. de Jong 2001 ad loc.

(*iterumque iterumque*),[55] no response by Ulysses is ever precisely the same.[56]

And what exactly does Ulysses's narrative consist of, at least this time around? The *praeceptor* tells us that Calypso expressed particular interest in the *Doloneia* (*Odrysii fata cruenta ducis*, 130), and that Ulysses, who was building his raft and so happened to be holding a stick, used this implement to sketch in the sand a depiction of the war, setting out a general plan of Troy, defined by the river Simois and city walls (131–38):

> ille leui uirga (uirgam nam forte tenebat),
>   quod rogat, in spisso litore pingit opus.
> "haec" inquit "Troia est" (muros in litore fecit),
>   "hic tibi sit Simois; haec mea castra puta.
> campus erat" (campumque facit), "quem caede Dolonis
>   sparsimus, Haemonios dum uigil optat equos.
> illic Sithonii fuerant tentoria Rhesi;
>   hac ego sum captis nocte reuectus equis—"

With a light stick (for by chance he was holding a stick) he draws a work of art on the thickly packed sand of the shore, as she asks. "This" he says "is Troy" (he made walls on the shore), "and let's make this the Simois; imagine that these are my camps. This was the plain" (and he drew a plain) "which we made wet with the slaughter of Dolon, while late at night he watched, hoping for the Haemonian horses. There were the tents of Sithonian Rhesus; that night I rode back with the captured horses—"

Several details of this scene and the speech it records are worth our attention. The most obvious point of connection occurs in verses 133–34, where Ulysses explains the topography of his sketch: the first precise

---

55. Another Alexandrian footnote: see chapter 2, n.32. Here, Ovid acknowledges the repetition of *iterum* by Virgil in the description of Dido's inability to tear herself away from Aeneas's narrative at *Aen.* 4.78–79: *Iliacosque* iterum *demens audire labores | exposcit pendetque* iterum *narrantis ab ore*; cf. also *Aen.* 4.413–14, *ire iterum in lacrimas, iterum temptare precando | cogitur*. On the appeal of this scene to Ovid, see also above, n.46. On repetition as a site for intertextuality in this episode, see also Armstrong 2005:102–3.

56. Sharon James has pointed out to me the contrast between Ulysses's straightforward style of speech (short, simple syntactical units) and Calypso's convoluted and repetitious speech (see below on her words at *Ars am.* 2.141–42)—an ironic effect, given Ulysses's *facunditas*.

feature he names is the Simois, in a line opening that echoes the words of *aliquis* at *Her.* 1.33, *hac ibat Simois*. Now, however, because he is tailoring his narrative to meet the particular request of Calypso, he locates himself front and center in this landscape: rather than the palace of Priam mentioned in the version of *aliquis* (*Her.* 1.34), his camp is most important here. And Ulysses keeps himself at the center of the episode, offering a version of the *Doloneia* that is as self-centered as Penelope's was partisan in *Heroides* 1—he presents himself as leader of the scheme (*sparsimus; ego sum . . . reuectus*), and Diomedes receives nary a mention.

The fact that it is the *Doloneia* in particular that is singled out here is itself curious: are we to suppose that Ovid thereby notes that the Homeric Odysseus otherwise does much more talking than acting, and that thus this episode must be featured *faute de mieux*? Is the episode's theme of deception what makes it so interesting to Ovid, helping to flesh out as it does the duplicitous character of his Ulysses? I suspect that in fact both considerations contribute to Ovid's use of the *Doloneia*, as does also the additional evidence it provides of Ovid's interest in the authenticity of the episode, an interest I have noted previously. The fact that Ulysses himself now narrates a version of the *Doloneia* also associates this narrative with the tales Odysseus tells *in propria persona* in the *Odyssey*, and so flirts with a different level of doubt about authenticity—that is, the question is not simply whether the *Doloneia* was composed by Homer, but also whether the *Doloneia* can be subjected to the same sort of scrutiny as the *Apologoi* vis-à-vis truth and tendentiousness.

The Ovidian *praeceptor* also displays remarkable interest in one other feature of this scene, namely, that Ulysses just happens to have a *uirga* conveniently to hand to help him with his storytelling: the repetition of *uirga/uirgam* just before and after the penthemimeral caesura insists that we notice and consider its presence. Sharrock emphasizes the role of *forte* in the parenthesis *uirgam nam forte tenebat* ("The *forte* is surely disingenuous") and sees in the mention of a *uirga* a nod to the Homeric episode with Calypso, in which Odysseus, standing on the shore, fills the raft with rushes and willow switches as Calypso delivers the sail (*Od.* 5.257[57]).

---

57. The fact that Homer's use of the word ὕλη (in the line πολλὴν δ' ἐπεχεύατο ὕλην, *Od.* 5.257) provoked scholiastic comment may be nothing more than coincidence; then again, it may suggest one reason Ovid includes this detail, as a metapoetic gesture to the "source" of his narrative: LSJ s. ὕλη III.1, 2, 3, *OLD* s. *silua* 5b. On the sense in Homer, see Hainsworth in Heubeck, West, and Hainsworth 1988 ad loc.

Thanks to *uirga*, Sharrock suggests, "the whole scene becomes sharply specific."[58]

Sharrock also notes in passing that Ovid's phrasing recalls Virgil's description in the final book of the *Aeneid* of Latinus preparing to take an oath.[59] As Latinus speaks, he gestures to the *sceptrum* he is holding (12.206–7):

> "... ut sceptrum hoc" (dextra sceptrum nam forte gerebat)
> "numquam fronde leui fundet uirgulta ... "

> "... just as this sceptre" (for he happened to be holding a sceptre in his right hand) "will never sprout as a branch with light foliage ..."

The repetition of the word *sceptrum*, its inclusion on its second appearance in a parenthesis, and the line ending *forte tenebat* all appear to have influenced Ovid;[60] but as Jeffrey Wills shows, the intertextual associations of this repetition do not stop here.[61] In the first place, Latinus's oath clearly alludes to the branchless σκῆπτρον by which Achilles swears at *Il.* 1.234–35; in Virgil, the *sceptrum* is now not only branchless but sheathed in bronze (*Aen.* 12.210–11), a treatment that suggests association with another metallic branch, the golden bough. As Wills observes, Virgil's description of this branch is likewise highlighted by repetition, parenthesis, and rhythm of line ending: "*at ramum hunc*" (*aperit ramum qui ueste latebat*) | "*agnoscas*" ("'But you should recognize this branch' (she revealed the branch that was hidden by her garment)," *Aen.* 6.406–7). The Ovidian adaptation held by Ulysses takes us back to the Homeric original in some ways, omitting any mention of metallic sheathing or color; simultaneously, Ovid suggests a controversion of the Homeric claim that the branch will never again sprout foliage, using *uirga* to indicate just the sort of new and flexible shoot that even an old stump might produce. Wills offers a metatextual

---

58. The quotes are from Sharrock 1987:409.

59. Sharrock 1987:409 n.10.

60. Indeed, in his note on Virgil's repetitive parenthesis, Tarrant 2012 on *Aen.* 12.206 comments: "[T]his type of parenthesis is more often found in Ovid, where it gently mocks the narrator's fondness for unnecessary explanations." I suggest that Ovid's substitution of *uirga* for *sceptrum* may also owe something to Latinus's use of *uirgulta* in *Aen.* 12.207.

61. I follow Wills 1996:338–39 closely here; Tarrant 2012 on *Aen.* 12.206, however, expresses some skepticism about Wills's argument for the relationship between the golden bough and the *sceptrum* of Latinus.

interpretation of this important alteration: "The substitution of *uirga* for *sceptrum* is no idle variation. Rather, Ovid cleverly grafts a branch to the sceptre which could supposedly never bear them again. Here, the reflexive allusion focuses on Ovid's nimble, new branch on the allusive tree of poetry, an image latent in Virgil."[62] I suggest a further detail that may help to explain Ovid's attention to the Virgilian examples, noting the strikingly human terms[63] in which Latinus describes the branch from which his sceptre was made: *"cum semel in siluis imo de stirpe recisum | matre caret posuitque comas et bracchia ferro"* (" 'when once, after having been cut in the forest from the base of its stock, it is parted from its mother and has set aside its tresses and limbs beneath the iron blade,' " *Aen.* 12.208–9). In Ovid, the motherless branch has been "adopted" and given a new lease on life.[64]

This string of associations is indicative of the connection between intertextuality and metatextuality that is so frequent in Ovid. I suggest, however, that we not stop with the "tree of poetry" imagery proposed by Wills. Ulysses, it will be recalled, is using the *uirga* to help him tell stories of the Trojan War to Calypso—in other words, he is doing the work of a rhapsode (ῥαψῳδός), the Homeric performer whose title is linked in ancient folk etymology with the ῥάβδος ("staff") with which such men are said to have performed.[65] Ovid thus offers his readers a Ulysses who, like

---

62. Wills 1996:339. Yet another association suggested throughout this passage is the rhetorical use of the word *silua* as "raw material," as used by Quint. *Inst.* 10.3.17, and most familiar from its appearance as the title of Statius's collection of occasional poems. See also n.57, above.

63. Cf. Tarrant 2012 on *Aen.* 12.209.

64. Wills 1996:338–39 notes that the Virgilian *sceptrum* may also be connected to the one with which Hector makes a promise to Dolon (*Il.* 10.328), and that the Ovidian imitation, embedded as it is in an allusion to the *Doloneia*, may gesture to that parallel.

65. For the ancient (false) etymology associating the word ῥαψῳδός etc. with ῥάβδος, see Pind. *Isthm.* 3[4].56–57 Snell-Maehler with scholia, Callim. *Aet.* fr. 26.5 Pf. (= fr. 30.5 Massimilla 1996 = fr. 26.5 Harder 2012), and other sources discussed by Harder 2012 ad loc. On the etymology of ῥαψῳδός etc. as derived from ῥάπτειν, "to stich or sew together," see Patzer 1952 and Ford 1988. For the equivalence of the *uirga* and a rhapsode's staff, see also Apul. *Fl.* 9.

The Latin word *uirga* is also used by the Augustan poets of the *caduceus* carried by Mercury: Virg. *Aen.* 4.242 (with Pease 1935 ad loc.); Hor. *Carm.* 1.10.18 and 1.24.16 (with Nisbet and Hubbard 1970 ad locc.), presumably translating Homer's ῥάβδος (*Il.* 24.344–45 and *Od.* 5.47–48). Ovid's redeployment of *uirga* = *caduceus* in an episode near the end of *Metamorphoses* Book 1, in which Mercury is sent by Jupiter to distract Argus from monitoring Io, may also have metatextual connotations. Ovid mentions Mercury's *uirga* three times, twice near the opening of the scene (*Met.* 1.671 and 675) and once at its climax, just before

his Homeric prototype, knows the stories so well that he can perform them himself; and this Ulysses becomes a figure for Ovid, performing his own distinctively original version of Homeric poetry and thereby challenging Homer himself for control of the corpus of epic story and song—only seconds later to destabilize even this assertion of authority with a description of how the visual aids created by the *uirga* to accompany Ulysses's story are in turn obliterated by the waves coming to shore (*Ars am.* 2.139–42):

> pluraque pingebat, subitus cum Pergama fluctus
>   abstulit et Rhesi sum duce castra suo.
> tum dea "quas" inquit "fidas tibi credis ituro,
>   perdiderint undae nomina quanta, uides."

And he was depicting more besides, when suddenly the wave stole Troy away and the camps of Rhesus, along with their master. Then the goddess said, "The waves which you believe will be trustworthy to you when you go—you see what great names they have destroyed."

Calypso comments on the untrustworthiness of the waves in the vain hope that she can keep Ulysses from leaving (and in the next couplet, the Ovidian *praeceptor* will use the transience of Ulysses's images in the sand to return to his ostensible theme, the transience of beauty); but we do not hear anything about Ulysses's reaction to the sudden termination of his narrative, as Ovid chooses to terminate this exemplum here and to return to general erotodidaxis.[66]

V. Circe

Ulysses's *facunditas* is fundamental to the exemplum of *Ars amatoria* Book 2. As I noted at the outset of the discussion of this exemplum, it opens with a reference to the goddesses who loved Ulysses (*aequoreas torsit amore*

Mercury beheads Argus (1.716). Between these two points Mercury takes up the panpipes and lulls Argus to sleep with the story of Pan and Syrinx—in other words, he becomes a (non-Homeric) rhapsode himself, all the while holding on to his *uirga* (1.675, *tantummodo uirga retenta est*).

66. It may be worthwhile to observe that the abrupt conclusion of this episode leaves the *uirga* in Ulysses's hand: he remains in possession of poetic power, and so may still be able to escape with words.

deas, "he racked the sea-goddesses with love," *Ars am.* 2.122). Ovid's use of the plural *deas* may be seen as simply a means to enhance Ulysses's non-physical appeal, but readers of the *Odyssey* already know that the Homeric hero did indeed have more than one divine lover in the course of his *nostos,* and will think of Circe, at least glancingly, here. Nonetheless, aside from a passing reference in a list of witches at 2.103, she never materializes in the *Ars amatoria;* and the abrupt conclusion of the exemplum strips the plural of its narrative potential.[67]

Then again, we might want to see in the plural *deas* a pledge or down payment of sorts—for Ovid does in fact somewhat later write a Circe exemplum to complement Calypso's, in the sequel to the *Ars amatoria,* the *Remedia amoris.*[68] It is tempting to think that, in this as in may other details, Ovid's goal with the *Remedia* is to suggest the completion of his career as an erotic elegist. Simultaneously, I suggest, he uses this opportunity to announce a new stage in his literary career and to anticipate the creative leap so aggressively foregrounded with the opening words of the *Metamorphoses, In noua fert animus.*[69] The Circe exemplum of *Rem. am.* 263–88 completes Ovid's reinterpretation of the women of the *Odyssey,* demonstrating even more strongly than his Penelope and Calypso a desire to assert control of the narrative and authority as a poet in the Homeric tradition.

The context for the Circe exemplum is almost predictable: the Ovidian *praeceptor* wishes to assert the scientific efficacy of his instruction, and in order to advance the medical status of his authority he draws a contrast between what he does on the one hand and the sham and ineffective claims proffered to lovers by practitioners of magic on the other (*Rem. am.* 249–90). Whereas the lover of the *Amores* had endorsed the power of magic, and especially of *carmina,* both to enthrall lovers and to liberate them (see especially *Am.* 2.1.23–28),[70] the Ovidian *praeceptor* of the *Remedia* forcefully rejects *carmina* in favor of his own *medicina* (establishing in the

---

67. On Ovid's allusion to two goddesses, see also chapter 1, n.48.

68. Parts of the following discussion are based on Boyd 2016a; see also Boyd 2009:116–17. Both of those essays, however, are more broadly concerned with questions of genre and didactic poetry and do not focus on Ovid's Homeric poetics per se.

69. See chapter 4 on the Homeric associations of this opening.

70. See also *Medic.* 35–42 and *Ars am.* 2.99–106 for other didactic rejections of magic; while similar in function, neither is as fully developed as the *Remedia* scene, and neither includes a mythological exemplum.

process a playful tension in the duality of *carmen*, "poem, charm, song").[71] Circe is, together with Medea, the archetypal model of erotic magic—and unlike Medea she is a fully developed character of Homeric epic. Thus, in using Circe's magic as a foil to his own *medicina*, Ovid simultaneously challenges the authority of Homeric poetry.

Nonetheless, this is a curious exemplum. First of all, while the characters are ostentatiously Homeric, the plot is decidedly not: no trace of Ovid's version of the story is to be found in Homeric epic—or elsewhere in the epic tradition, for that matter. In the Homeric Circe narrative of *Odyssey* Book 10, Circe wields her magic to transform Odysseus's men; Odysseus himself, however, gains the assistance of Hermes, and with the *moly* plant is able to avert Circe's power. In the subsequent resolution of their confrontation, Odysseus wins Circe as his sexual partner, and she, her toxic powers now neutralized, restores his men to their human forms. They then proceed to stay with Circe for an entire year, until Odysseus's men remind him of the purpose of their journey and urge him to bring them home. Circe expresses no dismay at their impending departure; rather, she offers her guidance, informing Odysseus that he must first visit the Underworld; and when he and his companions finally set sail at the start of Book 11, Circe sends a favorable wind to speed them on their way. In Ovid's version, on the other hand, Circe is emotionally distraught at the prospect of Ulysses's departure and swears her undying love; she not only expresses a desire to be his wife (*coniunx*, *Rem. am.* 274–75) but even offers him power over her kingdom (*Rem. am.* 284). Her behavior is in fact far closer to that of Homer's—or Ovid's—Calypso than it is to that of the Homeric Circe;[72] and as we shall see, Dido provides a Virgilian intertext as well. At the same time, the contrast with the Calypso exemplum of *Ars amatoria* Book 2 is also pointed: there, Ulysses could not stop talking, but here, he never utters a word. Instead, in a manner that recalls the absent Ulysses of *Heroides* 1, this Ulysses is virtually absent from the exemplum, preparing as he is to depart momentarily from Circe's life. Several scholars have observed that this exemplum bears a striking resemblance in some ways to the *Heroides*, except for the fact that its addressee is at least technically

---

71. Cf. Sharrock 1994b:50–67 for a discussion of Ovid's self-identification as "Doctor Love."

72. Perutelli 1994 draws attention to a similarly bold, albeit much briefer, revision of Calypso by Propertius, in the latter's elegy 1.15.9–14; her passivity and unceasing tears, along with her assumption of features Homer had initially assigned to Odysseus, may well have inspired Ovid to portray a version of Circe modeled on Calypso. See also above, chapter 1.

present;[73] in the following discussion, I shall suggest that even this technicality is prefigured in the *Heroides* themselves. In fact, in many ways the Circe exemplum of the *Remedia* brings this discussion full circle, taking us back to the point at which we left Penelope in *Heroides* 1, awaiting the return of Ulysses. Her desire endures, as does her frustration—emotions replicated by both Calypso and Circe. Though seen periodically in his role as rhapsode, Ovid's Ulysses, on the other hand, is evanescent, repeatedly escaping the grasp of his wife and lovers. But before we consider the broader implications of this pattern for Ovid's Homeric loves, let us examine in some detail the scene with Circe and the expectations it both arouses and frustrates, beginning with the extra-Homeric depictions of Circe that are likely to have been familiar to Ovid's readers.

In the midst of a moralizing interpretation of Ulysses's adventures, Horace suggests that Circe is to be considered a *meretrix* (*Epist.* 1.2.25); but that interpretation, while long-standing, does not seem to be in keeping with the characterization of Circe that Ovid suggests here.[74] The visual record is similarly unhelpful: it is clear from the famous "*Odyssey* landscapes" found on the Esquiline and usually dated to the mid-first century BCE[75] that the Homeric version of their encounter was well known in its details. In Panel 6 of this series, Ulysses can be seen approaching Circe's palace and then compelling her to kneel to him as he threatens her with his sword; the scene is carefully modeled on the encounter of the two at *Od.* 10.321–24.[76] And Ovid elsewhere shows himself intimately familiar with the details of the Homeric Circe narrative: in *Metamorphoses* Book 14, she is featured as both a voracious lover (more often rejected than not, as in the stories involving Glaucus and Picus) and a vindictive wielder of powerful magic (as in her transformations of Scylla and Picus) in the inset narrative of

---

73. Barchiesi 2001a:12–18 (1984:82–93); Casali 2009:345–46. Both point to *Heroides* 7 (Dido) as particularly close, since in that letter Dido addresses Aeneas at length even as he scurries away to his ships.

74. Horace's Ulysses is a product of a long tradition of philosophical readings of the *Odyssey*: see R. B. Rutherford 1986. For a survey of the influence and reception of several episodes from the *Odyssey* in a range of ancient authors, see Kaiser 1964.

75. For a detailed description of the "Odyssey landscapes," see Biering 1995 (for the Circe panel, 81–90 and plates 13–15); for detailed discussions and interpretation, see Leach 1988:27–49; Ling 1991:107–11; and O'Sullivan 2007; and cf. Vitr. 7.5.2, mentioning Ulysses's travels as likely subjects for painters.

76. For a Pompeian fresco depicting Circe's obeisance to Ulysses, see Schefold 1962: pl. 171.1. The scene also appears on the Tabula Iliaca Rondanini, now in Warsaw (Muzeum Narodowe Inv. 147975): Sadurska 1964:61–64; Weitzmann 1970:40–41 and fig. 8; Squire 2011:401.

Macareus, who thankfully recalls Ulysses's success in controlling her and thereby in restoring his men to themselves (*Met.* 14.293–307).[77]

The version of Circe who appears in the *Remedia*, on the other hand, is docile and submissive; the magic that she wields so effectively elsewhere has no force here, where her emotions have the best of her. And her six couplets of direct address to Ulysses—the first such instance of internal direct speech in the poem—bring her closer to characters like Catullus's Ariadne and Virgil's Dido than to the Homeric Circe (*Rem. am.* 273–84):

> "non ego, quod primo, memini, sperare solebam,
>   iam precor, ut coniunx tu meus esse uelis.
> et tamen, ut coniunx essem tua, digna uidebar,   275
>   quod dea, quod magni filia Solis eram.
> ne properes oro: spatium pro munere posco;
>   quid minus optari per mea uota potest?
> et freta mota uides, et debes illa timere:
>   utilior uelis postmodo uentus erit.   280
> quae tibi causa fugae? non hic noua Troia resurgit,
>   non aliquis socios rursus ad arma uocat.
> hic amor et pax est, in qua male uulneror una,
>   tutaque sub regno terra futura tuo est."

"I do not now pray for what I hoped for at first, I recall: that you might wish to be my spouse. Yet nonetheless, I thought I was worthy to be your spouse, I who was a goddess, the daughter of great Sol. I beg you, don't hurry; I ask for a bit of time as a favor; what less can be wished for through my prayers? You see that the waves are stirred, and you ought to fear them: later there will be a wind more useful for your sails. What is your reason for flight? Not here does a new Troy rise again, no one again calls his comrades to arms. Here there is love, and peace—in which I alone am wounded—and the land is destined to be safe under your rule."

In fact, this version of Circe offers just the sort of speech we might expect (but are never permitted to hear) from Calypso in *Ars amatoria* Book 2; and as I noted in my earlier discussion of that passage, Calypso's repeated

---

77. For a detailed collection and discussion of the Homeric echoes in this episode, see Myers 2009 on 14.243–307 and *passim*.

attempts to delay Ulysses by asking about the Trojan War (*iterumque iterumque, Ars am.* 2.127) also recall Dido's repetitive desire for Aeneas's stories (*iterum . . . iterum, Aen.* 4.78–79). Both Calypso and Dido, in these respective scenes, are responding to the seductive power of language as employed by the men they desire; in the *Remedia*, however, only Circe attempts to use language to seduce, and in the event she is entirely, and pitiably, unsuccessful. Ulysses's susceptibility to the power of language is gone.

Indeed, the Ulysses of the *Remedia* exemplum more closely resembles Virgil's Aeneas than his voluble self as depicted in *Ars amatoria* Book 2; and it will therefore be worthwhile to pursue the involvement of the Virgilian intertext alongside the Homeric one here. As I have already observed, Circe's abandonment corresponds in many ways to that of Dido by Aeneas (as opposed to anything in Homer). In fact, almost every detail of Circe's speech in this episode, with the exception of her self-identification as a goddess and daughter of Sol (*Rem. am.* 276),[78] recapitulates the central themes of Dido's speeches in *Aeneid* Book 4, sometimes even implying a (chronologically impossible) awareness of Dido's arguments and their rebuttal by Aeneas—arguments that the reader has already seen in the *Aeneid*, but that Circe herself cannot know, given the relative mythical relationship of the *Odyssey* and the *Aeneid*.[79] Circe alludes to the marriage between them that she had once desired, but of which she now only asks him to deem her worthy (273–76) in terms that recall—or anticipate—Dido's assertion of a promise of marriage by Aeneas, his refusal to acknowledge it, and her eventual abandonment of the claim (*Aen.* 4.314–19, 338–39, 431);[80] Circe's request for only the gift of a little more time with Ulysses ("*spatium pro munere posco,*" "I ask for time as a gift," 277) briefly recalls for the reader Dido's far more ominous wish for some time to come to terms with her loss ("*tempus inane peto, requiem spatiumque furori,* | *dum mea me uictam doceat fortuna dolere,*" "I ask only for time, a rest and release from my madness, until fate can teach me how to grieve in defeat," *Aen.* 4.433–34);

---

78. And *filia Solis* is itself a Virgilian epithet for Circe (i.e., not used for Dido), introduced as *Solis filia* at *Aen.* 7.11.

79. On Ovid's predilection for such chronological play, see especially Barchiesi 2001b (1993).

80. Cf. also the suggestion made by Hinds 1999 in a different context and noted earlier in my discussion of *Heroides* 1, viz., that in the *Tristia* Ovid experiments with the creation of a new subgenre of spousal love poetry: above, n.25. On the ambiguity of marriage in the *Aeneid*, cf. Gutting 2006.

Circe's repeated mention of Ulysses's eagerness to leave (266, 271, 277) closely parallels Dido's sense that Aeneas is acting in haste (*"properas . . . ?"*, "do you hurry?," *Aen.* 4.310; *"quo ruit?"*, "where does he rush?," 4.429), and, like Dido, Circe uses the stormy seas to argue for delay (279–80 ≈ *Aen.* 4.309–10, 428–30). Circe assures Ulysses that her land is a place of peace and love, where she alone has suffered harm (*"in qua male uulneror una,"* "where I alone am grievously wounded," 283), thus employing the image of love as a wound (*uulnus*) so closely associated with Dido (*Aen.* 4.1–2);[81] and she offers Ulysses the opportunity to be its sole ruler (283–84), unaware of the fact that the offer of joint rulership by Dido is not enough to keep Aeneas in Carthage (*Aen.* 4.374; cf. 1.572–74).[82] With the pointed imperfect of *illa loquebatur* ("she was speaking," *Rem. am.* 285) at the close of Circe's speech, Ovid reminds us how much longer Dido's speeches were in the *Aeneid*; and the other half of that line, *nauem soluebat Vlixes* ("Ulysses was unfastening the ship"), summarizes in three words both the uselessness of Circe's talk and the determined intransigence of Ulysses, who here has nothing whatsoever to say in response to her pleas. The general effect is of a Ulysses who provides a "precedent," in epic chronology, for Aeneas's taciturnity and evasiveness. Finally, we should recall that a major episode of *Aeneid* Book 4 is devoted to Dido's vain resort to magic (4.504–21). Dido thus provides a model for Ovid's Circe that itself looks back to Homer's Circe, but with a disconcertingly defamiliarizing result: through the mediation of Dido, the Ovidian Circe becomes almost the antithesis of the Homeric Circe. Ovid's didactic appropriation of a Homeric love affair simultaneously alludes to Circe's epic provenance and transforms her almost beyond recognition.

Ulysses is transformed in this episode, too: stripped of speech, he is stripped of the elaborate narrative that sustains his heroic identity and makes him desirable in the first place (recall, again, that in the Calypso episode in *Ars amatoria* Book 2, it was Ulysses's talent as Homeric bard that served to keep him and Calypso enthralled with each other). There is no Mercury here to give Ulysses *moly*, no men for him to lead safely home.

---

81. And also, of course, appropriate in a negative exemplum in a poem entitled *Remedia amoris*.

82. See also Casali 2009:345–46, observing the irony in Circe's comment that there is no need for Ulysses to flee, since there is no new Troy here (*non hic noua Troia resurgit*, 281): Circe "inadvertently anticipates with extreme precision the (intertextual) future in the exact moment when her situation of ignorance is most acute."

There is no *catabasis* to undertake, no advice from Circe about how to navigate Scylla, Charybdis, the Sirens, and so forth; Ulysses simply becomes a bored lover, eager to escape now that the thrill is gone. In fact, this Ulysses is much better suited to erotodidactic elegy, and his escape from Circe is best seen as a model of the successful escape from love recommended throughout the *Remedia*.[83] Ovid's Circe and Ulysses episode thus presents us with an ironically successful model of the transformative power of *carmina* in the *Remedia*. In the Circe exemplum, the journey of Ulysses exists solely so that Ulysses can meet and then abandon her; the telos of Homeric narrative disappears in the process, and Ulysses finally does become *Oûtis*, "Nobody"—or perhaps we might better locate him in the company of the nameless *aliquis* of *Heroides* 1, always just out of reach.

In this discussion of Ulysses's women we have seen Ovid's reception of Homer as a process involving both detailed observation and transformative revision: Ovid's Homeric women are transmuted by their new genre into elegiac women, even as they recapitulate their epic careers. Ulysses, too, is transformed, his definitive *polytropia* taken almost to the point of no return. He is always on the move, always preparing for the next episode in his story, never content to stay within the confines of a single poem; he is the master of his own narrative, and thus a fitting figure for the poets Homer and Ovid.

I began this chapter with a consideration of the feminine gender of poetic form and the roles it assumes as lover or spouse of its creator-poet. The complex emotions thus evoked—erotic desire, spousal devotion, the heartbreak of loss—can be seen to function as tropes for the relationship between a poet and his creation; and Ovid, like many poets before him, maps this complexity onto Homer, using the women loved by Ulysses to embody his transformative love for Homeric poetry, enabling as it does a seemingly endless series of Homeric offspring. I turn now to the erotic Homer of Ovidian repetition that can be located in the divine sphere inhabited by Venus and Mars.

---

83. Brunelle 2002:61–62 offers a strong description of Ulysses as didactic role model.

8

Homeric Desires

Come ho già accenato altrove di sfuggita, ritengo che
l'arte allusiva abbia la sua giustificazione storica nello
stile formulare dell'epos greco: i tardi imitatori ales-
sandrini di Omero che, come Callimaco o Arato, ne
hanno ripreso emistichi e clausole ricorrenti che tutti
avevano nell'orecchio, hanno voluto con questo ripro-
durre letterariamente una caratteristica che aveva le
sue radici nella poesia orale.

—ALESSANDRO RONCONI, "Sulla tecnica delle antiche
traduzioni latine di Omero"

I. Repeat after Me

At the risk of invoking an excessive degree of metatextual circularity,
I think it is worth noting—a final time—that Ovid's poetry thrives on
repetition. "Repetition with a difference" is central to Ovidian inter-
textuality; whether following his Homeric model reasonably closely, or
even ostentatiously so (as with, e.g., Briseis's version of the Embassy to
Achilles) or appearing to diverge widely (as with, e.g., the presence of
Phoenix in the Calydonian boar hunt) or even to throw all tradition to the
wind (as with, e.g., the lovelorn Circe), Ovid relies on his ideal reader's
ability to appreciate both his mastery of Homeric tradition and his dar-
ing innovativeness. In the introduction to this book, I noted the relatively
new appreciation of Ovidian repetition among scholars of Latin poetry,
and we have since seen how Ovid can repeat a single, crucial detail to
evoke in his reader a complex memory of a text's past; it is time now,
therefore, to look at an instance of repetition on the grand scale, as Ovid
puts on display his intimate understanding of the power of repetition to
transform its subject.

Let us turn to Ovid's repeated used of a single and unique Homeric narra-
tive, the betrayal of Hephaestus by his wife, Aphrodite, and her lover Ares as
told by Demodocus at the Phaeacian court in *Odyssey* Book 8.[1] The Homeric
story was something of a cause célèbre in ancient criticism, its notoriety
going back at least to the Alexandrian scholars who questioned the Homeric
authenticity of the episode on the basis of its language and of its scandalous
portrayal of illicit divine sex.[2] I suggest that Ovid, aware of the controversy,
draws pointed attention to it in each of his retellings of the story and uses
the very phenomenon of repetition to establish the story's Homeric creden-
tials.[3] Recognizing that the story is an outlier in the Homeric poems because
of its introduction of sexual burlesque into the world of heroic epic, and
that repetition—of words, phrases, themes, and type-scenes—is a central
feature of Homeric compositional technique, Ovid singles out a story that
so perfectly anticipates his own boundary-testing inclinations (surely it is
no coincidence that this is a story featuring the amorous exploits of Rome's
divine ancestors; see further below) precisely in order to assert its Homeric
provenance. Simultaneously, he exploits its didactic resonance both to dem-
onstrate its "educational" value in Homer and to reinterpret its lessons for
new audiences.

Before I turn to these narratives, a final preliminary consideration is
in order: the treatment that the two Ovidian versions of the story have
received in modern scholarship. Given Ovid's predilection toward self-
repetition, it is perhaps not surprising that his two versions of the Venus
and Mars tale have received relatively little attention as a pair, aside from
being seen as a further instantiation of the generic play thoroughly ana-
lyzed by Hinds with respect to Ovid's two versions of the *Homeric Hymn
to Demeter*.[4] Each of the two has been the object of individual analysis in

---

1. This discussion of Ovid's two versions of the loves of Venus and Mars draws extensively on
Boyd 2016b; I thank the University of Wisconsin Press for allowing me to reproduce parts of
that earlier discussion. Here, however, I develop the implications further, drawing connec-
tions between this narrative and other episodes in the gods' careers as elaborated by Ovid.

2. Cf. Feeney 1991:30; Halliwell 2008:82 n.75; and see the discussion below.

3. In this chapter I focus on Ovid's two extended repetitions of the Homeric tale; he refers
to the episode very briefly on several other occasions in his collected works, including *Am.*
1.9.39–40, *Mars quoque deprensus fabrilia uincula sensit:* | *notior in caelo fabula nulla fuit; Met.*
14.25–27, *At Circe (neque enim flammis habet aptius ulla* | *talibus ingenium, seu causa est huius
in ipsa,* | *seu Venus indicio facit hoc offensa paterno)* | . . . ; and *Tr.* 2.377–78, *quis, nisi Maeonides,
Venerem Martemque ligatos* | *narrat in obsceno corpora prensa toro?* See also below, n.20.

4. Hinds 1987b. The one substantial exception to this lack of critical interest in a comparison
of Ovid's two versions is offered by Petersen and Weiss 1985:48–49; its authors, however, are

the contexts in which they appear: the version of the tale given in *Ars amatoria* Book 2 has, not surprisingly, been read as in some way a comment on or response to the Augustan marriage legislation,[5] and the version in *Metamorphoses* Book 4 has received some (generally passing) comment from critics interested in the inset narratives of the Minyeides.[6] The way these two narratives interact not only with each other but also with their Homeric model, however, has been for the most part overlooked; a central goal of this discussion, therefore, is to articulate an understanding of Ovidian repetitive practice as a form of reception. As we have seen, Ovid figures himself as a (wayward) heir to Homeric tradition from the outset of the *Metamorphoses*; here I will suggest that in repeating a distinctive Homeric tale not once but twice, Ovid appropriates Homer's poetic distinctiveness, recognizing in the flexibility of formulaic verse a nuanced means for innovation within a traditional medium. In other words, he takes a cue from Homer himself in innovating upon a tale that is at once both traditional and exceptional.

II. The First Time: A Song Worth Repeating

Let us begin with Homer. *Odyssey* Book 8 finds Odysseus in the Phaeacian court, an as-yet unidentified guest of Alcinous and Arete. Alcinous initiates preparations for a ship to provide the newcomer with safe passage and then announces a period of feasting and entertainment in the interim. The blind singer Demodocus is summoned and proceeds to sing about an episode from the Trojan War—strife between Achilles and Odysseus, and its interpretation by Agamemnon as fulfillment of a prophecy about the impending end of the war (*Od.* 8.72–82).[7] Hearing about himself and his old comrades-in-arms, Odysseus hides his head and weeps; Alcinous, noticing the stranger's emotional reaction, halts the performance and proposes a series of outdoor games (8.83–103).

---

primarily concerned with cataloguing similarities and differences along generic lines and do not attempt to offer an explanation for or interpretation of Ovid's repetitive practice.

5. See, e.g., Stroh 1979; Holzberg 1990; Sharrock 1994a:113–22.

6. See, e.g., Leach 1974; von Albrecht 1982; Janan 1994.

7. Hainsworth in Heubeck, West, and Hainsworth 1988 on *Od.* 8.75 notes that this story is not attested elsewhere and suggests that it has been invented to suit the demands of the current narrative. The story has been central to recent work on oral poetics and Homer: for an overview, see J. S. Clay 1983:97–106, 241–46.

Taunted by the king's son Laodamas and his friend Euryalus because of an appearance of age and weariness, Odysseus responds with both strong words and an impressive hurling of the discus; to restore the festive air, Alcinous reconvenes the feast and summons Demodocus again (8.131–255). This time, the singer offers a very different song, not about Troy but about the love affair of Ares and Aphrodite (8.266–366). After Odysseus's positive response to this song (8.367–68), he is showered with gifts from Alcinous and the other lords of Phaeacia, and is offered a bath and fresh clothes by Arete (8.386–457). In yet another round of feasting, the newly refreshed stranger asks Demodocus to tell another Trojan War story—this time, about the Trojan horse; again he is moved to tears as he recalls his younger self and the comrades he has since lost (8.470–531). Now, rather than shielding his guest further, Alcinous invites the stranger to identify himself and explain the reason for his tears (8.431–586).

From this brief summary, it is worth noting in the first place that the song of Ares and Aphrodite is the central of three songs performed by Demodocus; and while the first and third stories are familiar to Odysseus, and so the source of sorrow, the tale of Ares and Aphrodite is both novel and distinctively non-epic in its themes. At the same time, it can be seen to offer a variation on the theme of marital fidelity (and the tensions surrounding it) that is generally recognized to be at the core of the poem's plot and that will echo, in unexpected ways, in Ovid's revisions. Finally, before we proceed to examine Ovid's two versions of the tale, a more detailed look at Homer's treatment of the story will illustrate how Odysseus inscribes repetition into the story and so invites its reinterpretation. This in turn will prepare the way for a demonstration of how Ovid's two versions continue this process.

The Homeric story establishes its themes early. After the two gods and their love affair are named (*Od.* 8.267), the poet quickly and with little elaboration describes their first rendezvous at the house of Hephaestus, in secrecy but with the provision of many gifts (8.268–70). Straightaway Helios, having witnessed their union, reports it to Hephaestus, who immediately heads to his forge to craft a snare for the lovers (8.270–75). The poet then slows the pace of the narrative somewhat, to detail the anger of the divine smith and his suspension of a fine net around and above the bed—a net so finely crafted that it recalls nothing so much as the work of a spider (8.276–81). While Hephaestus pretends to leave for Lemnos, Ares hastens back and urges Aphrodite to have sex with him again; again they go to bed together, only to find themselves trapped and, indeed, immobilized by Hephaestus's ruse (8.282–99).

Hephaestus comes back to catch them in flagrante delicto; at this visual confirmation of what Helios had reported, he bitterly apostrophizes Zeus and the other gods, lamenting his lameness and inferior looks and laying the fault at his parents' feet for having engendered him. Hephaestus then declares his intention to keep the two lovers ensnared until he is repaid the bride price he gave Zeus upon his marriage to Aphrodite (8.300–320). Meanwhile, the other male gods gather at the threshold of Hephaestus's house and burst into laughter at the result of the divine smith's craft; the witticisms that they share about the sorry plight of Ares and Aphrodite culminate in Hermes's declaration of his willingness to suffer three times as much at Hephaestus's hands in order to share Aphrodite's bed (8.321–43). Only Poseidon refrains from the bawdy exchange; instead, he promises, in return for a release of the two gods, to pay Ares's debt if Ares himself is somehow able to elude Hephaestus's demands. Once freed, the two lovers swiftly separate, each going to a familiar abode—Ares to Thrace, and Aphrodite to Paphos, where she is bathed and honored by the Graces (8.344–66).

While Ovid, we shall see, revisits in interesting ways several features of this story, the critical reception has tended to have a somewhat narrower focus, shaped in the first place by Homer's ancient readers.[8] The apparent frivolousness of the story has itself been cause for concern, a concern exacerbated by the unseemly nature of divine laughter in the face of divine immorality; and the references to bride price (ἔεδνα, 8.318) and payment of restitution (μοιχάγρια, 8.332) have contributed to scholarly curiosity about laws surrounding ancient marriage and the punishment of adultery.[9] While the last several decades of Homeric scholarship have dispelled earlier concerns about the episode's Homeric authenticity and have provided both cultural and intertextual frameworks in which to locate the tale's playful exposé, the primary focus has been on the resonance of the story within the larger context of the *Odyssey*; the juxtaposition of an episode of divine infidelity that concludes with humor and no serious consequences for any

---

8. See Hunzinger 1997 for a succinct and perceptive overview of the way in which critical subjectivity, from antiquity onward, has shaped criticism of the episode.

9. Concerns about the morality of the story are expressed by, e.g., Xenoph. 21 B 11 DK and Pl. *Rep.* 390c; see also above, n.2, and see further below on allegorical interpretations. On the language of bride price and restitution, see Garvie 1994 on *Od.* 8.318–19 and 330–32.

of the parties involved is generally appreciated as a reverse image of events on the human level, where Penelope's ability to continue to fend off the suitors is increasingly threatened and Odysseus's vengeance for the suitors' disrespect will culminate in slaughter. Other features of Demodocus's tale, meanwhile, are treated piecemeal in recent commentaries but do not generally feature prominently in Homeric studies.[10]

A consideration of the Homeric story from an Ovidian vantage point, however, suggests that there is more to be said both about Homer's tale itself and about its reception by Ovid.[11] As we turn to Ovid, I want to draw attention to several details in particular in the Homeric version of the story: the brevity of narration of the initial seduction and of Helios's role as informant vis-à-vis the detail devoted to the net crafted by Hephaestus, including a vivid simile; the active character of Ares's pursuit juxtaposed to Aphrodite's passive albeit willing compliance; the vengeful frustration of Hephaestus's response to his wife's infidelity, made prominent by the use of reported direct speech;[12] the elaborate reaction of the gods to the display of Ares and Aphrodite in flagrante, ranging as it does from naughty humor to moralizing to implied disapproval; and the hurried parting of Ares and Aphrodite, followed by a bath that helps to restore the goddess's allure. A calculated mixture of suppression, compression, and/or expansion of each of these aspects of the Homeric tale is used by Ovid to make each of his versions appropriate to its context and thematically coherent; at the same time, Ovid's manipulation of the story can be seen to function as a form of comment upon narrative repetition itself, as Ovid draws attention to the slippage between Homer's story and his versions of it. One of these details, in fact, provides an apt starting point for this investigation, as it illustrates that, in choosing to make this Homeric tale a locus of play with the idea of narrative repetition, Ovid takes a cue from the Homeric poem itself. While the way in which Demodocus draws the story to a close, namely, with a concluding scene of Aphrodite in the bath,

---

10. Burkert 1960 is fundamental to the modern reappraisal of the story; subsequent studies, prominent examples of which are Braswell 1982, Newton 1987, C. G. Brown 1989, Olson 1989, and Alden 1997, focus on the story's paradigmatic function. Rinon 2006a offers a fine appreciation of the role played by all three of Demodocus's songs as emblematic of the poem as a whole. The essays by Bierl 2012 and Hunter 2012, appearing in a recent companion to the ancient epyllion, consider generic features of the tale.

11. For a notable exception, see Baldo 1986:124–30.

12. While I have not focused on narratological niceties in this chapter, de Jong 2001 ad loc. draws attention to this story's incorporation of shifting narrative levels.

surrounded by attendant Graces, serves to restore a sense of decorum both to the story and to the gods featured in it, the bathing scene also opens up the potential for an entirely new, yet repetitious, episode of desire and seduction: freshly bathed and anointed, and clad in beautiful garments, Aphrodite brings the story to a close with a hint of anticipation for her next rendezvous with Ares. In fact, a nearly identical description of Aphrodite's journey to Paphos, where she is bathed and anointed by the Graces and clad in beautiful garments, appears in the *Homeric Hymn to Aphrodite* (58–63), in a passage detailing her preparations for the seduction of Anchises.[13] Ovid does not include the Homeric bath in either of the versions of the story that appear in his verse, but he nonetheless seizes on the suggestion of an erotic afterlife that the bathing scene holds as he revises this story of a divine assignation so that it occurs not once but repeatedly, incessantly, and repetitiously in his poetry.[14]

III. A Homeric Lesson in Adultery

In the second book of the *Ars amatoria*, the Ovidian *praeceptor* is at pains to offer his (male) readers advice on how to remain in the good graces of a beloved. A central theme is not to care too much about a lover's unfaithfulness, and to avoid mentioning it even if it is brought to one's attention: once the story is out, all concern for shame is lost, and the resulting open secret can hurt only the one who has been betrayed in the first place.

To enhance the persuasiveness of this rather convoluted advice, Ovid introduces the secret love affair of Venus and Mars, and the consequences of its outing for Vulcan (*Ars am.* 2.561–600). Ovid opens the episode with a couplet that both identifies it as a story with a distinguished pedigree and introduces its three protagonists:

---

13. For the bathing scene as a Homeric type-scene, see Arend 1933:124–26. On bathing as preliminary to love, compare *Il.* 14.166–86 (with Janko 1994 ad loc.): Hera begins her preparations for the seduction of Zeus by cleansing herself with ambrosia, anointing herself, and adorning her body with beautiful garments. Both the Iliadic and Odyssean scenes are connected, via Aphrodite, with the bath the goddess takes before her seduction of Anchises in the *Homeric Hymn to Aphrodite* (*h.* 5.58–68); on the last of these scenes, see Faulkner 2008; Richardson 2010; and Olson 2012 ad loc. Hunter 2012:91–101 sees in the bathing scene a generic association with hymnic style; see also Baumbach 2012. On the role of the bathing scene as a symbol of renewal and purification, see Tracy 1997:370–72.

14. Brillet-Dubois 2011:112 suggests that there is already an ironic humor in Demodocus's transposition of the preparatory scene to the time after intercourse in *Odyssey* Book 8: "far from being tamed by humiliation, the goddess is replying by getting provokingly ready for another round."

Fabula narratur toto notissima caelo,
   Mulciberis capti Marsque Venusque dolis.

A most famous tale is told in all of heaven, how Mars and Venus
were trapped by the tricks of Vulcan, god of fire.

The literary provenance of the story is not explicitly identified as Homer;
rather, Ovid simultaneously gestures to his literary model and implies the
broad familiarity—indeed, the notoriety—of the exemplum with the adjec-
tive *notissima*. The rapid succession of three names in the pentameter like-
wise insists on immediate recognition, and the framing of the line with
the words *Mulciberis . . . dolis* offers a visual cue to the story of entrapment
that is told by Homer.

   With the next couplet, however, the narrative begins to diverge from
its Homeric model, as Mars is transformed into an elegiac lover (*de
duce terribili factus amator*, "from a dread warrior a lover was made,"
2.564); and the story itself is now framed not as a tale of shared desire
(ἀμφ' Ἄρεος φιλότητος εὐστεφάνου τ' Ἀφροδίτης, "concerning Ares and
beautiful-crowned Aphrodite," *Od.* 8.267) but of tormented passion on
the part of Mars (*insano Veneris turbatus amore*, "distraught by his mad
love for Venus," 2.563).[15] Fortunately for Mars, Venus is not a harsh
mistress, but knowing and indulgent (*nec . . . | rustica . . . difficilisque*,
2.565–66).[16]

   The elegiac cast of the narrative is underscored in the next couplet
(2.567–68), which opens with the exclamatory words *a, quotiens* ("ah, how
often"): this line opening features repeatedly in emotionally overwrought
elegiac lament (e.g., *Am.* 2.19.11–14),[17] and often is spoken by a lover in
distress—but here, the distress appears to be expressed by the *praeceptor*,
as he recalls for his reader the shameless fun made of the lame smith-god
by his faithless wife. Shaming laughter is a central motif of the Homeric
tale, when the male gods gather on Hephaestus's threshold to laugh at the
ensnared lovers; here, however, the joke is private, enjoyed by the lovers

---

15. With *insanus amor*, Ovid cleverly inverts a Virgilian image: at *Ecl.* 10.44–45, Gallus's
"insane love of Mars" (i.e., war) keeps him from his beloved; see Clausen 1994 ad loc.; cf.
Janka 1997 on *Ars am.* 2.563–64, and see chapter 9 on the similar elegiac "disarming" of
Mars in the proem to Lucr. Book 1 and in *Fast.* 3.1–22.

16. Cf. Janka 1997 ad loc.

17. See also Hollis 1977 on *Ars am.* 1.313, citing Shackleton Bailey 1956:304–5.

alone, and the absent and ignorant Vulcan is its butt. The next couplet (2.569–70) develops the difference: Venus is said not only to have laughed at Vulcan, but even to have imitated his limp in the presence of Mars— and, the *praeceptor* continues, this mimicry itself was charming (*multaque cum forma gratia mixta fuit,* "much charm was mixed with her beauty"). Her limp, humorous in itself,[18] is also a marker of the scene's elegiac affiliation: her "defective" gait recalls a pun that Ovid uses elsewhere as a virtual signature for his elegy, beginning with Cupid's theft of a metrical "foot" in the very first poem of his early work, the *Amores* (*Am.* 1.1.1–4), and deployed later in the same collection as a defining—and charming—feature of personified Elegy: *uenit . . . Elegia . . . | et, puto, pes illi longior alter erat . . . . | et pedibus uitium causa decoris erat* ("Elegy came, and I believe one foot was longer than the other; and the flaw in her feet was a source of beauty," *Am.* 3.1.9–12).[19] The resulting picture of Venus, while embodying the generic difference between epic and elegy,[20] also points to a fundamental difference between the lesson taught by the Ovidian *praeceptor* and the lesson to be gleaned from the Homeric tale: now, Vulcan is just as open to divine mockery as were his antagonists in Homer. Venus too has a very different part to play in the Ovidian narrative: whereas she was a compliant but generally passive recipient of Ares' gifts and love in the *Odyssey,* here she is a willing partner, eager to entertain her lover even at the expense of her husband.[21]

---

18. Jolivet 2005:8–12 notes that this is not a detail of the Homeric version but suggests instead that it points both to the Homeric description of Hephaestus's limp at *Il.* 1.584 and to a scholion on this line, where Hephaestus himself is said to be imitating Ganymede and Hebe. Jolivet also posits the intriguing hypothesis that the emphasis on imitation by both the scholiast and Ovid may be seen as pointing to the theatricality of the scene of Hephaestus and Aphrodite, mentioned by Lucian (*De salt.* 63) as the subject of a pantomime. Evidence exists also for a much earlier comic *Hephaestus,* a satyr play by Euripides's approximate contemporary Achaeus of Eritrea (fr. 17 *TrGF* = fr. 17 Nauck; see also the testimonium fr. 16b *TrGF*); but the scanty remnants suggest that the plot concerned the god's return to Olympus after the fall he suffers in *Iliad* Book 18, rather than his interlude with Aphrodite. See also the discussion below and n.28.

19. On Ovid's depiction of Elegia, see Wyke 1989:117–34 (2006:172–82).

20. Elsewhere Ovid uses the pairing of Venus and Vulcan to characterize the combination of "perfect" and "defective" verses that constitutes the elegiac couplet: see *Am.* 2.17.19–22, *Vulcani Venus est, quamuis incude relicta | turpiter obliquo claudicet ille pede. | carminis hoc ipsum genus impar, sed tamen apte | iungitur herous cum breuiore modo,* with L. Morgan 2012: 210.

21. We may also suspect a sly joke regarding the absence of gifts—the expectation of gift giving by a lover to his *puella* is one of the many topics upon which the Ovidian *praeceptor* offers solemn—and stingy—advice to his male readers, e.g., *Ars am.* 1.405–36.

Venus' epithet *lasciua* (2.567) underscores this difference: in erotic con-
texts it often indicates a degree of sexual aggressiveness, and is frequently
therefore used by Ovid to describe Cupid himself.[22]

Two further differences in this part of Ovid's narrative also invite
notice: the implication in the word *quotiens* that Venus and Mars met in
secret not once before discovery but repeatedly; and the curious attribution
to tradition of the details of Venus' mockery of her husband (*risisse . . . |
dicitur*, "she is said to have laughed," 2.567-68). The first of these novelties
is made explicit shortly thereafter, when Ovid uses the plural *concubitus
primos* to describe their initial assignations; that this is not simply a poetic
plural is implicit in the three imperfect verbs that describe Venus, and
Mars's response to her (*decebat, celare solebant, erat*, 2.569–72). In Homer,
one sexual encounter is enough for Helios, who immediately reports what
he has seen to Hephaestus (*Od.* 8.268–71). With the Alexandrian foot-
note[23] *risisse . . . | dicitur*, meanwhile, Ovid invites his readers to appreciate
the joke: if the story told here is really "the most (in)famous tale in all of
heaven" (*fabula . . . toto notissima caelo*, 2.561), then surely his readers will
know that the details given here are not in fact part of Homer's narrative
at all (and indeed there is no extant authority for this aspect of the story
besides Ovid himself).[24] Ovid thus calls attention to his own revision of
the Homeric story by radically reinterpreting it; the emphasis on repe-
tition in the story, meanwhile, is a neat metatextual comment on Ovid's
repetition—with a difference—of the Homeric original.

Yet another difference from the Homeric version emerges in the
next couplet (*Ars am.* 2.573–74): while the Homeric Helios was intro-
duced quickly into the tale and just as quickly brought the sorry news
to Hephaestus, the Ovidian Sol has been noticeably absent until now—
perhaps because his presence earlier in the story would have made
repeated assignations less likely (or might Ovid wish slyly to suggest that
Sol lingered voyeuristically before informing on the lovers?). The *prae-
ceptor*, who has already expressed a certain dismay at the story with his
exclamatory "*a*," now intrudes fully into the narrative to apostrophize Sol

---

22. E.g., *Ars am.* 2.497, *Met.* 1.456; cf. also *Am.* 1.4.21, 1.8.98. Quint. *Inst.* 10.1.93 uses the
adjective to describe Ovid himself.

23. See chapter 2, n.32.

24. *Risisse . . . | dicitur* in the same *sedes* appears also in the programmatic first poem of the
Amores, characterizing the troublesome god Cupido (*Am.* 1.1.3–4); on the use of the phrase
there, see McKeown 1989 ad loc.

(575–76)—not to chastise him for his late appearance, however, but rather to find fault with the bad example he sets by becoming an informer; much better, the *praeceptor* continues, to remain silent, and to extract an appropriate reward from Venus for doing so (*pete munus ab ipsa*, "request a gift from her," 2.575). The word *munus* appears often in elegy, as gift giving is a tried-and-true technique for winning a *puella*'s favor;[25] but it can also be used of the particular powers of a god that that god can bestow on others—with the implication here that Venus could well offer sex to Sol in return for his silence.[26]

In keeping with the altered function of Ovid's version of the story, the Homeric emphasis on Hephaestus's skilled craftsmanship and clever trickery (i.e., τέχνη and δόλος, *Od.* 8.276, 282, 286, 297, 317, 327, 332), culminating in a simile comparing the snare to a spider's web so fine that not even the gods could detect it (*Od.* 8.280–81), is now, if not entirely elided, yet very much reduced: the snare (*laquei, Ars am.* 2.578 and 580) is described as difficult to see (*obscuros*, 2.577) and as able to deceive the eye (*lumina fallit opus*, "the work tricks the eyes," 2.578)—but no potential divine viewers are mentioned, and no spider simile is present to enhance the fine work of Vulcan. Instead, the *praeceptor* moves quickly to the next phase of the story: Vulcan feigns a trip to Lemnos, the lovers quickly resume their affair, and just as quickly they are caught in the smith-god's snare, all in a single couplet (2.579–80) instead of the more than twenty hexameters of Homeric narrative devoted to these events. Again, the shared desire of the two lovers is bypassed; instead, Ovid moves rapidly to the gathering of gods and the spectacle (*spectacula*, 2.581) created by the ensnared divinities.

Not surprisingly, the treatment of this gathering and its conclusion also differs in the two poems. First, the *Odyssey*: in Demodocus's song, the assembling of the gods is a response to Hephaestus's aggrieved outburst to Zeus and the other gods; Aphrodite bears the brunt of his wrath because she shames him ("ἐμέ . . . | αἰὲν ἀτιμάζει," " 'she always disgraces me,' " *Od.* 8.308–9), preferring the handsome and surefooted Ares to her ungainly husband, and Hephaestus vows not to release the two gods from their unseemly situation until he receives restitution of the marriage price from his wife's (and his own) father, Zeus (8.315–20). The transference to the

---

25. Cf. above, n.21.

26. E.g., *Am.* 3.1.60 (and cf. the context of *pretium* at *Am.* 2.8.21–28); cf. Janka 1997 ad loc., *OLD* s.v. *munus* 5b, Adams 1982:164.

divine sphere of a declaration of desire to divorce following human legal procedures is, as Alexander Garvie notes, comical;[27] and the incongruity of this demand is emphasized by the arrival of the divine witnesses Poseidon, Hermes, and Apollo (8.321–23). The latter two laugh—but their laughter is aimed not at Hephaestus, who earns from them acknowledgment of his skill in catching the lovers (8.329–32), but at Aphrodite and Ares; that they are the target is elaborated and made explicit by a ribald exchange between Apollo and Hermes, the latter of whom expresses his willingness to be ensnared by three times as many snares and to be exposed in this position to all the other gods in exchange for an opportunity to have sex with Aphrodite (8.334–43). Only Poseidon—the eldest and, presumably, most sober-minded of the three witnesses—restores a semblance of seriousness to the story, asking for Ares's release (not Aphrodite's, however) and promising to pay compensation himself if Ares somehow can avoid paying the debt (8.344–56). Now presumably satisfied, Hephaestus agrees and releases the lovers; Ares departs straightaway for Thrace, while Aphrodite goes to Paphos, where her nymphs bathe and anoint her and then clothe her in beautiful garments (8.357–66). With this bathing scene, as we have noted, Demodocus draws his song to a close, leaving a vision of Aphrodite's beauty as the last thing to be imagined by his audience (θαῦμα ἰδέσθαι, "a marvel to look upon," 8.366).

In the *Ars amatoria*, on the other hand, suppression of some details and expansion of others effect a very different ending. The *spectacula* mentioned in 2.581, it turns out, do not simply consist of the two exposed and immobilized gods but have Venus at their center—a naked and embarrassed Venus, unable to cover her face in shame or conceal her private parts (2.582–84). The word *spectacula* relocates the scene quite clearly in a Roman world where spectacles—Circus races, *uenationes*, and lewd mimes—constitute a distinct class of public entertainment; indeed, the exposure of Venus's genitalia, identified clearly with the term *partes obscenae* a few lines later (584), suggests nothing so much as the May festival of the Floralia, during which prostitutes are said to have performed nude onstage.[28] And it is this sight that stirs the gods' bawdy humor, as one of

27. Garvie 1994 on *Od.* 8.318–19.

28. Valerius Maximus (2.10.8) and Seneca (*Ep.* 97.8) both tell how Cato absented himself from naughty stage shows at the Floralia in order not to put a damper on the festive spirits of the *populus*; see also Wiseman 1999 and 2002:293–99. On *partes obscenae*, cf. Varro's

them—never named,[29] but providing the only example of direct speech in the episode apart from the *praeceptor*'s comments—offers to relieve Mars of his troublesome chains and to take them upon himself. In focusing on Venus and obscuring Mercury's identity, Ovid has not only stripped the story down to its bare essentials but also reframed it in elegiac terms with the translation of Homer's δεσμοί as *uincula* (2.586), so suggesting the cliché of *seruitium amoris* that is common elegiac imagery.[30] He also elides the language of bride price and financial compensation for adultery that was central to Hephaestus's vindication in the *Odyssey*; the *Ars amatoria*, after all, is intended to assist the adulterer, not to frame him, and so the liberation of the lovers is effected in a single couplet (2.587–88). The only reminder that actual payment might have been involved is a faint one indeed, embedded in the connotation of "repayment" that the verb *resoluere* can have; but the association with "freeing" (i.e., from imprisonment) that the verb also has seems to be the dominant one here, since Neptune is described as using prayers (*precibus, Neptune, tuis*, "through your prayers, Neptune," 2.587) to end their entrapment.[31]

Ovid's treatment of the story in the *Ars amatoria* also closes very differently from Homer's: whereas the earlier treatment had promised Hephaestus at least financial compensation and had ended with the lovers separated—at least for now—the final word in *Ars amatoria* Book 2 is a rebuke of Vulcan for his foolishness in bringing their dalliance into

---

etymology for *obscenus* (*obscaenum dictum ab scaena, Ling.* 7.96). Jolivet 2005:8–12 posits pantomime as the theatrical form of choice here, primarily on the basis of a passage in Lucian (see above, n.18); but the historically earlier forms of Roman farce discussed by Wiseman lend themselves equally well to the theme and are more securely identifiable as types of performance with which Ovid would have been familiar, especially mime. For good discussions of the now fragmentary tradition, see McKeown 1979; Fantham 1989; and Viarre 2009; and see the discussion in chapter 9.

29. In yet another instance of compression: Demodocus mentions a τις among the gods who utter witticisms at the sight of the ensnared twosome (328), but then specifies that Hermes is the one who is willing to change places with Ares; Ovid's *praeceptor*, on the other hand, invites his readers to remember, or to guess at, the identity of the unnamed voyeur—and in the process to become voyeurs themselves. Jolivet 2005:6–8 nicely observes that the anonymity of *aliquis* may also be a sort of mock διόρθωσις on Ovid's part, responding as it does to the charge of τὸ ἀπρεπές lodged against Hermes's laughter by some ancient critics: see the T scholia on *Od.* 8.332 and the H scholia on *Od.* 8.333–42.

30. For a recent survey of the conventional imagery of elegy, see Kennedy 2012.

31. Cf. *OLD* s.v. *resoluo* 2 and 6.

the public eye; all he will get for his trouble, concludes the *praeceptor*, is shame, since now the lovers will simply continue their affair in public rather than trying to conceal it (2.589–92):

> hoc tibi perfecto, Vulcane: quod ante tegebant,
>   liberius faciunt, et pudor omnis abest:
> saepe tamen demens stulte fecisse fateris,
>   teque ferunt artis paenituisse tuae.

> This is your doing, Vulcan; what they concealed previously, they now do more freely, and all shame is gone; you often, though in a frenzy, confess that you acted foolishly, and they say that you became ashamed of your skill.

For the Ovidian *praeceptor*, the mad love of Mars (2.563) gives way to the far more consequential madness of Vulcan (*demens*), the only character to emerge from the episode permanently shamed. The lovers now can enjoy the openly available luxury of repetition into the permanent present of myth (*liberius faciunt*), but the only repetition available to Vulcan is the incessant reminder of his own foolishness (*saepe . . . stulte fecisse fateris*). And in a final scathing revision of the moral expressed by Homer's gods, "οὐκ ἀρετᾷ κακὰ ἔργα" ("'ill deeds prosper not,'" *Od.* 8.329), it is now the *ars* of Vulcan that should be blamed for the trouble—an *ars* that, following the *praeceptor*'s logic, can clearly be seen to be inferior to the *Ars amatoria* of Ovid.[32]

IV. A Homeric Lesson Not Learned

While the tale of Venus and Mars that appears in *Ars amatoria* Book 2 has a clear, if surprising, didactic trajectory, its retelling in *Metamorphoses* Book 4 is all but entirely devoid of any explicit lesson (though, as we shall see, we are invited by Ovid to tease both didactic and metapoetic functions out of the story). It appears as the introduction to one of three inset narratives, narrated one by one by the daughters of Minyas: the Theban sisters are the only women in the city who reject the worship of Bacchus,

---

32. Cf. Jolivet 2005:4–6, noting that one form of interpretation taken in allegorical readings of Homer is didactic; indeed, the beginnings of didactic reading can be traced to the scholia themselves. Cf. also Giannini 1995 on Eustathius's reading of the lessons to be learned from the scene.

and to enact their distaste for the new cult, they not only refuse to follow the other women who leave their homes and duties to participate in the god's worship (*Met.* 4.1–12) but decide to pass their time indoors, spinning and working at their looms (4.32–35). Their domestic activities evoke traditional women's work as seen repeatedly in ancient literature, beginning with Homeric women like Helen and Penelope; but unlike their Homeric predecessors, they will find that this demonstration of domestic virtue is powerless in the face of the power of Bacchus.

The work of spinning and weaving is slow and decidedly repetitive: the careful fingering of clumped wool, drawn piecemeal off the distaff, and its gradual transformation into slender thread as it passes over the spindle; the up-and-down interlacing of the thread as the shuttle carries it row by row across the warp set up on the loom—in its necessary attention to detail and to the establishment of a rhythm, wool-working ensures that its practitioners will be focused on their task and fixed in place for long periods of time.[33] Gianpiero Rosati has shown in rich detail how the semantic field of the language used to describe this craft intersects with metaphors for poetic composition in ancient literature, using the episode of the daughters of Minyas in *Metamorphoses* Book 4 (along with the Arachne and Minerva story in Book 6) to illustrate Ovid's play with the simultaneity of poetry and wool-working in his narrative.[34] As the sisters spin and weave wool, so they spin and weave song; and the *textus* that results is in both instances a work of refined and discerning art.

By paralleling the work of spinning and weaving with that of composing poetry, Ovid suggests that the sisters' compositions are verbal tapestries—and so approximates their songs to ecphrastic poems that use language to articulate detailed descriptions of works of art.[35] And in keeping with their rejection of the mass psychology of the women of Thebes, the daughters of Minyas go out of their way to reject common stories; thus, the first tale, narrated by an unnamed sister, is chosen precisely because it is uncommon ("*quoniam uulgaris fabula non est*," "'since the tale is not common,'" *Met.* 4.53): this is the story of the love of Pyramus and Thisbe, set in an

33. For a helpful introduction to the techniques involved, see Barber 1992; for their literary deployment, Snyder 1981 provides a useful introduction. Pantelia 1993 is rightly insistent about the very different work of spinning on the one hand and weaving on the other, but the differences she emphasizes are not central to the scene in the *Metamorphoses*.

34. Rosati 1999.

35. On the ecphrastic character of their work, see Leach 1974:107–11.

exotic locale and filling more than one hundred verses (4.55–166).[36] The
second tale, almost as long, is narrated by Leuconoe, and her theme is
almost as unusual as the first: the loves of the god Sol (4.169–270), focus-
ing on the story of Leucothoe, an Eastern princess loved by Sol, and her
jealous competitor Clytie.[37] The love story of Venus and Mars serves as a
preface to the central narrative of Leuconoe, the connection being Sol's
pivotal role in the exposure of the two lovers; while I shall return to this in
some detail shortly, it is worth noting here the subordination of the famil-
iar Venus and Mars story to a tale known first to us from Ovid.[38] A third
sister, Alcithoe, brings up the rear in this sequence, offering a third story
of roughly similar length (4.276–388) and yet again set in an exotic locale
(Caria, 4.296–97). Like the first sister to perform, Alcithoe opens her nar-
rative with an explicit rejection of familiar themes ("*uulgatos taceo . . . pas-
toris amores,*" " 'I pass over the common loves of the shepherd,' " 4.276) and
then launches into the story of Salmacis and Hermaphroditus—a tale that,
if not entirely unknown before Ovid, here receives distinctively Ovidian
treatment.[39] Further contributing to the symmetry of the sequence is the
way in which both the first and the last story are selected by their narra-
tors only after the rejection of several other possibilities: before the first
sister takes up Pyramus and Thisbe as her theme, she considers, and
rejects, the obscure loves of the Babylonian divinity Dercetis, of Dercetis's
unnamed daughter,[40] and of an unnamed nymph (4.44–50); the last narra-
tor, Alcithoe, considers and rejects the unhappy loves of Daphnis, the sex-
ual transformation of Sithon, and then finally—in an outburst that recalls
Ovid's earlier comment about the first sister, *nam plurima norat* ("for she
knew very many tales," 4.43)—packs not one but four other rejected pos-
sibilities into three verses: the transformations of Celmis, of the Curetes,
of Crocus, and of Smilax (4.281–83).[41]

---

36. Knox 1988b considers carefully the possibility that other versions of the story were
known in antiquity, though we have no evidence of a source before Ovid.

37. For the combination of Eastern setting and arcane stories, Myers 1994:79–80.

38. Though Ovid may well have found some version of the story of Leucothoe and Clytie in
an earlier source: see Cameron 2004:290–303. In any case, there is certainly some irony, as
Laurel Fulkerson has pointed out to me, in the use of the name Clytie, "renowned female,"
for such an obscure character; see also below, n.49.

39. For Ovid's version of the story, see Labate 1993 and Robinson 1999; and cf. the collection
of references in Barchiesi and Rosati 2007 ad loc.

40. Identified elsewhere as Semiramis: see Bömer vol. 2, 1976 ad loc.

41. See Bömer vol. 2, 1976 and Barchiesi and Rosati 2007 ad locc. for the ancient evidence
relating to each of these myths.

It is in this context—amid a cluster of stories, both told and untold, linked by exotic locales and arcane characters—that the *Metamorphoses* version of the story of Venus and Mars finds itself: strange bedfellows indeed. The central position of the story clearly recalls the tale's central position in the *Odyssey*—but there, it was the novelty, framed by two tales intimately familiar to Odysseus. Ovid further marks the inversion of the novel and the traditional by featuring the story here not as a central narrative but as a prelude, subordinate to the second sister's primary tale. I have already noted that the first and last of the three daughters of Minyas make a point of the novelty of their chosen stories (*Met.* 4.53 and 276); the latter of these, Alcithoe, makes the point a second time when, after listing all the stories she plans *not* to tell, she concludes, *"praetereo dulcique animos nouitate tenebo"* ("'I bypass them, and will hold your attention with sweet novelty,'" 4.284). Then, still not quite done with the point, she begins her description of Salmacis with an indirect question, *"unde sit infamis"* ("'whence comes her notoriety,'" 4.285): though *infamis* clearly is intended to anticipate the notoriety that Salmacis will bring upon herself through her sexual aggressiveness, if we think of the adjective as composed of the negative (rather than intensifying) prefix *in* + *fama*, it also suggests another meaning: "without fame," that is, "unknown"—an appropriate designation for a recherché story. It is striking, then, to revisit the version of the love of Venus and Mars narrated by Leuconoe, marked at both its opening and conclusion by indications of its repetitive nature. Leuconoe begins by explaining that the loves of Sol will be her theme (*"cepit amor Solem: Solis referemus amores,"* "'love seized the Sun; of the Sun's loves we shall tell,'" 4.170)—an explanation that, enhanced by the repetition of Sol's name, would lead her audience to expect that, with the next line, one of these unfamiliar tales will begin. And the first word of the next verse, *primus*, is promising: it recalls the striking transition Ovid makes from the cosmic narrative with which *Metamorphoses* Book 1 opens to the first love story in the poem, that of Apollo and Daphne (*Primus amor Phoebi Daphne Peneia,* "the first love of Phoebus was Daphne, daughter of Peneus," *Met.* 1.452),[42] and its repetition at the end of the following hexameter would seem to underscore the point: *"primus adulterium Veneris cum Marte putatur | hic uidisse deus; uidet hic deus omnia primus"* ("'This god is thought to have been the first to see the adultery of Venus with

---

42. The repetition of *primus* is noted by Barchiesi and Rosati 2007 ad loc.; on the pivotal role of the Apollo and Daphne story, see Nicoll 1980.

Mars; this god sees all things first,'" 4.171–72). This fleeting echo, how-
ever, proves to be false: with the next phrase, "'adulterium Veneris cum
Marte,'" Leuconoe reveals that her real first topic is not an obscure erotic
tale about Sol but, rather, a story with a long literary pedigree; and by the
last word of this hexameter, putatur, it is clear that the story is a familiar
one indeed—the Alexandrian footnote points Leuconoe's audience indu-
bitably back to Homer. After this opening, Leuconoe's audience has been
reoriented and can be reasonably sure what to expect; and confirmation of
their expectation, implicit in the story itself, is underscored with the tale's
final line, announcing the story's fame (and its notoriety) as it echoes the
very first line of the version seen in Ars amatoria Book 2: Leuconoe's sig-
nature "haec fuit in toto notissima fabula caelo" ("'this was the most famous
tale in all of heaven,'" Met. 4.189) repeats everything but the verbal tense
of the praeceptor's introductory fabula narratur toto notissima caelo (Ars am.
2.561). Repetition of the mirroring line, opening one version and closing
the other, signals not only the repetitiousness of the story but the very
incessant character of the activities it details: the love affair of Venus and
Mars, already revealed in Ars amatoria Book 2 to be habitual, is now used
as a foil for the unheard-of stories told by Leuconoe and her sisters, who
engage in the repetitious work of weaving as they narrate stories without
a history of repetition.[43]

Leuconoe's compact version of the story (only twenty-one hexameters,
and including no direct speech whatsoever) also betrays its reliance on
repetition.[44] She needs only four unadorned words, "adulterium Veneris
cum Marte," to introduce the tale, and a single verse to explain Sol's role
as informer, thereby connecting the tale to her ostensible theme, Solis
amores. Sol's informing to Vulcan is similarly summary (4.173–74), and
only when she arrives at Vulcan's response to the news does Leuconoe
linger over the details: in a humorous syllepsis,[45] the smith-god loses both
his mind and the object he had been crafting, as the latter falls from his
hands ("at illi | et mens et quod opus fabrilis dextra tenebat | excidit," "'from
his control fell both his mind and the work his crafty right hand held,'"

---

43. On the reversal of beginnings and endings as "a convention of Alexandrian and neoteric
poetry," see Zetzel 1983:261.

44. Bömer vol. 2, 1976 on 4.167–89 notes the speed and brevity of this version; cf. also his
n. on 4.186.

45. Tissol 1997 is the standard discussion of this rhetorical device in Ovid; for other examples
with excidit, see Bömer vol. 2, 1976 ad loc.

4.174–76), and then—in an implicit but markedly quick recovery—immediately sets to work on a new project, a snare in which to catch the lovers.

This snare, described with not one but three words (*"catenas | retiaque et laqueos,"* " 'chains and nets and snares,' " 4.176–77), is in many ways the centerpiece of the story.[46] Its fine execution is illustrated not only by the invisibility of the mesh (*"quae lumina fallere possent,"* " 'of the sort that was able to deceive the eyes,' " 177, echoing *Ars am.* 2.578, *lumina fallit opus*) but also by its comparability to the web of a spider: *"non illud opus tenuissima uincant | stamina, non summo quae pendet aranea tigno"* (" 'nor would the finest webs surpass that work, not the spider web that hangs from the highest beam,' " 4.178–79). The use of this simile may be seen as a demonstration of Leuconoe's familiarity with the Homeric version, but she has in fact already shown that with the Alexandrian footnote of 4.171; in singling out this elaborate simile for inclusion in her narration—a simile not found, as we have seen, in the *Ars amatoria* Book 2 version of the story—Leuconoe also wants to remind her sisters of the weaving they are engaged in as they tell stories, and of the way in which their stories can be seen as ecphrastic narratives that they weave with words. Leuconoe thus characterizes the story of Venus and Mars and the handiwork of the Minyeides as simultaneously didactic and metapoetic forms of narrative: on the didactic level, she implies that their sophisticated storytelling, as finely crafted as Vulcan's snare, can immobilize even gods; and on the metapoetic level, Ovid uses the story of Venus and Mars to assert the parity of Leuconoe's song with Homeric poetry.[47] Of course, these audacious parallels also draw attention to an inherent tension on both the didactic and metapoetic levels of the narrative: in didactic terms, the outcome of the sisters' resistance to Bacchus suggests that their handiwork, unlike Vulcan's, is neither an effective prophylactic nor a vindication in the face of Bacchus's superior skills; and in metapoetic terms, Ovid draws attention to the power that *ars* can have, while leaving unanswered the question of whether his appropriation of the Homeric tale, together with its subordination to other distinctly non-Homeric stories, constitutes an act of aggression on his part or rather an acknowledgemnt of the inescapability of Homer as model—or both.

---

46. On the concept of the ecphrastic centerpiece, see Thomas 1983.

47. Cf. Rinon 2006a:212–13 for a discussion of the parallels between Hephaestus's craftsmanship and Demodocus's singing.

I shall return shortly to the implications of this interpretation; but first let us complete our reading of the version of the story in *Metamorphoses* Book 4. After lingering over the Homeric simile, Leuconoe returns to narrating in summary fashion Vulcan's setting of the snare and the hapless lovers' subsequent entrapment (4.180–84); Leuconoe's repeated emphasis on Vulcan's *ars* (4.181, 183) suggests that he regains his ability to plot revenge very quickly after the shock of Sol's report (cf. *extemplo*, 4.175). The speed of her narrative is foregrounded by the reappearance of *extemplo* a few lines later (4.185), as Vulcan throws open the doors to expose the two ensnared lovers and to admit an assembly of expectant gods (gods who, perhaps because of the repetitions of this very story, now appear to be waiting at the door rather than needing to be summoned, as they were in the Homeric version: compare *Met.* 4.186 with *Od.* 8.305–21). The economy of Leuconoe's narrative culminates in her concluding focus on the witticism made by one of the divine witnesses about willingly being disgraced in a manner similar to Venus and Mars (*"illi iacuere ligati | turpiter, atque aliquis de dis non tristibus optat | sic fieri turpis,"* " 'they lay disgracefully, bound, and one of the gods—not one of the gloomy ones—wishes he might be thus disgraced,' " 4.186–88): none of the gods present is named, and only the designation *de dis non tristibus* hints at the joker's identity, while the repetition in *turpiter* and *turpis* both glosses over and trivializes the nature of the exposé. Leuconoe's version ends with divine laughter (*"superi risere,"* " 'the ones above laughed,' " 4.188), even as it leaves the two lovers apparently trapped permanently by Vulcan's snare—there is now no hurried departure for Thrace or Paphos on the part of Mars and Venus, respectively, no restorative bath for Venus, and Vulcan is neither promised compensation for the loss of honor to his marriage nor chastised for revealing his shame. The story is an entertainment—for its internal audience of gods, for Leuconoe's sisters, and for Ovid's readers—and the fact of its repetitious history, on both the didactic and metapoetic levels,[48] makes it the perfect foil for the novelty to follow.

Before we close discussion of this episode, however, it is worth wondering whether Ovid may not well have given this tale to Leuconoe with one other connection in mind. The sisters, we recall, pass the time as

---

48. Note the adverb in the closing frame *"diuque | haec fuit in toto notissima fabula caelo,"* 4.188–89: it acknowledges the story's long pedigree while hinting that it has recently been, or may soon be, replaced.

they tell stories with wool-working; and the webs they weave strongly resemble, I have suggested, the tales they tell as they avoid the Bacchic revelry that possesses the rest of Thebes. The story of the entrapment of Venus and Mars, however, suggests yet a further narrative inversion, as the sister-storytellers in turn become the subject of song—Ovid's song—with their transformation into bats. One of the many potential lessons of the Venus and Mars tale concerns the omniscience of the gods (Sol, in the Homeric tale); another concerns the gods' ability to entrap those who have offended them (Vulcan, in the Homeric tale). These two lessons are in turn transferred to the Minyeides themselves by the Ovidian narrator, as he describes how the sounds of the Bacchic procession, though invisible, fill their room, the air becomes fragrant (4.391–93), and—incredibly—the looms themselves and the webs they support are overpowered and transformed by ivy and grapevines, so that the threads become vines (4.394–98):

> resque fide maior, coepere uirescere telae
> inque hederae faciem pendens frondescere uestis;
> pars abit in uites et, quae modo fila fuerunt,
> palmite mutantur; de stamine pampinus exit;
> purpura fulgorem pictis adcommodat uuis.

> Then an event greater than belief: the webs began to turn green and the fabric began to get leaves, hanging in the appearance of ivy; a part turns into vines, and what had recently been threads are exchanged for shoots; a vine-stalk comes forth from the loom; the purple in colored grapes complements the textile's brilliance.

The sisters are thus caught in the act, just as were Venus and Mars; and like Venus and Mars, they are trapped by a divine net, their transformation paralleling in its swiftness the speed of Leuconoe's earlier narration (cf. *subito*, 4.391). But, as the Homeric story, so often repeated, makes clear to its readers, the humiliation of the two gods is ephemeral, and they—and the gods who observe them—will have all of eternity to repeat this episode if they wish; these same readers also know, however, that on the plane of human experience, exemplified in the *Odyssey* by the story of Odysseus himself, such events can have only the most dire consequences. The tale that ends in divine laughter (4.188) will bring no similar laughter to the Minyeides, who are instead swept along by the power of Bacchus to become the objects of song rather than its creators. Unlike the readers of the *Ars amatoria*, for whom the story of adultery exposed and of Vulcan's disgrace is intended as an apotropaic warning, the listeners in this episode are drawn by their weaving and singing into the web of the poem itself.

V. *The Moral of the Story*

I began this chapter with some general thoughts about Ovidian repetition and proceeded to demonstrate how Ovid interrogates, rewrites, and sometimes challenges his Homeric model. The centrality of repetition to the Ovidian *ars canendi* is a familiar point of entry to the interpretation of Ovid's poetry because it allows—indeed, demands—that his attentive readers question his choices and consider his models even as they make sense of his transformative rewriting. Everything that is new in Ovid's retelling of the story of the loves of Venus and Mars is set into relief against the background provided by the Homeric model; Ovid's sheer delight in his own inventiveness is made almost palpable in the details.

But this is not the end of Ovid's repetitiveness; that is, he does not simply revisit Homer in order to "correct" him or to initiate a display of poetic one-upsmanship in which he will inevitably trump a static and fixed model. Rather, what I have tried to show is that Ovid actively enters into the spirit of Homeric composition, finding in the tale of the loves of Venus and Mars a perfect opportunity to engage with Homeric repetitiousness in its own terms. Ovid finds in Homeric narrative itself, I suggest, an invitation to join in the retelling of the tale, a tale that opens up the possibility of endless repetition while never being entirely the same as any of its previous forms.

In so doing, Ovid may well intend simultaneously, if momentarily, to recall yet another repetition of the Homeric tale, the version that appears, only briefly and in a highly allusive context, in the fourth *Georgic* (4.333–47). There, Virgil has begun the story of Aristaeus's appeal to his mother, Cyrene, for her assistance in resuscitating the bees that have inexplicably died. Cyrene hears him as she is sitting in her marine dwelling, surrounded by beautiful nymphs engaged in wool-working; another nymph, Clymene,[49] is entertaining the group with a narrative song to accompany

---

49. E. L. Harrison 1989 observes that Clymene is an apt name for a female counterpart of Homer's Demodocus, called περικλυτός (*Od.* 8.367; see also Thomas 1988 on *Geo.* 4.345–47), and follows it with an appealing suggestion: "Is it not possible that Clymene seemed a

their task. Before turning his focus on Aristaeus, Virgil describes briefly
the contents of Clymene's song (4.345–47):

> . . . curam Clymene narrabat inanem
> Volcani, Martisque dolos et dulcia furta,
> aque Chao densos diuum numerabat amores.

> . . . Clymene was narrating the foolish love of Vulcan, and the tricks
> and sweet deceits of Mars, and starting from Chaos was recounting
> the incessant loves of the gods.

Her song concerns the loves of the gods, going all the way back to the
beginning of time and of myth (*aque Chao*); presumably it is a long story
indeed, as the epithet *densos* suggests, although Virgil's readers, unlike the
sea nymphs, are not privileged to hear any more of it.[50] But Virgil provides
just enough detail to suggest that her song began with a prelude of sorts,
in which she told of "the futile love of Vulcan, and Mars' deceptions and
stolen pleasures"—in other words, a version of the Homeric story of the
loves of Venus and Mars.[51] Both recent English-language commentators
on the *Georgics* draw attention to the rather non-Homeric emphases of
this Homeric tale in its new context;[52] but neither tries to account for the

---

suitable name in such a context because its bearer was familiar enough with Helios to have
had a son by him [i.e., Phaethon], and he, after all, was the one who blew the whistle on Ares
in the first place?" See also Ziogas 2013:82, who observes that Clymene also appears as the
name of one of the many former lovers rejected by Sol in favor of Leucothoe at *Met.* 4.204–
08—namely, Clymene, mother of Phaethon.

50. Perhaps because, as Servius notes in a comment on *Aen.* 1.742, such songs are appro-
priate only when the audience consists only of women, as the internal audience does here;
the implication is that its sexual content is not appropriate for mixed company. In an ironic
twist, Ovid appears to anticipate Servius's concern, when he makes the tale of Venus and
Mars an entertainment for the puritanical Minyeides. See also chapter 9, n.12, on Servius's
sensitivity to inappropriate sexual conduct on the part of the gods.

51. Ziogas 2013:109–10 notes a number of significant connections between and among
Virgil's Clymene and the weaving storytellers of Ovid (i.e., the Minyeides and Arachne),
arguing that they all perform Hesiodic catalogue poetry; he does not, however, attempt to
account for the nonsequential placement of the Venus and Mars story in the song of Virgil's
Clymene. A somewhat more complex and nuanced—albeit also far more hypothetical—view
of the poetic affiliations of Clymene's song is offered by Fabre-Serris 2014:6–7, who sees it
as part of a larger complex of Empedoclean themes in Augustan poetry and suggests that
Gallus may have been a crucial conduit in the reception of Empedocles at Rome, perhaps
even narrating the *amores* of Venus and Mars in his *Amores*. On the Empedoclean hypoth-
esis, see chapter 9.

52. Thomas 1988 and Mynors 1990 ad loc.

singling out of this story from all the other *diuum amores*, or for its primary position in the narrative in spite of Chaos's status as first beginning of the universe, at least in Hesiodic tradition.[53] It may well be that this tale earns special treatment by Virgil because of its status as what Ovid will later call a *notissima fabula* (though that identification in itself contains a bit of circular logic); but Ovid's reception of the story may also allow us to see in the Virgilian allusion a recognition of the tale's boundless ability to be begun anew, and in the process, to be made new again.

53. Nor, for that matter, does Erren 2003 ad loc., although he comments extensively on the register of the diction in the scene.

9

Homer's Gods in Rome

πῶς δὲ οὐκ ἂν πᾶσαν ἀρετὴν ἀναθείημεν Ὁμήρῳ ὅπου καὶ
ὅσα αὐτὸς μὴ ἐπετήδευσε ταῦτα οἱ ἐπιγενόμενοι ἐν τοῖς
ποιήμασιν αὐτοῦ κατενόησαν; καὶ χρῶνται μέν τινες πρὸς
μαντείαν τοῖς ἔπεσιν αὐτοῦ καθάπερ τοῖς χρησμοῖς τοῦ
θεοῦ· ἄλλοι δὲ ἑτέρας ὑποθέσεις προθέμενοι ἁρμόζουσιν
ἐπ' αὐτὰς τα ἔπη μετατιθέντες καὶ συνείροντες.

—[PLUTARCH] DE HOMERO 54B.218[1]

I. Strange Bedfellows?

Ovid's repetition of the Homeric tale of Aphrodite and Ares plays with the
possibility of repetition embedded in the Homeric scene itself. Yet as all
Homer's audiences, ancient and modern, would know, there is no such
repetition in the Homeric poems; indeed, as we have seen, the tale's many
exceptional features caused Homer's first professional critics to question
its authenticity. But equally remarkable—yet generally overlooked—is the
degree of personification experienced by Ares in this episode, who is else-
where in Homer rarely presented as much other than an embodiment of
or metonymy for war. The one significant exception that proves the rule
occurs in *Iliad* Book 5, when Ares is wounded on the battlefield (*Il.* 5.835–
909): his wounding echoes and in some ways parallels the wounding of
Aphrodite that preceded it (*Il.* 5.311–430), but neither his wrath at the insult
nor his complaint to his father, Zeus, is as memorable as the richly devel-
oped scene in which the wounded Aphrodite seeks out her mother for

---

1. "How then could we possibly not attribute every virtue to Homer, when those who have
come after him have even found in his poetry all the things he did not himself think to
include? Some use his poetry for divination, just like the oracles of god, while others put
forth entirely different subjects and ideas and fit the verses to them, transposing them and
stringing them together in new ways" (trans. Keaney and Lamberton 1996).

consolation. The conclusion of each of these parallel episodes is particularly worth noting: Aphrodite is received sympathetically by her mother, Dione, who strokes and soothes the hand of the wounded young goddess; Ares, on the other hand, is reproached by Zeus, who expresses a deep-seated dislike for his hateful son ("μή τί μοι ἀλλοπρόσαλλε παρεζόμενος μινύριζε. | ἔχθιστος δέ μοί ἐσσι θεῶν οἳ Ὄλυμπον ἔχουσιν: | αἰεὶ γάρ τοι ἔρις τε φίλη πόλεμοί τε μάχαι τε," "'Do not sit by me and whine, you trouble-maker; for most hateful to me are you of the gods who dwell on Olympus, for strife and wars and battles are dear to you,'" Il. 5.890–91).[2]

The parallelism between the two gods marked by the wounding scenes of Iliad Book 5 is thus exceptional and hints at an unusual complementarity between the two. It is almost as if Aphrodite's provocative episodes of human interference, so clearly reflected in her power to arouse physical desire, are complemented by the interference of Ares, who drives mortals mad with bloodlust; but only in Iliad Book 5 and Odyssey Book 8 does Homer depict them as matched gods, who not only express similar emotions but also interact similarly with humans—or serve humans as subjects of the same song.

Of course, all the gods distinguish themselves by the degree of their involvement in—or detachment from—human affairs; divine interference (often complicated by divine competition) fuels at least to some degree all of the major traditions of mythological narrative we know from the classical world. These wounding episodes, however, isolate and unite the two, simultaneously, if incongruously, also linking them to a third god, Hephaestus, another member of the younger generation of Olympian gods and the one other divinity whose corporeal integrity is compromised in the divine world of the Homeric epics. Hephaestus is, famously, the lame god; as such, his injury cannot be cured easily and quickly, as are the wounds of Aphrodite and Ares, but is rather a permanent and defining feature of his physique, at least within the narrative time of the Iliad's

---

2. The link between Aphrodite and Ares that is constructed by the two wounding scenes in Iliad Book 5 finds a rationale in a tradition not provided by Homer—aside, that is, from the illicit union of the two in Odyssey Book 8—but by Hesiod, who portrays the two gods as spouses (at least insofar as they have children together) at Th. 933–38: αὐτὰρ Ἄρηι | ῥινοτόρῳ Κυθέρεια Φόβον καὶ Δεῖμον ἔτικτε | δεινούς, οἵτ' ἀνδρῶν πυκινὰς κλονέουσι φάλαγγας | ἐν πολέμῳ κρυόεντι σὺν Ἄρηι πτολιπόρθῳ, | Ἁρμονίην θ', ἣν Κάδμος ὑπέρθυμος θέτ' ἄκοιτιν. This is virtually all Hesiod has to say about Ares, aside from an earlier inclusion of him among the three children of Hera and Zeus (Th. 921–23; the others are Eileithyia and Hebe). Meanwhile, Homer identifies Hephaestus as Aphrodite's husband, although elsewhere the wife of the craftsman-god is identified as Charis (Il. 18.382). West 1966 on Th. 933 notes other early evidence for the association/marriage of Ares and Aphrodite.

present.³ Hephaestus offers an indirect aetiology for his limp in the divine banqueting scene with which *Iliad* Book 1 concludes, when he warns his mother, Hera, to avoid Zeus's wrath: on an earlier occasion, the father of gods and men, angered at Hephaestus's support of his mother, had taken the younger god by the ankle and thrown him from Olympus to earth (*Il.* 1.571–94). The fall was so cataclysmic that he lost almost all of his θυμός, he says, and was only restored by the Sintians of Lemnos. The permanence of Hephaestus's resulting handicap seems to be underscored by the later mention of a second fall from Olympus, this time at the hands of Hera herself, who wanted to conceal her son's imperfection (*Il.* 18.394–99). Whether we see the second fall as an instance of Homeric invention or of two alternate traditions concerning the god's lameness,⁴ Homer leaves the god's vulnerability in no doubt: like Ares and Aphrodite, he is immortal, but also like them he can be—and has been—physically damaged. In their cases, the damage is temporary; in his, permanent.⁵

The three gods thus present us with an unlikely sort of triangle, one that is made literal by the erotic relationships that link Aphrodite to each of the other two. Indeed, when Hephaestus crafts the spiderweb-like net that traps the other two gods in bed, the three are quite explicitly triangulated. At the same time, Hephaestus is clearly marginalized by the results of his own craft: forever on the outside, forever looking in. This odd interdependence is underscored by the repetition of desire embedded in the story itself, as well as by the permanent present inhabited by the gods: Hephaestus is always set apart in some way (as he was physically set apart from the other gods when he was thrown from Olympus), even as he remains Aphrodite's husband; and Ares is always at the heart of strife—domestic strife on the divine plane, but a far more destructive form of strife among mortals. Last but not least, there is Aphrodite, never finished with the work of humbling others through desire.

When we look at Ovid's reception of these Homeric divinities, therefore, the story of the loves of Venus and Mars is only the most explicit

---

3. On Hephaestus's distinctive characterization in Homer, see Rinon 2006b, in a reading that very much complements the one I offer here.

4. Braswell 1971:19–21 suggests that this second fall is an instance of Homeric invention (endorsed by Edwards 1991 on 18.394–409); cf. Kirk 1985 on *Il.* 1.586–94.

5. See also the astute observations of Purves 2006, who concerns herself primarily with the similarities between Hephaestus and Ares as the two "falling" gods in the *Iliad*. Although she limits her discussion to these two, many of her observations are relevant, mutatis mutandis, to Aphrodite as well.

result. Ovid's internalization of Homeric repetition should not make us lose sight of other variations on the theme; I therefore shall close this chapter with a consideration of several other instances of Homeric resonance in Ovid that cluster around these gods. My primary focus will be on Mars, who in the transition from the Greek world to Roman culture develops a literary "personality" at least somewhat more dynamic than that offered by Homer and Hesiod.[6] His union with Venus, too, takes on a new complexion, while remaining a constant in his career; and while Vulcan will remain an outsider in this discussion, his silent presence will nonetheless be felt, as Ovid manipulates the narrative tradition to which he is heir.

II. Becoming Roman

The love affair of Aphrodite and Ares is not only an engaging novelty in the universe of Homeric epic; it takes on a far greater, albeit entirely different, significance in the philosophy of Empedocles, who characterizes the energy infusing and making possible the cosmos as the interaction of Neikos (Νεῖκος, "Strife") and Philôtes or Philia (Φιλότης or Φιλία, "Love"), cosmic forces generally to be identified as abstract equivalents of Ares and Aphrodite.[7] According to Empedocles, these divine forces alternately come together (when Philôtes dominates) and are driven apart (when Neikos dominates), in an unceasing cycle of creation and destruction.[8] Although the remains of Empedocles's work are so fragmentary as to limit our understanding of how he developed these cosmic forces as personifications, his influence on later thought, and especially in Latin poetry, helps to flesh out the basics. Empedocles wrote in hexameters;[9] his adaptation of this meter to the articulation of natural philosophy received what is

---

6. Sapph. fr. 111.6–7, with its playful comparison of a new bridegroom to Ares, hints at an Homeric afterlife for the god that develops his character at least as a lover; but only the hint survives.

7. Wright 1995:30–34 offers a good introduction to the place of Love and Strife in Empedocles's thought.

8. Emped. fr. 8(17).7–8 Wright 1995 is the basic statement of the idea: ἄλλοτε μὲν φιλότητι συνερχόμεν' εἰς ἓν ἅπαντα, | ἄλλοτε δ' αὖ δίχ' ἕκαστα φορεύμενα νείκεος ἔχθει.

9. Aristotle's verdict on Empedocles's poetry, Poet. 47b18, is perhaps more well known than it is well understood: οὐδὲν δὲ κοινόν ἐστιν Ὁμήρῳ καὶ Ἐμπεδοκλεῖ πλὴν τὸ μέτρον διὸ τὸν μὲν ποιητὴν δίκαιον καλεῖν, τὸν δὲ φυσιόλογον μᾶλλον ἢ ποιητήν. Janko 1987 ad loc. suggests that Aristotle's judgment is based on the nonrepresentational quality of Empedocles's poetry.

perhaps its clearest pre-Ovidian response in Lucretius, whose opening hymn to Venus as generative force of all living things, with the power to overcome even Mars (1.1–40), has been shown to offer a powerful evocation of Empedoclean Love and so to assert Lucretius's place in a genealogy of scientific poetry headed by Empedocles.[10]

Virgil too knows and develops this tradition; indeed, he does so in a far more complex and nuanced manner, even as he responds to his predecessors. Philip Hardie has explored this theme in a number of books and articles, beginning with his study of traditions of cosmology in the *Aeneid*;[11] while Empedoclean echoes reverberate throughout the Virgilian corpus, certainly the most striking instance—simultaneously revealing how Virgil innovates upon the tradition, drawing links to Homer and Lucretius as well—occurs in *Aeneid* Book 8, when Venus turns to her husband, Vulcan, and invokes his aid in providing armor for her son Aeneas (*Aen.* 8.370–406). Indeed, the details of her artful seduction of Vulcan suggest that the scene not only has Homeric models in the equally artful seduction of Zeus by Hera in *Iliad* Book 14 and in the appeal made by Thetis to Hephaestus for new armor for her son Achilles in *Iliad* Book 18 but also functions as a narrative sequel[12] to the betrayal sung of by Demodocus in *Odyssey* Book 8. There, in receiving Venus's embrace, Vulcan succumbs to the desire with which she inflames him, a desire he has known many times before (*Aen.* 8.387–90, 404–6):

---

10. Sedley 1989; *idem* 1998:1–34. Sedley follows Furley 1970, but moves away from Furley's suggestion that Lucretius's philosophy has a truly Empedoclean cast; rather, Sedley makes the case that Lucretius positions himself as a philosopher joining philosophy and poetry in Latin just as had Empedocles in Greek. See also the general discussion of D. Clay 1983:82–95, and Fabre-Serris 2014.

11. Hardie 1986 (particularly relevant are his discussions of the song of Iopas at *Aen.* 1.52–66 and of Aeneas's shield at *Aen.* 8.360–62); *id.* 1995. See also Farrell 1991:258–62.

12. Servius *ad Aen.* 8.373 [*dictis diuinum inspirit amorem*] clearly reads the scene in this way, drawing attention to Venus's infidelity not only with Mars but with Anchises, who fathered Aeneas: *petitura pro filio de adulterio procreato orationem suam ingenti arte conposuit: quod etiam Vulcanus ipse testatur, dicens "quid causas petis ab alto?"* [395]. *non enim aperta est eius petitio sed longo prooemio peruersam amore mariti circumuenit mentem. ergo quaestionem hanc quae nascitur ex petitione Veneris inpudica, soluimus his modis: primo quod Vulcanum amore circumuenit . . . , deinde quod nacta est occasionem eius temporis quo Marti arma faciebat, quem fuisse sciebat adulterum: per quod datur intellegi Vulcanum iam omnem suspitionem et iram quam habuit circa Venerem, deposuisse, adeo ut arma etiam ipsi fabricaret adultero. praeterea Vulcanum uxorium fuisse testatur et ipse Vergilius dicens "tum pater aeterno fatur deuinctus amore"* [394]. Servius concludes with reference to an ongoing scholarly discussion of when precisely in relation to her marriage to Vulcan Venus slept with Anchises, concluding that Venus and Vulcan were married "from the beginning" (*a principio*). See also Macrob. *Sat.* 1.24.6–7.

dixerat et niueis hinc atque hinc diua lacertis
cunctantem amplexu molli fouet. ille repente
accepit solitam flammam, notusque medullas
intrauit calor et labefacta per ossa cucurrit, . . .

. . .

ea uerba locutus
optatos dedit amplexus placidumque petiuit
coniugis infusus gremio per membra soporem.

She finished speaking, and she fondles him in her soft embrace as
he lingers, her snowy arms around him. He suddenly felt the famil-
iar fire, and the well-known warmth penetrated his marrow and ran
through his melting frame . . .

. . .

Having said these words, he gave her the embraces she desired,
and melting in the arms of his wife sought peaceful rest throughout
his body.

Venus's earlier infidelity seemingly forgotten, Vulcan cannot resist the famil-
iar (*solitam; notus*) charms of his divine spouse. In fact, Mars re-enters the
scene shortly thereafter—now, however, not as Venus's lover but as the god
of war. When Vulcan goes to his workshop after making love with Venus, he
orders the Cyclopes to stop their other work on weapons of various sorts for
the gods, among whom Mars is named (*Aen.* 8.433–34);[13] and the image of
Mars serves Vulcan as an embodiment of the martial valor that will enable
Rome's greatness to emerge. Vulcan crafts a great shield for Aeneas, on
which is depicted a tendentious history of Rome; three times Mars appears
on the shield, as divinity of the cave in which the she-wolf cares for the res-
cued twins (*Mauortis in antro*, "in the cave of Mars," 630); as a metonym for
the gathering of troops on the brink of the battle of Actium (*instructo Marte*,
"once the armies had been arrayed for war," 676); and as the god who takes
central place, both on the field and on the shield, as the battle of Actium
rages (*medio in certamine Mauors | caelatus ferro*, "and Mars, worked in iron,
in the midst of the struggle," 700–701). Virgil too, then, brings the three

---

13. Astutely observed by Servius: see the preceding note.

gods into close association, but now the sexual desire that drives Vulcan's creativity is transformed not by an intimate betrayal but by Rome's destiny.

Virgil's remarkable joining of erotic desire with the origins of Rome reflects (and reflects upon) a traditional linking of Venus and Mars as Rome's patron deities.[14] Virgil's allusion to "the cave of Mars" as he begins the description of Aeneas's shield (8.630) foregrounds the mythical tradition making Mars the father of Rome's founder Romulus, even as it carefully avoids any explicit allusion to the rape that enabled Mars's paternity. In a similar vein, the two remaining mentions of Mars's presence on the shield occur in the context of Virgil's description of the battle of Actium (8.676 and 700), and the second of these explicitly positions Mars between the divine defenders of Rome and the theriomorphic gods who preside over the Egyptian pantheon, where he functions as a sort of nonpartisan patron of total war (*saeuit medio in certamine Mauors*, "Mars rages in the midst of the struggle"); this Mars has no apparent erotic career or interests in a poem that explores Rome's divinely guarded destiny.[15] Venus, too, no longer abandons fidelity and decorum, both of which are strikingly absent from her characterization in the Homeric poems; rather, she is first and foremost a wife and mother, with an immovable focus on her son Aeneas's destiny as Rome's first and greatest ancestor.[16] Of course, this shift in perspective does not alter the essential features of Venus's divine character: from her first appearance in the *Aeneid*, when she conceals her true identity from her son (*Aen.* 1.314–417), through the cunning game of intellectual chess she plays with Juno (*Aen.* 4.90–128), to the scene of her seduction of Vulcan that we have just considered,

---

14. See Weinstock 1971:128–30 for pre-Caesarian references to the two gods; and cf. Herbert-Brown 1994:81–95.

15. Cf. Gurval 1995:238, with n.42.

16. It is tempting to suggest that, in rewriting the seduction scene as the marital union of Venus and Vulcan rather than an illicit rendezvous between Venus and Mars, Virgil is also reacting to scholiastic criticism of the Homeric scene: for a similar interpretation of other scenes in the *Aeneid* with clear Homeric predecessors, see Nelis 2010; also Hexter 2010. The decorum of Virgil's scene was nonetheless not immune to criticism of its own; the comments by Servius quoted in n.12 may be interpreted in this way, and an anecdote reported by Aulus Gellius (9.10) offers insight into the scrutiny to which the Virgilian scene was subjected: after noting approvingly the modesty with which Virgil describes the union of Venus and Vulcan (*uerecunda quadam translatione uerborum*), he quotes the scholar Annaeus Cornutus's "silly and hateful" (*insulsa nimis et odiosa*) criticism: " '*membra*,' tamen," inquit, "*paulo incautius nominauit*." Cf. also Schmit-Neuerburg 1999:251–52 and O'Rourke 2014:3.

she remains manipulative and slippery, often using her sexual appeal to achieve her ends;[17] thus, she remains true to the essential character we first encountered in Homer, the goddess whose maternal instincts led to the wound with which this discussion began. Indeed, the maternal bond lies at the heart of the continuity between the Homeric Aphrodite and the Virgilian Venus, even as it serves to highlight a fundamental difference between the Homeric poems and Virgil: the goddess who intrudes on the human battlefield in the *Iliad* to help her son continues to do so throughout the *Aeneid*, although while her Homeric motivation appears to have been purely personal, in the *Aeneid* it becomes closely linked with a national identity and a prophetic destiny. Lucretius's designation of the goddess as *Aeneadum genetrix* ("mother of the descendants of Aeneas," 1.1) inspires the rhetoric of Venus's request to Vulcan: with the words *"arma rogo, genetrix nato"* ("'I request arms, a mother for her son,'" *Aen.* 8.383), the goddess merges war and sexual desire, maternity and politics.[18]

The resulting realignment of our view of Venus and Mars complements what we know about the representation of the two divinities in the visual art and architecture of the late republic and early principate. Julius Caesar's inclusion of a temple to Venus Genetrix in the Forum Iulium, begun in 54 BCE (temple dedicated in 46 BCE), is easily recognized as an assertion of divine ancestry;[19] but his qualification of the divine ancestor as *genetrix* also provides the raw material for his adopted son Octavian Augustus to promote Venus's maternal dimension as part of a coherent program of imagery ornamenting new structures in Rome and throughout its empire.[20] Most explicit is the presentation of Venus in at least somewhat modest attire adjacent to Mars both on the pediment of the temple

---

17. Schmit-Neuerburg 1999:248–50 discusses the parallel between Hera's ἀπάτη of Zeus in *Iliad* Book 14 and Venus's employment of *dolus* here (*Aen.* 8.393).

18. See O'Rourke 2014:3–4 for a slightly more skeptical reading of the scene. Leach 1997 sets out in detail the prominent differences between Homeric Aphrodite (and Thetis) and Virgilian Venus as mothers. Cf. also Gutting 2009, emphasizing the contradictions in Venus's Virgilian character; Smolenaars 2004, focusing on the humor of Virgil's scene; and Lada-Richards 2006, exploring the polics of gender in the episode.

19. On the Julian cult of Venus Victrix/Genetrix, see Weinstock 1971:80–87 and Kuttner 1995: 22–32; further on the decoration of the Forum Iulium and the temple of Venus Genetrix, Ulrich 1993.

20. Julius Caesar is the first to have given Venus this epithet: Weinstock 1971:84 suggests that he borrowed it directly from Lucretius.

of Mars Ultor (dedicated in 2 BCE) and as one of three cult figures (along with Mars and Diuus Iulius) within its *cella*.[21] The two are united, but now the union is not explicitly erotic; rather, their oversight as protective divine parents is what matters. Finally, the very fact of so central a dedication to Mars Ultor as a god of vengeance does not invite reflection on his amatory history. Even when a period of war is itself over, as it is by the time of the construction of the forum of Augustus, Mars remains a vigilant and defensive god: wearing helmet and cuirass, he models the prudent and strategic general rather than the naughty lover, while the image of Venus depicted next to him is modestly clothed (in the *cella*) or portrayed as mother and ruler (i.e., with Cupid and scepter in the temple pediment). Finally, there is the bountiful female divinity protecting the two infants on her lap amid a landscape of fertility and abundance on a relief on the Ara Pacis Augustae (dedicated in 9 BCE); while inviting a range of interpretations, the image certainly allows at least the possibility of an identification with Venus.[22]

Thus, the ancestral importance of Venus and Mars is on prominent display throughout the period; their sexual escapades, on the other hand, as so memorably recounted by Demodocus in *Odyssey* Book 8, are not. In this context, Ovid's treatment of the loves of Venus and Mars in Book 2 of the *Ars Amatoria* appears as a striking, even daring, aberration; its inclusion there, to demonstrate, at least ostensibly, why exposing your wife's infidelity can only have negative repercussions for you—in fact, why your silence is much better for all involved!—certainly might be thought to lend support to the theory that the *Ars amatoria* was a, if not the, primary reason for Ovid's eventual *relegatio*.[23]

---

21. I follow the conventional dating of the forum of Augustus and temple of Mars Ultor, although some questions remain about its late completion: see P. Zanker 1988:193–203 for an influential view, and cf. Gurval 1995:282–83 and Galinsky 1996:198–202. Our knowledge of the decorative program of the temple is based on several later reliefs: a relief from the Claudian Ara Pietatis Augustae depicts the pediment (Galinsky 1996: fig. 47), and a first-century CE relief from Algiers depicts the triad of divinities worshipped with cult statues in the temple (Galinsky 1996: fig. 120). For a good discussion of the variation in details in these and related images, see Kuttner 1995:22–34.

22. As strongly argued by Galinsky 1992; for other views, see the exhaustive study of Spaeth 1996.

23. While Ovid's own allusions to the causes of his exile are often vague, he does, as we have seen (above, chapter 5), identify the three books of *Ars amatoria* as the real culprits. See also Sharrock 1994a and Holzberg 1990. I suspect, however, that the straw that broke the camel's back is to be found instead in the *Fasti*: the discussion below will introduce the transgressive poetics of Ovid's calendar poem.

The impression of divine irresponsibility and treachery that Ovid's appropriation of the Homeric tale creates for its readers does not end there, however; I turn now, therefore, to consider how Ovid continues to revise the careers of these gods in the *Fasti*. Indeed, it is tempting to suggest that, when he returns in both *Ars* and *Metamorphoses* to the depiction of these divinities as seen in Homer, Ovid reasserts their Homeric identities by stripping away any evidence of their Augustan rehabilitation. In the *Fasti*, conversely, Ovid makes the Romanness of these two divine ancestors a prominent and recurring motif, only to reveal points of rupture in the tendentious fabric where the Homeric presence peeks through.

III. Mars in Love

In his valuable discussion of Ovid's poetics in his calendar poem, Alessandro Barchiesi has drawn attention to the implicit but obvious presence of Homer's tale of Aphrodite and Ares behind the Venus and Mars of the *Fasti*.[24] Aside from Book 2, each of the books of the *Fasti* opens with an invocation of or prayer to its patron divinity (or stages a debate over that divinity's identity); Books 3 and 4, dedicated to Mars and Venus, respectively, are thus juxtaposed in the poem as they are on the calendar. That this juxtaposition is meaningful—indeed, that it constitutes a double entendre—is suggested in Ovid's description of the adjacency of Mars to Venus in the forum of Augustus: *formosa Venus . . . | utque solet, Marti continuata suo est* ("And, as usual, lovely Venus adjoins her Mars," 4.129–30). As Barchiesi comments: "[A]dultery is what binds them together, and *continuata* is not just a simple allusion to the fact that March is 'coupled' with April in the calendar."[25]

This coupling poses a challenge, however, for the elegiac poet. Venus is perfectly at home in the genre defined by the elegiac couplet; Mars, on the other hand—despite Ovid's frequent play with the trope of *militia amoris*—is really out of his depth here.[26] And, fittingly, he is entirely absent from the first two books of the *Fasti*, until in the final four couplets of Book

---

24. Barchiesi 1997b:61.

25. See also J. F. Miller 1997:396–97.

26. The point is made in strongly generic terms by Hinds 1992; I am indebted to his discussion, as also to that of Merli 2000:37–48, although I here pursue a different line of inquiry. For an interesting association of the trope of *militia amoris* with the poetics of Empedoclean Venus and Mars, see O'Rourke 2014.

2 (2.857–64) the Ovidian narrator announces the advent of Mars as his eponymous month begins. Virtually nothing about these verses suggests anything other than the battle god known from Homer: he comes in a chariot heralding the Equirria, chariot races in his honor that, like the *lusus Troiae* described by Virgil (*Aen.* 5.545–603), suggest military exercises; and he is addressed with the epithet Gradiuus, which, while of uncertain origin and etymology,[27] seems quite clearly to be used of Mars when he is at his most fierce. In the opening of *Aeneid* Book 3, Aeneas describes the arrival of the Trojans in wild Thrace, where he encounters the dread apparition of the bleeding shrub; this inauspicious beginning leads him to try to appease the local gods, including Gradiuus, with prayer (3.35); and in his comment on *Aen.* 1.292, in a long discussion of the god Quirinus, Servius mentions that the name Gradiuus is used of the fierce aspect of Mars (*Mars . . . cum saeuit Gradiuus dicitur*, "When he rages, Mars is called Gradivus").

The Ovidian narrator thus sets the stage for the opening of *Fasti* Book 3, and the first word in the book appears to confirm the implication: the book of Mars and of March opens with the invocation *Bellice*. But with the very next word, the narrator seems to contradict the mood he has established, so that by the end of the first couplet Mars is disarmed both physically and metaphorically (*Fast.* 3.1–2):[28]

> Bellice, depositis clipeo paulisper et hasta,
>   Mars, ades et nitidas casside solue comas.

> Be present, warrior Mars, set aside your shield and spear for a little while, and release your glossy tresses from the helmet.

The narrator then proceeds to promote the disarming of Mars by using Minerva as an exemplum: Mars is urged to set aside his warlike persona from time to time just as she does (5–8). She has things to do when she

---

27. Paul. Fest. p. 86.15 suggests an etymological link with the verb *gradior* (*a gradiendo in bella*); after strong words regarding the views of other scholars on this and other etymologies, Horsfall 2006 on *Aen.* 3.35 concludes, "At least the associations of G. are clearly bellicose and therefore admirably suited to Thrace."

28. The gesture is repeated at *Fast.* 3.171 (*sic posita dixit mihi casside Mauors*), but, as Hinds 1992:98–99 observes, this is an instance of "limited arms reduction," as in the following verse Mars keeps his *hasta* at the ready. The removal of the helmet as a means of displaying a less terrifying presence is of course Homeric: Hector does so to allay the fright of the young Astyanax at *Il.* 6.468–70 (discussed above, chapter 4).

is not at war, suggests the narrator (*num minus ingenuis artibus illa uacat?*, "she has no less free time than you for the liberal arts, does she?," 6); following her example, Mars too should be able to find something to do that does not involve armor (*inuenies et quod inermis agas*, "you will also find something you may do without weapons," 8).

The poet's use of the phrase *ingenuae artes* to describe Minerva's non-military interests is both perfectly accurate and studiedly misleading: the "liberal arts" she is known for include wool-working and carpentry, that is, the crafts practiced by hard-working but peaceful citizens, male and female;[29] in Mars's case, however, we quickly learn that the "arts" he can practice off the battlefield include impregnating a Vestal virgin (9–10):

> tum quoque inermis eras, cum te Romana sacerdos
>   cepit, ut huic urbi semina magna dares.

> Then too you lacked weapons, when the Roman priestess captivated you, so that you might give your great seed for this city.

With this couplet, the poet launches into a narrative about the Vestal Silvia (elsewhere known as Rhea Silvia or Ilia), who fell asleep one morning, presumably while some distance away from any local inhabitants who might protect her, and was raped by the lascivious Mars as she slept (11–22). Her inevitable pregnancy, of which she was not at first even aware, resulted in a dream about twin palm trees that sprang from the fillet she wore as a Vestal, and that were protected by a woodpecker and a wolf; some months later she found herself the mother of the twins Romulus and Remus (23–46).[30]

Mars is thus introduced as yet another in a long line of divine seducers: even in the ostensibly non-erotic *Fasti*, his act is preceded by the sexual assaults carried out—or at least planned—by Priapus (1.415–40), Jupiter (2.155–92), Faunus (2.303–58), Typhon (2.459–74), Jupiter again (2.583–98), and Mercury (2.599–616)—not to mention the mortal rapist Tarquinius (2.685–852).[31] By including the story of Silvia's rape as the very first of Mars's activities described in the *Fasti*, the narrator sets the

---

29. Burkert 1985:141–42.

30. Silvia's/Ilia's dream is examined in its literary-historical context by Krevans 1993 and Connors 1994, the latter of whom also offers a useful suggestion about the metatextuality of the scene: see further below.

31. Cf. Fantham 1983, who focuses on episodes of "frustrated seduction" in the *Fasti*.

tone for what will be a series of other erotic encounters—or attempts at encounters—in the remainder of Book 3. The Ovidian narrator thus suggests that Mars's first entry into the Roman calendar, and into a Romanocentric view of the world broadly conceived, is not as Homeric warrior but as Roman lover: his Roman identity begins at the moment when he desires Silvia.[32]

With the mention of the twins, the Ovidian narrative moves quickly through time, summarizing briefly the events surrounding their birth and childhood and, in a single oblique couplet (69–70), the demise of Remus. The first major event over which the narrator lingers is Romulus's establishment of the calendar and naming of the months, and Mars once again resumes his identity as a fighter, not a lover: initially, the first month is designated by Romulus as the month of his father, Mars, and the narrator observes that this is an appropriate beginning for a warlike people (77–80, 85–86):

> uox rata fit, patrioque uocat de nomine mensem:
> dicitur haec pietas grata fuisse deo.
> et tamen ante omnes Martem coluere priores;
> hoc dederat studiis bellica turba suis.
>
> . . .
>
> Mars Latio uenerandus erat, quia praesidet armis:
> arma ferae genti remque decusque dabant.

His speech is validated, and he calls the month by his father's name; this act of piety is said to have pleased the god. And yet, even those before [Romulus] cultivated Mars before all the other gods; in this the warlike populace had given themselves over to their own desires.

. . .

Mars was to be worshipped in Latium, since he presides over arms; arms gave a fierce people both a state and glory.

Mars's warlike personality is thus returned to center stage and reasserted, as his erotic history fades into a patriotic version of the Roman past.

---

32. Connors 1994:100 comments: "In Roman myth, Mars's penetration of Ilia's body sets Roman history in motion." Ovid emphasizes that this is Rome's and Mars's starting point by making it the starting point of his narrative, too. Cf. Newlands 1995:49.

Indeed, this continues as Ovid's narrative moves into the sequence of festivals on the March calendar: the narrator's description of the Matronalia, occurring on the first of the month (167–258), opens with a request that Mars Gradiuus himself explain how it is that a holiday so closely identified with women should be celebrated in his month, since he is so interested in manly affairs: *cum sis officiis, Gradiue, uirilibus aptus,* | *dic mihi matronae cur tua festa colant* ("Since you are suited to masculine observance, Gradivus, tell me why married women observe your holiday," 169–70). Mars responds directly, matching action to intent by removing his helmet (but not letting go of his spear; 171–72), explaining that he is useful in peacetime, too (*"studiis pacis deus utilis armis,"* "'a god skilled with weapons [now called upon] in the pursuits of peace,'" 173): in his capacity as the herald of spring, he presides over the fertility of all living things, and in particular of young brides hoping to become pregnant. The position of this holiday in the calendar links the military and amatory sides of his character, either one of which, says Mars, can be seen as an explanation for the ritual (231–34):

> "aut quia committi strictis mucronibus ausae
>   finierant lacrimis Martia bella suis;
> uel quod erat de me feliciter Ilia mater
>   rite colunt matres sacra diemque meum."

> "Either because the women, having dared to be exposed to drawn swords, had put an end to martial fighting with their tears, or because Ilia was made a mother auspiciously by me, women celebrate with ritual my cult and my day."

In addition to offering a rationale for Mars's association with the Matronalia, this speech also cleverly revises the episode of rape just narrated: whereas the first mention of this event captures the aggressive violence of Mars's desire (*Mars uidet hanc uisamque cupit potiturque cupita,* "Mars sees her, and desires her once seen, and overpowers her once desired," 21), it is now presented as if the intercourse necessarily involved is an unimportant footnote to the story. What matters, rather, is that Silvia/Ilia has become a mother, and has done so *feliciter* (233)—that is, in a manner propitious for the day and for all those who are pious in their performance of the ritual. Thus Mars subtly rehabilitates his reputation, framing his lustful assault as an act fundamental to the success of the Roman state.

The Ovidian narrator follows this episode with yet another devoted to Mars; focusing again on the god's association with war and military affairs, the poet offers a lengthy aetiology for the Salian cult, incorporating stories about Faunus and Picus as well (259–398). This episode too emphasizes the martial aspect of the god, particularly in the concluding vignette about the divine *ancile* and its multiple copies as articles closely associated both with the cult of Mars and with Rome's earliest days. With the conclusion of this episode, Mars recedes into the background, no longer a featured character in the myths and rituals the poet describes. The attention shifts to various constellations that are harbingers of spring, lingering over one of the several sequels to Ariadne's story that Ovid revisits throughout his career (459–516),[33] and then moves to the Ides, with a lengthy narrative about Anna Perenna, the Carthaginian refugee who became a beloved Roman god (523–696).

Anna's odyssey in her exile from Carthage is just that—an odyssey, modeled on the odyssey of Aeneas that is itself modeled on the Homeric *Odyssey*.[34] At the same time, it allows Ovid to indulge in one of his most playful interactions with Virgil, as he imagines a sequel and offers a portrait of Aeneas that is far from entirely complimentary. Anna wanders for years, seeking hospitality; during a storm at sea, she wishes she were dead and avoids dying in a shipwreck by the skin of her teeth, only to wash up on the Laurentian shore of Italy. There, it seems that Aeneas, having defeated the locals, is in power, and married to Lavinia; but now, perhaps nostalgic for the more hazardous and adventure-filled days of yore, he is apparently wont to relive the past on occasion by wandering the shore accompanied by faithful Achates alone (603–4).[35] One day, engaged in this pastime, he espies Anna wandering on the shore and can hardly believe his eyes: what a coincidence (605–7)! But she, knowing all too well the effect he had on her sister, is only conciliated to him

---

33. Boyd 2010, developing Conte 1986:60–63.

34. Littlewood 1980 offers many fine observations on the Virgilian intertext for Ovid's narrative; see also Newlands 1996:328–30.

35. Cf. Bömer 1958 on *Fast.* 3.603, noting that Achates appears to be a specifically Virgilian invention and comparing the use of *comitatus* here with that at *Aen.* 1.312. The playfulness of the reminiscence is heightened, I suggest, by Ovid's description of their solitary stroll as *secretum . . . iter*: the participle at least hints at the scene in *Aeneid* Book 1 in which Aeneas and Achates observe their companions unseen, concealed in a cloud provided by Venus (see especially *Aen.* 1.516–19 and 579–87). Cf. also Newlands 1996:328, who interprets Aeneas's furtiveness here as an indication of "Ovid's reversal of Aeneas' heroic qualities."

after he explains his continuing dismay at Dido's fate and offers her his hospitality; after all, she has no other realistic choice but to accept his offer (608–26).

The momentary reprieve offered by Aeneas is, however, brief indeed: no sooner does he take her to his home and entrust her to the care of his new wife, Lavinia, than that the Latin princess, overpowered by fear and jealousy of the new arrival, begins to think Medea-like thoughts (627–38). Warned to flee by Dido, who appears to her in a dream, Anna jumps out of a window and races through the woods until reaching the river Numicius, where she disappears, only to emerge as a nymph who, because she hides in the ever-flowing stream (*amne perenne*), is now called Anna Perenna (639–54).

The Ovidian narrator brings this episode to an apparent close with a learned disquisition on alternative aetiologies for Anna Perenna's cult and her origins, and explains the helpful role she plays in one of these alternatives, involving the secession of the plebs (657–74). Just when her exit from the narrative would appear to be imminent, however, the narrator adds a final vignette to her story, ostensibly to explain why the singing of obscene ditties is associated with this festival; this otherwise casually motivated narrative, until now entirely set off from the opening scenes of *Fasti* Book 3, then circles back to that opening and in a single couplet establishes a link between Anna Perenna and Mars (677–78):[36]

> nuper erat dea facta: uenit Gradiuus ad Annam,
>   et cum seducta talia uerba facit . . .

She had been made a god recently. Lord Gradivus came to Anna, and taking her aside he says words such as these . . .

As we have seen, the epithet Gradiuus solemnly introduces the god into the poem at *Fast.* 2.861; its repetition here now recalls that introduction and recalls as well the incongruous lasciviousness the god had shown in the first scene of Book 3, with the rape of Silvia. The circular movement of the narrative is underscored by the double entendre that characterizes Anna when Mars addresses her: she is *seducta*, "taken aside," by him; but

---

36. A good example of what I have elsewhere referred to as "narrative patterning" in the *Fasti*: Boyd 2000.

as Ovid's readers will shortly discover, she is also "seduced" by his charms and will soon act upon her feelings.[37]

Mars, however, sees Anna as essentially a means to an end rather than an end in herself. After pointing out their shared space on the calendar, he reveals to Anna the real reason for his wanting to talk with her: he needs help in seducing Minerva. They are, he suggests, meant for each other (*"armifer armiferae correptus amore Mineruae | uror,"* " 'a warrior myself, I burn, seized by love for the warrior goddess Minerva,' " 681–82), and he claims to have been enamored for quite some time (*"hoc longo tempore uulnus alo,"* " 'I've been nursing this wound for a long time,' " 682). He sees Anna not as a potential lover, in fact, but as a matchmaker or procuress (*"comis anus,"* " 'dear old woman,' " 684) who can help him to bed the goddess. The narrative thus moves Ovid's readers forward in the calendar, as Mars's encounter with Silvia fades into the past, but also has a circular rhythm, as it returns to a point very much like the one with which *Fasti* Book 3 had opened; the only difference now is that Mars needs help because his latest would-be mate is not, like Silvia, disarmed by sleep but is divine, and a militant virgin at that.[38]

Scholars have long noted the possibility—indeed, the likelihood—that Ovid's inspiration for the scene that follows is to be found in the Roman theater, in particular, the tradition of mime, and Laberius's *Anna Peranna* has been identified as a likely source.[39] Certainly Ovid's text itself invites readers to think about a theatrical setting: the opening of the Anna Perenna narrative establishes the general idea that the festivities have a theatrical flavor (535–40); recalling that introduction, Ovid now uses the word *obscena* to describe the songs sung by girls at the festival of Anna Perenna (*Nunc mihi, cur cantent, superest, obscena puellae,* "It remains for me now to explain why the girls sing naughty songs," 675; cf. 695), a word the popular etymology of which is active as well in the Venus and Mars scene from *Ars amatoria* Book 2 discussed in the

---

37. For the sexual innuendo, compare *Met.* 3.379 (of Narcissus).

38. The circularity of the narrative is underscored by the fact that Minerva in fact had been mentioned in the opening of the book, as a good example of a god who knows how to do something other than carry weapons and wage war (*Fast.* 3.5–8).

39. McKeown 1979:75–76 is tentative; Fantham 1983:185 confidently asserts the origins of Ovid's narrative in Laberius; for a more cautious assessment, see Panayotakis 2010:115–23 for the meager fragments of *Anna Peranna* and their interpretive limits.

preceding chapter;[40] and in asking for her help, Mars tells Anna that
the role of procuress suits her ("*conueniunt partes hae tibi, comis anus,*"
"'This role suits you, my dear old lady,'" 684). Certain features of the
action also suggest mythological burlesque: even in the first aetiology
for Anna Perenna's cult, long before this scene with Mars, Anna's self-
defenestration (643–44) invites a comic reading of her character; and the
trick she plays on Mars, disguising herself as his would-be bedmate (*ut
noua nupta*, "like a new bride," 690), is not only sexually suggestive but
humorously grotesque. Finally, Ovid's readers are invited to observe the
entire scenario from a divine perspective—now, however, not that of the
male divinities who had laughed at the entrapment of Venus and Mars
but that of Anna Perenna herself, as well as of one other aptly chosen
female divinity, Venus (693–94):

> ridet amatorem carae noua diua Mineruae,
>   nec res hac Veneri gratior ulla fuit.

> The new goddess laughs at the lover of dear Minerva, nor was any-
> thing more pleasing to Venus than this.

With the mention of Venus, the narrator not only reminds us of the
Homeric tale and its Ovidian descendants but also sets the stage for what
is to follow in Book 4, when Venus takes center stage and her union with
Mars is reasserted as proper and enduring, from an archly Roman point
of view (*Fast.* 4.57–60).

And so at last the story of Anna Perenna's escapades, both mortal and
divine, does truly come to an end, and with it ends Mars's involvement in
Fasti Book 3.[41] The last view readers have of him here shows us how far
he, and we, have traveled from the god's Homeric beginnings: now no
longer the envy of the other gods, he feels only shame and anger (*nunc
pudor elusum, nunc subit ira, deum*, "now shame, now anger overcomes
the god who had been fooled," 692) and must endure the mockery of
both goddesses and the human worshippers of Anna, who immortalize
this story with jokes and song (*ioci ueteres obscenaque dicta*, "old jokes and
dirty remarks," 695). Indeed, with the epithet *ueteres* the Ovidian narrator

---

40. See above, chapter 8, n.28, for the etymology given by Varro.

41. Cf. the discussion of Merli 2000:117–29 on the disappearance of Mars from the narrative
of March, with further observations on the relationship of Mars and Minerva (esp. 126 n.77).

reminds his readers that versions of this story have been circulating for a very long time, and that he is following in a tradition that began with Homer's tale of Ares and Aphrodite: an old and naughty tale indeed, but one worth repeating.

IV. Old Scars

The literary history of the association of Venus and Mars is an old one, going back to Homer; and Ovid offers a final nod to their Homeric characters when he complements their proximity in the calendar (and in his calendar-poem) with a subtle reminder of their Homeric exceptionality as the two gods wounded by mortals in *Iliad* Book 5. I return once more to Mars's words to Anna at *Fast.* 3.682: *"hoc longo tempore uulnus alo."* The wound of love is a cliché of erotic poetry that connects Mars to a long line of desperate lovers, of whom Dido is surely the most memorable example: *At regina graui iamdudum saucia cura | uulnus alit uenis* ("But the queen, hurt for some time now by her grievous desire, nurses the wound in her veins," *Aen.* 4.1–2); even Mars's diction reflects her influence (*longo tempore* ≈ *iamdudum*;[42] *uulnus alo* ≈ *vulnus alit*).[43] But context is everything; and whereas Virgil's description offers us a vivid impression of Dido's simmering and self-destructive desire, the same language on Mars's lips is almost incongruous, if not entirely false. After all, how long, exactly, is the period of infatuation that is implied in the words *longo tempore*? At the beginning of this book, after all, it was Silvia rather than Minerva who occupied Mars's lascivious desires; so his representation of himself here as a longtime unrequited lover of Minerva is at best hyperbole.[44] On the other hand, the old wound of which he here complains may instead be construed as a veritable wound indeed, the

---

42. On the interpretation of *iamdudum*, see the useful notes ad loc. of Pease 1935 and R. G. Austin 1955.

43. See *TLL* 1.1711.60–70 (s.v. *alo*). The phrase *uulnus* (or *uulnera*) *alere* appears first at Lucr. 3.64, but the metaphorical range of *uulnus* there is general, i.e., "tribulations"; *Aen.* 4.1 is the first example we have of the expression in an erotic sense, perhaps a bold extension of Catull. 68.23–24, *gaudia . . . | . . . alebat amor*. Ovid uses the expression on one other occasion (*Tr.* 5.2.13), but the context is not erotic.

44. It is also strikingly at odds with the Homeric relationship of the two gods: at *Il.* 5.825–86, Athena instigates Diomedes's attack on Ares; note especially Ares's description of Athena in his words to Zeus at *Il.* 5.874–75, "σὺ γὰρ τέκες ἄφρονα κούρην | οὐλομένην, ἣ τ' αἰὲν ἀήσυλα ἔργα μέμηλεν." Cf. also Hinds 1992:101, developed by Merli 2000:132–35, for the suggestion that another implication of *longo tempore* would be "since the time of the Trojan War."

one inflicted a long time ago, by Diomedes, in *Iliad* Book 5. In Homer's narrative, that wound was quickly healed, and the divine impermeability of the god restored; but in Ovid's narrative, it re-emerges, like an old scar, neither entirely forgotten nor entirely gone, but repurposed, as Ovid rewrites the Homeric Ares.

A similarly Homeric scar can be traced on Venus, too. As Book 4 of the *Fasti* opens, she addresses her poet, asking him why he is interested in her; could it be, she wonders, that he still bears "the old wound" (*uetus . . . uulnus*, 4.4)? Her reference here looks to the Ovidian narrator of the *Amores*, who senses himself to be suffering from the wound of love, and to the *praeceptor* of the *Ars amatoria*, who cites his own experience with the wounds of love as a basis for his didactic authority;[45] in other words, she recognizes the conventions of elegy. Here, Venus uses the trope to ask him what he wants with the goddess of elegiac love now that he is engaged upon something greater. But the poet of the *Fasti* replies with words meant to remind her that wounds are not originally an elegiac occurrence but in fact are borrowed by elegy from epic itself. She should know, he suggests; after all, she herself knows about wounds (*Fast.* 4.3–6):

> "quid tibi" ait "mecum? certe maiora canebas.
>   num uetus in molli pectore uulnus habes?"
> "scis, dea," respondi "de uulnere." risit, et aether
>   protinus ex illa parte serenus erat.

> "What business have you with me? Surely you were singing of greater things. You don't still have the old wound in your tender breast, do you?" "You know about a wound, goddess," I replied. She laughed, and straightaway the upper air was calm in that region.

The wound she knows about is in the first place the wound of love: she has been responsible for inflicting many such wounds herself, as well as for bidding her son Cupid to do so on her behalf. But with his knowing use of the verb *scis*, the Ovidian narrator also points to her own experience— experience that begins with the wound she received on the battlefield in *Iliad* Book 5 (and which my readers will recognize from the opening

---

45. E.g., *Am.* 2.9.1–4; *Ars am.* 1.23–24, both noted by Fantham 1998 on *Fast.* 4.4.

chapters of this study of Ovid's Homeric reception). Her response is tell-
ing: she laughs (and so recalls her Homeric epithet φιλομμειδής), rec-
ognizing the joke, as clever as it is bold, made by her interlocutor. She
has long since recovered, but with her laugh she acknowledges that the
Homeric scar is with her still and helps to ensure her intimate familiarity
with the passions of human lovers.

The two gods wounded on the epic battlefield of Homer have changed
location, from Greece to Italy and from epic to elegy; in the process, the
nature of their wounds has changed, too, to conform to their new envi-
ronment. But the Homeric resonance of their origins is loud and clear,
and the pattern of repetition already observed indicates that it is only a
matter of time until we find them again where Homer first joined them,
in the bed of Vulcan. Ovid offers a subtle but acute indication of this
potential with an allusion to Vulcan in *Fasti* Book 3 that occurs immedi-
ately before the adventures of Anna Perenna.[46] The narrator of the *Fasti*
offers to explain the aetiology of the constellation Corona: it is the crown
of Ariadne, given to the Minoan princess by Bacchus as a gift to mark
their union and her transformation into a goddess. The explanation is
familiar, and the association of the constellation Corona with Ariadne
and Bacchus is known from a variety of other sources;[47] but the narrator,
speaking through Bacchus, offers one small—and entirely unnecessary—
detail that makes for a conclusion to their love story that is ambiguous at
best (*Fast.* 3.511–14):

> "tu mihi iuncta toro mihi iuncta uocabula sumes,
>   nam tibi mutatae Libera nomen erit,
> sintque tuae tecum faciam monimenta coronae,
>   Volcanus Veneri quam dedit, illa tibi."

"Since you are joined with me in my bed, we are now joined names,
for now that you have been transformed, your name will be Libera;
and with you I shall make your crown an enduring reminder—the
crown which Vulcan gave to Venus, and Venus to you."

---

46. Vulcan is mentioned in passing on one other occasion in this book, at *Fast.* 3.82, in a list
of the various tutelary divinities worshipped in different places throughout the ancient world.

47. See Ovid *Met.* 8.177–82 with Kenney 2011 ad loc.; Bömer 1958 on *Fast.* 3.459f. notes earlier
allusions.

The crown Bacchus offers to Ariadne as a memorial of their love is, it seems, a creation of Vulcan: although Bacchus says no more, he implies that it was a wedding gift, crafted by the divine artisan for his beautiful wife.[48]

The only other extant ancient source that makes mention of Vulcan's crown for Venus is Pseudo-Eratosthenes *Catast.* 5, according to whom it was the work of Hephaestus, and Ariadne received it from the Graces and Aphrodite.[49] Although this work in its current form postdates Ovid, it is quite likely that both its author and Ovid are working from an earlier text on catasterisms; and the involvement of Hephaestus as the crown's creator is both logical and plausible, given the wide variety of female ornaments, as well as female *automata*, that he is described as creating in *Iliad* Book 18 (400–402; 417–21).[50] Indeed, Hephaestus creates another crown of ambiguous significance in Hesiod's *Theogony*: that which yet another of his creations wears, the clay woman crafted as an evil thing (κακόν, 570) in return for Prometheus's theft of fire (*Th.* 578–84):[51]

ἀμφὶ δέ οἱ στεφάνην χρυσέην κεφαλῆφιν ἔθηκε,
τὴν αὐτὸς ποίησε περικλυτὸς Ἀμφιγυήεις
ἀσκήσας παλάμῃσι, χαριζόμενος Διὶ πατρί.
τῇ δ' ἐνὶ δαίδαλα πολλὰ τετεύχατο, θαῦμα ἰδέσθαι,
κνώδαλ' ὅσ' ἤπειρος δεινὰ τρέφει ἠδὲ θάλασσα,
τῶν ὅ γε πόλλ' ἐνέθηκε, χάρις δ' ἐπὶ πᾶσιν ἄητο,
θαυμάσια, ζῳοῖσιν ἐοικότα φωνήεσσιν.

And [Athena] placed around her on her head a golden diadem, which the lame god himself had made, renowned Hephaestus, fashioning it with his hands, so pleasing father Zeus. And on it were worked many intricate things, a marvel to see, as many fearful creatures as the land and the sea produce; and many of these

---

48. A *stephanê* is typically worn by a bride about to be married: see Oakley and Sinos 1993:12, 16–19.

49. Hardie 2015 on *Met.* 14.849–51 notes the connection between the *corona* of Ariadne and the *coma Berenices* found at Catull. 66.59–62, and evidently modeled on Callim. *Aet.* fr. 110.59–64 Pf.: Callimachus celebrates the recent marriage of Berenice by suggesting that her lock of hair will ascend to the heavens, where it will join Ariadne's crown.

50. On Hephaestus's *automata* and ancient magic, see Faraone 1987.

51. I quote the text as it appears in West 1978; he comments on the verses but has little to say about the crown itself. Francis 2009:13–16 discusses the crown in ecphrastic terms and provides further bibliography.

marvels he included, resembling living creatures with voices; and charm breathed upon them all.

The clay woman's crown is a suitable ornament for a bride-to-be, and an indication of divine favor; we may suppose, therefore, that in bestowing on Ariadne the crown Vulcan had originally made for Venus, Ovid's Bacchus signifies the impending divinity of his new bride. Yet as readers of this episode well know—or should at least suspect—this is not in fact the conclusion of a love story for the ages, nor a token of Bacchus's undying devotion; rather, as we learn from the opening of the episode, Ariadne's distress is caused not by the departure of Theseus—an event in her mythical career that long precedes the scene in *Fasti* Book 3—but by Bacchus himself, who had saved her from the lonely abandonment so famously imagined by Catullus (poem 64) and elsewhere by Ovid himself (*Heroides* 10, *Ars am.* 1.525–64, and *Met.* 8.169–82).[52] In fact, in *Fasti* Book 3 Ovid's narrator introduces a version of Ariadne who is at first almost unrecognizable, when she declares herself delighted to have been able to trade in Theseus for Bacchus (461–64):

> iam bene periuro mutarat coniuge Bacchum
> quae dedit ingrato fila legenda uiro;
> sorte tori gaudens "quid flebam rustica?" dixit;
> "utiliter nobis perfidus ille fuit."

And now she who had given an ungrateful man the thread to follow had gotten Bacchus in exchange for her treacherous mate; delighting in the lucky choice of a bed, she said, "Why was I crying like a country girl? That man was usefully treacherous for me."

Ariadne's satisfaction does not last long, however; it seems that, in his peregrinations through the East, Bacchus has met yet another pretty princess and has therefore driven his wife to a new round of lamentation (465–506). It is only after listening to her repetitive lament that Bacchus takes her in his arms, dries her tears, and promises her the crown made by Vulcan for Venus: presumably, a symbol of marital bliss for them, but not entirely pristine, since it cannot help but simultaneously evoke Venus's betrayal of the husband who gave it to her in the first place.

---

52. Boyd 2010.

The gods thus depicted by Ovid are inseparable, it seems, from the mythical narratives in which they appear; and the one feature they all share is a repetitious predictability. Both the repetitious desire of Venus and Mars and the repetitious craft of Vulcan work their way through numerous marvelous stories, all different, yet all the same, as Ovid combines poetic desire and poetic craft in an unceasing renewal of Homeric poetry.

Bibliography

Adams, J. N. 1982. *The Latin Sexual Vocabulary*. Baltimore: Johns Hopkins University Press.

Aicher, P. 1989. "Ennius' Dream of Homer." *AJP* 110:227–32.

Alden, M. J. 1997. "The Resonances of the Song of Ares and Aphrodite." *Mnemosyne* 50:513–29.

———. 2000. *Homer beside Himself: Para-narratives in the Iliad*. Oxford: Oxford University Press.

Allen, A., ed. 1993. *The Fragments of Mimnermus: Text and Commentary*. Stuttgart: Steiner.

Andersen, Ø. 1978. *Die Diomedesgestalt in der Ilias*. Symbolae Osloenses Suppl. Vol. 25. Oslo: Universitetsforlaget.

Apthorp, M. J. 1980. *The Manuscript Evidence for Interpolation in Homer*. Heidelberg: C. Winter.

Arend, W. 1933. *Die typischen Scenen bei Homer*. Berlin: Weidmann.

Armstrong, R. 2005. *Ovid and His Love Poetry*. London: Duckworth.

Ashby, T. 1910. "The Classical Topography of the Roman Campagna, Part III, Section II." *PBSR* 5:215–425.

Asquith, H. 2005. "From Genealogy to *Catalogue*: The Hellenistic Adaptation of the Hesiodic Catalogue Form." In *The Hesiodic Catalogue of Women: Constructions and Reconstructions*, edited by R. Hunter, 266–86. Cambridge: Cambridge University Press.

Austin, N. 1969. "Telemachos Polymechanos." *California Studies in Classical Antiquity* 2:45–63.

Austin, R. G., ed. 1955. *P. Vergili Maronis Aeneidos Liber Quartus*. Oxford: Oxford University Press.

———, ed. 1977. *P. Vergili Maronis Aeneidos Liber Sextus*. Oxford: Oxford University Press.

Baldo, G. 1986. "Il codice epico nelle *Metamorfosi* di Ovidio." *MD* 16:109–31.

———. 1995. *Dall'Eneide alle Metamorfosi: Il codice epico di Ovidio*. Padua: Imprimitur.

Barbara, S. 2006. "Le 'Diomède' de l'*Énéide* ou le bon roi selon Virgile." *REA* 108:517–58.

Barber, E. J. W. 1992. "The Peplos of Athena." In *Goddess and Polis: The Panathenaic Festival in Ancient Athens*, edited by J. Neils, 103–17. Princeton, NJ: Princeton University Press.

Barchiesi, A. 1984. *La traccia del modello: Effetti omerici nella narrazione virgiliana.* Pisa: Giardini. (= 2015. *Homeric Effects in Vergilian Narrative.* Translated by I. Marchesi. Princeton, NJ: Princeton University Press.)

———. 1989. "Voci e istanze narrative nelle *Metamorfosi* di Ovidio." *MD* 23:55–97.

———, ed. 1992. *P. Ovidii Nasonis Epistulae Heroidum I–III.* Florence: Felice Le Monnier.

———. 1994. *Il poeta e il principe: Ovidio e il discorso augusteo.* Rome: Laterza.

———. 1997a. "Endgames: Ovid's *Metamorphoses* 15 and *Fasti* 6." In *Classical Closure: Reading the End in Greek and Latin Literature*, edited by D. H. Roberts, F. M. Dunn, and D. Fowler, 181–208. Princeton, NJ: Princeton University Press.

———. 1997b. *The Poet and the Prince: Ovid and Augustan Discourse.* Berkeley: University of California Press.

———. 1999. "Venus' Masterplot: Ovid and the *Homeric Hymns*." In Hardie, Barchiesi, and Hinds 1999:112–26.

———. 2001a. "Continuities." In *Speaking Volumes: Narrative and Intertext in Ovid and Other Latin Poets*, 9–28. London: Duckworth. (= 1984. "Problemi d'interpretazione in Ovidio. Continuità delle storie, continuazione dei testi." *MD* 16:77–107.)

———. 2001b. "Future Reflexive: Two Modes of Allusion and Ovid's *Heroides*." In *Speaking Volumes: Narrative and Intertext in Ovid and Other Latin Poets*, 105–27. London: Duckworth. (= 1993. *HSCP* 95:333–65.)

———. 2002. "Narrative Technique and Narratology in the *Metamorphoses*." In *The Cambridge Companion to Ovid*, edited by P. Hardie, 180–99. Cambridge: Cambridge University Press.

———, ed. 2005. *Ovidio, Metamorfosi volume I: Libri I–II.* Turin: Mondadori.

Barchiesi, A., and G. Rosati, eds. 2007. *Ovidio, Metamorfosi volume II: Libri III–IV.* Turin: Mondadori.

Baumbach, M. 2012. "Borderline Experiences with Genre: The Homeric *Hymn to Aphrodite* between Epic, Hymn and Epyllic Poetry." In *Brill's Companion to Greek and Latin Epyllion and Its Reception*, edited by M. Baumbach and S. Bär, 135–48. Leiden: Brill.

Beaumont, L. A. 1994. "Constructing a Methodology for the Interpretation of Childhood Age in Classical Athenian Iconography." *Archaeological Review from Cambridge* 13:81–96.

———. 1995. "Mythological Childhood: A Male Preserve? An Interpetation of Classical Athenian Iconography in Its Socio-historical Context." *ABSA* 90:339–61.

———. 2012. *Childhood in Ancient Athens: Iconography and Social History.* London: Routledge.

Beck, D. 1999. "Speech Introductions and the Character Development of Telemachus." *CJ* 94:121–41.

Beekes, R. 2010. *Etymological Dictionary of Greek.* 2 vols. Leiden: Brill.

Bekker, I., ed. 1833. *Apollonii Sophistae Lexicon Homericum.* Berlin: Reimer.

Belmont, D. E. 1969. "Athena and Telemachus." *CJ* 65:109–16.

Benediktson, D. T. 1985. "Propertius' 'Elegiacization' of Homer." *Maia* 37: 17–26.

Bérard, J. 1957. *La colonization grecque de l'Italie méridionale et de la Sicile dans l'antiquité.* Paris: Presses universitaires de France.

Berthet, J. F. 1980. "Properce et Homère." In *L'élégie romaine: Enracinement, thèmes, diffusion: Actes du colloque international organisé par la Faculté des lettres et sciences humaines de Mulhouse,* edited by A. Thill, 141–55. Mulhouse: Ophrys.

Beschi, L. 1967–68. "Il monumento di Telemachos, fondatore dell'Asklepieion ateniense." *ASAA* 45–46:381–436.

Bickel, E. 1950. "Syllabus indiciorum quibus Pseudovergiliana et Pseudoovidiana carmina definiantur: Symbolae ad Cirin, Culicem, Aetnam." *RhM* 93:289–324.

Biering, R. 1995. *Die Odysseefresken vom Esquilin.* Munich: Biering & Brinkmann.

Bierl, A. 2012. "Demodokos' Song of Ares and Aphrodite in Homer's *Odyssey* (8.266–366): An Epyllion?—Agonistic Performativity and Cultural Metapoetics." In *Brill's Companion to Greek and Latin Epyllion and Its Reception,* edited by M. Baumbach and S. Bär, 111–34. Leiden: Brill.

Bing, P. 1988. *The Well-Read Muse: Present and Past in Callimachus and the Hellenistic Poets.* Göttingen: Vandenhoeck & Ruprecht.

———. 1993. "The *Bios*-Tradition and Poets' Lives in Hellenistic Poetry." In *Nomodeiktes: Greek Studies in Honor of Martin Ostwald,* edited by R. M. Rosen and J. Farrell, 619–31. Ann Arbor: University of Michigan Press.

Blänsdorf, J., ed. 1995. *Fragmenta poetarum latinarum, post W. Morel et K. Büchner.* Stuttgart: Teubner.

Block, E. 1982. "Poetics in Exile: An Analysis of *Epistulae ex Ponto* 3.9." *CA* 1: 18–27.

Bloom, H. 1973. *The Anxiety of Influence: A Theory of Poetry.* Oxford: Oxford University Press.

Bolton, M. C. 1997. "Elegy Upside Down: The Inversion of Elegiac and Epic Elements in *Heroides* III." In *Studies in Latin Literature and Roman History VIII,* edited by C. Deroux, 218–30. Brussels: Éditions Latomus.

Bömer, F., ed. 1958. *P. Ovidius Naso: Die Fasten.* 2 vols. Heidelberg: C. Winter.

———, ed. 1969–2006. *P. Ovidius Naso: Metamorphosen.* 8 vols. Heidelberg: C. Winter.

Bonner, S. F. 1977. *Education in Ancient Rome.* Berkeley: University of California Press.

Boyancé, P. 1953. "Properce." In *L'influence grecque sur la poésie latine de Catulle à Ovide,* 169–209. Entretiens sur l'antiquité classique vol. 2. Vandœuvres: Fondation Hardt.

Boyd, B. W. 1992. "Vergil's Camilla and the Traditions of Catalogue and Ecphrasis (*Aeneid* 7.803–817)." *AJP* 113:213–34.

———. 1997. *Ovid's Literary Loves: Influence and Innovation in the Amores.* Ann Arbor: University of Michigan Press.

———. 2000. "'*Celabitur auctor*': The Crisis of Authority and Narrative Patterning in Ovid, *Fasti* 5." *Phoenix* 54:64–98.

———. 2003. "*Itala nam tellus Graecia maior erat*: 'Poetic Syncretism' and the Divinities of Ovid, *Fasti* 4." *Mouseion*, ser. III.3:13–35.

———. 2006. "Two Rivers and the Reader in Ovid, *Metamorphoses* 8." *TAPA* 136:171-206.

———. 2009. "Ovid's *Remedia amoris*." In *Blackwell's Companion to Ovid*, edited by P. E. Knox, 104–19. Oxford: Wiley-Blackwell.

———. 2010. "Island-Hopping: Reading Ovid's Ariadne and Her Texts." In *Approaches to Teaching the Works of Ovid and the Ovidian Tradition*, edited by B. W. Boyd and C. Fox, 225–33. New York: Modern Language Association.

———. 2012. "On Starting an Epic (Journey): Telemachus, Phaethon, and the Beginning of Ovid's *Metamorphoses*." *MD* 69:101–18.

———. 2015. "Ovidian Encounters with the Embassy to Achilles: Homeric Reception in *Metamorphoses* 8 and *Heroides* 3." *Paideia: Rivista di filologia, ermeneutica e critica letteraria* 70:27–41.

———. 2016a. "Ovid's Circe and the Revolutionary Power of *carmina* in the *Remedia amoris*." In *Roman Literary Cultures: Domestic Politics, Revolutionary Poetics, Civic Spectacle*, edited by A. Keith and J. Edmondson, 111–23. Toronto: University of Toronto Press.

———. 2016b. "Repeat after Me: The Loves of Venus and Mars in *Ars amatoria* 2 and *Metamorphoses* 4." In Fulkerson and Stover 2016b:47–68.

Braswell, B. K. 1971. "Mythological Innovation in the *Iliad*." *CQ* 21:16–26.

———. 1982. "The Song of Ares and Aphrodite: Theme and Relevance in *Odyssey* 8." *Hermes* 110:129–37.

Bremmer, J. 1988. "La plasticité du mythe: Méléagre dans la poésie homérique." In *Métamorphoses du mythe en Grèce antique*, edited by C. Calame, 37–56. Geneva: Labor et Fides.

Bright, D. F. 1971. "A Tibullan Odyssey." *Arethusa* 4:197–214.

Brillet-Dubois, P. 2011. "An Erotic *Aristeia*: The *Homeric Hymn to Aphrodite* and Its Relationship to the Epic Tradition." In *The Homeric Hymns: Interpretive Essays*, edited by A. Faulkner, 105–32. Oxford: Oxford University Press.

Brink, C. O., ed. 1971. *Horace on Poetry: The Ars Poetica.* Cambridge: Cambridge University Press.

———. 1972. "Hellenistic Worship of Homer." *AJP* 93:547–67.

Broccia, G. 1974. *Ricerche su Livio Andronico epico.* Padua: Antenore.

Brown, C. G. 1989. "Ares, Aphrodite, and the Laughter of the Gods." *Phoenix* 43:283–93.

Brown, R. 1987. "The Palace of the Sun in Ovid's *Metamorphoses*." In *Homo Viator: Classical Essays for John Bramble*, edited by M. Whitby, P. Hardie, and M. Whitby, 211–20. Bristol: Bristol Classical Press.

Brunelle, C. 2002. "Pleasure, Failure, and Danger: Reading Circe in the *Remedia*." *Helios* 29:55–68.

Büchner, K. 1979. "Livius Andronicus und die erste künstlerische Übersetzung der europäischen Kultur." *SO* 54:37–70.

Burkert, W. 1960. "Das Lied von Ares und Aphrodite." *RhM* 103:130–44.

———. 1985. *Greek Religion*. Cambridge, MA: Harvard University Press.

Cairns, D.L. 1993. *Aidôs: The Psychology and Ethics of Honour and Shame in Ancient Greek Literature*. Oxford: Oxford University Press.

Calhoun, G. M. 1933 (actually published in 1944). "Homeric Repetitions." *University of California Publications in Classical Philology XII (1933 [1944])*: 1–25.

Cameron, A. 1995. *Callimachus and His Critics*. Oxford: Oxford University Press.

———. 2004. *Greek Mythography in the Roman World*. Oxford: Oxford University Press.

Camps, W. R., ed. 1965. *Propertius, Elegies Book IV*. Cambridge: Cambridge University Press.

———, ed. 1966. *Propertius, Elegies Book III*. Cambridge: Cambridge University Press.

Casali, S. 1997. "*Quaerenti plura legendum*: On the Necessity of 'Reading More' in Ovid's Exile Poetry." *Ramus* 26:80–112.

———. 2009. "Ovidian Intertextuality." In *A Companion to Ovid*, edited by P. E. Knox, 341–54. Oxford: Wiley-Blackwell.

Caspers, C. L. 2006. "The Loves of the Poets: Allusions in Hermesianax fr. 7 Powell." In *Beyond the Canon*, edited by M. A. Harder, R. F. Regtuit, and G. C. Wakker, 21–42. Leuven: Peeters.

Christensen, J. P. 2009. "The End of Speeches and a Speech's End: Nestor, Diomedes, and the *telos muthôn*." In *Reading Homer: Film and Text*, edited by K. Myrsiades, 136–62. Madison, NJ: Fairleigh Dickinson University Press.

Christensen, J. P., and E. T. E. Barker. 2011. "On Not Remembering Tydeus: Agamemnon, Diomedes, and the Contest for Thebes." *MD* 66:9–43.

Ciappi, M. 2000. "La narrazione ovidiana del mito di Fetonte e le sue fonti: L'importanza della tradizione tragica." *Athenaeum* 88:117–68.

Citroni, M. 1984. "Ovidio, *Ars* 1, 2–4 e Omero, *Iliade* 23, 315–18: L'analogia tra le *artes* e la fondazione del discorso didascalico." *Sileno* 10:157–67.

———. 1986. "Le raccomandazioni del poeta: Apostrofe al libro e contatto col destinario." *Maia* 38:111–46.

Claassen, J.-M. 1990. "Ovid's Wavering Identity: Personification and Depersonalisation in the Exilic Poems." *Latomus* 49:102–16.

Clark, M. 2001. "Was Telemachus Rude to His Mother? *Odyssey* 1.356–59." *CP* 96:335–54.

————. 2004. "Formulas, Metre and Type-scenes." In *The Cambridge Companion to Homer*, edited by R. Fowler, 117–38. Cambridge: Cambridge University Press.

Clarke, H. W. 1963. "Telemachus and the *Telemacheia*." *AJP* 84:129–45.

Clarke, W. M. 1978. "Achilles and Patroclus in Love." *Hermes* 106:381–96.

Clausen, W., ed. 1994. *Virgil: Eclogues*. Oxford: Oxford University Press.

Clay, D. 1983. *Lucretius and Epicurus*. Ithaca, NY: Cornell University Press.

Clay, J. S. 1983. *The Wrath of Athena: Gods and Men in the Odyssey*. Princeton. NJ: Princeton University Press.

————. 2005. "The Beginning and End of the *Catalogue of Women* and Its Relation to Hesiod." In *The Hesiodic Catalogue of Women: Constructions and Reconstructions*, edited by R. Hunter, 25–34. Cambridge: Cambridge University Press.

Clément-Tarantino, S., and F. Klein. 2015. "Introduction." In *La représentation du «couple» Virgile-Ovide dans la tradition culturelle de l'Antiquité à nos jours*, edited by S. Clément-Tarantino and F. Klein, 11–35. Villeneuve d'Ascq: Septentrion.

Clinton, K. 1994. "The Epidauria and the Arrival of Asclepius in Athens." In *Ancient Greek Cult Practice from the Epigraphical Evidence*, edited by R. Hägg, 17–34. Proceedings of the Second International Seminar on Ancient Greek Cult, 22–24 November 1991. Stockholm: Paul Åström.

Cole, T. 2004. "Ovid, Varro, and Castor of Rhodes: The Chronological Architecture of the *Metamorphoses*." *HSCP* 102:355–422.

Collard, C., and M. Cropp, eds. 2008. *Euripides, Fragments (Aegeus–Meleager)*. Cambridge, MA: Harvard University Press.

————, eds. 2009. *Euripides, Fragments (Oedipus–Chrysippus; Other Fragments)*. Cambridge, MA: Harvard University Press.

Collard, C., M. J. Cropp, and K. H. Lee, eds. 1995. *The Plays of Euripides: Selected Fragmentary Plays, Volume I*. Warminster: Aris & Phillips.

Connors, C. 1994. "Ennius, Ovid, and Representations of Ilia." *MD* 32:99–112.

Conte, G. B. 1986. *The Rhetoric of Imitation: Genre and Poetic Memory in Virgil and Other Latin Poets*. Translated by C. Segal. Ithaca, NY: Cornell University Press.

Coppola, A. 1990. "Diomede in età augustea: Appunti su Iullo Antonio." *Hesperia: Studi sulla Grecità di Occidente* 1:125–38.

Courtney, E., ed. 1993. *The Fragmentary Latin Poets*. Oxford: Oxford University Press.

Cozzoli, A.-T. 2011. "The Poet as Child." In *Brill's Companion to Callimachus*, edited by B. Acosta-Hughes, L. Lehnus, and S. Stephens, 407–28. Leiden: Brill.

Cribiore, R. 1994. "A Homeric Writing Exercise and Reading Homer in School." *Tyche* 9:1–8.

Crotty, K. 1994. *The Poetics of Supplication: Homer's Iliad and Odyssey*. Ithaca, NY: Cornell University Press.

Curley, D. 2013. *Tragedy in Ovid: Theater, Metatheater, and the Transformation of a Genre*. Cambridge: Cambridge University Press.

Currie, B. 2006. "Homer and the Early Epic Tradition." In *Epic Interactions: Perspectives on Homer, Virgil, and the Epic Tradition Presented to Jasper Griffin by Former Pupils,* edited by M. J. Clarke, B. G. F. Currie, and R. O. A. M. Lyne, 1–45. Oxford: Oxford University Press.

Currie, H. M. 1973. "Propertius IV.8—A Reading." *Latomus* 32:616–22.

Curtius, E. R. 1953. *European Literature and the Latin Middle Ages.* Translated by W. R. Trask. New York: Pantheon.

Dalzell, A. 1980. "Homeric Themes in Propertius." *Hermathena* 129:29–36.

Davies, M. 1989. *The Greek Epic Cycle.* Bristol: Bristol Classical Press.

Davisson, M. H. T. 1984. "Parents and Children in Ovid's Poems from Exile." *CW* 78:111–14.

Degl'Innocenti Pierini, R. 2008. *Il parto dell'orsa: Studi su Virgilio, Ovidio e Seneca.* Bologna: Pàtron.

de Jong, I., ed. 2001. *A Narratological Commentary on the Odyssey.* Cambridge: Cambridge University Press.

Dekel, E. 2012. *Virgil's Homeric Lens.* New York: Routledge.

Delebecque, E., ed. 1970. *Xénophon: l'Art de la Chasse.* Paris: Les Belles Lettres.

Detienne, M., and J.-P. Vernant. 1974. *Les ruses de l'intelligence: La mètis des Grecs.* Paris: Flammarion.

Dickey, E. 2007. *Ancient Greek Scholarship: A Guide to Finding, Reading, and Understanding Scholia, Commentaries, Lexica, and Grammatical Treatises, from Their Beginnings to the Byzantine Period.* Oxford: Oxford University Press.

Diggle, J., ed. 1970. *Euripides: Phaethon.* Cambridge: Cambridge University Press.

Dorandi, T., ed. 1982. *Filodemo, Il buon re secondo Omero.* Naples: Bibliopolis.

Dover, K. J., ed. 1980. *Plato, Symposium.* Cambridge: Cambridge University Press.

Drinkwater, M. O. 2007. "Which Letter? Text and Subtext in Ovid's *Heroides*." *AJP* 128:367–87.

———. 2013a. "An Amateur's Art: Paris and Helen in Ovid's *Heroides*." *CP* 108:111–25.

———. 2013b. "*Militia amoris*: Fighting in Love's Army." In *The Cambridge Companion to Latin Love Elegy*, edited by T. S. Thorsen, 194–206. Cambridge: Cambridge University Press.

Dué, C. 2002. *Homeric Variations on a Lament by Briseis.* Lanham, MD: Rowman & Littlefield.

Dué, C., and M. Ebbott. 2010. *Iliad 10 and the Poetics of Ambush: A Multitext Edition with Essays and Commentary.* Cambridge, MA: Harvard University Press.

Ebbott, M. 2010. "Error 404: Theban Epic Not Found." *Trends in Classics* 2:239–58.

Edelstein, E., and L. Edelstein. 1945 (reissued with a new introduction in 1998). *Asclepius: Collection and Interpretation of the Testimonies.* Baltimore: Johns Hopkins University Press.

Edmunds, L. 1997. "Myth in Homer." In *A New Companion to Homer*, edited by I. Morris and B. Powell, 415–41. Leiden: Brill.

Edwards, M. W., ed. 1991. *The Iliad: A Commentary. Volume I: Books 17–20.* Cambridge: Cambridge University Press.

Eisenberger, H. 1960. "Der innere Zusammenhang der Motive in Tibulls Gedicht 1, 3." *Hermes* 88:188–97.

Elliott, J. 2013. *Ennius and the Architecture of the Annales*. Cambridge: Cambridge University Press.

Erbse, H., ed. 1969–88. *Scholia Graeca in Homeri Iliadem*. 7 vols. Berlin: De Gruyter.

Erren, M., ed. 2003. *P. Vergilius Maro, Georgica. Band 2: Kommentar*. Heidelberg: C. Winter.

Evans, H. 1983. *Publica Carmina: Ovid's Books from Exile*. Lincoln: University of Nebraska Press.

Evans, S. 1971. "Odyssean Echoes in Propertius IV.8." *G&R* 18:51–53.

Fabre-Serris, J. 2014. "La réception d'Empédocle dans la poésie latine: Virgile (*Buc.* 6), Lucrèce, Gallus et les poètes élégiaques." *Dictynna* 11:2–21.

Fantham, E. 1983. "Sexual Comedy in Ovid's *Fasti*: Sources and Motivation." *HSCP* 87:185–216.

———. 1989. "Mime: The Missing Link in Roman Literary History." *CW* 82:153–63.

———, ed. 1998. *Ovid, Fasti Book 4*. Cambridge: Cambridge University Press.

Faraone, C. 1987. "Hephaestus the Magician and Near Eastern Parallels for Alcinous' Watchdogs." *GRBS* 28:257–80.

Farrell, J. 1991. *Vergil's Georgics and the Traditions of Ancient Epic: The Art of Allusion in Literary History*. Oxford: Oxford University Press.

———. 1999. "The Ovidian *Corpus*: Poetic Body and Poetic Text." In Hardie, Barchiesi, and Hinds 1999:127–41.

———. 2001. "The Vergilian Century." *Vergilius* 47:11–28.

———. 2004. "Ovid's Virgilian Career." *MD* 52:41–55.

———. 2012. "Calling Out the Greeks: Dynamics of the Elegiac Canon." In *A Companion to Roman Love Elegy*, edited by B. K. Gold, 11–24. Malden, MA: Wiley-Blackwell.

Faulkner, A., ed. 2008. *The Homeric Hymn to Aphrodite: Introduction, Text, and Commentary*. Oxford: Oxford University Press.

Fedeli, P., ed. 1980. *Sesto Properzio: Il primo libro delle elegie*. Florence: Leo S. Olschki.

———, ed. 1985. *Properzio: Il libro terzo delle elegie*. Bari: Adriatica.

Feeney, D. C. 1991. *The Gods in Epic: Poets and Critics of the Classical Tradition*. Oxford: Oxford University Press.

———. 2016. *Beyond Greek: The Beginnings of Latin Literature*. Cambridge, MA: Harvard University Press.

Felson, N. 1997. *Regarding Penelope: From Character to Poetics*. Norman: University of Oklahoma Press.

Fenno, J. 2005. "'A Great Wave against the Stream': Water Imagery in Iliadic Battle Scenes." *AJP* 126:475–504.

Finlay, R. 1980. "Patroklos, Achilleus, and Peleus: Fathers and Sons in the *Iliad*." *CW* 73:267–73.

Fish, J. 1999. "Philodemus on the Education of the Good King (*PHerc*. 1507, col. 23)." In *Satura: Collectanea philologica Italo Gallo ab amicis discipulisque dicata*, edited by G. Abbamonte, A. Rescigno, A. Rossi, and R. Rossi, 71–77. Naples: Arte tipografica.

Fletcher, K. F. B. 2006. "Vergil's Italian Diomedes." *AJP* 127:219–59.

Flower, H. I. 1996. *Ancestor Masks and Aristocratic Power in Roman Culture*. Oxford: Oxford University Press.

Ford, A. 1988. "The Classical Definition of ΡΑΨΩΙΔΙΑ." *CP* 83:300–307.

Fowler, R. 2004. "The Homeric Question." In *The Cambridge Companion to Homer*, edited by R. Fowler, 220–32. Cambridge: Cambridge University Press.

Fraenkel, E. 1931. "Livius." In *Paulys Real-Encyclopädie der classischen Altertumswissenschaft*, suppl. V, cols. 598–607. Stuttgart: J. B. Metzler.

———, ed. 1950. *Aeschylus: Agamemnon*. Oxford: Oxford University Press.

Frame, D. 2009. *Hippota Nestor*. Cambridge, MA: Harvard University Press.

Francis, J. A. 2009. "Metal Maidens, Achilles' Shield, and Pandora: The Beginnings of 'Ekphrasis.'" *AJP* 130:1–23.

Fränkel, H. 1932. "Griechische Bildung in altrömischen Epen." *Hermes* 67:303–11.

Frings, I. 2005. *Das Spiel mit eigenen Texten: Wiederholung und Selbszitat bei Ovid*. Munich: C. H. Beck.

Fulkerson, L. 2005. *The Ovidian Heroine as Author: Reading, Writing, and Community in the Heroides*. Cambridge: Cambridge University Press.

———. 2013. "*Servitium amoris*: The Interplay of Dominance, Gender, and Poetry." In *The Cambridge Companion to Latin Love Elegy*, edited by T. S. Thorsen, 180–93. Cambridge: Cambridge University Press.

Fulkerson, L., and T. Stover. 2016a. "Introduction." In Fulkerson and Stover 2016b: 3–25.

———, eds. 2016b. *Repeat Performances: Ovidian Repetition and the Metamorphoses*. Madison: University of Wisconsin Press.

Furley, D. 1970. "Variations on Themes from Empedocles in Lucretius' Proem." *BICS* 17:55–64.

Gaisser, J. H. 1969. "A Structural Analysis of the Digressions in the *Iliad* and the *Odyssey*." *HSCP* 73:1–43.

Gale, M. 1994. *Myth and Poetry in Lucretius*. Cambridge: Cambridge University Press.

Galinsky, G. K. 1969. *Aeneas, Sicily, and Rome*. Princeton, NJ: Princeton University Press.

———. 1975. *Ovid's Metamorphoses: An Introduction to the Basic Aspects*. Berkeley: University of California Press.

———. 1992. "Venus, Polysemy, and the Ara Pacis Augustae." *AJA* 96:457–75.

———. 1996. *Augustan Culture: An Interpretive Introduction*. Princeton, NJ: Princeton University Press.

Gantz, T. 1993. *Early Greek Myth*. Baltimore: Johns Hopkins University Press.

Garani, M. 2013. "Lucretius and Ovid on Empedoclean Cows and Sheep." In *Lucretius: Poetry, Philosophy, Science*, edited by D. Lehoux, A. D. Morrison, and A. Sharrock, 233–59. Oxford: Oxford University Press.

Garvie, A. F., ed. 1994. *Homer: Odyssey Books VII–VIII*. Cambridge: Cambridge University Press.

Gebhard, E. R. 2001. "The Gods in Transit: Narratives of Cult Transfer." In *Antiquity and Humanity: Essays on Ancient Religion and Philosophy Presented to Hans Dieter Betz on His 70th Birthday*, edited by A. Y. Collins and M. M. Mitchell, 453–75. Tübingen: Paul Mohr.

Geyssen, J. 2007. "Ovid's Addresses to the Book in *Tristia* 1,1." *Latomus* 66:374–83.

Giannini, P. 1995. "Eustazio e il serio-comico nell'episodio degli amori di Ares ed Afrodite: La scelta del tema poetico nell'*Odissea*." In *Studia classica Iohanni Tarditi oblata, Volume II*, edited by L. Belloni, G. Milanese, and A. Porro, 1281–92. Milan: Vita e Pensiero.

Gibson, B. 1999. "Ovid on Reading: Reading Ovid. Reception in Ovid *Tristia* II." *JRS* 89:19–37.

Gibson, R. K. 1999. "Aeneas as *hospes* in Vergil, *Aeneid* 1 and 4." *CQ* 49:184–202.

———. 2007. *Excess and Restraint: Propertius, Horace, and Ovid's Ars Amatoria*. London: Institute of Classical Studies.

Goldberg, S. M. 1995. *Epic in Republican Rome*. Oxford: Oxford University Press.

Gössl, S. 1981. "Ovid, *Amores* I.7." *GB* 10:165–80.

Gow, A. S. F., and D. L. Page, eds. 1968. *The Greek Anthology: The Garland of Philip*. 2 vols. Cambridge: Cambridge University Press.

Gowers, E. 2005. "Virgil's Sibyl and the 'Many Mouths' Cliché (*Aen.* 6.625–7)." *CQ* 55:170–82.

Greene, T. 1963. *The Descent from Heaven: A Study in Epic Continuity*. New Haven, CT: Yale University Press.

Grethlein, J. 2007. "Diomedes redivivus: A New Reading of Mimnermus fr. 14 W^2." *Mnemosyne* 60:102–11.

Griffin, J., ed. 1995. *Homer, Iliad Book Nine*. Oxford: Oxford University Press.

Grossardt, P. 2001. *Die Erzählung von Meleagros: Zur literarischen Entwicklung der Kalydonischen Kultlegende*. Leiden: Brill.

Gurval, R. A. 1995. *Actium and Augustus: The Politics and Emotions of Civil War*. Ann Arbor: University of Michigan Press.

Gutting, E. 2006. "Marriage in the *Aeneid*: Venus, Vulcan, and Dido." *CP* 101:263–79.

———. 2009. "Venus' Maternity and Divinity in the *Aeneid*." *MD* 61:41–55.

Hainsworth, B., ed. 1993. *The Iliad: A Commentary. Volume III: Books 9–12*. Cambridge: Cambridge University Press.

Hall, E. 2000. "Female Figures and Metapoetry in Old Comedy." In *The Rivals of Aristophanes: Studies in Athenian Old Comedy*, edited by D. Harvey and J. Wilkins, 407–18. London: Duckworth and the Classical Press of Wales.

Halliwell, S. 2008. *Greek Laughter: A Study of Cultural Sociology from Homer to Early Christianity*. Cambridge: Cambridge University Press.

Halperin, D. M. 1990. *One Hundred Years of Homosexuality*. New York: Routledge.

Hamdi-Ibrahim, M. 1976–77. "The Study of Homer in Graeco-Roman Education." *Athena* 76:187–95.

Harder, A., ed. 2012. *Callimachus: Aetia*. 2 vols. Oxford: Oxford University Press.

Hardie, P., A. Barchiesi, and S. Hinds, eds. 1999. *Ovidian Transformations: Essays on Ovid's Metamorphoses and Its Reception*. Cambridge: Cambridge Philological Society.

Hardie, P., and H. Moore. 2010. "Literary Careers: Classical Models and Their Reception." In *Classical Literary Careers and Their Reception*, edited by P. Hardie and H. Moore, 1–16. Cambridge: Cambridge University Press.

Hardie, P. 1986. *Virgil's Aeneid: Cosmos and Imperium*. Oxford: Oxford University Press.

———. 1988. "Lucretius and the Delusions of Narcissus." *MD* 21:71–89.

———. 1993. *The Epic Successors of Virgil: A Study in the Dynamics of a Tradition*. Cambridge: Cambridge University Press.

———, ed. 1994. *Virgil, Aeneid Book IX*. Cambridge: Cambridge University Press.

———. 1995. "The Speech of Pythagoras in Ovid *Metamorphoses* 15: Empedoclean Epos." *CQ* 45:204–14.

———. 2002. *Ovid's Poetics of Illusion*. Cambridge: Cambridge University Press.

———. 2007a. "Contrasts." In *Classical Constructions: Papers in Memory of Don Fowler, Classicist and Epicurean*, edited by S. J. Heyworth, 141–73. Oxford: Oxford University Press.

———. 2007b. "Lucretius and Later Latin Literature in Antiquity." In *The Cambridge Companion to Lucretius*, edited by S. Gillespie and P. R. Hardie, 111–27. Cambridge: Cambridge University Press.

———. 2012. *Rumour and Renown: Representations of Fama in Western Literature*. Cambridge: Cambridge University Press.

———, ed. 2015. *Ovidio, Metamorfosi volume VI: Libri XIII–XV*. Turin: Mondadori.

Hardwick, L. 2003. *Reception Studies*. Greece and Rome New Surveys in the Classics 33. Oxford: Oxford University Press.

Harries, B. 1990. "The Spinner and the Poet: Arachne in Ovid's *Metamorphoses*." *PCPhS* 36:64–82.

Harrison, E. L. 1989. "Clymene's Song (*Georgics* 4.345–7)." *LCM* 14.8:115.

Harrison, S. J. 1995. "Horace, Pindar, Iullus Antonius, and Augustus: *Odes* 4.2." In *Homage to Horace: A Bimillenary Celebration*, edited by S. J. Harrison, 108–27. Oxford: Oxford University Press.

Heath, J. 2001. "Telemachus ΠΕΠΝΥΜΕΝΟΣ: Growing into an Epithet." *Mnemosyne* 54:129–57.

Heinze, R. 1919. *Ovids elegische Erzählung*. Berichte der Sächsischen Akademie zu Leipzig, philologisch-historisch Klasse, 71.7. Leipzig: Teubner.

————. 1993. *Virgil's Epic Technique*. Translated from the German by H. and D. Harvey and F. Robertson (translation of the 3rd edition, published in 1928). Berkeley: University of California Press.

Held, G. F. 1987. "Phoinix, Agamemnon and Achilleus: Parables and Paradeigmata." *CQ* 37:245–61.

Herbert-Brown, G. 1994. *Ovid and the Fasti: An Historical Study*. Oxford: Oxford University Press.

Heslin, P. 2016. "Ovid's Cycnus and Homer's Achilles Heel." In Fulkerson and Stover 2016b:69–99.

Heubeck, A., S. West, and J. B. Hainsworth, eds. 1988. *A Commentary on Homer's Odyssey, Volume I: Introduction and Books I–VIII*. Oxford: Oxford University Press.

Hexter, R. 2010. "On First Looking into Vergil's Homer." In *A Companion to Vergil's Aeneid and Its Tradition*, edited by J. Farrell and M. C. J. Putnam, 26–36. Malden, MA: Wiley-Blackwell.

Heyworth, S. J. 1994. "Some Allusions to Callimachus in Latin Poetry." *MD* 33:51–79.

————. 2007a. *Cynthia: A Companion to the Text of Propertius*. Oxford: Oxford University Press.

————, ed. 2007b. *Sexti Properti Elegi*. Oxford: Oxford University Press.

Higbie, C, 1995. *Heroes' Names, Homeric Identities*. New York: Garland.

Hinds, S. E. 1985. "Booking the Return Trip: Ovid and *Tristia* 1." *PCPhS* 31:13–32.

————. 1987a. "Generalising about Ovid." *Ramus* 16:4–31.

————. 1987b. *The Metamorphosis of Persephone: Ovid and the Self-Conscious Muse*. Cambridge: Cambridge University Press.

————. 1992. "*Arma* in Ovid's *Fasti* Part 1: Genre and Mannerism." *Arethusa* 25:81–112.

————. 1993. "Medea in Ovid: Scenes from the Life of an Intertextual Heroine." *MD* 30:9–47.

————. 1998. *Allusion and Intertext: Dynamics of Appropriation in Roman Poetry*. Cambridge: Cambridge University Press.

————. 1999. "First among Women: Ovid, *Tristia* 1.6 and the Traditions of 'Exemplary' Catalogue." In *Amor: Roma: Love and Latin Literature*, edited by S. M. Braund and R. Mayer, 123–42. Cambridge: Cambridge Philological Society.

Hollis, A. S., ed. 1970. *Ovid, Metamorphoses Book VIII*. Oxford: Oxford University Press.

————, ed. 1977. *Ovid: Ars Amatoria Book I*. Oxford: Oxford University Press.

————. 1996. "Ovid, *Metamorphoses* 1.445ff.: Apollo, Daphne, and the Pythian Crown." *ZPE* 112:69–73.

————. 1997. "A New Fragment on Niobe and the Text of Propertius 2.20.8." *CQ* 47:578–82.

————, ed. 2007. *Fragments of Roman Poetry c. 60 BC–AD 20*. Oxford: Oxford University Press.

Holzberg, N. 1990. "Ovids Version der Ehebruchsnovelle von Ares und Aphrodite (Hom. *Od*. 8.266–366) in der *Ars amatoria* (2.561–92)." *WJA* 16:137–52.

———. 1998. "*Ter quinque volumina* as *carmen perpetuum*: The Division into Books in Ovid's *Metamorphoses*." *MD* 40:77–98.

Hopkinson, N., ed. 2000. *Ovid, Metamorphoses Book XIII*. Cambridge: Cambridge University Press.

Horsfall, N. 1979. "Epic and Burlesque in Ovid, *Met.* viii.260ff." *CJ* 74:319–32.

———. 1981. "Some Problems of Titulature in Roman Literary History." *BICS* 28:103–14.

———. 1991. *Virgilio: L'epopea in alambicco*. Naples: Liguori.

———, ed. 2000. *Virgil, Aeneid 7: A Commentary*. Leiden: Brill.

———, ed. 2003. *Virgil, Aeneid 11: A Commentary*. Leiden: Brill.

———, ed. 2006. *Virgil, Aeneid 3: A Commentary*. Leiden: Brill.

Housman, A. E. 1890. "Emendations in Ovid's *Metamorphoses*." *TCPhS* 3:140–53.

———. 1897. "Ovid's *Heroides*." *CR* 11:102–6, 200–204, 238–42, 286–90, 425–31.

Houston, G. W. 2014. *Inside Roman Libraries: Book Collections and Their Management in Antiquity*. Chapel Hill: University of North Carolina Press.

Howie, J. G. 1995. "The *Iliad* as Exemplum." In *Homer's World: Fiction, Tradition, Reality*, edited by Ø. Andersen and M. Dickie, 141–73. Bergen: Paul Åström.

Hubbard, M. 1974. *Propertius*. London: Duckworth.

Hunter, R. 2004. *Plato's Symposium*. Oxford: Oxford University Press.

———. 2005. "The Hesiodic *Catalogue* and Hellenistic Poetry." In *The Hesiodic Catalogue of Women: Constructions and Reconstructions*, edited by R. Hunter, 239–65. Cambridge: Cambridge University Press.

———. 2012. "The Songs of Demodocus: Compression and Extension in Greek Narrative Poetry." In *Brill's Companion to Greek and Latin Epyllion and Its Reception*, edited by M. Baumbach and S. Bär, 83–109. Leiden: Brill.

Hunter, R. and D. Russell, eds. 2011. *Plutarch: How to Study Poetry*. Cambridge: Cambridge University Press.

Hunzinger, C. 1997. "Comment décider qu'un passage est interpolé: Les interprétations des *Amours d'Arès et d'Aphrodite*: Bilan bibliographique." *Lalies (actes des sessions de linguistique et de littérature)* 17:125–38.

Huskey, S. 2002. "Ovid at the Fall of Troy in *Tristia* 1.3." *Vergilius* 48:88–104.

———. 2006. "Ovid's *Metamorphoses* in *Tristia* I,1." In *Studies in Latin Literature and Roman History XIII*, edited by C. Deroux, 335–57. Brussels: Éditions Latomus.

Hutchinson, G., ed. 2006. *Propertius: Elegies Book IV*. Cambridge: Cambridge University Press.

Imperio, O. 2012. "Personificazioni dell'arte poetica e metafore parentali: la maternità letteraria tra commedia e filosofia." In *Persona ficta: La personificazione allegorica nella cultura antica fra letteratura, retorica e iconografia*, edited by G. Moretti and A. Bonandini, 29–51. Trento: Università di Trento, Dipartimento di studi letterari, linguistici e filologici.

Ingleheart, J., ed. 2010. *A Commentary on Ovid, Tristia, Book 2*. Oxford: Oxford University Press.

————. 2012. "Ovid's *Scripta Puella*: Perilla as Poetic and Political Fiction in *Tristia* 3.7." *CQ* 62:227–41.

Jacobson, H. 1971. "Ovid's Briseis: A Study of *Heroides* 3." *Phoenix* 25:331–56.

————. 1974. *Ovid's Heroides*. Princeton, NJ: Princeton University Press.

James, S. 2003. *Learned Girls and Male Persuasion: Gender and Reading in Roman Love Elegy*. Berkeley: University of California Press.

Janan, M. 1994. "'There beneath the Roman ruin where the purple flowers grow': Ovid's Minyeides and the Feminine Imagination." *AJP* 115:427–48.

Janka, M., ed. 1997. *Ovid, Ars Amatoria Buch 2: Kommentar*. Heidelberg: C. Winter.

Janko, R., ed. 1987. *Aristotle: Poetics; with the Tractatus Coislinianus, Reconstruction of Poetics II, and the Fragments of On Poets*. Indianapolis, IN: Hackett.

————, ed. 1994. *The Iliad: A Commentary, Volume IV: Books 13–16*. Cambridge: Cambridge University Press.

Jocelyn, H. D., ed. 1967. *The Tragedies of Ennius*. Cambridge: Cambridge University Press.

Johnson, P. J. 1996. "Constructions of Venus in Ovid's *Metamorphoses* V." *Arethusa* 29:125–49.

————. 2008. *Ovid before Exile: Art and Punishment in the Metamorphoses*. Madison: University of Wisconsin Press.

Jolivet, J.-C. 1999. "La dispute d'Ovide et des Alexandrins ou Briséis γραμματικωτάτη: Trois problèmes homériques et une *Quaestio Ovidiana* dans la troisième *Héroïde*." In *Élégie et épopée dans la poésie ovidienne (Héroïdes et Amours), en hommage à Simone Viarre*, edited by J. Fabre-Serris and A. Deremetz, 15–39. Villeneuve d'Ascq: Université Charles-de-Gaulle-Lille 3.

————. 2004. "*Nyctegresiae Romanae*: Exégèse homérique et *retractio* de la *Dolonie* chez Virgile et Ovide." *Dictynna* 1:2–17.

————. 2005. "Les amours d'Arès et Aphrodite, la critique homérique et la pantomime dans l'*Ars amatoria*." *Dictynna* 2:1–16.

Jones, P. V. 1988. "The ΚΛΕΟΣ of Telemachus: *Odyssey* 1.95." *AJP* 109:496–506.

Kaiser, E. 1964. "Odyssee-Szenen als topoi." *MH* 21:109–36, 197–224.

Kaster, R. A. 1992. *Studies on the Text of Suetonius De grammaticis et rhetoribus*. Atlanta: Scholars Press.

————, ed. 1995. *C. Suetonius Tranquillus, De grammaticis et rhetoribus*. Oxford: Oxford University Press.

Keaney, J. J., and R. Lamberton, eds. 1996. *[Plutarch] De Homero: Essay on the Life and Poetry of Homer*. Atlanta: Scholars Press.

Kearns, J. M. 1990. "Σεμνότης and Dialect Gloss in the *Odussia* of Livius Andronicus." *AJP* 111:40–52.

Keith, A. M. 1992. *The Play of Fictions: Studies in Ovid's Metamorphoses Book 2*. Ann Arbor: University of Michigan Press.

————. 1999. "Versions of Epic Masculinity in Ovid's *Metamorphoses*." In Hardie, Barchiesi, and Hinds 1999:214–39.

———. 2008. *Propertius: Poet of Love and Leisure*. Bristol: Bristol Classical Press.

Kennedy, D. F. 1984. "The Epistolary Mode and the First of Ovid's *Heroides*." *CQ* 34:413–22.

———. 2012. "Love's Tropes and Figures." In *A Companion to Roman Love Elegy*, edited by B. K. Gold, 189–203. Oxford: Wiley-Blackwell.

Kenney, E. J. 1958. "The 'Praestantissimus Puteanus' Again." *SIFC* 30:172–74.

———. 1959. "Notes on Ovid: II." *CQ* 9:240–60.

———. 1965. "The Poetry of Ovid's Exile." *CCJ* 11:37–49.

———. 1993. "Ovidiana." *CQ* 43:458–67.

———. 2002. "Ovid's Language and Style." In *Brill's Companion to Ovid*, edited by B. W. Boyd, 27–89. Leiden: Brill.

———, ed. 2011. *Ovidio, Metamorfosi volume IV: Libri VII–IX*. Trans. G. Chiarini. Turin: Mondadori.

Kirk, G. S., ed. 1985. *The Iliad: A Commentary. Volume I: Books 1–4*. Cambridge: Cambridge University Press.

———, ed. 1990. *The Iliad: A Commentary. Volume II: Books 5–8*. Cambridge: Cambridge University Press.

Klein, F. 2009. "La réception de Lycophron dans la poésie augustéenne: Le point de vue de Cassandre et le dispositif poétique de l'Alexandra." In *Lycophron: Éclats d'obscurité*, edited by C. Cusset and E. Prioux, 561–92. St.-Étienne: Publications de l'Université de St.-Étienne.

Knauer, G. N. 1964. *Die Aeneis und Homer*. Göttingen: Vandenhoeck & Ruprecht.

Knox, P. E. 1986. *Ovid's Metamorphoses and the Traditions of Augustan Poetry*. Cambridge: Cambridge Philological Society.

———. 1988a. "Phaethon in Ovid and Nonnus." *CQ* 38:536–51.

———. 1988b. "Pyramus and Thisbe in Cyprus." *HSCP* 92:315–28.

———. 1993. "Philetas and Roman Poetry." In *Papers of the Leeds International Latin Seminar*, vol. 7, edited by F. Cairns and M. Heath, 61–83. Leeds: Francis Cairns.

———, ed. 1995. *Ovid, Heroides: Select Epistles*. Cambridge: Cambridge University Press.

———. 2016. "Metamorphoses in a Cold Climate." In Fulkerson and Stover 2016b:176–95.

Kouklanakis, A. 1999. "Thersites, Odysseus, and the Social Order." In *Nine Essays on Homer*, edited by M. Carlisle and O. Levaniouk, 35–53. Lanham, MD: Rowman & Littlefield.

Krevans, N. 1993. "Ilia's Dream: Ennius, Virgil, and the Mythology of Seduction." *HSCP* 95:357–71.

Kruschwitz, P. 2005. "Phaethon, Clymene, und Merops: zu Ov. *Met*. 1.762–764." *GB* 24:151–54.

Kuttner, A. 1995. *Dynasty and Empire in the Age of Augustus: The Case of the Boscoreale Cups*. Berkeley: University of California Press.

Labate, M. 1993. "Storie di instabilità: L'episodio di Ermafrodito nelle *Metamorfosi* di Ovidio." *MD* 30:49–62.

Lada-Richards, I. 2006. "*Cum femina primum . . .*": Venus, Vulcan, and the Politics of Male *Mollitia* in *Aeneid* 8." *Helios* 33:27–72.

Lang, M. L. 1983. "Reverberation and Mythology in the *Iliad*." In *Approaches to Homer*, edited by C. A. Rubino and C. W. Shelmerdine, 140–64. Austin: University of Texas Press.

Lateiner, D. 1984. "Mythic and Non-mythic Artists in Ovid's *Metamorphoses*." *Ramus* 13:1–30.

Lawton, C. L. 2007. "Children in Classical Attic Votive Reliefs." In *Constructions of Childhood in Ancient Greece and Italy*, edited by A. Cohen and J. B. Rutter, 41–60. Princeton, NJ: Princeton University Press.

Leach, E. W. 1974. "Ekphrasis and the Theme of Artistic Failure in Ovid's *Metamorphoses*." *Ramus* 3:102–42.

———. 1988. *The Rhetoric of Space: Literary and Artistic Representations of Landscape in Republican and Augustan Rome*. Princeton, NJ: Princeton University Press.

———. 1997. "Venus, Thetis and the Social Construction of Maternal Behavior." *CJ* 92:347–71.

Lee-Stecum, P. 1998. *Powerplay in Tibullus: Reading Elegies Book One*. Cambridge: Cambridge University Press.

Lewis, A.-M. 2012. "Reconsidering Ovid's Relationship to Perilla (*Tristia* III, 7)." In *Studies in Latin Literature and Roman History XVI*, edited by C. Deroux, 367–97. Brussels: Éditions Latomus.

LiDonnici, L. R. 1995. *The Epidaurian Miracle Inscriptions: Text, Translation, and Commentary*. Atlanta: Scholars Press.

Lightfoot, J. L., ed. 1999. *Parthenius of Nicaea*. Oxford: Oxford University Press.

———, ed. 2009. *Hellenistic Collection: Philitas, Alexander of Aetolia, Hermesianax, Euphorion, Parthenius*. Cambridge, MA: Harvard University Press.

Ling, R. 1991. *Roman Painting*. Cambridge: Cambridge University Press.

Littlewood, R. J. 1980. "Ovid and the Ides of March (*Fasti* 3.523–710): A Further Study in the Artistry of the *Fasti*." In *Studies in Latin Literature and Roman History II*, edited by C. Deroux, 301–21. Brussels: Éditions Latomus.

———, ed. 2006. *A Commentary on Ovid, Fasti Book VI*. Oxford: Oxford University Press.

Livingston, I., ed. 2004. *A Linguistic Commentary on Livius Andronicus*. New York: Routledge.

Loehr, J. 1996. *Ovids Mehrfacherklärungen in der Tradition aitiologischen Dichtens*. Stuttgart: Teubner.

Lord, A. 1960. *The Singer of Tales*. Cambridge, MA: Harvard University Press.

Louden, B. 2006. *The Iliad: Structure, Myth, and Meaning*. Baltimore: Johns Hopkins University Press.

Luck, G., ed. 1967. *P. Ovidius Naso, Tristia. Band I: Text und Übersetzung*. Heidelberg: C. Winter.

———, ed. 1977. *P. Ovidius Naso, Tristia. Band II: Kommentar*. Heidelberg: C. Winter.

Lynn-George, M. 1988. *Epos: Word, Narrative and the Iliad*. Basingstoke: Macmillan.

Mackie, C. J. 1997. "Achilles' Teachers: Chiron and Phoenix in the *Iliad*." *G&R* 44:1–10.

Malkin, I. 1998. *The Returns of Odysseus: Colonization and Ethnicity*. Berkeley: University of California Press.

Maltby, R. 1991. *A Lexicon of Ancient Latin Etymologies*. Leeds: Francis Cairns.

———, ed. 2002. *Tibullus: Elegies. Text, Introduction and Commentary*. Cambridge: Cambridge University Press.

March, J. R. 1987. *The Creative Poet: Studies on the Treatment of Myths in Greek Poetry*. BICS Supplement 49. London: Institute of Classical Studies.

Mariotti, S. 1986. *Livio Andronico e la traduzione artistica*. 2nd, revised edition (originally published 1952). Urbino: Pubblicazioni dell'Università di Urbino.

———. 1991. *Lezioni su Ennio*. 2nd, expanded edition (originally published 1951). Urbino: QuattroVenti.

Marks, J. 2005. "The Ongoing *neikos*: Thersites, Odysseus and Achilles." *AJP* 126:1–31.

Marrou, H. I. 1956. *A History of Education in Antiquity*. Translated by G. Lamb. New York: Sheed and Ward.

Martindale, C., and R. F. Thomas, eds. 2006. *Classics and the Uses of Reception*. Oxford: Wiley-Blackwell.

Massimilla, G., ed. 1996. *Callimaco: Aitia Libri Primo e Secondo*. Pisa: Giardini.

Mayer, R., ed. 1994. *Horace, Epistles Book I*. Cambridge: Cambridge University Press.

Mazurek, E. F. 2013. "Homer and the Epic Cycle in Ovid, *Heroides* 16–17." *TAPA* 143:153–70.

McCauley, M. 2016. *Reproducing Rome: Motherhood in Virgil, Ovid, Seneca, and Statius*. Oxford: Oxford University Press.

McElduff, S. 2013. *Roman Theories of Translation: Surpassing the Source*. New York: Routledge.

McGinn, T. A. J. 1998. *Prostitution, Sexuality, and the Law in Ancient Rome*. Oxford: Oxford University Press.

McKeown, J. C. 1979. "Augustan Elegy and Mime." *PCPhS* 25:71–84.

———, ed. 1989. *Ovid, Amores: Text, Prolegomena, and Commentary. Volume II: A Commentary on Book One*. Leeds: Francis Cairns.

———, ed. 1998. *Ovid, Amores: Text, Prolegomena, and Commentary. Volume III: A Commentary on Book Two*. Leeds: Francis Cairns.

McNelis, C., and A Sens. 2016. *The Alexandra of Lycophron: A Literary Study*. Oxford: Oxford University Press.

Merli, E. 2000. *Arma canant alii: Materia epica e narrazione elegiaca nei fasti di Ovidio*. Florence: Università degli studi di Firenze, Dipartimento di scienze dell'antichità Giorgio Pasquali.

Mikalson, J. D. 1984. "Religion and the Plague in Athens, 431–423 B.C." In *Studies Presented to Sterling Dow on His Eightieth Birthday*, edited by K. J. Rigsby, 217–25. *GRBS* Monographs 10. Durham, NC: Duke University Press.

Miller, J. F. 1993. "Ovidian Allusion and the Vocabulary of Memory." *MD* 30:153–64.

———. 1997. "Lucretian Moments in Ovidian Elegy." *CJ* 92:384–98.

———. 2009. *Apollo, Augustus, and the Poets.* Cambridge: Cambridge University Press.

Miller, P. A. 2010. "Sex and Violence in *Amores.*" In *Approaches to Teaching the Works of Ovid and the Ovidian Tradition,* edited by B. W. Boyd and C. Fox, 161–69. New York: Modern Language Association.

Mills, D. H. 1974. "Tibullus and Phaeacia: A Reinterpretation of 1.3." *CJ* 69: 226–33.

Mitchell-Boyask, R. 2008. *Plague and the Athenian Imagination: Drama, History, and the Cult of Asclepius.* Cambridge: Cambridge University Press.

Morgan, L. 2003. "Child's Play: Ovid and His Critics." *JRS* 93:66–91.

———. 2010. *Musa Pedestris: Metre and Meaning in Roman Verse.* Oxford: Oxford University Press.

———. 2012. "Elegiac Meter: Opposites Attract." In *A Companion to Roman Love Elegy,* edited by B. K. Gold, 204–18. Oxford: Wiley-Blackwell.

Morgan, T. 1998. *Literate Education in the Hellenistic and Roman Worlds.* Cambridge: Cambridge University Press.

Morrison, J. S. 1964. "Four Notes on Plato's *Symposium.*" *CQ* 14:43–55.

Morrison, J. V. 1992. "Literary Reference and Generic Transgression in Ovid, *Amores* I.7: Lover, Poet, and *Furor.*" *Latomus* 51:571–89.

Most, G. W. 1989. "The Structure and Function of Odysseus' *Apologoi.*" *TAPA* 119:15–30.

———, ed. 2007. *Hesiod: The Shield, Catalogue of Women, Other Fragments.* Cambridge, MA: Harvard University Press.

Muecke, F. 1974. "*Nobilis historia?* Incongruity in Propertius 4.7." *BICS* 21:124–32.

Murgatroyd, P., ed. 1980. *Tibullus I.* Pietermaritzburg: University of Natal Press.

Murray, P. 2005. "The Muses: Creativity Personified?" In *Personification in the Greek World: From Antiquity to Byzantium,* edited by E. Stafford and J. Herrin, 147–59. Aldershot: Ashgate.

Musgrove, M. W. 1998. "Nestor's Centauromachy and the Deceptive Voice of Poetic Memory (Ovid *Met.* 12.182–535)." *CP* 93:223–31.

Myers, K. S. 1994. *Ovid's Causes: Cosmogony and Aetiology in the Metamorphoses.* Ann Arbor: University of Michigan Press.

———, ed. 2009. *Ovid, Metamorphoses Book XIV.* Cambridge: Cambridge University Press.

Mynors, R. A. B., ed. 1990. *Virgil: Georgics.* Oxford: Oxford University Press.

Nagler, M. N. 1990. "Ethical Anxiety and Artistic Inconsistency: The Case of Oral Epic." In *Cabinet of the Muses: Essays on Classical and Comparative Literature in Honor of Thomas G. Rosenmeyer,* edited by M. Griffith and D. Mastronarde, 225–39. Atlanta: Scholars Press.

Nagy, G. 1979. *The Best of the Achaeans: Concepts of the Hero in Archaic Greek Poetry.* Baltimore: Johns Hopkins University Press.

————. 2001. "Homeric Poetry and Problems of Multiformity: The 'Panathenaic Bottleneck.'" *CP* 96:109–19.

————. 2004. *Homer's Text and Language*. Urbana: University of Illinois Press.

Nelis, D. P. 2010. "Vergil's Library." In *A Companion to Vergil's Aeneid and Its Tradition*, edited by J. Farrell and M. C. J. Putnam, 13–25. Malden, MA: Wiley-Blackwell.

Newby, Z. 2007. "Reading the Allegory of the Archelaos Relief." In *Art and Inscriptions in the Ancient World*, edited by Z. Newby and R. Leader-Newby, 154–78. Cambridge: Cambridge University Press.

Newlands, C. E. 1995. *Playing with Time: Ovid and the Fasti*. Ithaca, NY: Cornell University Press.

————. 1996. "Transgressive Acts: Ovid's Treatment of the Ides of March." *CP* 91:320–38.

Newton, R. M. 1987. "Odysseus and Hephaestus in the *Odyssey*." *CJ* 83:12–20.

Nicoll, W. S. M. 1980. "Cupid, Apollo and Daphne (Ovid, *Met.* 1.452ff.)." *CQ* 30:174–82.

Nisbet, R. G. M., and M. Hubbard, eds. 1970. *A Commentary on Horace, Odes Book I*. Oxford: Oxford University Press.

————, eds. 1978. *A Commentary on Horace, Odes Book II*. Oxford: Oxford University Press.

Notopoulos, J.A. 1951. "Continuity and Interconnexion in Homeric Oral Composition." *TAPA* 82:81–101.

Nünlist, R. 2009. *The Ancient Critic at Work: Terms and Concepts of Literary Criticism in Greek Scholia*. Cambridge: Cambridge University Press.

Oakley, J. H. 2013. "Children in Archaic and Classical Greek Art: A Survey." In *The Oxford Handbook of Childhood and Education in the Classical World*, edited by J. Evans Grubbs and T. Parkin, with R. Bell, 147–71. Oxford: Oxford University Press.

Oakley, J. H., and R. H. Sinos. 1993. *The Wedding in Ancient Athens*. Madison: University of Wisconsin Press.

Ogden, D. 2013. *Drakōn: Dragon Myth and Serpent Cult in the Greek and Roman Worlds*. Oxford: Oxford University Press.

O'Hara, J. J. 1993. "Medicine for the Madness of Dido and Gallus: Tentative Suggestions on *Aeneid* 4." *Vergilius* 39:12–24.

————. 1996. *True Names: Vergil and the Alexandrian Tradition of Etymological Wordplay*. Ann Arbor: University of Michigan Press.

Olson, S. D. 1989. "*Odyssey* 8: Guile, Force, and the Subversive Poetics of Desire." *Arethusa* 22:135–45.

————. 1995. *Blood and Iron: Stories and Storytelling in Homer's Odyssey*. Leiden: Brill.

————, ed. 2012. *The Homeric Hymn to Aphrodite and Related Texts*. Berlin: De Gruyter.

O'Rourke, D. 2014. "Lovers in Arms: Empedoclean Love and Strife in Lucretius and the Elegists." *Dictynna* 11:1–18.

O'Sullivan, T. M. 2007. "Walking with Odysseus: The Portico Frame of the Odyssey Landscapes." *AJP* 128:497–532.

Page, D. L. 1959. *History and the Homeric Iliad*. Berkeley: University of California Press.

Palmer, A., ed. 1880. *Sex. Propertii Elegiarum Libri IV*. Oxford: Oxford University Press.

Panayotakis, C., ed. 2010. *Decimus Laberius: The Fragments*. Cambridge: Cambridge University Press.

Pannuti, U. 1984. "L'apotheosi d'Omero." *Monumenti antichi (Serie miscellanea)* 3:43–61.

Pantelia, M. C. 1993. "Spinning and Weaving: Ideas of Domestic Order in Homer." *AJP* 114:493–501.

Papaioannou, S. 2000. "Vergilian Diomedes Revisited: The Re-evaluation of the *Iliad*." *Mnemosyne* 53:193–217.

———. 2005. *Epic Succession and Dissension: Ovid, Metamorphoses 13.623–14.582, and the Reinvention of the Aeneid*. Berlin: De Gruyter.

———. 2006. "'*Opus est . . . Apolline nato*': Liminality and Closure in the Aesculapius Episode in *Metamorphoses* 15.626–744." *C&M* 57:125–56.

Parker, R. 1996. *Athenian Religion: A History*. Oxford: Oxford University Press.

Parry, M. 1971. *The Making of Homeric Verse: The Collected Papers of Milman Parry*. Ed. A. Parry. Oxford: Oxford University Press.

Paton, W. R., ed. 1916–18. *The Greek Anthology*. 5 vols. London: Heinemann.

Patzer, H. 1952. "ΡΑΨΩΙΔΟΣ." *Hermes* 80:314–25.

———. 1991. "Die Reise des Telemach." *ICS* 16:17–35.

Pavlock, B. 2009. *The Image of the Poet in Ovid's Metamorphoses*. Madison: University of Wisconsin Press.

Pease, A. S., ed. 1935. *Publi Vergili Maronis Aeneidos Liber Quartus*. Cambridge, MA: Harvard University Press.

Pender, E. 1992. "Spiritual Pregnancy in Plato's *Symposium*." *CQ* 42:72–86.

Perutelli, A. 1994. "Calipso e Ulisse (Prop. 1.15.9 ss.)." *MD* 32:169–71.

Petersen, O., and H. Weiss. 1985. "Ovids Einsatz mythologischer Stoffe: Ein Vergleich ausgewählter Mythen in den *Metamorphosen* und der *Ars amatoria*." *AU* 28:42–51.

Petrain, D. 2014. *Homer in Stone: The Tabulae Iliacae in their Roman Context*. Cambridge: Cambridge University Press.

Pfeiffer, R. 1968. *History of Classical Scholarship from the Beginnings to the End of the Hellenistic Age*. Oxford: Oxford University Press.

Pinkwart, D. 1965. *Das Relief des Archelaos von Priene und "Die Musen des Philiskos."* Kallmünz: Lassleben.

Platnauer, M. 1951. *Latin Elegiac Verse*. Cambridge: Cambridge University Press.

Porte, D. 1976. "Ovide et la tradition homérique dans *Hér.* I, 15 et 91." *RPh* 50:239–46.

Possanza, D. M. 2004. *Translating the Heavens: Aratus, Germanicus, and the Poetics of Latin Translation*. New York: Peter Lang.

Postlethwaite, N. 1988. "Thersites in the *Iliad*." *G&R* 35:123–36.

Pratt, L. 2007. "The Parental Ethos of the *Iliad*." In *Constructions of Childhood in Ancient Greece and Italy*, edited by A. Cohen and J. B. Rutter, 25–40. Princeton, NJ: Princeton University Press.

———. 2009. "Diomedes: The Fatherless Hero of the *Iliad*." In *Growing Up Fatherless in Antiquity*, edited by S. Hübner and D. Ratzan, 141–61. Cambridge: Cambridge University Press.

Purves, A. 2006. "Falling into Time in Homer's *Iliad*." *CA* 25:179–209.

Race, W. R. 1982. *The Classical Priamel from Homer to Boethius*. Leiden: Brill.

Rankin, H. D. 1972. "Thersites the Malcontent: A Discussion." *SO* 47:36–60.

Ready, J. L. 2004. "A Binding Song: The Similes of Catullus 61." *CP* 99:153–63.

Redfield, J. 1994. *Nature and Culture in the Iliad: The Tragedy of Hector*. Expanded edition (originally published in 1975). Durham, NC: Duke University Press.

Renaud, J.-M. 1993. *Le mythe du Meleagre: Essais d'interpretation*. Liége: s.n.

Richardson, N., ed. 1993. *The Iliad: A Commentary, Volume VI: Books 21–24*. Cambridge: Cambridge University Press.

———, ed. 2010. *Three Homeric Hymns: To Apollo, Hermes, Aphrodite*. Cambridge: Cambridge University Press.

Rinon, Y. 2006a. "*Mise en abyme* and Tragic Signification in the *Odyssey*: The Three Songs of Demodocus." *Mnemosyne* 59:208–25.

———. 2006b. "Tragic Hephaestus: The Humanized God in the *Iliad* and *Odyssey*." *Phoenix* 60:1–20.

Robb, K. 1994. *Literacy and Paideia in Ancient Greece*. Oxford: Oxford University Press.

Robinson, M. 1999. "Salmacis and Hermaphroditus: When Two Become One (Ovid, *Met.* 4.285–388)." *CQ* 49:212–23.

———, ed. 2011. *A Commentary on Ovid's Fasti, Book 2*. Oxford: Oxford University Press.

Roisman, H. 1988. "Nestor's Advice and Antilochus' Tactics." *Phoenix* 42:114–20.

———. 1990. "*Kerdion* in the *Iliad*: Profit and Trickiness." *TAPA* 120:23–35.

———. 1994. "Like Father Like Son: Telemachus' ΚΕΡΔΕΑ." *RhM* 137:1–22.

Ronconi, A. 1962. "Sulla tecnica delle antiche traduzioni latine da Omero." *SIFC* 34:5–20.

Rosati, G. P. 1999. "Form in Motion: Weaving the Text in the *Metamorphoses*." In Hardie, Barchiesi, and Hinds 1999: 240–53.

———. 2002. "Narrative Techniques and Narrative Structures in the *Metamorphoses*." In *Brill's Companion to Ovid*, edited by B. W. Boyd, 271–304. Leiden: Brill.

Rose, G. P. 1967. "The Quest of Telemachus." *TAPA* 98:391–98.

Rose, P. W. 1988. "Thersites and the Plural Voices of Homer." *Arethusa* 21:1–23.

Rosen, R. M. 2007. *Making Mockery: The Poetics of Ancient Satire*. Oxford: Oxford University Press.

Rosenmeyer, P. A. 1999. "Tracing *medulla* as a *locus eroticus*." *Arethusa* 32:19–47.

Rosner, J. A. 1976. "The Speech of Phoenix: *Iliad* 9.434–605." *Phoenix* 30:314–27.

Ross, D. O. 1975. *Backgrounds to Augustan Poetry: Gallus, Elegy and Rome.* Cambridge: Cambridge University Press.

Rossi, A., and B. W. Breed. 2006. "Introduction: Ennius and the Traditions of Epic." *Arethusa* 39:397–425.

Rudd, N., ed. 1989. *Horace: Epistles, Book II, and Epistle to the Pisones (Ars Poetica).* Cambridge: Cambridge University Press.

Ruesch, A., ed. 1908. *Guida Illustrata del Museo Nazionale di Napoli.* Naples: Richter.

Russell, D. A., ed. 2002. *Quintilian: The Orator's Education, Volume V: Books 11–12.* Cambridge, MA: Harvard University Press.

Russo, J., M. Fernández-Galiano, and A. Heubeck, eds. 1992. *A Commentary on Homer's Odyssey Volume III: Books 17–24.* Oxford: Oxford University Press.

Rutherford, I. 2000. "Formulas, Voice, and Death in *Ehoie*-Poetry, the Hesiodic *Gunaikon Katalogos*, and the Odyssean *Nekuia*." In *Matrices of Genre: Authors, Canons, and Society*, edited by M. Depew and D. Obbink, 81–96, 263–66. Cambridge, MA: Harvard University Press.

Rutherford, R. B. 1986. "The Philosophy of the *Odyssey.*" *JHS* 106:145–62.

Sadurska, A. 1964. *Les Tables Iliaques.* Warsaw: Panstwowe Wydawnictwo Naukowe.

Schefold, K. 1962. *Vergessenes Pompeji.* Bern: Francke.

Schlunk, R. R. 1974. *The Homeric Scholia and the Aeneid: A Study of the Influence of Ancient Homeric Literary Criticism on Vergil.* Ann Arbor: University of Michigan Press.

Schmit-Neuerburg, T. 1999. *Vergils Aeneid und die antike Homerexegese: Untersuchungen zum Einfluss ethischer und kritischer Homerrezeption auf imitatio und aemulatio Vergils.* Berlin: De Gruyter.

Schouler, B. 1980. "Dépasser le Père." *REG* 93:1–24.

Sciarrino, E. 2006. "The Introduction of Epic in Rome: Cultural Thefts and Social Contests." *Arethusa* 39:449–69.

Scodel, R. 1982. "The Autobiography of Phoenix: *Iliad* 9.444–95." *AJP* 103:128–36.

———. 2008. *Epic Facework: Self-Presentation and Social Interaction in Homer.* Swansea: Classical Press of Wales.

Seaman, K. 2005. "Personifications of the *Iliad* and *Odyssey* in Hellenistic and Roman Art." In *Personification in the Greek World*, edited by E. Stafford and J. Herrin, 173–89. Aldershot: Ashgate.

Sedley, D. 1989. "The Proems of Empedocles and Lucretius." *GRBS* 30:269–96.

———. 1998. *Lucretius and the Transformation of Greek Wisdom.* Cambridge: Cambridge University Press.

Segal, C. 1999. "Ovid's Meleager and the Greeks: Trials of Gender and Genre." *HSCP* 99:301–40.

Seng, H. 2007. "Ovids Phaethon-Tragödie (*Met.* 1,747–2,400)." In *Ovid: Werk— Kultur— Wirkung*, edited by M. Janka, U. Schmitzer, and H. Seng, 163–81. Darmstadt: Wissenschaftliche Buchgesellschaft.

Severy, B. 2003. *Augustus and the Family at the Birth of the Roman Empire.* New York: Routledge.

Shackleton Bailey, D. R. 1956. *Propertiana.* Cambridge: Cambridge University Press.

Shapley, J. 1923. "Another Sidamara Sarcophagus." *ABull* 5:61–75.

Sharrock, A. R. 1987. "*Ars Amatoria* 2.123–42: Another Homeric Scene in Ovid." *Mnemosyne* 40:406–12.

———. 1991. "Womanufacture." *JRS* 81:36–49.

———. 1994a. "Ovid and the Politics of Reading." *MD* 33:97–122.

———. 1994b. *Seduction and Repetition in Ovid's Ars Amatoria II.* Oxford: Oxford University Press.

Sheets, G. A. 1981. "The Dialect Gloss, Hellenistic Poetics and Livius Andronicus." *AJP* 102:58–78.

Sheffield, F. C. C. 2001. "Psychic Pregnancy and Platonic Epistemology." *Oxford Studies in Ancient Philosophy* 20:1–33.

Sheppard, J. T. 1940. "The Heroic Sophrosyne and the Form of Homer's Poetry." *JHS* 20:47–67.

Skiadas, A. D. 1965. *Homer im griechischen Epigramm.* Athens: Griechische Humanistische Gesellschaft.

Skinner, M. 1993. "Perillus at Tomis." In *Tria Lustria: Essays and Notes Presented to John Pinsent, Founder and Editor of Liverpool Classical Monthly, by Some of Its Contributors on the Occasion of the 150th Issue,* edited by H. D. Jocelyn with the assistance of H. Hurt, 301–10. Liverpool: Liverpool Classical Monthly.

Skutsch, O., ed. 1985. *The Annals of Q. Ennius.* Oxford: Oxford University Press.

Slatkin, L. 2011. "Theban Traces at Troy." In *The Power of Thetis and Selected Essays,* 99–119. Washington, DC: Center for Hellenic Studies.

Smolenaars, J. J. L. 2004. "A Disturbing Scene from the Marriage of Venus and Vulcan: *Aeneid* 8.370–415." *Vergilius* 50:96–107.

Snyder, J. M. 1981. "The Web of Song: Weaving Imagery in Homer and the Lyric Poets." *CJ* 76:193–96.

Solodow, J. 1977. "Ovid's *Ars Amatoria*: The Lover as Cultural Ideal." *WS* 11:106–27.

Sommerstein, A. H. 2005. "A Lover of His Art: The Art-Form as Wife and Mistress in Greek Poetic Imagery." In *Personification in the Greek World,* edited by E. Stafford and J. Herrin, 161–71. Aldershot: Ashgate.

Spaeth, B. S. 1996. *The Roman Goddess Ceres.* Austin: University of Texas Press.

Spoth, F. 1992. *Ovids Heroides als Elegien.* Munich: C. H. Beck.

Squire, M. 2011. *The Iliad in a Nutshell: Visualizing Epic on the Tabulae Iliacae.* Oxford: Oxford University Press.

Stafford, E. 1998. "Masculine Values, Feminine Forms: On the Gender of Personified Abstractions." In *Thinking Men: Masculinity and Its Self-Representation in the Classical Tradition,* edited by L. Foxhall and J. Salmon, 43–56. London: Routledge.

Stanley, K. 1993. *The Shield of Homer: Narrative Structure in the Iliad.* Princeton, NJ: Princeton University Press.

Stok, F. 1992. "La rivincita di Esculapio." In *Ovidius παρῳδήσας*, edited by G. Brugnoli and F. Stok, 135–80. Pisa: Edizioni ETS.

Stokes, M. C. 1986. *Plato's Socratic Conversations*. Baltimore: Johns Hopkins University Press.

Stroh, W. 1979. "Ovids Liebeskunst und die Ehegesetze des Augustus." *Gymnasium* 86:323–52.

Suerbaum, W. 2005. "L. Andronicus." In *Brill's New Pauly: Antiquity*, vol. 7, edited by H. Cancik and H. Schneider, cols. 745–49. Leiden: Brill.

Swain, S. C. R. 1988. "A Note on *Iliad* 9.524–99: The Story of Meleager." *CQ* 38:271–76.

Tarrant, R., ed. 2012. *Virgil: Aeneid Book XII*. Cambridge: Cambridge University Press.

Thalmann, W. G. 1988. "Thersites: Comedy, Scapegoats, and Heroic Ideology in the *Iliad*." *TAPA* 118:1–28.

Theodorakopoulos, E. 1999. "Closure and Transformation in Ovid's *Metamorphoses*." In Hardie, Barchiesi, and Hinds 1999:142–61.

Thomas, R. F. 1983. "Virgil's Ecphrastic Centerpieces." *HSCP* 87:175–84.

———. 1986. "Virgil's *Georgics* and the Art of Reference." *HSCP* 90:171–98.

———, ed. 1988. *Virgil: Georgics*. 2 vols. Cambridge: Cambridge University Press.

———, ed. 2011. *Horace, Odes Book IV and Carmen Saeculare*. Cambridge: Cambridge University Press.

Thompson, H. A. 1954. "Excavations in the Athenian Agora: 1953." *Hesperia* 23:31–67.

Thorsen, T. S. 2014. *Ovid's Early Poetry: From His Single Heroides to His Remedia amoris*. Cambridge: Cambridge University Press.

Tissol, G. 1997. *The Face of Nature: Wit, Narrative, and Cosmic Origins in Ovid's Metamorphoses*. Princeton, NJ: Princeton University Press.

———. 2005. "Maimed Books and Maimed Authors: *Tristia* 1.7 and the Fate of the *Metamorphoses*." In *Defining Genre and Gender in Latin Literature: Essays Presented to William S. Anderson on His Seventy-Fifth Birthday*, edited by W. W. Batstone and G. Tissol, 97–112. New York: Peter Lang.

Toher, M. 2001. "Telemachus' Rite of Passage." *PP* 56:149–68.

Tolkhien, J. 1991. *Omero e la poesia latina*. Translated from the German edition of 1900 and revised by M. Scaffai. Bologna: Pàtron.

Torres-Guerra, J. B. 1995. *La Tebaida Homérica como fuente de Ilíada y Odisea*. Madrid: Fundación Pastor de Estudios Clásicos.

Tracy, S. V. 1997. "The Structures of the *Odyssey*." In *A New Companion to Homer*, edited by I. Morris and B. Powell, 360–79. Leiden: Brill.

Traina, A. 1970. *Vortit barbare: Le traduzioni poetiche da Livio Andronico a Cicerone*. Rome: Edizioni dell'Ateneo.

Tsitsiou-Chelidoni, C. 2003. *Ovid, Metamorphosen Buch VIII: Narrative Technik und literarischer Kontext*. Frankfurt: Lang.

Ulrich, R. B. 1993. "Julius Caesar and the Creation of the Forum Iulium." *AJA* 97:49–80.

van Otterlo, W. A. A. 1944. "Eine merkwürdige Kompositionsform der älteren griechischen Literatur." *Mnemosyne* 12:192–207.

van Wees, H. 1992. *Status Warriors: War, Violence and Society in Homer and History*. Amsterdam: J. C. Gieben.

Verducci, F. 1985. *Ovid's Toyshop of the Heart: Epistulae Heroidum*. Princeton, NJ: Princeton University Press.

Viarre, S. 2009. "Ovide, *Fastes* III, 524–695: De la mise en scène de la fête d'Anna Perenna à l'animation théâtrale de deux sujets de mime." In *La théâtralité de l'œuvre ovidienne*, edited by I. Jouteur, 225–31. Paris: De Boccard.

Vogt-Spira, G. 2007. "Homer—Virgil Comparison." In *Brill's New Pauly: Classical Tradition*, vol. 2, edited by M. Landfester et al., cols. 983–90. Leiden: Brill.

von Albrecht, M. 1961. "Zum Metamorphosenprooem Ovids." *RhM* 104:269–78.

———. 1968. "Ovids Humor und die Einheit der *Metamorphosen*." In *Ovid*, edited by M. von Albrecht and E. Zinn, 405–37. Darmstadt: Wissenschaftliche Buchgesellschaft. (= 1963. *Der altsprachliche Unterricht* 6.2: 47–72.)

———. 1980. "Rezeptionsgeschichte im Unterricht: Ovids Briseis-Brief." *AU* 23:37–53.

———. 1982. "Venus in Ovids *Metamorphosen*." *Vichiana* 11:318–31.

von Glinski, M. L. 2012. *Simile and Identity in Ovid's Metamorphoses*. Cambridge: Cambridge University Press.

Warmington, E. H., ed. 1935. *Remains of Old Latin I: Ennius and Caecilius*. Cambridge, MA, and London: Heinemann and Harvard University Press.

———, ed. 1936. *Remains of Old Latin II: Livius Andronicus, Naevius, Pacuvius and Accius*. Cambridge, MA, and London: Heinemann and Harvard University Press.

Weinstock, S. 1971. *Diuus Iulius*. Oxford: Oxford University Press.

Weitzmann, K. 1970. *Illustrations in Roll and Codex: A Study of the Origin and Method of Text Illustration*. Princeton, NJ: Princeton University Press.

West, M. L., ed. 1966. *Hesiod: Theogony*. Oxford: Oxford University Press.

———, ed. 1978. *Hesiod: Works and Days*. Oxford: Oxford University Press.

———. 1985. *The Hesiodic Catalogue of Women: Its Nature, Structure, and Origins*. Oxford: Oxford University Press.

———. 1999. "The Invention of Homer." *CQ* 49:364–82.

———. 2001. *Studies in the Text and Transmission of the Iliad*. Munich and Leipzig: K. G. Saur.

———, ed. 2003. *Greek Epic Fragments: From the Seventh to the Fifth Centuries BC*. Cambridge, MA: Harvard University Press.

Wheeler, A. L., ed. 1924. *Ovid: Tristia, Ex Ponto*. Cambridge, MA, and London: Heinemann and Harvard University Press.

Wheeler, S. 2000. *Narrative Dynamics in Ovid's Metamorphoses*. Tübingen: Narr.

Whitman, C. H. 1958. *Homer and the Heroic Tradition*. Cambridge, MA: Harvard University Press.

Wickkiser, B. L. 2005. "Augustus, Apollo, and an Ailing Rome: Images of Augustus as a Healer of State." In *Studies in Latin Literature and Roman History XII*, edited by C. Deroux, 267–89. Brussels: Éditions Latomus.

———. 2008. *Asklepios, Medicine, and the Politics of Healing in Fifth-Century Greece: Between Craft and Cult*. Baltimore: Johns Hopkins University Press.

Wilkinson, L. P. 1953. "Greek Influence on the Poetry of Ovid." In *L'influence grecque sur la poésie latine de Catulle à Ovide*, 223–43. Entretiens sur l'antiquité classique vol. 2. Vandœuvres: Fondation Hardt.

Willcock, M. M. 1964. "Mythological Paradeigma in the *Iliad*." *CQ* 14:141–54.

———, ed. 1978. *The Iliad of Homer: Books I–XII*. New York: St. Martin's.

———. 1983. "Antilochus in the *Iliad*." In *Mélanges Édouard Delebecque*, 477–85. Aix-en-Provence: Publications Université de Provence.

Williams, F., ed. 1978. *Callimachus: Hymn to Apollo*. Oxford: Oxford University Press.

Williams, G. D. 1994. *Banished Voices: Readings in Ovid's Exile Poetry*. Cambridge: Cambridge University Press.

———. 2010. "Apollo, Aesculapius and the Poetics of Illness in Ovid's *Metamorphoses*." In *Papers of the Langford Latin Seminar*, vol. 14, edited by F. Cairns and M. Griffin, 63–92. Cambridge: Cambridge University Press.

Wills, J. 1996. *Repetition in Latin Poetry: Figures of Allusion*. Oxford: Oxford University Press.

Wimmel, W. 1960. *Kallimachos in Rom*. Wiesbaden: F. Steiner.

———. 1968. *Der frühe Tibull*. Munich: W. Fink.

Wise, V. 1977. "Flight Myths in Ovid's *Metamorphoses*: An Interpretation of Phaethon and Daedalus." *Ramus* 6:44–59.

Wiseman, T. P. 1999. "The Games of Flora." In *The Art of Ancient Spectacle*, edited by B. Bergmann and C. Kondoleon, 194–203. Studies in the History of Art 56. Washington, DC: National Gallery of Art.

———. 2002. "Ovid and the Stage." In *Ovid's Fasti: Historical Readings at Its Bimillennium*, edited by G. Herbert-Brown, 275–99. Oxford: Oxford University Press.

Wissmann, J. 2009. "Athena's 'Unreasonable Advice': The Education of Telemachus in Ancient Interpretations of Homer." *GRBS* 49:413–52.

Wöhrle, G. 1999. *Telemachs Reise: Väter und Söhne in Ilias und Odyssey, oder ein Beitrag zur Erforschung der Männlichkeitsideologie in der homerischen Welt*. Göttingen: Vandenhoeck & Ruprecht.

———. 2009. "Sons (and Daughters) without Fathers: Fatherlessness in the Homeric Epics." In *Growing Up Fatherless in Antiquity*, edited by S. Hübner and D. M. Ratzan, 162–74. Cambridge: Cambridge University Press.

Wright, M. R., ed. 1995. *Empedocles: The Extant Fragments*. 2nd ed. Bristol: Bristol Classical Press.

Wyatt, W. F. 1989. "The Intermezzo in *Odyssey* 11 and the Poets Homer and Odysseus." *SMEA* 27:235–53.

Wyke, M. 1987. "Written Women: Propertius' *Scripta Puella*." *JRS* 77:47–61.

———. 1989. "Reading Female Flesh: *Amores* 3.1." In *History as Text: The Writing of Ancient History*, edited by A. Cameron, 111–43. London: Duckworth. (= 2006. In *Oxford Readings in Classical Studies: Ovid*, edited by P. Knox, 169–204. Oxford: Oxford University Press.)

Yamagata, N. 1991. "Phoenix's Speech—Is Achilles Punished?" *CQ* 41:1–15.

Yardley, J. C. 1977. "Cynthia's Ghost: Propertius 4.7 Again." *BICS* 24:83–87.

Zanker, G. 1994. *The Heart of Achilles: Characterization and Personal Ethics in the Iliad.* Ann Arbor: University of Michigan Press.

Zanker, P. 1988. *The Power of Images in the Age of Augustus.* Translated by A. Shapiro. Ann Arbor: University of Michigan Press.

———. 1995. *The Mask of Socrates: The Image of the Intellectual in Antiquity.* Translated by A. Shapiro. Berkeley: University of California Press.

Zeitlin, F. I. 2001. "Visions and Revisions of Homer." In *Being Greek under Rome: Cultural Identity, the Second Sophistic and the Development of Empire*, edited by S. Goldhill, 195–266. Cambridge: Cambridge University Press.

Zetzel, J. E. G. 1983. "Catullus, Ennius, and the Poetics of Allusion." *ICS* 8:251–66.

Ziogas, I. 2013. *Hesiod and Ovid: The Metamorphosis of the Catalogue of Women.* Cambridge: Cambridge University Press.

Zumwalt, N. 1977. "*Fama subversa*: Theme and Structure in Ovid, *Metamorphoses* 12." *CSCA* 10:209–222.

Index Locorum

This index gathers all the most important and extended quotations of ancient texts contained within the body of the book and the notes. Discussions of single words, however, are not included here; the most significant individual words appear instead in the general index. If a phrase or verse appears repeatedly in the course of several pages, only the first instance is included here.

General Index